FARM MANAGEMENT

Decisions, Operation, Control

John E. Kadlec
Purdue University

Prentice-Hall, Inc., Englewood Cliffs, New Jersey 07632

Library of Congress Cataloging in Publication Data

Kadlec, John E. (date)
   Farm management.

   Includes bibliographies and index.
   1. Farm management. I. Title.
S561.K24 1985   630'.68   84–3315
ISBN 0-13-305053-X

Editorial/production supervision and
   interior design: Paula J. Martinac
Cover design: Lundgren Graphics, Ltd.
Manufacturing buyer: John Hall
Title page photo: USDA

© 1985 by Prentice-Hall, Inc., Englewood Cliffs, New Jersey 07632

Printed in the United States of America

10 9 8 7 6 5 4 3 2 1

ISBN 0-13-305053-X   01

PRENTICE-HALL INTERNATIONAL, INC., *London*
PRENTICE-HALL OF AUSTRALIA PTY. LIMITED, *Sydney*
EDITORA PRENTICE-HALL DO BRASIL, LTDA., *Rio de Janeiro*
PRENTICE-HALL CANADA INC., *Toronto*
PRENTICE-HALL OF INDIA PRIVATE LIMITED, *New Delhi*
PRENTICE-HALL OF JAPAN, INC., *Tokyo*
PRENTICE-HALL OF SOUTHEAST ASIA PTE. LTD., *Singapore*
WHITEHALL BOOKS LIMITED, *Wellington, New Zealand*

Contents

22   TAX MANAGEMENT   396

23   PROFESSIONAL FARM MANAGEMENT   406

Preface

We have entered a new era in agriculture—the *management era*. There are now and there will continue to be excellent profit opportunities for those who are prepared to operate effectively in this new era.

The management era involves: (1) greater emphasis on *continual analysis* for key decisions and the adjustment of the farm business to changes in technology, market conditions, laws, and regulations. Computers and electronic information systems will be tools for accomplishing continual analysis; (2) increased importance of *gaining control of adequate capital* to have an economic-sized farm; (3) greater need for *control* of all aspects of the farm business; (4) increased *market orientation*—choice of time, place, and method of selling and buying; (5) more emphasis on hiring and supervising workers and *dealing with people;* (6) increased importance of business *legal organization* and *tax management;* (7) continued emphasis on *efficiency* of crop and livestock production.

This book is designed to help readers compete in the management era.

Approximately 80 farm situations are used to illustrate key principles for successfully managing a farm business. Most of these examples are about real farmers (their names have been changed) and the situations they faced. These vignettes make learning easier and more interesting for the beginning student. In addition, the illustrations emphasize the importance of the people associated with each particular farm business; personal goals, strengths, and weaknesses must be taken into account when making farm management decisions.

The mini-cases also illustrate the characteristics of a successful farm manager, including the ability to: produce crops and/or livestock efficiently; manage money, keep records, and prepare budgets; manage people, machinery, land, and buildings;

market farm products effectively and purchase inputs economically; manage taxes; plan, organize, and analyze with a constant awareness of changing technology, laws, and economic conditions; and, finally, tolerate risk, make decisions, and take action.

Although some background in the elements of farm management would be helpful to the reader, no previous study of business management, accounting, or economics is required. This book is written to provide those who are beginning their study of farm management with an understanding of key farm management principles and concepts. "How-to-do-it" procedures are presented to aid in the application of principles for making important farm management decisions such as investing in land, machinery and buildings, and choosing crops and livestock. Readers are especially encouraged to apply the principles to their own farms or farms in their home communities.

All aspects of farm management cannot be treated adequately in a single textbook. Related readings are provided in each chapter for teachers and students who wish to pursue particular topics in greater depth.

While there are numerous sequences in which the contents of this book may be studied effectively, there are four "sets" of chapters which should be read sequentially:

Chapters 2–4:   farm organization and decision-making principles

Chapters 5–7:   record keeping and financial management

Chapters 9–12: planning crops and livestock and budgeting farm profit and cash flow

Chapters 16–17: machinery and building production systems.

Chapter 8, "Decision Making Methods," provides procedures that are used in Chapters 9 through 19 and therefore should precede these chapters. Chapters 13 through 21 are devoted to farm management and organization decisions: the best farm size; how to acquire and manage land, machinery, buildings, and labor; marketing and purchasing; and legal organization with corporations or partnerships. Tax management is covered in Chapter 22 and professional farm management in Chapter 23.

I am indebted to many people for important contributions. My wife, Mary Nell, reviewed and edited various drafts. My son, John, made helpful suggestions for the farm records chapters. Numerous colleagues reviewed sections and provided comments: Earl Kehrberg and Gene Nelson, decision principles; Julian Atkinson, Timothy Baker, and Freddie Barnard, farm records and financial management; Craig Dobbins and Steven Sonka, decision-making methods; David Bache, Howard Doster, Bob Jones, David Petritz, and Paul Robbins, farm organization and resource acquisition; Bernard Erven and Milton Holcomb, labor management; Steven Erickson, Christopher Hurt, Joseph Uhl, and William Uhrig, farm marketing; Neil Harl, Gerald Harrison, George Patrick, and Robert Suter, legal organization and tax management; Lawrence Bohl and Robert Taylor, style of presentation for undergraduates. The reviewers—John Holt, Alfred B. Kelly, James

B. Kliebenstein, James D. Libbin, and Joseph E. Williams, Oklahoma State University—made helpful suggestions.

I am also grateful for the encouragement of Paul Farris and Richard Kohls, Department Head and Dean, respectively, when this book was initiated.

John E. Kadlec

CHAPTER OPENING PHOTO CREDITS

Chapter 1 USDA   *Chapter 2* William G. Congleton Family   *Chapter 3* J. C. Allen and Son   *Chapter 4* USDA   *Chapter 5* USDA   *Chapter 6* USDA   *Chapter 7* D. Howard Doster   *Chapter 8* University of Missouri *Chapter 9* USDA *Chapter 10* USDA   *Chapter 11* Samuel Washburn   *Chapter 12* John E. Kadlec *Chapter 13* USDA   *Chapter 14* Robert Halderman   *Chapter 15* J. C. Allen and Son   *Chapter 16* USDA   *Chapter 17* William G. Congleton Family   *Chapter 18* USDA   *Chapter 19* USDA   *Chapter 20* John Pickering *Chapter 21* USDA *Chapter 22*   J. C. Allen and Son   *Chapter 23* USDA   *Appendix A* USDA   *Appendix B* USDA

Farm Management:
Decisions, Operation,
Control

1

INTRODUCTION

In 1810 Roger Johnson I purchased the farm on which Roger Johnson V presently lives with his parents. Roger is eighteen years old and would like to prepare himself to be an outstanding farm manager and operator and to continue to keep the farm in the family. The Johnsons have been excellent managers over the generations. This is why the farm is still operated by the family.

But the kind of management understanding needed by Roger V to enable him to be a successful manager is quite different from that required by his grandfathers. Today's successful farmer must above all excel as a business manager. The years 1860 to 1940 were a period of organizational stability on farms. Only moderate changes occurred in farming during that time. The average U.S. yield of corn for the period 1866 to 1875 was 26 bushels per acre; for 1930 to 1940 it was 24 bushels per acre. Skills and technical knowledge learned from past generations tended to apply to current generations with only minor modification. Answers to many farm management questions tended to remain the same, hence answers rather than methods of analysis were often taught. The ability to do specific jobs correctly and efficiently was a key criterion for success in farming.

From 1940 to the present we have witnessed a technological revolution. There has been a flow of new and improved fertilizers, seeds, feed additives, insecticides, herbicides, machines, buildings, and so on. By 1982 the average yield of corn in the U.S. had increased to 115 bushels per acre. Each farm worker provided agricultural products for himself and ten other people in 1940; by 1981 this number had increased to 78. Those who were the first to identify accurately and adopt new technologies were the ones who profited. Most farmers who were late in adopting new technologies are no longer in business.

In the future, technological change will continue, but it will cease to be a revolution; it is now a part of farmers' expectations. Farmers know sources of information that help them to identify relevant new technologies: bankers, extension specialists, fertilizer salesmen, machinery dealers, feed suppliers, and others. The time lag between introduction and adoption of new technologies will be so short that profits from early adoption will be reduced. Adoption of new technology will be crucial but will not guarantee success to the extent that it has in the past.

At present a new revolution is occurring in agriculture, the management revolution. Changes in agricultural technology, communications, transportation, management methods, data handling, human abilities, and size and nature of farm-related

2

industries have set the stage for this new era. There are now, and will continue to be, tremendous profit opportunities in farming for those who have the knowledge and ability to operate effectively in this new era, the era of management.

The management revolution involves:

- Greater emphasis on continual analysis for key decisions to be made and the adjustment of the farm business to changes in technology and market conditions. Computers and electronic information systems will be important tools for accomplishing continual analysis.
- Increased importance of gaining control of adequate capital to have an economic-sized farm.
- Greater importance of control of capital and production costs.
- Increased market orientation—choice of time, place, and method of selling and buying.
- More emphasis on hiring and supervising workers and dealing with people.
- Increased importance of business legal organization and tax management.
- More complex and sophisticated farm businesses.

This book is designed to help readers compete in the management era. The first four chapters deal mainly with background and principles for farm management decision making and the next three with record keeping and financial management. Methods for making farm management decisions are presented in Chapter 8. In Chapters 9 through 18 principles and methods are applied in making important farm management decisions, such as crop planning, livestock choice, size, securing and improving land, building and machinery investments, and marketing. The final five chapters are concerned with getting started in farming, legal organization, labor management, tax management, and professional farm management.

The remainder of this chapter will set forth the meaning of the term *management* and briefly explain what it takes to make money in the farm business.

MANAGEMENT

Management is important to everyone. All people are required to be their own personal managers. Management, in simplest terms, is using what you have to get what you want most.

We all have things that we want—our goals. These goals may include wealth, good health, a happy family life, a nice home, yearly vacations, and social prestige, to name but a few.

We also have certain resources with which to pursue our goals: time (hours, days, weeks, years), physical abilities, and mental abilities. In addition, some people have savings, land, stocks, bonds, a good credit profile, training for a particular profession, and other assets.

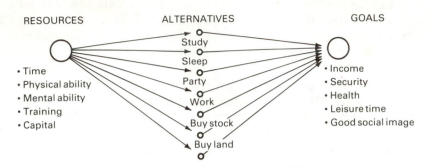

Figure 1.1 Illustration of the basic parts of management.

Finally, our resources can be used in a variety of ways, and each of these uses has a different payoff in terms of the things we want (see Figure 1.1). The science of management includes the *decisions and actions* that allocate limited resources among alternative uses so that achievement of goals is maximized.

Farm management is the science of allocating land, buildings, machinery, operating capital, and labor among different crops, livestock, production systems, buying systems, and selling systems so that goals such as income, income stability, risk minimization, as well as personal goals, are attained (see Figure 1.2). Differences in *decisions* about the use of resources and differences in the ability to put these decisions into action can have a great impact on farm profit.

Figure 1.2 Basic parts of farm management.

MAKING MONEY IN THE FARM BUSINESS

Some farms consistently make relatively high returns to the operator and the capital invested in the business, while other farms consistently make low returns. Table 1.1 shows earnings summaries from farm records.

Income variations of similar magnitude to those in the table can be observed between high-profit and low-profit groups of farms of different types in various locations of the country. *There are eight basic factors under the manager's control that explain most of these profit differences.* Several other chance factors, such as

TABLE 1.1   Farm Earnings Summary[a]

	1967		1972		1978		1982	
	No. of Farms	Farm Income[b]	No. of Farms	Farm Income	No. of Farms	Farm Income	No. of Farms	Farm Income
High-profit group	31	$27,756	16	$69,389	16	$165,317	23	$120,450
Low-profit group	30	−1,510	16	−2,982	16	5,582	23	6,039

[a]*Source:* Indiana Farm Business Summaries, Purdue University.
[b]Incomes are average for all farms in each group.

weather, difficult-to-control crop and livestock disease, and unpredictable price changes, cause some of this variation. The factors under the manager's control, as well as those outside his control, will be discussed and illustrated throughout this book.

Here is a brief summary of the eight key factors that can be controlled by a manager and that largely determine income level. Each will be discussed in detail in later chapters.

1. *Efficiency:* getting high output from given resources. Some farm operators consistently get greater-than-average output from given resources. This greater output is the result of knowing what to do, having the skill to do it, and having the self-discipline, organizational ability, and determination to do it at the right time. Farmers who are above average in efficiency make more money. The impact of efficiency is discussed throughout the book, especially in Chapters 3, 5, 6, 10, 11, and 13.

2. *Volume.* Farmers who do a good job with efficiency and make a profit per unit can increase total profits by producing more units. Also, increasing farm size to at least moderate levels allows farmers to take advantage of labor-saving machinery and equipment that may be too expensive for use on smaller farms. Buying and selling large volumes often enables farmers to get better prices. Decisions about business size are considered in Chapter 13. Specific expansion alternatives are discussed in Chapters 14, 15, 16, and 17.

3. *Combination of enterprises.* Some enterprises fit given land, labor, management, and capital resources better than others. Farmers who can best fit enterprises to available resources and markets will make more money. Enterprise choice is covered in Chapters 3, 9, 10, and 11.

4. *Production systems.* There are several systems for producing most products (for example, slotted-floor buildings versus pasture for hogs). These systems require different amounts of labor, management, and capital. Farmers who can do a better-than-average job of fitting the production system to resources will make more money. Chapters 3, 9, 10, 11, 16, and 17 all include a discussion of production systems.

5. and 6. *Buying and selling.* Farmers who purchase given resources at a lower-than-average price and/or sell for a higher-than-average price usually make

greater profits. Even though the extent to which a farmer can influence price is limited, the relatively small effect is nevertheless very important and can have a great impact on profit. Specific marketing strategy alternatives are covered in Chapter 18.

7. *Labor productivity.* Some farmers get more done by organizing their time better and/or by working longer hours. Farmers who have above-average labor productivity make higher incomes by saving on labor costs. Labor management is discussed in Chapter 21.

8. *Net worth.* As capital is saved and replaces borrowed money or leased capital items, interest or other capital costs are reduced and income is increased. Strategies for increasing net worth are presented in Chapter 7.

Forecasting the Changing Environment

The "best" production methods, size, enterprise choice, production system, and buying and selling place and time are determined by the goals of the operator, the management ability of the operator, the resources available, and the operating environment (the state of technology, economic conditions, and laws and regulations). Hence, to make good management decisions it is important to assess and forecast the economic, social, and technological environment on a continuous basis.

Deciding and Acting

Successful management requires sound decisions and implementation of those decisions. Unless a manager acts, good decisions are of no value. To act, a manager must have the courage to take a calculated risk. Decision making and risk are discussed in Chapters 3 and 4.

Entrepreneurship

The ability to "put it all together" is a need shared by all farmers and is a must for operators of large, growing farms. Someone must secure capital and labor and also coordinate and organize.

The principles for developing a plan or strategy for the farm business are presented in Chapter 2.

DISCUSSION QUESTIONS

1. How does farm management today differ from farm management fifty years ago? How is farm management in the future likely to differ from farm management today?
2. In the years ahead, being a successful farm manager will require what kind of education and what kinds of abilities?
3. What are the three key elements of management?

4. Why is every person required to be a manager?
5. Last year Rich Smith had a net farm profit of $78,263. His neighbor I. M. Broke had a net farm profit of $3,000. Do variations of this magnitude really occur? What could have caused these differences? List the key factors that cause large differences in farm business incomes.
6. Is the ability to make good decisions the main requirement for success as a farm manager? Explain.

RELATED READINGS

GILES, TONY and MALCOLM STANSFIELD. *The Farmer as Manager.* London: George Allen and Unwin Ltd., 1980.

HARSH, STEPHEN B., LARRY J. CONNOR, and GERALD D. SCHWAB. *Managing the Farm Business,* chap. 1. Englewood Cliffs, N.J.: Prentice-Hall, 1981.

HERBST, J. H. *Farm Management: Principles, Budgets, Plans* (6th ed.), chap. 1. Champaign, Ill.: Stipes Publishing Co., 1983.

JOHNSON, GLENN L., ALBERT N. HALTER, HARALD R. JENSEN, and D. WOODS THOMAS. *A Study of Managerial Processes of Midwestern Farmers.* Ames, Ia.: Iowa State University Press, 1961.

WARREN, G. F. *Farm Management.* pp. 1–13. New York: Macmillan, 1918.

Developing a Strategy
for the Farm Business

2

How should the farm business be organized? Should the farm be specialized in crops or livestock, or should it be diversified with both crops and livestock? Should high-investment labor-saving buildings and machinery be purchased, or should low-investment high-labor-requirement buildings and equipment be used? How big should the farm be and how fast should it grow? What crops and livestock should be produced? Should land be purchased or rented? How much capital should be borrowed? The answers to these and other similar questions are the farm strategy or long-range plan.

To develop a "good" strategy or the "best" strategy, the manager should consider four factors. First, what are the *goals* of the owners and operators? Second, what are the unique *strengths of the management?* Third, what *resources* are available? Finally, what are the characteristics of the *operating environment?*

GOALS

Well-defined goals enable a good manager to do a more effective job than goals that are not well defined. Since management involves making decisions about resource use to attain objectives, the manager must know the objectives in detail in order to make a wise choice of alternatives that will attain desired goals.

Farm businesses usually involve only a few managers and owners, so the definition of goals is largely an individual matter. The people involved with the business should list their goals, and these lists should be integrated to develop a set of goals for the business.

Goals and goal formulation are complex. It is often difficult for individuals to identify what they do want. Goals are long-range and short-range, tangible and intangible, specific and general, monetary and nonmonetary. Good management requires well-defined goals. Here are some considerations that may be helpful in defining and achieving goals.

1. *Recognize that when goals are well defined it is more likely that they will be achieved.*

Make a list of the things you want to achieve in the next day and the next week. Arrange this list in order of importance. Observe this list at least three times each day and cross off the things you have accomplished.

After the first day and the first week, review this list of goals to see how many you have accomplished. Did you do more than you have been doing without the goals listing? Did you accomplish some things that you had intended to do for a long time but had put off?

This same success in goal attainment can be achieved with long-range business goals if they are well defined and reviewed frequently.

2. *The process of writing goals encourages specificity and permits frequent goal review.*

You probably learned from consideration 1 that well-defined written goals that are reviewed often are more likely to be accomplished than are vague unwritten goals. Complete the checklist in Table 2.1 and then make a list of the personal goals you would like to accomplish during the next year, five years, and twenty years.

TABLE 2.1 Goals Checklist
How important is each of the following?

	Very Important 10	8	6	4	2	Not Important 0
A. Income and wealth						
1. Make $10,000/year	—	—	—	—	—	—
2. Make $20,000/year	—	—	—	—	—	—
3. Make $50,000 or more/year	—	—	—	—	—	—
4. Accumulate $500,000 (lifetime)	—	—	—	—	—	—
5. Accumulate $1,000,000 or more (lifetime)	—	—	—	—	—	—
6. Save 5% of income/year	—	—	—	—	—	—
7. Save 10% of income/year	—	—	—	—	—	—
8. Know the lower limit of my income for this year	—	—	—	—	—	—
9. Have a farm business that produces a stable income	—	—	—	—	—	—
10. Have a family income comparable to what my spouse and I could make if we lived in town	—	—	—	—	—	—
B. Risk						
1. Avoid bankruptcy	—	—	—	—	—	—
2. Debt load:						
Less than $100,000 debt	—	—	—	—	—	—
Less than $500,000 debt	—	—	—	—	—	—
Less than 50% of net worth	—	—	—	—	—	—
Less than 100% of net worth	—	—	—	—	—	—
No limit on debt	—	—	—	—	—	—
3. Insurance						
Life	—	—	—	—	—	—
Health	—	—	—	—	—	—
Homeowner's	—	—	—	—	—	—

TABLE 2.1 (continued)

	Very Important 10	8	6	4	2	Not Important 0
Farm liability	—	—	—	—	—	—
Crops	—	—	—	—	—	—
4. Make mortgage and loan payments on time	—	—	—	—	—	—
C. Family and personal life						
1. Spend 1 hour/day with family	—	—	—	—	—	—
Spend 2 hours/day with family	—	—	—	—	—	—
Spend 4 hours/day with family	—	—	—	—	—	—
Spend 8 hours/day with family	—	—	—	—	—	—
2. Take a vacation each year	—	—	—	—	—	—
3. Time to do anything you want						
1 hour/day	—	—	—	—	—	—
2 hours/day	—	—	—	—	—	—
4 hours/day	—	—	—	—	—	—
6 hours/day	—	—	—	—	—	—
10 hours/day	—	—	—	—	—	—
4. Own my home	—	—	—	—	—	—
5. Own a nice automobile	—	—	—	—	—	—
6. Set aside money for retirement	—	—	—	—	—	—
7. Contribute to the community	—	—	—	—	—	—
8. Live close to home	—	—	—	—	—	—
9. Recreation						
Together as a family	—	—	—	—	—	—
Individually	—	—	—	—	—	—
Own recreational vehicle	—	—	—	—	—	—
10. Cultural development for family	—	—	—	—	—	—
11. Increase my family's living standard quickly	—	—	—	—	—	—
D. Farm characteristics						
1. Rapidly growing farm	—	—	—	—	—	—
2. Efficient, well-managed farm	—	—	—	—	—	—
3. Owning land	—	—	—	—	—	—
4. Sufficient size to bring children into the business	—	—	—	—	—	—
5. Be recognized as a top farmer in the community	—	—	—	—	—	—
E. Job satisfaction						
1. Outdoors work	—	—	—	—	—	—
2. Indoors work	—	—	—	—	—	—
3. Plenty of freedom	—	—	—	—	—	—
4. Required to make many tough decisions	—	—	—	—	—	—
5. Job security	—	—	—	—	—	—
6. Physical activity	—	—	—	—	—	—
7. Work with others	—	—	—	—	—	—
8. Work alone	—	—	—	—	—	—

3. *If farm business goals and objectives strongly conflict with goals of persons associated with the business, there is potential for difficulty.*

Tom and Donna were interested in farming. They were short on land and capital, so it was decided that an intensive livestock program was needed to generate sufficient income for living. In the beginning there was not sufficient income for hiring labor to give Tom and Donna free time. Donna's father owned a cottage on the lake, and one of Donna's goals was to spend weekends at the lake. Tom tried to raise livestock and spend time at the lake too. As a result, livestock efficiency was low, and the farm was unprofitable. After two years of losses, Tom and Donna sold out and moved to town.

Situations in which there are strongly conflicting goals among individuals and the business can lead to decision deadlock and frustration. It is important for all the key people associated with a business to define their goals carefully. The goals of individuals are the main ingredients in developing goals for the farm business.

There may be situations when, in the development of lists of goals for all key persons in the business, it is determined that the goals are incompatible. It may not be possible to have business goals that satisfy all parties. In such cases, the earlier the goal conflict can be determined, the less costly and frustrating the situation will be.

Jerry returned to the home farm and started a partnership with his father Marshall. Jerry wanted to expand the business rapidly in order to provide a very good income for two families and to increase prestige in the community. Marshall had worked most of his life to reduce the farm debt, which was now down to a level at which Marshall felt comfortable.

Jerry kept expanding the business at a moderate rate. But each time money was borrowed to buy land, add buildings, or use as operating capital, the lender required Marshall's signature.

Marshall began to feel the pressure of debt that he did not want. He and Jerry squabbled more and more about farm decisions. The efficiency of the business began to decline as a result of their disagreements. After five years they decided to dissolve their partnership. Jerry had not accumulated sufficient capital to allow him to start farming with an income level similar to his friends, so he took a job in town.

The desires of both Jerry and Marshall could have been more adequately met if they had discussed their goals more carefully before they started farming together.

4. *Managers may become completely absorbed in day-to-day activities and lose sight of long-range goals.*

The daily problems and decisions that emerge in a farm business often distract a manager from longer-range goals. The tractor tire is flat, cows need to be milked, feed must be ground, the fence needs repair, more help must be located—the list goes on and on. Such problems as these occur from day to day, month to month, and year to year on most farms, and as a result, longer-range goals are often neglected. It is important, therefore, that farm managers take time to develop goals for themselves and for their businesses and to periodically review these goals.

5. *Goals change over time.*

Fred Keeler graduated from college in 1959 and was determined to get started farming and to own a farm. Fred worked such long hours and so intensely that he did not have time to explain things about the business to his two sons, who viewed the farm as a place for hard, dirty work. The sons had little, if any, influence over farm decisions.

Now Fred is ready to slow down and transfer the farm responsibilities to his sons, but they are not interested. Both sons are in college majoring in pharmacy. If Fred could have anticipated the way his goals would change over time, he might have been able to keep his sons interested in the farm.

Goals change with age, family obligations, net worth, social position in the community, experience, health, and other circumstances. Managers who can anticipate these changes can organize their business to attain both current and future goals.

6. *Goals may be the result of a challenge.*

A young man who graduated from a university and established a successful farm business was motivated to these accomplishments by his high school principal, who told him, "You do not have the ability to get a college degree and manage a business. You should plan to do more routine work." The young man was so irritated by the principal's comment that he enrolled in farm management, graduated with high grades, and now operates several hundred acres and produces thousands of hogs and cattle.

7. *Be careful that goals do not become a limit.*

Some managers stop short of their management potential because they set limits on themselves. They never dream of a business different from a fixed concept that they have always had. A listing of goals can be limiting in that it may not reflect managers' real objectives had they taken into account *all* the possibilities. Too many managers make plans without considering opportunities available to them.

It is helpful to observe what others are doing, read, attend field days, and do other research in developing goals. The purpose of observation is not to copy others but to consider what they are doing as alternatives.

8. *Farm family goals.*

The following goals are often listed by farm families.

a. Having a farm business that leads to a feeling of satisfaction. Characteristics of a farm business that provide satisfaction may include:
- Progressive, up-to-date, with new technology
- Neat appearance

- High crop yields and livestock production rates
- Large size
- Profitable unit
- Avoid bankruptcy or financial difficulty
- Respected in the community.

b. Maintaining an income level at least as high as that of friends and associates.

c. Enjoying personal freedom and independence.

d. Having financial independence.

e. Having a comfortable, attractive home.

f. Making a contribution to the community.

g. Spending time together as a family.

Management is using what you have to get what you want most. To use what you have wisely, you must know what you want.

MANAGEMENT STRENGTHS AND WEAKNESSES

Agriculture is a competitive business. Managers who are better than average usually make money, and those who are below average generally do not make money. It is very important for managers to determine the above-average abilities they have and then organize their businesses to use these strengths to best advantage. It is also desirable to identify weak points and to select a farm plan that has low requirements in these areas.

Two cattle feeders capitalize on their own unique abilities. John Williams is very skillful at obtaining efficient feedlot gains with his cattle. He is a good observer of animal health and keeps sickness and death loss to a minimum. John has the ability to prepare a feed ration that results in fast, cheap gains. He is only average in buying and selling ability. John buys 450-pound feeders and feeds them to weights of 1,050 pounds or more. He emphasizes producing beef.

Bill Gilson, on the other hand, has average feedlot management ability but is very perceptive about the cattle market. Bill buys heavier feeders (700–900 pounds) and turns them over often. As long as Bill is feeding cattle and adding pounds, he has no advantage over other cattle feeders. But when he is buying and selling, he has an advantage. So Bill spends more time and effort in buying and selling.

Components of Management Ability

It is important to evaluate several aspects of management in order to determine the type of farm business organization that will best fit your management ability.

1. Crop and livestock management.   Some operators are able to attain more output per unit of input with crops and livestock than an average manager can attain. The better-than-average managers get more output from given resources by doing the "right thing at the right time." Since farming is a competitive industry, long-range price tends to equal the cost of production of the average operator. Managers who are above average in efficiency and have below-average costs of production make a profit over time.

> Abe is below average in efficiency, Bill is average, and Calvin is above average. Efficiency has affected their cost of wheat production as shown in Figure 2.1. When price is $4.50 per bushel ($P_1$), Calvin is making $1.50 profit per bushel and Abe is breaking even. Profit encourages efficient and average operators to expand production. As they expand, price declines (P_2). But Abe cannot continue to operate for a long period of time with costs of $4.50 and a price of $3.75 or less. Many producers with costs similar to Abe's will quit production. Supply will decrease and price increase. Because of his efficiency, Calvin continues to make a profit even during low-price periods.

Operators who have the skill and desire to be above average in efficiency will make high returns. It is important for a manager to maintain a high level of technical efficiency in the products produced, either through the manager's ability or by hiring operators who can keep efficiency high.

The manager's ability with various types of crops and livestock relative to the ability of other managers should affect the types of enterprises produced. Crop and livestock management decisions are considered in Chapters 10 and 11.

2. Mechanical and building construction ability.   Machinery is one of the major investments and costs of crop production. Buildings and equipment are major investments and costs of livestock production.

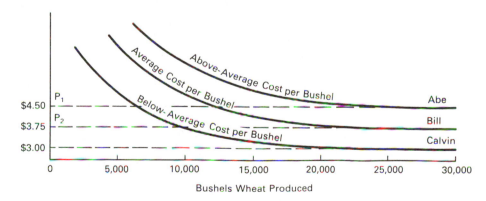

Figure 2.1   Costs of wheat production for three levels of management (hypothetical).

Farmers who are skillful in repairing machinery and identifying good used machinery can reduce costs substantially compared to operators who buy only new machinery and hire repairs. However, if used and self-repaired machinery breaks down at critical times, the money lost in crop efficiency may be greater than the money saved in reduced machinery costs.

Jim Fix started farming with limited capital. As an agricultural engineering graduate, he had a long-time interest in machinery and engineering. Jim was able to get started with minimum investment and cost because he had the ability to identify *good* used machinery and to make it run by overhauling it during less busy seasons. Jim has now farmed for several years and operates a large unit. He still buys some used machinery and does all of his machinery repair work. He even builds and sells to other farmers some specialized equipment that was initially developed for his own operation.

Ralph Thumbs does not have mechanical ability and recognizes his limitation. He buys new equipment from a dealer who is known for the good service he provides. Ralph's main skill is with crop production, and he devotes most of his attention to technical crop practices rather than machinery. He has a successful operation but was not able to buy land as easily as Jim because he has had more money invested in machinery. If, however, Ralph tried to use Jim's strategy of buying used machinery and repairing it himself, it is likely that his timeliness with crop planting and harvesting would be seriously hampered, and he might even fail in the farming business.

Just as Jim is skillful with machinery and Ralph is not, some farmers have the ability to construct their own crop and livestock buildings and others do not. Farmers who have the skill to coordinate and supervise the construction of their own buildings usually save 25% to 40% of a contractor's bid price.

Bill Craig supervised construction of his own high-investment cattle facility. The contractor bid price was $100,000, but the facility cost Bill only $73,000, and this cost included a charge for Bill's labor.

Sometimes constructing one's own buildings may conflict with the existing farming operation and delay growth of the business. Also, if an operator does not have building skills, an unsatisfactory building may result.

Forrest Smith constructed a completely slatted floor swine finishing unit. The slats were not finished correctly, and the pigs injured their feet. Hog performance was poor, and eventually commercial slats had to be purchased. Forrest would have been much better off to contract for the construction of the building rather than constructing it himself.

Machinery and building decisions are discussed in Chapters 16 and 17.

3. Buying and selling management.   For most farm commodities and re-sources, prices can be affected only to a limited extent. However, even a limited influ-ence on prices of items purchased and sold can have a major impact on farm profit.

For example, records of returns for a cattle feeder may show a net return of $27 per head after costs of $623 and receipts of $650 per head. If, through shopping, bar-gaining, selecting the best time of selling, and other marketing practices, sale price could be increased 5%, profit would increase by $32.50. In other words, profit could be more than doubled by effective selling.

The opportunity for gain from buying and selling is greater in some enterprises than in others. It is important for operators to select enterprises that enable them to capitalize on good marketing skills or to avoid losses from marketing management weaknesses. It is also important for operators to work to improve their marketing and purchasing management skills. Marketing and purchasing management are dis-cussed in Chapter 18.

4. Personnel management.   With good production skills and marketing and purchasing management, an operator can have a profitable one-person unit. If that unit is expanded to include more people, it is essential to be able to select, supervise, and motivate people. Personnel management is discussed in depth in Chapter 21.

5. Securing resources and financial management.   Capital re-quirements per person in farming range from $200,000 to $2 million, in most cases, depending on the type of operation. A successful farmer must gain control of needed resources through family, partners, rental, or borrowing. Rental or borrowing re-quires ability to project income and cash flow and to monitor receipts and expenses and make adjustments so that financial commitments can be met. Persons who do not have these abilities must find a partner or associate who has expertise in financial management and acquisition or must work for someone who has these abilities. Chapters 5, 6, 7, 13, 14, 15, 16, and 17 all relate to financial management and resource acquisition.

6. Analytical ability.   Alternative farm plans and practices must be iden-tified and evaluated in light of the manager's ability in production, marketing, finan-cial management, personnel management and other aspects of management. Infor-mation about these alternatives must be collected. Projections of future prices, costs and technology must also be made. Appropriate analytical methods must be used to evaluate alternatives. The manager's analytical ability is one of the keys to his or her success.

7. Decision making and action.   When the analyses are completed, deci-sions must be made and action must be taken.

Doug Manawish was an intelligent person who was very perceptive at analyzing and budgeting alternatives. But after all the analyses were completed, Doug could not make up his mind and move ahead. His farm business stagnated and generated very little income. Doug eventually took a job working in a farm supply store, where he was given specific instructions about what to do. He is happier and making more money.

Some managers make decisions but then fail to act. This failure is often due to reluctance to accept risk. Any business transaction has some element of risk associated with it. Risk can be controlled somewhat by the type of operation planned and by effective financial management and marketing practices. Persons who have strong risk-avoidance preferences should probably be workers for a business rather than owners or managers. Decision making and risk are discussed in Chapters 3 and 4.

8. Physical and emotional endurance.   The physical and emotional demands of farming can be substantial. The physical and emotional strengths and limitations of the farm managers and workers are important considerations in planning the farm business.

John Roberts cannot operate a combine because he is allergic to dust. Anne Axel experiences respiratory difficulties when she works in confined livestock buildings. Joe Arch cannot sleep at night when he owes large amounts of money.

Take inventory of your own management strengths and weaknesses. Figure 2.2 may be helpful for this inventory. What are your major strengths? What are your major weaknesses? What management areas are still unknown? How can you learn more about your unknown management strengths and weaknesses? How can you organize your business to capitalize on your management strengths? Can you and should you try to improve weak areas? Can you hire management to compensate for your weak areas?

Evaluating Management

The most reliable indicator of management ability is performance. Various tests and interview systems have been developed, and these tests can be useful indicators. But nothing can beat a track record for assessing management. What kind of crop yields and livestock efficiency did the manager attain compared to similar operations? What price was received for crops and livestock compared to other operators and to the average? What is the rate of labor turnover? How good is the morale and labor productivity of workers? Are resources being secured at the rate specified by the farm plan or strategy?

Successful managers organize the business to capitalize on their particular

		High				Average				Low	
		10	9	8	7	6	5	4	3	2	1
1.	Crop management	___	___	___	___	___	___	___	___	___	___
2.	Livestock management	___	___	___	___	___	___	___	___	___	___
3.	Marketing	___	___	___	___	___	___	___	___	___	___
4.	Purchasing	___	___	___	___	___	___	___	___	___	___
5.	Mechanical ability	___	___	___	___	___	___	___	___	___	___
6.	Building construction skills	___	___	___	___	___	___	___	___	___	___
7.	Personnel management	___	___	___	___	___	___	___	___	___	___
8.	Financial management	___	___	___	___	___	___	___	___	___	___
9.	Securing resources	___	___	___	___	___	___	___	___	___	___
10.	Physical endurance	___	___	___	___	___	___	___	___	___	___
11.	Emotional Endurance	___	___	___	___	___	___	___	___	___	___
12.	Analytical ability	___	___	___	___	___	___	___	___	___	___
13.	Decision making	___	___	___	___	___	___	___	___	___	___
14.	Ability to act and accept risk	___	___	___	___	___	___	___	___	___	___

Figure 2.2   Evaluation of farm management strengths and weaknesses.

management strengths. Financial gains are made by doing things that can be done exceptionally well or at least better than the average manager.

ADJUSTING TO THE CHANGING ENVIRONMENT

There is an old campus story about a college professor whose course is considered difficult because "he gives the same test *questions* each year, but he changes the *answers*!"

If this professor is teaching a farm management course, he may be doing a good job: In farm management, the questions remain the same but the answers change. Changes in technology, economic conditions, government laws and regulations, and the attitude of society all change the answers to such basic farm management questions as:

- What crops and livestock should be produced?
- How big should the business be?
- What production system should be used?
- When, where, and how should resources be purchased and crops and livestock be sold?

An important ability of a manager is to forecast the changing environment and adjust the business to those changes. Many operators adjust the business to *current* conditions. But production takes time, and by the time crops and livestock are produced, conditions may have changed. Because of the lag between the time when plans are made and the time when production is completed, a manager must always look to the future.

To make plans for a farm business on the basis of the current environment rather than the future is like going duck hunting and shooting directly at a flying duck. By the time the shot arrives, the duck has moved on. The hunter must *anticipate* the duck, but if he anticipates it too much, the shot will be ahead of the duck. The successful manager must plan the business for the future environment—but not *too* far in the future.

Technical Changes

Most farmers are aware of technological changes and make adjustments accordingly. New seed varieties, fertilizers, weed-control chemicals, disease-control chemicals, machinery, and livestock equipment are evolving from research stations, industry, and farms. Managers who can identify technological changes that cut costs or save a limiting resource and who can adopt that change early can usually make a profit. But managers who are late in adopting the change will experience a reduction in profit as a result of the change.

> Charlie First is operating a crop farm with cost C_1 and receiving price P_1 (see Figure 2.3). Charlie has included in the costs a charge for his labor, management, and capital. Because farming is a competitive industry, in most instances price equals average total cost. Professor Jetsun at State University has developed a new seed variety that increases crop yields from 100 to 130 bushels per acre. Cost per bushel is reduced substantially with the new seed. Initially most farmers do not know much about the new seed, and the new seed is difficult to obtain. But Charlie First keeps aware of technical changes. He has been following Jetsun's experiments, and when the new seed was released, he ordered early. Charlie also keeps on good personal terms with his seed dealer.
>
> Using the new seed, Charlie cut his costs to C_2, thus gaining a profit of C_1 minus C_2 times Q_1. Over time, more farmers learn about the new seed and greater quantities become available. Production increases because of the profit possibilities, and eventually the price declines to P_2. By this time, however, Charlie has found another technology that will help him reduce costs further.
>
> Charlie's neighbor, Jim Lag, likes to be certain that a new technology will work before adopting it. He waited until almost all farmers were using the new seed before using it himself. Because Jim operated for three years with cost C_1 and price P_2, he had a loss of P_1 minus P_2 times Q_1. If Jim continues to be the last to adopt new methods, his business will not survive.

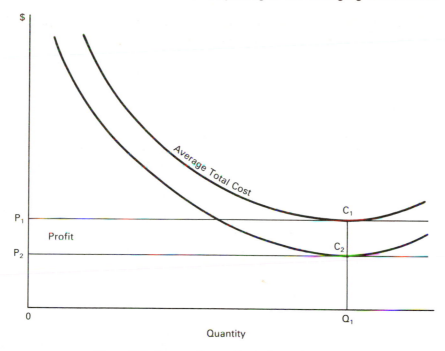

Figure 2.3 Impact of new technologies on farm profit.

Some technical innovations may not reduce cost but provide more alternative combinations of resources that can be used in the production of a product. An example of this type of change is slotted floors for hogs. Slotted floors reduce the amount of labor per hog but increase building costs and capital requirements. Costs per hog produced are generally about the same with slotted floors or with conventional lower-investment buildings. While the slotted-floor technology did not change the average cost of producing hogs, many swine producers have built higher-investment slotted-floor units. Why? The slotted-floor units have enabled good swine managers to produce more hogs with their limited labor. It is possible, however, for a farmer with limited capital to be competitive in producing hogs with the lower-investment systems.

New technologies can provide cost advantages to larger size and can encourage expansion. Large field machinery is an example of this type of technology. Machinery cost per acre remains approximately the same for large machinery as for small machinery if the large machinery and small machinery are operated the same number of hours. But since large machinery covers more acres with the same amount of total labor as small machinery, labor cost per unit of production is decreased with large machinery. This is one of the reasons there has been a trend toward larger machinery and increased size of crop farms. In some cases, the new technology will create such an advantage for a larger enterprise that a small enterprise will not be able to survive. Larger farms will increase production until price decreases to equal their cost of production. The lower price resulting from increased production may be below the cost of production for small farms.

The strategy of a farm manager with regard to new technology can be summarized as follows:

1. Be aggressive about studying and experimenting with new technologies that do not require large capital outlays or organizational changes (such as new fertilizers, seeds, chemicals, and feeds), but do not assume that everything new is better. Be a very early adopter of these new methods if they cut cost or have other advantages.
2. Study very carefully new technologies that require substantial long-term capital investments. Before adding a big new machine or an expensive building, make observations of others who are using similar ones and carefully budget returns for your farm. Be sure this technology fits the farm before making the investment.

Economic Changes

Continuing changes in the supply and demand for farm products and farm resources change product and input prices. The manager who is not alert to changes will fail to attain possible gains. Strategies for dealing with some changes in the economic environment will be discussed in Chapter 18.

Because of natural resources, climatic conditions, products markets, input markets, and transportation costs, different geographic areas have certain advantages for producing different products. This explains why we find concentrations of corn, soybeans, wheat, pasture, cotton, rice, vegetables, beef cattle, and dairy cattle in different geographic areas. Managers must be aware of the products for which their area has an advantage compared to other areas and products for which the area has a disadvantage.

> List the products for which your geographic area has an advantage and those for which it has a disadvantage. Why do these advantages and disadvantages exist?

Political and Social Changes

The actions of farmers have an impact on present and future society. The desires and preferences of society have an impact on farms and farm management. With increasing numbers of people in the world and improved ways of measuring and dealing with the interface of different groups, the social and political issues will become increasingly important to agriculture. Farmers who can accurately assess political and social changes can avoid problems and in some cases gain a profit.

What should a farm manager do to minimize losses and problems and/or increase profits in light of the situations described below? For each of the following situations, list the advantages and disadvantages to society and to farm operators.

- Congress passes a new feed grain law that guarantees a price and certain other benefits to farmers who set aside 20% of their land in an acreage reserve.
- Nitrites are banned for use as a pork preservative.
- Minimum wages and fringe benefit requirements are increased for all farm workers, resulting in a labor cost increase of 20%.
- A special license is required for operators who apply chemicals to land and crops.
- An animal rights law is passed that requires increased square footage of housing for dairy cows, beef cattle, hogs, and poultry.
- A certain type of chemical is banned; this cuts production 20%.
- Clean air and water laws require special processing of livestock waste.
- Law requires soil loss to be limited to 20 tons per acre per year.
- A new estate-tax law results in the sale of many farms at the death of the owners.
- Low-interest money is made available for young starting farmers to purchase land.

Political and Social Responsibility

While most people dislike regulatory restraints, a business must be operated within the framework of the preferences of the people in the country where that business is located. It would seem wise for farmers as a group to support programs that educate society about the advantages and disadvantages of certain policies. It also would seem wise for farmers to work to improve the political and social decision-making structure. They may do this by becoming personally involved in improving the political process or by supporting someone who is involved.

The Local Environment

The manager should assess characteristics of the local environment as well as the broader national or world environment.

Bill Wilkie's farm is located close to a university that has a large agriculture school. There is also an excellent milk market in the area. Bill has learned to operate with part-time help from the agriculture students whom he hires at a relatively low cost. He also calls on researchers and extension specialists for technical and management information. Bill has used the management counseling, low-cost labor, and good milk market to establish a very profitable dairy herd. Like Bill Wilkie, farm operators should strive to capitalize on the advantages of the local environment.

PHYSICAL RESOURCES

Finally, in addition to goals, management ability, and the environment, the physical resources of the farm affect the strategy. Land, buildings, machinery, and equipment are discussed in detail in Chapters 10, 11, and 14 through 17. The principle is to use resources in the enterprise that provide the greatest return per unit of resource.

The application of the concepts presented in this chapter is the heart of farm management. Decision-making principles are discussed in Chapter 3.

DISCUSSION QUESTIONS

1. What are the important basic factors that should be taken into consideration when planning farm strategy?
2. What are your main management strengths, the things at which you consider yourself to be above average? At what things do you consider yourself to be below average?
3. Why is it important that a farm business have goals?
4. Indicate one important current innovation or change in each of the following areas of the operating environment: technology, economics, sociopolitics. How should the farm strategy be adjusted as a result of these changes?
5. How might farm business goals change over time? What impact should these changing goals have on a farm strategy?

RELATED READINGS

BARNA, TIBOR. *Agriculture toward the Year 2000: Production and Trade in High-Income Countries,* preamble. Sussex, England: Sussex European Research Centre, University of Sussex, 1980.

CHRISTENSEN, C. R., K. R. ANDREWS, and J. L. BOWER. *Business Policy, Text, and Cases* (4th ed.), book 1. Homewood, Ill.: Richard D. Irwin, Inc., 1978.

DRUCKER, P. F. *The Practice of Management.* New York: Harper and Row, 1954.

GILES, TONY, and MALCOLM STANSFIELD. *The Farmer as Manager,* chap. 1. London: George Allen and Unwin, Ltd., 1980.

HUTCHINSON, JOHN G. *Management Strategy and Tactics,* chap. 4–5. New York: Holt, Rinehart and Winston, Inc., 1971.

KRAUSE, L. R. and P. L. WILLIAMS. *Personality Characteristics Related to Managerial Success*. South Dakota Agricultural Experiment Station Technical Bulletin 30, 1971.

NEWMAN, WILLIAM H. and JAMES P. LOGAN. *Strategy, Policy, and Central Management* (6th ed.), part 1. Cincinnati, Ohio: Southwestern Publishing Co., 1971.

PETERS, THOMAS J. and ROBERT H. WATERMAN, JR. *In Search of Excellence*. New York: Harper and Row, 1982.

Decision-Making Principles

3

An important attribute of a successful manager is the ability to make decisions that will enable the business to attain its goals. This chapter is devoted to concepts that can help a manager make wise choices for the business.

AWARENESS OF CHOICES

The success or failure of many managers is determined by their ability or lack of ability to seek out possible management alternatives.

A group of managers of grain elevators was surveyed. Information was collected about the profitability of each elevator and also about a number of other characteristics. One question asked was "How many problems do you now have?" The number of problems was then related to profit. Which do you think had more problems, the high-profit grain elevators or the low-profit grain elevators? The high-profit elevators! Why? Because the more capable managers were identifying choices and decisions, whereas the less capable managers were not cognizant of many of their alternatives.

A farm manager must continue to maintain awareness of possible choices. New developments in seed varieties, chemicals, machines, buildings, enterprises, computers, labor management methods, marketing methods, government programs, and others present themselves each year. To make the best decisions, a manager must first know his or her alternatives.

Some farmers are establishing "boards of directors" for their farms (whether they are incorporated or not) as a way to generate new ideas and alternatives. These directors might be other farmers, farm loan representatives, managers of agribusiness firms, or anyone who is a good observer and an innovative thinker. Farmers read farm magazines, attend university extension and professional meetings, and participate in workshops as a means of keeping well informed.

Managers who hope to be most successful must have a constant alertness to new ideas and choices.

Make a list of ways that would enable you to be more aware of your alternatives.

Make a list of five new choices that have emerged for you during the past two years.

ASSIGNING PRIORITIES

Some decisions are more important than others, and the most successful managers know that the payoff to time and management is usually greater for more important decisions. When T. K. Cowden was dean of agriculture at Michigan State University, he explained his ideas about setting priorities under the title ''The Big Problem in Life'':

As the years go by, I have become increasingly convinced that one of the most important things in determining a person's success is the ability to separate out the important from the unimportant. Most people work hard enough. The question is, are they working on important things?

Some of us seem to take great pride in being busy. The question is, are we busy on the important things? I am satisfied that we could put a radish marketing specialist on our staff and he could be extremely busy. Our job is to be sure that we are spending the public's money for the most important things we can do with the resources made available for our use. To concentrate on the important things is not easy. About once every day I find myself getting excited about something that really doesn't amount to anything. To me, separating out the important from the unimportant is one of the keys to success.

Herman Krannert, chairman of the board of Inland Container Company, said to a graduating class:

When I was young and had just finished my engineering studies at the University of Illinois, I thought I had time to do everything there was to do in the world. I thought I could run the best company, read all the good books, see all the beautiful paintings—in other words, do everything I considered worth doing. Now I know there isn't enough time for everything. . . . You will need to establish priorities. . . . If you set out to do the things which are really important you will find that your job isn't nearly as complicated as some people make it. . . . I don't know why some people persist in using 90% of their efforts on projects which will give them 10% of the potential rewards. Your real job is to figure out the important things to get done and to spend your effort doing the things which will give you 90% of the potential return. The other 10% may never get done, and I don't think you should worry too much about this. In fact, sometimes I like to measure people by the things they leave undone. The persons who insist on getting 100% of their job done either do not have enough to do or do not have the kind of stuff it takes to succeed in business today.[1]

[1]*Source:* Krannert, Herman C., *Krannert on Management,* Krannert Graduate School of Management, Purdue University, West Lafayette, IN., 1974.

> Make a list of the things that you have to do in the next week. Make your list as complete as possible. Mark each of the things on your list in order of importance for attaining your objectives. Can you get all of these things done? What will be the consequences if you do not do the last 20% of the things on your list?

IMPORTANCE OF DECISIONS

What makes a decision important? One criterion is the *degree of impact on goals*. For instance, if one goal is higher income, and a large amount of money hinges on making the right decision, the decision is important. The make of pickup truck to be purchased might have as much as $1,000 impact on farm profit. But the choice of seed variety or types of crops might have a $10,000 impact on profit. The purchase of a building could affect profit $50,000, and the purchase of a farm $100,000.

The importance of a decision is also affected by *frequency*. Determining the lowest-cost feeder cattle ration might save only 3 cents per steer per day. If you are feeding only one steer, you would save $10.95 per year by constantly calculating the least-cost ration. Other uses for your time might be more important. But if 10,000 steers are fed every day of the year, annual profit will be affected to the tune of $109,500 by ration choice.

Decisions that are not easily changed are more important than decisions that can easily be changed. If a dairyman does not make the best decision about a feed ration, it can be changed easily. Fertilization of an annual crop will take a year to change. A building decision usually would be very difficult to change.

Finally, *decisions that have time urgency are more important than decisions that do not have time urgency*. Some decisions can be delayed with little cost and perhaps a gain, whereas other decisions result in losses if they are delayed.

> John Keystone and Bill Hall are both considering building a new slotted-floor thirty-sow farrowing house. Bill plans to farrow his first group of sows in one year. By delaying his decision about the type of slats and other details of the building, Bill may have an opportunity to observe the experiences of others and make a better decision. John, on the other hand, has already bred his first group of sows. Unless he begins building soon, he will likely lose some pigs at farrowing time. A decision about the building is more important for John than Bill—even though both are facing the same decision.

> Which is more important in each of the following? Why?
>
> 1. Deciding on a new $50,000 cattle-feeding facility or buying a $50,000 combine.

2. Deciding on the kind of new tires for the pickup truck or deciding on the acreage of corn and soybeans to grow.
3. Deciding on the best ration for 200 dairy cows with a payoff of 25 cents per day per cow or deciding on purchase of a $10,000 feed storage center.
4. Deciding on the purchase of a 500-acre farm or the rental of a 500-acre farm.

PRODUCTION ECONOMICS AS A DECISION-MAKING FRAMEWORK

Production economics provides a framework for making such decisions as:

- How much to produce or how many inputs to use.
- The most profitable combination of inputs to use.
- The most profitable combination of products to produce.

The answers can be found if you know

- The physical relationships among inputs and outputs.
- Prices of inputs and outputs.
- Production economics criteria for determining the most profitable situation.

The Law of Variable Proportions

The physical relationships among inputs and outputs are determined by the *law of variable proportions,* which is sometimes referred to as the *law of diminishing returns.*

> If the input of one resource is increased while the inputs of other resources are held constant, the amount of additional (or marginal) product resulting from each successive unit of input will first increase, then decrease, and finally become negative.

This law is illustrated in terms of total output from increasing variable input in Figure 3.1 and in terms of additional output in response to additional input in Figure 3.2. As the amount of variable input is increased, starting from 0, each additional unit of input initially results in a greater amount of output. First, total product is increasing at an increasing rate, and additional product is increasing (A). Then, total output increases at a decreasing rate and additional product decreases (B). Finally, as more and more units of variable inputs are added, total product decreases and additional product becomes negative (C).

The law of variable proportions applies to the entire farm business. It applies not only to fertilizer on crops and feed to livestock but also to the use of labor and

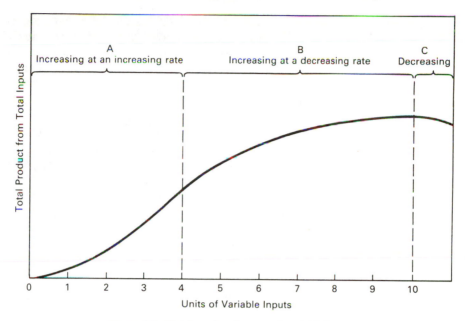

Figure 3.1   Total product from total variable inputs.

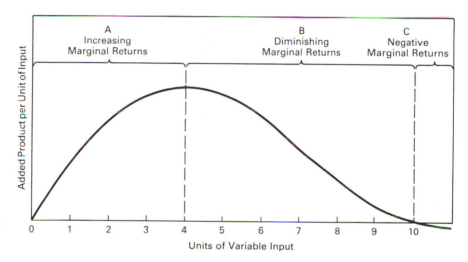

Figure 3.2   Additional product per unit of added variable input.

capital. From a practical standpoint, conditions on a farm are seldom such that they permit increasing rates of return or negative returns. Increasing rates of return could occur in some extreme cases of depleted soils, underfed animals, underemployed workers, or unused capital. The most usual situation is that of decreasing or diminishing rates of return from additional inputs. For example, as 20-pound increments of nitrogen were added to Odell soil (Figure 3.3) starting from 0 and increasing to 200 pounds, the marginal or additional corn from 20-pound increments of nitrogen decreased from 16 bushels to 1 bushel. If the addition of nitrogen had been continued, there would have been some point at which production of corn would have actually decreased.

The law of variable proportions explains the physical relationship a manager is most likely to find. Input and product prices are determined by supply, demand, and institutional forces. Production economics principles, which require information about physical relationships and prices, can determine the maximum profit level of output or input, kinds of inputs, and kinds of output. These principles will now be discussed. Although the three decisions are interrelated, the analysis for making these decisions is most easily understood by examining each production decision individually.

The Most Profitable Level of Production

Decisions on how much to produce or how much input to use must be made every day by farm managers. Examples of these decisions are:

- How much fertilizer should I use?
- How heavy should I feed my hogs?

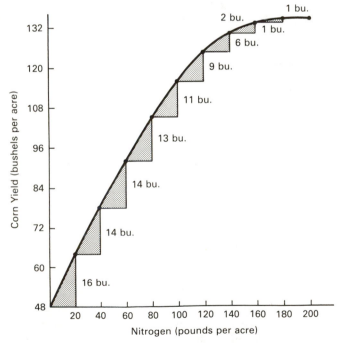

Figure 3.3 Corn response to nitrogen in Odell silt loam in central Indiana. (Based on data reported by R. K. Stivers, Agronomy Department, Purdue University, 1963.)[a]

[a]Data are from an early study but are representative of corn yield response to nitrogen application.

- Should I set the tractor fuel injector up?
- Should I rent 200 more acres?
- Would another hired worker pay?
- How big should my farm business be?
- What is the most profitable level of grain to feed to my dairy cows?

Many levels of input and output are physically possible, but there is usually only *one* level that is most profitable.

A farmer may not choose the most profitable level of production because of limited capital, risk involved, or other factors, but profit is one important consideration for making level-of-output decisions.

The rule for determining the most profitable level of output or resource use in a competitive industry[2] such as agriculture is:

Continue to add inputs until the value of the product gained from an additional unit of input is equal to the cost of an additional unit of input.

VMP (value of marginal product)[3] = CUI (cost of an added unit of input)[4]

The law of variable proportions states that as more and more of a given input is added to fixed amounts of other inputs, marginal product (product gained from adding one unit of input) eventually decreases. Therefore, the value of the marginal product (marginal product times the price of the product) also decreases.

As long as the value of the marginal product (VMP) is greater than the cost of an added unit of input (CUI), it is profitable to add inputs. Eventually, the VMP becomes equal to the cost of an added unit of input; this is the most profitable level of output and input.

For example, when nitrogen is added to corn, the VMP is at first greater than CUI (Figure 3.4). The difference between VMP and CUI, when VMP is greater than CUI, is added to profit. More and more profit is obtained by increasing nitrogen use as long as VMP is greater than CUI. To stop before VMP equals CUI, point P, would result in sacrificing some profit. To add nitrogen after the VMP is below CUI results in a reduction in profit. Therefore, the most profitable level of production is where VMP equals CUI. Table 3.1 shows profit figures for various levels of nitrogen application.

Another way to determine the most profitable level of production is to equate marginal cost and marginal revenue.

MC (marginal cost) = MR (marginal revenue)

[2]In a competitive industry the actions of a single firm do not affect the price of inputs or outputs.

[3]In a competitive industry the value of the marginal product (VMP) is the same as marginal revenue product.

[4]In a competitive industry the cost per added unit of input (CUI) is the same as input price, marginal factor cost (MFC), or marginal input cost (MIC).

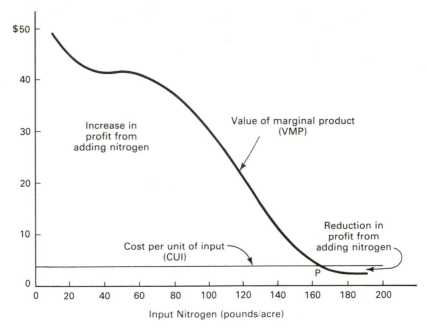

Figure 3.4 Most profitable level of nitrogen use per acre on corn.

TABLE 3.1 Corn Response and Returns to Nitrogen Fertilizer—The Most Profitable Rate of Nitrogen Application[a]

Total Input	Total Product	Marginal Input	Marginal Product	Marginal Input Cost	Value Marginal Product		Total Net Returns
Nitrogen (pounds/acre)	Corn Yield (bushels/acre)	Added Nitrogen (pounds/acre)	Added Yield (bushels/acre)	Added Nitrogen Cost	Added Corn Returns	Added Net Return	from Adding Nitrogen
0	48	—	—	—	—	—	—
20	64	20	16	$4	$48	$44	$44
40	78	20	14	4	42	38	82
60	92	20	14	4	42	38	120
80	105	20	13	4	39	35	155
100	116	20	11	4	33	29	184
120	125	20	9	4	27	23	207
140	131	20	6	4	18	14	221
160	133	20	2	4	6	2	223
180	134	20	1	4	3	−1	222
200	135	20	1	4	3	−1	221

[a]These data are calculated with nitrogen at $0.20/pound and corn at $3.00/bushel.

TABLE 3.2   Marginal Cost with Various Levels of Nitrogen

Nitrogen Input Pounds/Acre	Total Product, Yield /Acre	Marginal Product, Δ Total Product	Cost/Unit Input, Δ Total Cost	Marginal Cost, Δ Total Cost Divided by Δ Total Product	Marginal Revenue, Δ Total Revenue/ Unit Corn Increase
0	48	—	—	—	—
20	64	16	$4.00	$0.25	$3.00
40	78	14	4.00	0.29	3.00
60	92	14	4.00	0.29	3.00
80	105	13	4.00	0.31	3.00
100	116	11	4.00	0.36	3.00
120	125	9	4.00	0.44	3.00
140	131	6	4.00	0.67	3.00
160[a]	133	2	4.00	2.00	3.00
180	134	1	4.00	4.00	3.00
200	135	1	4.00	4.00	3.00

[a]Most profitable level of production.

Marginal cost is the cost of producing one additional unit of production. Marginal cost can be determined by dividing the change in total cost (TC) by the change in total production (TP):

$$MC = \frac{\Delta\ TC}{\Delta\ TP}$$

As noted in Table 3.2, the addition of the first 20 pounds of nitrogen results in a change in total cost of $4.00 and a change in total production of 16 bushels:

$$\text{Marginal cost} = \frac{\$4.00}{16\ \text{bushels}} = \$0.25/\text{bushel}$$

Marginal revenue is the change in total returns from selling one more unit of production. If corn price is $3.00, marginal revenue is $3.00. Since corn is produced for $0.25 and sold for $3.00, it is profitable to add the first 20 pounds of nitrogen. Marginal cost continues below marginal revenue until nitrogen use is increased to 160 pounds. Beyond this point, MC is greater than MR, so the most profitable level of nitrogen is 160 pounds. This marginal cost, marginal revenue, and profit relationship is illustrated in Figure 3.5. The most profitable levels of input use occur when VMP equals CUI or MC equals MR.

The Most Profitable Combination of Inputs

It is usually possible to use different combinations of inputs to produce a given amount of a particular product, but only one of these combinations is cheapest to buy. Farmers face many decisions about the combination of inputs, such as:

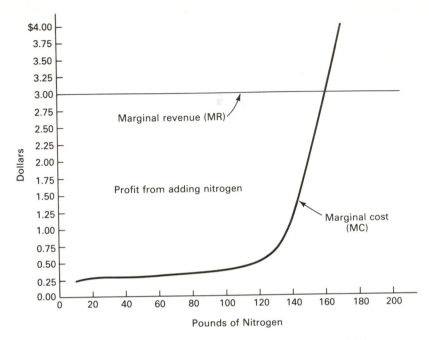

Figure 3.5 Most profitable level of nitrogen use for corn production.

- What combination of grain and protein supplement should be used to feed cattle or hogs?
- What ingredients should be included in the poultry ration?
- Should a high-investment dairy barn be built to reduce labor, or should more labor be used with a low-investment system?
- Should more land be rented or purchased to produce soybeans, or should drainage and fertilization be added to increase production from existing land?

Myron Korse has found from university research data that he can feed various combinations of corn and soybean meal (SBOM) to his hogs and they will still gain the same number of pounds (Table 3.3). He is currently feeding 10 pounds of soybean meal and 421.7 pounds of corn to produce 100 pounds of gain on his 60-pound pigs. Myron has concluded from Table 3.3 that if he increases soybean meal to 15 pounds, he will need only 336.5 pounds of corn to produce a hundredweight of gain on his 60-pound pigs. Thus, 5 pounds of soybean meal (increase from 10 to 15 pounds) reduces corn use by 85.2 pounds (from 421.7 pounds to 336.5 pounds). Each pound of soybean meal replaces 17.04 pounds of corn (85.2 pounds of corn ÷ 5 pounds SBOM). The amount of corn that one pound of SBOM replaces in the ration is called the *marginal rate of substitution* (MRS) of soybean meal for corn, and it is determined by dividing the pounds of corn replaced by the pounds of SBOM added:

TABLE 3.3 Soybean Meal and Corn Combinations to Produce 100 Pounds of Gain for Pigs of 60, 110, and 175 Pounds

60-Pound Pigs

Feed Quantities to Produce 100-Pounds Gain		Marginal Rate of Substitution SBOM for Corn
Pounds SBOM	Pounds Corn	Pounds Corn Replaced by 1 Pound SBOM
10	421.7	
15	336.5	17.04
20	286.7	9.96
25	253.1	6.72
30	228.7	4.88
35	209.8	3.78
40	194.8	3.00
45	182.4	2.48
50	172.0	2.08
55	163.1	1.78
60	155.4	1.54
65	148.6	1.36
70	142.6	1.20
75	137.2	1.08

110-Pound Pigs

Feed Quantities to Produce 100-Pounds Gain		Marginal Rate of Substitution SBOM for Corn
Pounds SBOM	Pounds Corn	Pounds Corn Replaced by 1 Pound SBOM
10	356.8	
15	336.3	4.10
20	319.0	3.46
25	306.0	2.60
30	295.0	2.20
35	287.5	1.50
40	280.6	1.38
45	274.6	1.20
50	269.2	1.08
55	264.4	0.96
60	260.2	0.84
65	256.4	0.76
70	252.9	0.70

175-Pound Pigs

Feed Quantities to Produce 100-Pounds Gain		Marginal Rate of Substitution SBOM for Corn
Pounds SBOM	Pounds Corn	Pounds Corn Replaced by 1 Pound SBOM
10	387.0	
15	370.5	3.30
20	359.3	2.24
25	350.7	1.72
30	344.0	1.32
35	338.2	1.16
40	333.3	0.98
45	329.1	0.84
50	325.4	0.74
55	322.2	0.64
60	319.0	0.64
65	316.4	0.52

Source: Heady, Earl O., Roger Woodworth, Damon V. Catron and Gordon Ashton, Iowa State University A.E.S. Research Bulletin 409, May 1954.[a]
[a]Data are from an early study, but SBOM-Corn substitution relationships are still applicable.

$$\underset{\text{(SBOM for corn)}}{\text{MRS}} = \frac{\Delta \text{ corn}}{\Delta \text{ SBOM}}$$

Because of the law of variable proportions, as more and more of one input is added, it eventually replaces less and less of the other inputs. Myron Korse observed that if he increases SBOM in the ration even more, from 15 to 20 pounds, corn will be reduced only 49.8 pounds. In other words, the marginal rate of substitution of soybean meal for corn is 9.96. Each pound of SBOM replaces 9.96 pounds of corn. As more and more SBOM is added, it replaces less and less corn.

As long as one pound of soybean meal costs less than the corn it replaces, money can be made by substituting SBOM for corn. Myron can purchase SBOM for 12.5 cents per pound and corn for 5 cents per pound. The addition of one more pound of SBOM will cost 12.5 cents and will replace 9.96 pounds of corn, which is worth 49.8 cents (9.96 times 5 cents). Thus Myron can reduce costs for 60-pound pigs by 37.3 cents for each pound of SBOM he substitutes for corn (in the 15–20 pound SBOM range).

But as Myron adds more SBOM to the ration, each pound replaces less and less corn. Eventually the value of the SBOM added equals the value of the corn replaced. If further additions of SBOM are made, the cost of the meal would be greater than the value of the corn replaced, and profit would be decreased by adding SBOM.

> The least-cost combination of inputs for producing a given amount of product occurs when a dollar's worth of one input replaces a dollar's worth of other inputs.

Soybean meal costs 2.5 times as much per unit as corn. Therefore, as long as one unit of soybean meal will replace more than 2.5 units of corn, it will be profitable to substitute bean meal for corn. However, if one unit of soybean meal replaces less than 2.5 units of corn, it will be profitable to substitute corn for bean meal. Hence, the least-cost ration for producing 100 pounds of pork with 60-pound pigs is the combination of corn and soybean meal at which the marginal rate of substitution of soybean meal for corn is 2.5. This is approximately 42.5 pounds of bean meal and 188.6 pounds of corn.

1. Marginal rate of substitution of soybean meal for corn = $\dfrac{\text{Change in corn}}{\text{Change in bean meal}}$

2. Inverse price ratio = $\dfrac{\text{Price of bean meal}}{\text{Price of corn}}$

3. Least-cost ration = $\dfrac{\text{Price of bean meal}}{\text{Price of corn}} = \dfrac{\text{Change in corn}}{\text{Change in bean meal}}$

4. $\dfrac{\$12.50}{\$\ 5.00} = \dfrac{12.5 \text{ pounds}}{5 \text{ pounds}} = 2.5$

5. Least-cost ration is approximately 42.5 pounds soybean meal and 188.6 pounds of corn (taken from Table 3.3 where MRS equals 2.5).

The solution of the least-cost ration may also be found graphically (Figure 3.6). An isoproduct contour indicating the various combinations of corn and soybean meal that can be used to produce 100 pounds of pork is plotted. The slope of the isoproduct curve is the marginal rate of substitution of soybean meal for corn. The isoproduct contour is convex to the origin because the more of one resource included in the ration in relation to other resources, the greater the additional amount of the first resource needed to substitute for a given amount of the second resource. An isocost line is then drawn, indicating combinations of corn and SBOM of equal value. Since the price of soybean meal is 2.5 times the price of corn, the slope of the line will be in a 2.5 to 1 ratio. Thus, 250 pounds of corn has the same value as 100 pounds of soybean meal; any combination of corn and soybean meal denoted by this line has the same value. At the point at which the isocost line is tangent to the isoproduct contour, the

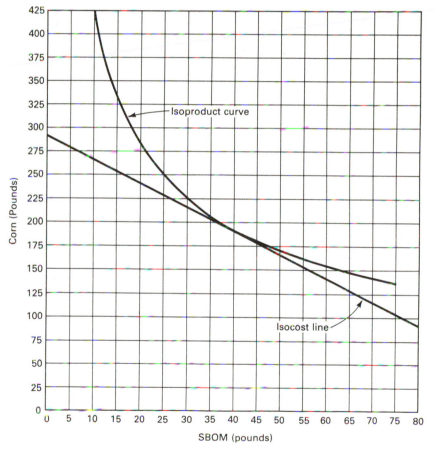

Figure 3.6 Isoproduct curve for producing 100 pounds of pork with 60-pound pigs with corn and soybean meal and isocost line for corn and soybean meal.

marginal rate of substitution is equal to the inverse price ratio; this, therefore, indicates the least-cost combination of corn and soybean meal.

The Most Profitable Combination of Products

Some of the most important decisions a farm manager must make involve planning the kinds of crops and livestock to be produced. Several chapters of this book are devoted to enterprise choice and enterprise size. The economic principle for enterprise-choice decisions is presented here. For maximum profit, resources should be allocated first to the product that will bring the greatest value of marginal product. In accordance with the law of variable proportions, it is likely that VMP will eventually decrease for a given product. If VMP to additional resources decreases below the level of VMP to additional resources for another product, resources should then be allocated to the second product. This allocation should be continued as long as the value of the marginal product is greater than the value of additional inputs or until resources are exhausted.

When the allocation of resources to various enterprises is completed, an additional or marginal unit of resource used in the production of any product will result in an equal value of production.

This situation is attained when:

$$\frac{\text{VM product 1}}{\text{CUI input 1}} = \frac{\text{VM product 2}}{\text{CUI input 1}} = \frac{\text{VM other products}}{\text{CUI input 1}}$$

As an illustration, Table 3.4 shows the returns from two enterprises, crops and livestock, that can be obtained by a manager. He has $50,000 to invest. Following the profit-maximizing allocation procedure presented above, he allocates the first $10,000 unit to crops because they bring the greatest net return. The same is true of the second unit. The addition of the third unit of capital, however, will bring the same return in either crops or livestock; if it is allocated to crops, the next two units of capital would be allocated to livestock. Capital has been allocated between crops and livestock so that it will give the greatest possible return. If $10,000 were taken from the crop enterprise and allocated to livestock, net returns would be decreased. The

TABLE 3.4 Value Marginal Products from Capital Invested in Alternative Uses (Hypothetical)

Total Capital Input	Marginal Capital Input		Value Marginal Product from $10,000	
			Crops	Livestock
10,000	10,000		$16,750	$14,000
20,000	10,000		14,500	14,000
30,000	10,000	3 units	14,000	2 units 13,000
40,000	10,000		13,500	9,000
50,000	10,000		13,000	8,000

same would be true if capital were changed from livestock to crops. Thus, there is no way to reallocate capital to increase net returns. The solution to resource allocation is expressed graphically (Figure 3.7). If the five units of capital are allocated so that the value of marginal product of the last unit of resource in either enterprise is equal, three units of capital will be allocated to crops and two to livestock.

Types of Relationships among Products

The product choice discussed in the preceding section is for the usual case in which products compete for resources. With a given amount of total resource, an increase in the production of one product results in a decrease in the production of other products. Two other types of relationships are the complementary and the supplementary relationship.

Complementary relationships. An increase in the production of one product results in an increase in the production of other products using a given amount of resources. Complementary relationships exist for certain crops. Continuous soybeans may result in decreased yield on a given farm. The addition of corn, wheat, or hay into the rotation may result in more bushels of soybeans grown on fewer acres of land.

Supplementary relationships. The production of one product might be increased without changing the production of other products using a given amount of resources. A small amount of livestock might be added to a crop farm to utilize salvage feed, buildings, labor, and management not used by the crop enterprises.

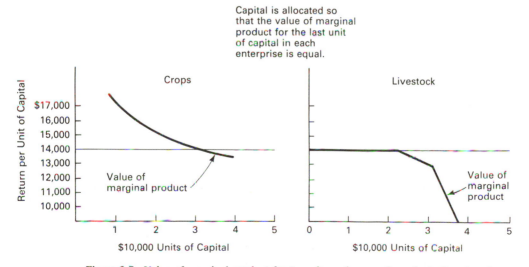

Figure 3.7 Value of marginal product for two alternative uses (hypothetical) and optimum allocation.

If a complementary or supplementary relationship exists, it is always profitable to produce the complementary or supplementary product until it becomes competitive with other products. Then the principles for enterprise choice described in the preceding section apply.

Joint products.   Two or more products are sometimes produced from a single production process. Wheat and straw or mutton and wool are examples. Joint products are treated as a single product.

Summary and Management Implications

1. Produce products in such a combination that an additional unit of resource used in the production of any product will result in an equal value of production.
2. Use such a combination of resources for the production of any product that an additional dollar invested in each resource will result in the additional production of the same amount of product.
3. Add inputs to the business until the last unit of input produces just enough to cover cost of the input or until capital is exhausted.

The preceding may be stated as follows:

1. Produce product combinations: $\dfrac{VMP_1}{CUI} = \dfrac{VMP_2}{CUI}$
2. Use resource combination: Marginal rate of substitution of resource 1 for resource 2 $= \dfrac{\text{Price of 1}}{\text{Price of 2}}$
3. Produce an output: VMP = Cost per unit of input or where MC = MR (assuming capital is unlimited).

If we knew with certainty the prices of products at the time that they will be sold, prices of inputs at the time they will be purchased, and the physical relationship between inputs and output for all farm products, farm decision making would be an exact science. Managers could determine the "best" level of output, combination of resources, and products to produce.

But production takes time, and farm product prices can change between the time a decision is made and the time the product is produced. Likewise, a new planter, purchased to be used several years, may become obsolete the first year. Also, the physical relationship between input and output is affected by weather, disease, the farm operator, and new technologies. It is essential, therefore, that the manager be perceptive in making judgments about prices and the physical relationship between input and output. Much of the needed information cannot be determined precisely at the time the decision must be made (see Chapter 4). The theoretical concepts presented in this chapter are used for decision making, though not with the precision illustrated. Nevertheless, these principles are used by good managers as a decision-making framework or guide and are used for making analyses for farm management decisions.

To make good decisions, a manager needs not only to understand the principles for decision making but also be able to make good judgments regarding technology, prices of inputs at the time they are purchased, and prices of products at the time they are sold. The manager must also recognize that there are wide variations in the ability of operators to manage crops and livestock and, consequently, in operators' abilities to convert inputs into output.

COSTS AND DECISION MAKING

The profitability of each farm management decision is determined by the costs and returns resulting from that decision. Costs and returns for three types of decisions were discussed in the preceding section. Types of costs and their relationship to farm decision making are presented here.

Types of Costs

An important principle is that only variable costs should be considered in decision making. Variable costs change as production changes. Fixed costs do not change. The length of the planning period is critical for determining whether a cost is fixed or variable. The following example illustrates decision making with variable and fixed costs.

Bill Ritz is trying to decide if he should feed cattle this fall and has prepared a budget of expected costs and returns (situation 1, Table 3.5). Bill expects the usual operating costs (items 1 through 5). He will need some extra part-time labor and plans to rent his neighbor's feedlot, which will hold about 100 cattle (items 6 and 7).

All costs are variable. If Bill does not feed cattle, he will not incur any of the costs. If he feeds the cattle, Bill will incur all of the costs shown in situation 1. The net returns above variable costs would be $3,000. Bill feels that $3,000 is satisfactory, so he agrees to hire the extra labor and rents the feedlot. After making these commitments for labor and buildings, however, Bill learns that the cattle price outlook has changed and that the most likely price he will receive is only $65 per hundredweight rather than the original $68 he had planned. This lower beef price would eliminate his net returns! Bill said, "I will not feed cattle for nothing!"

A friend helped Bill prepare a budget for "not feeding cattle" (Table 3.6). Although Bill does not have other uses for the labor and buildings, he has made a commitment for them, so he must pay for them whether they are used or not—these costs are now fixed. Because they do not change as production changes, fixed costs are not

TABLE 3.5   Costs and Returns from Feeding 100 Cattle, Bill Ritz

		Situation 1 100 Calves Fed	Situation 2 100 Calves Fed
A.	Returns		
	10 cwt. each at $68.00 and $65.00	$68,000	$65,000
	Total received	$68,000	$65,000
B.	Variable Costs		
	1. Feed, $191 each	$19,100	$19,100
	2. Feeders purchased at $324 each	32,400	32,400
	3. Veterinarian and medical expenses, $7.00 each	700	700
	4. Power, fuel, misc., $25 each	2,500	2,500
	5. Interest, insurance, taxes	3,800	3,800
	6. Labor	1,500	0
	7. Buildings and equipment, rent	5,000	0
		$65,000	$58,500
	Return above variable costs	$ 3,000	$ 6,500

considered for decision making. After he has rented the feedlot and hired labor, Bill's return above variable costs for feeding cattle with the lower beef price is $6,500 (situation 2, Table 3.5). This is because he will lose $6,500 if he does not feed cattle but will break even if he feeds cattle. Thus the gain from feeding cattle is $6,500.

- *Opportunity value or cost* is the value of a resource in the best use other than the one for which a budget is being prepared. The opportunity value or cost of a resource is the one that should be used for decision making.

In Bill Ritz's cattle-feeding situation 1, all resources could be sold for the amount listed. In situation 2 the labor and buildings could not be used for anything else, so they had an opportunity value or cost of 0.

Time is very important in determining the opportunity value of resources. The longer the time period, the more likely a resource is to have an opportunity value. For example, once Bill Ritz contracted for hiring labor and renting buildings, these resources had no opportunity value for the present feeding year, but they had an opportunity value equal to their rental cost for the next year.

TABLE 3.6   Costs and Returns Without Cattle Feeding, Bill Ritz

A.	Returns	0
B.	Costs	
	1. Labor	$1,500
	2. Rent	5,000
		$6,500
	Net returns above variable cost	−$6,500

Are the following resources likely to be fixed or variable for the time periods given?

Resource	6 Months Fixed or Variable?	1 Year Fixed or Variable?	10 Years Fixed or Variable?
Fertilizer	_____	_____	_____
Seed	_____	_____	_____
Machinery	_____	_____	_____
Feed	_____	_____	_____
Buildings	_____	_____	_____
Farm Operator	_____	_____	_____
Hired labor	_____	_____	_____
Rented land	_____	_____	_____
Owned land	_____	_____	_____

- *Total costs* include all costs of producing a given amount of product.
- *Total variable costs* include all variable costs involved in producing a given amount of product.
- *Total fixed costs* include all fixed costs involved in producing a given amount of product.
- *Average total, variable, and fixed costs* are the above three costs divided by the number of units produced.

Bill Ritz calculated his total fixed and variable costs and average fixed and variable costs for feeding 100 head of cattle.

Total costs:

$$\begin{aligned}
\text{Total variable costs} &= \$58,500 \\
\text{Total fixed costs} &= \underline{\$\ 6,500} \\
\text{Total costs} &\ \$65,000
\end{aligned}$$

Average costs:

$$\text{Average variable cost} = \frac{\$58,500}{100} = \$585$$

$$\text{Average fixed costs} = \frac{\$6,500}{100} = \$65$$

$$\text{Average total cost} = \frac{\$65,000}{100} = \$650$$

The gross return that Bill expects to receive is $650 per head. Bill observed that average variable cost is $585, while gross return per animal is expected to be $650. Bill's question is, "Would it pay me to crowd the feedlot with more than 100 cattle?"

The answer to Bill's question is, "We must calculate marginal cost and compare this to marginal revenue before we know whether or not feeding more than 100 cattle would be profitable."

TABLE 3.7 Cattle-Feeding Costs and Returns for 100–180 Cattle

Number of Cattle Fed	Total Fixed Cost	Total Variable Cost	Total Cost	Average Fixed Cost	Average Variable Cost	Average Total Cost	Marginal Cost	Marginal Revenue	Total Revenue	Return Above Variable Cost	Return Above All Costs
100	$6,500	$ 58,500	$ 65,000	$65.00	$585.00	$650.00	$590	$650	$ 65,000	$6,500	$ 0
110	6,500	64,400	70,900	59.09	585.45	644.55	600	650	71,500	7,100	600
120	6,500	70,400	76,900	54.17	586.67	640.83	615	650	78,000	7,600	1,100
130	6,500	76,550	83,050	50.00	588.85	638.85	635	650	84,500	7,950	1,450
140	6,500	82,900	89,400	46.43	592.14	638.57	660	650	91,000	8,100	1,600
150	6,500	89,500	96,000	43.33	596.67	640.00	690	650	97,500	8,000	1,500
160	6,500	96,400	102,900	40.63	602.50	643.13	730	650	104,000	7,600	1,100
170	6,500	103,700	110,200	38.24	610.00	648.24	790	650	110,500	6,800	300
180	6,500	111,600	118,100	36.11	620.00	656.11		650	117,000	5,400	-1,100

46

- *Marginal cost* is the change in total cost associated with a one-unit change in output. Since fixed costs do not change, marginal cost is also the change in total variable costs associated with a one unit change in output.

- *Marginal revenue* is the change in total revenue associated with a one-unit change in sales. When product price is constant regardless of the amount of product sold, marginal revenue is equal to price. If price increases as quantity increases, marginal revenue is greater than price of product.

It is profitable to increase production if marginal revenue is greater than marginal cost.

To find if it would be profitable to feed more than 100 cattle, Bill estimated cost and return information for numbers of cattle from 100 to 180 (Table 3.7). Bill judged that as cattle numbers increase above 100, the crowding of cattle in the feedlot will result in decreased efficiency and increased costs per head. This is the working of the law of variable proportions.

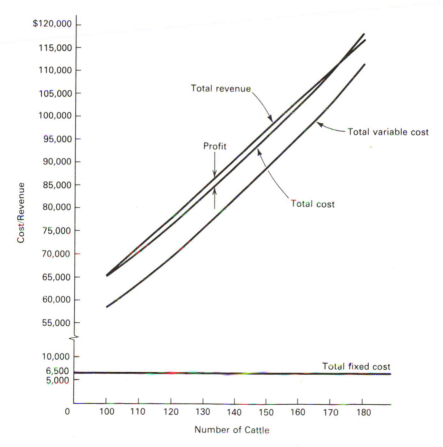

Figure 3.8 Total fixed costs, total variable costs, total costs, and total revenue for feeding cattle, Bill Ritz.

Bill sketched total costs, total fixed costs, total variable costs, and total revenue (Figure 3.8). Bill also plotted average fixed, variable, and total cost and marginal cost and revenue (Figure 3.9). These graphs illustrate what Bill found in the table analysis, that the most profitable number of cattle (when marginal cost = marginal revenue) is 140 head.

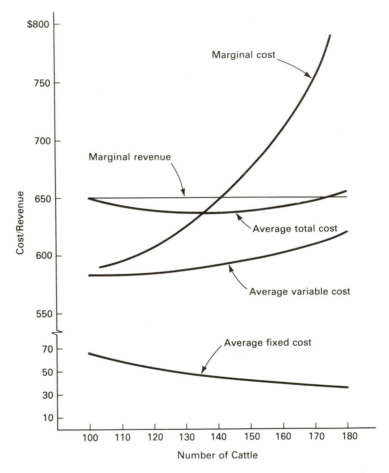

Figure 3.9 Average fixed, average variable, average total marginal costs, and marginal revenue for feeding 100–180 cattle.

FARM CAPITAL INVESTMENT DECISIONS

Capital resources are resources that last more than one year, such as land, buildings, machinery, equipment, and breeding stock. In evaluating capital resource purchase decisions, the manager must determine costs and returns over the planning period for which the purchase is being made. Estimates of costs and returns should reflect changes over time due to price-level change, new technologies, and so on. Income tax should not be overlooked in the decision-making process of capital resource investments. Another important factor is timing—*when* the returns are received and *when* the costs are expended. A dollar received early is more valuable than a dollar received later because the dollar received early can be used to earn interest or to meet other goals.

In making capital resource decisions, the manager should ask these questions: Will it pay? Can I pay for it? and Am I willing to accept the risk? The following procedures should be helpful in making decisions regarding capital resource investments.

Calculate Net Worth at the End of the Planning Period[5]

A useful and simple method of evaluating capital investment decisions is to project farm business net worth[6] for the end of the planning period for each of three situations: (1) the farm operated without the capital investment, (2) the farm with a particular capital item purchased, and (3) another good investment, farm or nonfarm, that may be available. In projecting ending net worth the manager must:

1. Decide on the length of the planning period. The planning period should not be longer than the life of the capital resource. It may be shorter if the manager expects the farm to close operations before the investment resource has been fully used or to sell the investment resource before it has been fully used. Generally speaking, managers use 15 to 20 years for land decisions, 7 to 15 years for buildings, 3 to 10 years for machinery and equipment and 2 to 5 years for cattle and swine breeding stock.

2. Project cash receipts and cash expenses for each year of the planning period. This involves adjustments for price level changes, technological changes and other factors which influence costs and returns. Taxes must be considered as should family living, principal payments, interest on debts and interest received on cash balance.

3. Calculate assets, liabilities and net worth for the end of the planning period. A net worth estimate for each year is useful information for the manager. To determine net worth adjust the net cash flow for changes in the value of all capital assets and inventory items as well as changes in the amount of debt. Finally, compare the projected net worth of the business at the end of a planning period in which a capital investment has been considered with the projected net worth when no capital investment is considered.

4. Take into account the variability that could occur in costs and returns and the impact that different prices and costs could have on farm profit, cash flow, and

---

[5]Two other methods that account for the timing of cash flows are net present value and internal rate of return. For a discussion of these methods, see Peter J. Barry, John A. Hopkins, and C. B. Baker, *Financial Management in Agriculture,* chaps. 9–11 (Danville, Ill.: Interstate Printers and Publishers, 1983).

[6]For an explanation of net worth, see Chapter 5.

TABLE 3.8 Present Operation Compared to Renting 400 Additional Acres, and Investing $100,000 in Machinery: Changes in Cash Flow, Profit, and Net Worth, Charles Scott Farm

	1 Cash Receipts	2 Cash Expense	3 Machinery and Building Depreciation	4 Net Farm Profit 1 − (2 + 3)	5 Family Living	6 Income and Social Security Taxes	7 Net Worth Change 4 − (5 + 6)	8 Principal Payments	9 Net Cash Flow[a] 1 − (2 + 5 + 6 + 8)
Present Plan									
Year									
1	$150,000	$ 90,000	$30,000	$30,000	$15,000	$ 5,000	$10,000	$30,000	$10,000
2	156,000	95,000	30,000	31,000	16,000	5,200	9,800	30,000	9,800
3	162,000	100,000	30,000	32,000	17,000	5,400	9,600	30,000	9,600
Total for 3 years							$29,400		$29,400
Rent 400 More Acres									
Year									
1	$250,000	$150,000	$50,000	$50,000	$15,000	$ 6,500	$28,500	$55,000	$23,500
2	260,000	158,000	50,000	52,000	16,000	13,000	23,000	55,000	18,000
3	270,000	166,000	50,000	54,000	17,000	13,500	23,500	55,000	18,500
Total for 3 years							$75,000		$60,000

[a]Net cash is used to repay debts; this in turn reduces interest costs and cash expenses.

the survival of the farm business (see Chapter 4). Because a capital investment often requires a large outlay of capital at the outset of the planning period, substantial risk may be involved especially if a large amount of money is borrowed. The manager must assess this risk and decide if projected gains are sufficient to warrant the risk.

Capital Investment Analysis

Charles Scott farms 600 acres in Missouri and has the opportunity to rent 400 more acres. In evaluating his machinery situation, he found that he will need to increase machinery size at a cost of $100,000 to efficiently operate the additional 400 acres (see Chapter 16). Charlie can get a three-year rental lease on the land and has decided that three years would be the length of his planning period.

An important consideration in estimating costs and returns is whether Charlie can be as efficient with 1,000 acres as he is with his present 600 acres (see Chapter 13). Efficiency often declines when a major expansion is made. After careful study and thought, Charlie judged that with the larger machinery he has planned, his performance should be just as effective on 1,000 as on 600 acres.

Using a three-year planning period, Charlie projected cash costs, cash returns, and depreciation for the present operation as well as for the proposed plan, which includes the rental of 400 acres and the purchase of machinery valued at $100,000 (Table 3.8). Next he calculated farm profit and then estimated change in net worth by subtracting family living expenses and taxes from net farm income. His analysis shows that continuing his present operation would result in a net worth increase of $29,400 during the next three years, whereas expanding his acreage would result in an increase of $75,000. Thus the answer to the question "Will it pay?" is yes, if events materialize as budgeted.

Cash-flow problems can arise if an investment is unprofitable; if adverse events occur, such as lower-than-expected yields due to unfavorable weather; or if loan principal repayment terms require higher payments than the cash generated by the investment. Charlie calculated net cash flow by subtracting expenses, family living, taxes, and principal payments from cash income. The analysis shows that expansion will make Charlie better off from a cash-flow standpoint with net cash flow for the three years increasing from $29,400 with the present operation to $60,000 with the added 400 acres. Thus the answer to the question "Can I pay for it?" is yes!

Charlie then evaluated the effect that adverse yields or prices might have on profit and cash flow. He judged that costs were not likely to change greatly but that yields and prices could affect cash receipts by as much as 30%. Charlie judged that one year of adverse returns over the three-year period was a distinct possibility. He thought that there was only a small chance of two unfavorable years. In calculating the effect of a 30% reduction in the second year, Charlie observed:

1. Net cash flow in the unfavorable year would be − $43,000 with the expansion but − $27,800 with the present operation (Table 3.9).

TABLE 3.9 Present Operation Compared to Renting 400 Additional Acres, and Investing $100,000 in Machinery: Changes in Cash Flow, Profit, and Net Worth with a 30% Yield Reduction in Year Two, Charles Scott Farm

	1 Cash Receipts	2 Cash Expense	3 Machinery and Building Depreciation	4 Net Farm Profit $1 - (2 + 3)$	5 Family Living	6 Income and Social Security Taxes	7 Net Worth Change in $4 - (5 + 6)$	8 Principal Payments	9 Net Cash Flow[a] $1 - (2 + 5 + 6 + 8)$
Present Plan									
Year									
1	$150,000	$ 90,000	$30,000	$30,000	$15,000	$ 5,000	$10,000	$30,000	$10,000
2	109,200	95,000	30,000	−15,800	12,000	0	−27,800	30,000	−27,800
3	162,000	104,000	30,000	28,000	17,000	2,400	8,600	30,000	8,600
Total for 3 years							−$ 9,200		−$ 9,200
Rent 400 More Acres									
Year									
1	$250,000	$150,000	$50,000	$50,000	$15,000	$ 6,500	$28,500	$55,000	$23,500
2	182,000	158,000	50,000	−26,000	12,000	0	−38,000	55,000	−43,000
3	270,000	173,000	50,000	47,000	17,000	6,500	23,500	55,000	18,500
Total for 3 years							$14,000		−$ 1,000

[a]Net cash is used to repay debts; this in turn reduces interest costs and cash expenses.

52

2. Net farm profit in the unfavorable year would be $-$26,000$ with the expansion but $-$15,800$ without the expansion (Table 3.9).
3. Over the entire three-year period, net worth would increase more and cash flow would decrease less with the expansion than without the expansion because of gains from expansion in the good years.

In making his decision, Charlie had to consider the possibility of the first year's being adverse and determine if he could survive under such circumstances. He also had to weigh the possibility (even though odds were small) of more than one bad year.

Believing that more than one bad year out of three would be highly unlikely and that he could survive one bad year, Charlie decided to accept the risk. He purchased the machinery and rented the 400 acres.

The foregoing analysis included these assumptions: (1) Crops are not stored from one year to the next, (2) 6% investment tax credit could be obtained on the machinery purchase (see Chapter 22), and (3) the added machinery can be sold for the depreciated value of $40,000 after three years. The storage of crops until the next year would affect cash flow by reducing receipts and taxes. If the machinery cannot be sold, it should be depreciated at the rate of 33% per year rather than the 20% used in the analysis.

A manager should use the procedure illustrated to investigate all reasonable capital investment alternatives. Computer programs are available to help farm managers do the calculations necessary to estimate the impact of capital investment on profit, cash flow, and net worth over time.

Two other methods used in evaluating capital investments are simple rate of return and payback period. Both methods are easy to use but are not as informative or as accurate for investment decisions as net worth at the end of the planning period, net present value, or internal rate of return. Neither method accounts for year-to-year differences as to when money is expended and when income is received. This can lead to erroneous conclusions, especially in the evaluation of alternatives with different timing in expenditures and receipts. For example, investment in an orchard requires early expenditures, and receipts follow years later. On the other hand, investment in vegetable production results in receipts soon after expenditures. Simple rate of return and payback period evaluation of Charlie's expansion alternative would be less accurate than net worth at the end of the planning period. Nevertheless, simple rate of return and payback period are useful methods for making quick analyses.

Simple Rate of Return on Investment

$$SRR = \frac{P + ip}{AI} \times 100$$

SRR = Annual percentage return on the investment

P = Annual increase in profit resulting from the investment

ip = Interest paid on borrowed funds used to make the investment

AI = Average investment over the time period

For example, in the Charlie Scott case, net farm profit increased from an average of $31,000 per year before the $100,000 investment to an average of $52,000 after the investment. Interest on borrowed money averaged $5,000 per year without expansion and $15,000 with expansion. For Charlie Scott's expansion:

$$\text{SRR} = \frac{\$21,000 + \$10,000}{(\$100,000 + \$40,000) \div 2} = \frac{\$31,000}{\$70,000} = 44\%$$

This return is quite attractive and is consistent with the large increase in net worth determined previously.

Payback Period

The payback period is the number of years it takes for an investment to pay for itself. To calculate payback period, divide the total investment by net farm profit with depreciation deleted from the costs.

$$\text{PP} = \frac{I}{P + \text{Depreciation of the investment}}$$

PP = Payback period

I = Initial investment

Depreciation is excluded because it is not a cash cost, and the amount of annual depreciation can be used to pay for the investment.

In the Charlie Scott case,

$$\text{PP} = \frac{\$100,000}{\$21,000 + \$20,000} = 2.44 \text{ years}$$

This rapid payback period verifies the results of both the ending net worth and the return on investment analyses.

INFORMATION FOR FARM DECISIONS

Decisions are no better than the information on which they are based. The economic decision-making framework enables a manager to determine the most profitable decision *provided* the prices of resources, prices of products, and quantities of inputs and outputs are projected correctly. Each manager must develop procedures for securing needed information and a policy regarding the amount of information to collect before making decisions. The manager must plan for the kinds of information

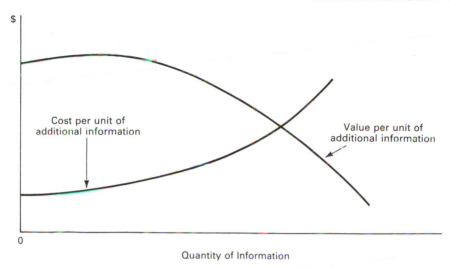

$

Cost per unit of
additional information

Value per unit of
additional information

0

Quantity of Information

Figure 3.10   Cost and returns from information for making management decisions.

needed, the alternative sources of needed information, the cost of securing information from alternative sources, and the value of needed information.

The law of variable proportions applies to information gathering; the cost of additional amounts of information increases and the value declines as more and more information is collected (Figure 3.10).

Managers can become more efficient in collecting information and can reduce information costs by carefully defining information needs and sources.

> Check in Figures 3.11 and 3.12 your best sources of various kinds of information. Make a more detailed listing of types of information needed for making sound management decisions.

DECISIONS AND ACTION

Making the right decisions is a critical aspect of good management. Managers must continuously make themselves aware of the choices or decisions available to them and must be able to identify the most important ones. To make good decisions a manager must not only collect relevant information but must also have an understanding of the application of production economics, cost concepts, and capital investment concepts.

Finally, although good decisions are essential to successful management, they are useful only if they are put into action.

Information about	Past Experience	Trial and Error on Whole Operation	Experimentation on a Limited Scale	Observing the Experience of Others	Reasoning from Information Known to Be True	Keeping Written Records
Prices of Things Sold Past prices and price trends						
Current prices and changes in prices						
Price outlook						
Prices of Things Bought Past prices and their trends						
Current prices and changes in costs						
Price outlook						
Production Factors Existing varieties of crops and livestock						
Existing methods of producing crops and livestock						
Climate, soil, and disease conditions						
New Development New inventions, developments, and discoveries						
Human Factors People you must deal with in running your farm						
People whose reactions may be important to you in running your farm						
Political, Social, and Religious Factors Chances for depression or prosperity						
Actions and attitudes of local informal groups that may affect your farm						
Actions of nongovernment groups (e.g., Farm Bureau, American Legion, etc.)						
Federal, state, and local government actions affecting farming						

Figure 3.11 General information sources for farm management decision making. *Source:* Johnson, Glenn L., Albert N. Halter, Harald R. Jensen, and D. Woods Thomas. *A Study of Managerial Processes of Midwestern Farmers.* Ames, Iowa: The Iowa State University Press, 1961.

DISCUSSION QUESTIONS

1. Is it possible for a manager to be unaware of a decision that needs to be made? How can this occur? What are some examples?
2. How can a manager determine which decisions are most important?
3. Have you made any personal observations that illustrate the law of diminishing return or variable proportions? Can you think of any areas where the law of variable proportions does not apply?

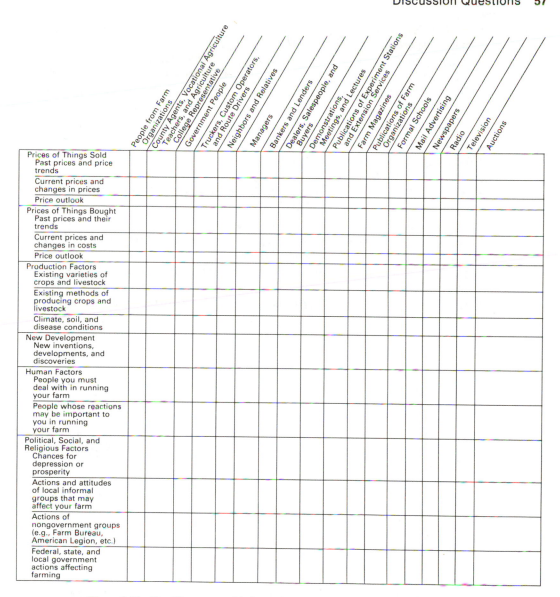

Figure 3.12 Specific sources of information for farm management decision making. *Source:* Johnson, Glenn L., Albert N. Halter, Harald R. Jensen, and D. Woods Thomas. *A Study of Managerial Processes of Midwestern Farmers.* Ames, Iowa: The Iowa State University Press, 1961.

4. Is the highest possible yield per acre the most profitable yield per acre? How can one determine most profitable yield per acre?

5. Is there one specific "best" ration that should be fed to livestock, or does the "best" ration vary with the price of the components? How can one determine the least-cost ration?

6. Should farms produce only one product, or should they have several enterprises? Explain.

7. How should a manager decide which crops to produce?

8. If a manager understands production economics and can apply this understanding to important management decisions, will this assure that the manager makes good decisions?

9. In making a management decision, what determines the value that the manager should place on a resource?

10. Is it possible for a particular resource, such as a building, to have different values for different decision-making periods? Explain.

11. Define: total cost, fixed cost, variable cost, opportunity cost, average cost, marginal cost.

12. How do the analyses required for making these two decisions differ: How much fertilizer should I use? Should I build a new cow barn?

13. Should a manager collect all the information possible before making a management decision? Explain.

14. What kinds of information does a manager need? What are the sources of information?

15. Does making good decisions assure success?

RELATED READINGS

BARNARD, C. S., and J. S. NIX. *Farm Planning and Control* (2nd ed.), chap. 2. Cambridge: Cambridge University Press, 1980.

BARRY, PETER J., JOHN A. HOPKIN and C. B. BAKER. *Financial Management in Agriculture* (3rd ed.), chaps. 10–11. Danville, Ill.: The Interstate Printers and Publishers, Inc., 1983.

DOLL, J. P., and F. ORAZEM. *Production Economics: Theory with Applications,* chaps. 2–5. Columbus, Ohio: Grid Inc., 1978.

FERGUSON, C. E., and J. P. GOULD. *Microeconomic Theory* (4th ed.), chaps. 6–8. Homewood, Ill.: Richard D. Irwin, 1975.

HARSH, STEPHEN B., LARRY J. CONNOR, and GERALD D. SCHWAB. *Managing the Farm Business.* Englewood Cliffs, N.J.: Prentice-Hall, 1981.

HEADY, EARL O. *Economics of Agricultural Production and Resource Use.* New York: Prentice-Hall, 1952.

JOHNSON, GLENN L., ALBERT N. HALTER, HARALD R. JENSEN, and D. WOODS THOMAS. *A Study of Managerial Processes of Midwestern Farmers.* Ames, Iowa: The Iowa State University Press, 1961.

KRANNERT, HERMAN C. *Krannert on Management.* West Lafayette, Ind.: Purdue University, Krannert Graduate School of Industrial Administration, 1966.

Uncertainty and Farm Decision Making

4

The future cannot be predicted with certainty. The variation in the possible results of a decision is called uncertainty. Sometimes results of a decision are better than expected and sometimes the results are worse than expected. One key requirement of a successful farm manager is the ability to make decisions and act even though the outcome of the decision is not certain.

The inability to tolerate uncertainty keeps many people from the ownership and management of businesses. A farm management student asked a seasoned businessman about the most important thing that determines success in business. The businessman's reply was, "It takes guts to succeed in business. Lots of people have good ideas, but only a few have the courage to implement them."

Each farm business manager or owner must be willing to accept some uncertainty. A greater understanding of the sources of uncertainty, principles for decision making under uncertainty, and methods of protecting the business against adverse uncertainty are helpful to a manager and will be discussed in this chapter.

SOURCES OF UNCERTAINTY IN FARMING

- *Production uncertainty*. Crop yields per acre and livestock production vary greatly because of weather, disease, pests, and so on. Small variations in production have a major impact on profits.
- *Price uncertainty*. Prices of crops and livestock vary widely because of supply and demand conditions. Likewise, price variations occur for inputs that farmers purchase. These variations have a major impact on farm profit.
- *Obsolescence*. Farmers must often make investments in resources such as machinery and buildings which last for several production periods. Sometimes major improvements are made in durable resources, and as a result the usefulness and return of physically sound but obsolete buildings and equipment is reduced. A farmer might have made a major investment in ear-corn storage just before the introduction of the picker-sheller. Many farmers made major investments in confinement livestock facilities before information was available about slotted floors.
- *Political and social uncertainty*. Changes in laws and regulations are a major source of uncertainty for farmers. Regulations about such things as crop chemical use, feed additives, and waste disposal may result in increased costs,

investments, and management requirements. New laws and regulations are sometimes enacted because of changes in social attitudes.

- *Human uncertainty.* Changes in the goals, health, or behavior of persons working on a farm are unpredictable and have a major impact on the operation, costs, and profit.
- *Financial uncertainty.* Variation in the availability, cost, and rate of payback for capital affects the business. Also, availability of rented land may be uncertain because of decisions made by the landlord.
- *Mechanical uncertainty.* Machines break down from time to time, and these breakdowns have an impact on crop timeliness and production, livestock efficiency, and costs.
- *Casualty loss uncertainty.* Buildings, machinery, crops, and livestock may be damaged or destroyed as a result of fire, wind, water, hail, or vandalism.

> List some examples of variations in farm profit that have occurred as a result of the factors listed above.

FARM DECISION MAKING UNDER UNCERTAINTY

Uncertain conditions create risks for managers. To a manager, risk means increased chances of having an income below expectations, perhaps so low that the business is unable to meet financial commitments.[1] Income might even be so low that the business must be liquidated.

The good manager is able to recognize situations in which risk tends to be greater—for example:

- When the costs or prices or yields of the enterprise fluctuate widely
- When the percent borrowed relative to owned is high
- When experience with a particular type of business is limited
- When a commitment is made for a high-cost fixed asset which lasts a long time and is difficult to sell
- When large amounts of money are involved.

In a particular year, some events may materialize better than expected and others may be worse than expected. There is often some compensation or balancing of "better" and "worse" events. Low crop yields may be offset by higher prices. Low prices of one commodity might be offset by higher prices of another com-

---

[1]Other definitions of risk are presented in economic literature. The definition given here is one of the most common used by farm managers.

modity. Thus much of the impact of uncertainty is reduced, and total results are close to total expectations even though many aspects of the farm business are better or worse than anticipated. But at certain times, unfavorable events will outweigh the favorable events, and the business will make less money than expected.

Although uncertainty creates great risks for farmers, it also provides opportunities for profit if the manager uses appropriate management strategies. The opportunity for profit (and loss) is usually higher in uncertain industries than in more certain industries. Managers who have the fortitude and management skill to operate in a risky environment will likely be paid for their capabilities.

GUIDELINES FOR DECISION MAKING IN AN UNCERTAIN ENVIRONMENT

Identify your risk-profit preference. Higher-profit farm business organizations often (but not always) have more risk than lower-profit organizations. It is important for each manager to assess the optimum trade-off between income and risk. What level of risk can be tolerated? What is the value in personal satisfaction of an additional $1,000 income? How does this gain in satisfaction from an additional $1,000 compare to the loss in satisfaction from a $1,000 income decrease? (See Table 2.1 for estimating your own risk-profit preference.)

Assign probabilities to various outcomes that could result from a decision. Each decision a manager makes has not one but a series of possible outcomes, depending on external events. In budgeting, farmers often use the "most likely" yield or price, recognizing that actual outcome may be higher or lower. When making decisions in an uncertain environment, farmers must think in terms of the range in outcomes that could result from a decision and the probability and consequences of each occurrence. These probabilities are difficult to estimate accurately, but they are the heart of decision making under uncertainty, and good estimates are necessary for good decisions. Farmers who have the ability to assess the environment accurately can be more effective managers under uncertainty.

Ralph Williams considered purchasing land in 1983. Ralph calculated the returns he expected under various yield and price situations that he thought could occur (Table 4.1)

Ralph assigned probabilities to the corn yields and prices in Table 4.1 and calculated the probability of each corn yield–price combination by multiplying each corn yield probability by each price probability (Table 4.2).

In assigning yield probabilities, Ralph studied his records to determine experiences he had with similar soil. He obtained a listing of yield variability on farms that kept records in cooperation with his state extension service. He read the long-range weather forecasts of climatologists. After all of his study, Ralph

TABLE 4.1 Cash Remaining after All Costs, Including Mortgage Payments[a]

Corn Yield	Corn Price			
	$2.20	$2.60	$3.00	$3.40
	Dollars per Acre Remaining[b]			
130	− $35	$17	$69	$121
110	− 71	− 27	17	61
90	− 107	− 71	− 35	1

[a]$1,000/acre borrowed at 9% over 20 years.

[b]After all costs, including machinery depreciation, operator labor and management, and land interest, principal, and tax payments. No charge is made for the $1,000 equity in land.

concluded the most likely event was an "average" year (70% chance) with a normal distribution of good and bad years (15% chance of each) around the average years.

In assigning prices, Ralph was almost certain that the government would support corn prices above $2.50, so he gave the $2.20 price only a 1% chance. Ralph judged that corn prices most likely will be in the $2.60 to $3.00 range (80% probability). Ralph thought there was a 19% chance that unfavorable world weather or very rapid inflation would increase corn prices to $3.40.

Ralph multiplied each of the probabilities in Table 4.2 times the income associated with that probability in Table 4.1 and totaled all of these figures to determine that his long-run expected return after mortgage payments was:

Sum of Table 4.1 returns × Table 4.2 probabilities = $6.88

If Ralph's return estimates and yield and price probabilities are correct and if he can stay in business over time, his long-run cash flow from the purchased farm will be $6.88 per acre. Ralph must weigh this return against the 41% probability that he will have a negative cash flow in particular years. On

TABLE 4.2 Probabilities of Various Crop Yields and Corn Prices

Corn Yield		Corn Price			
		$2.20	$2.60	$3.00	$3.40
	Yield Probabilities[a]	Price Probabilities[a]			
		.01	.40	.40	.19
130	.15	.0015	.06	.06	.0285
110	.70	.0070	.28	.28	.1330
90	.15	.0015	.06	.06	.0285

Positive cash flow probability   Negative cash flow probability
of 59%   of 41%

[a]It is assumed in this example that yield and price probabilities are independent. With some crops in some geographic areas, price may be dependent to some extent on the yield.

the other hand, there is some chance of making much higher than expected returns. Ralph, then, must match his risk tolerance and profit goals with potential returns and losses in deciding if he should purchase the land. Of course, if Ralph has surplus income from other parts of his farm operation or from off-farm sources, this surplus could be used as a cushion in bad years, thus reducing the risk. The total farm cash flow and profit situation must be considered.

Decision trees can be helpful to a manager for visualizing alternatives and consequences. The main branches of a decision tree represent the choices that a manager can make. The subbranches extending from the main branches show the results of the decisions with alternative environmental occurrences.

Robbie Echer is trying to decide if he should feed cattle. Two types of uncertainty he is facing are price and performance due to the weather. Robbie developed a decision tree for his cattle-feeding decision (Figure 4.1). Robbie found that his odds

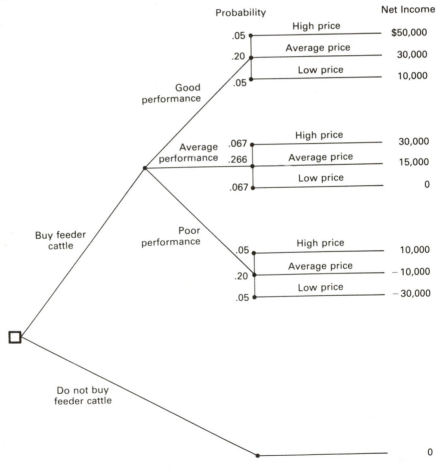

Figure 4.1 Decision tree for Robbie Echer cattle-feeding decision.

of making money would be 68.3%, his odds of losing money would be 25%, and his odds of just breaking even would be 6.7%. He decided to feed cattle.

Decision trees can be useful for visualizing the consequences of many other types of decisions, such as amount of fertilizer application, land rental, land purchase, and so on.

Choose a farm strategy consistent with your risk-profit preference.
Some strategies for decision making under uncertainty follow.

1. Maximize expected income. A manager can calculate the expected incomes for various alternatives, the way that Ralph Williams did for his land purchase alternative in the preceding section, and choose the alternatives that have the highest expected incomes. This is the strategy that is most likely to be profitable if a manager has sufficient financial resources to survive in adverse times. If a manager does not have sufficient reserves and encounters unfavorable years early, he or she may not be in business to experience more favorable years.

2. Select the farm organization with the highest possible income.
This strategy best fits a manager who receives much satisfaction from making extra money and is not greatly worried by the prospect of losing money.

In Figure 4.2, Pete has organized his farm for an expected annual income of $43,000. In a year of extremely favorable events, income could reach $100,000, but in a year of unfavorable events, losses could run to $30,000. Pete enjoys managing this type of business. He shoots for the maximum chance of highest income. Pete is a *maximaxer*.[2]

Pete feeds heavy cattle, raises fresh vegetables, and rapidly increases the size of his business with borrowed capital. He recognizes that if unfavorable conditions persist over a period of time, his business could go bankrupt.

3. Select the farm organization that minimizes maximum losses. Joe does not like the prospect of unpaid bills or bankruptcy. He likes to know where he stands. He likes events to materialize as planned. Joe would prefer a $15,000 expected income with little chance of income falling below $5,000 to Pete's $43,000 income with a chance of bankruptcy (Figure 4.2).

Joe wants to minimize maximum losses; he is a *minimaxer*.[2] Joe has a dairy herd with an irrigated land unit. He doesn't expand his farm business unless he has most of the cash to pay for expansion. He has considered selling out and taking a government job with an assured income and guaranteed retirement plan.

4. Select the organization with the highest expected income but a selected level of minimum income. Bill is part maximaxer and part minimaxer (Figure 4.2). He would like a high income but would not like to chance bankruptcy.

[2]Suter, Robert C., "The Management Process," *Journal of the American Society of Farm Managers and Rural Appraisers,* XXVII (October 1963), 5–18.

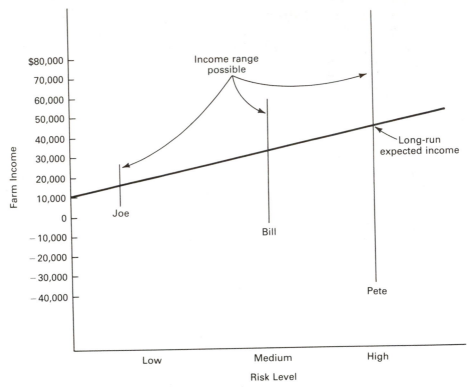

Figure 4.2   Gain and loss possibilities from alternative farm organizations (illustrative).

He has organized his business for a $30,000 expected income but with little chance of income falling below zero.

The "best" strategy depends on the risk-profit preferences of those who own and manage the business.

> Make estimates of production, price, and profit variability for the major en-terprises in your area (see example in Table 4.3).
>
> Make a listing of the enterprises, production systems, marketing prac-tices, debt level, and growth characteristics that should be followed by a maximaxer and a minimaxer. Which are you? What are your risk-profit pref-erences?

Astute managers look for alternatives with high expected earnings and low risk. *Although risk is associated with profitability, it does not follow that all risky choices have a high expected profit.* A manager must carefully evaluate the risk and profit potential of alternative choices for any farm business.

TABLE 4.3 Variability of Real Farm Labor Income, 1965–1979 for Selected States and Types of Farms[a]

State and Type of Farm	Mean Income	Standard Deviation	Coefficient of Variation
Kansas farms	18,013	21,376	118.7
Michigan			
Specialized dairy	15,765	12,057	76.5
All farms	15,423	13,811	89.6
Illinois			
Northern Grain	27,246	21,744	79.8
Southern Grain	23,408	12,354	52.8
Northern Hog	31,513	30,744	97.6
Southern Hog	29,624	18,295	61.8
Northern Beef	9,954	24,699	248.1
Indiana (per operator)			
Hog	42,573	29,380	69.0
Dairy	22,024	7,679	34.9
Crop	34,867	27,704	79.5
Crop-Hog	40,472	30,430	75.2
State	36,390	24,996	68.7

[a]Derived from annual farm record summaries in the selected states. Incomes have been adjusted to 1979 dollars by the index of prices paid by farmers for commodities, interest, taxes, and wages.
Source: Steven T. Sonka and George F. Patrick, *Risk Management in Agriculture,* Chapter 8, Ames, Iowa: Iowa State University Press, 1984.

Control risk at acceptable levels.   Farmers can take steps to reduce their risk. The two most important steps are things that should be done in any event, and they are discussed first.

Keep the efficiency level high.   Efficiency is not only important for increasing farm profit (Chapter 1), but it is also a good strategy for minimizing risk. Efficiency with crops, livestock, labor, and machinery will reduce risk.

For example, cattle feeders are subject to risk as cattle prices and production costs cycle. The average cattle feeder experiences alternating periods of profit and loss as a result of price and cost fluctuations (Figure 4.3). A few highly efficient cattle feeders have costs of production as much as $7 per hundredweight or approximately $50 per head below average. Many feeders drop out of production as cattle returns fall below the break-even level. As a result, supplies decrease and prices increase. Losses experienced by producers with costs of production $50 below average are much less severe than the losses of the average cattle feeder. Because of the wide range of efficiency that exists in agriculture, high-cost producers often drop out and prices increase before low-cost producers suffer severe losses. A high level of efficiency increases profit and decreases risk at the same time.

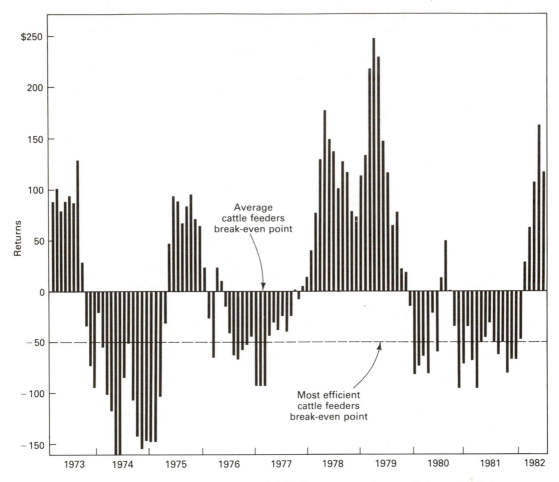

Figure 4.3 Net returns variability for average and most efficient cattle feeders.

Do a good job of buying and selling. Doing a good job of buying and selling has an effect on risk similar to efficiency. If a cattle feeder reduces costs 5% by doing a better job of purchasing cattle and feed and obtains 5% higher prices by more carefully evaluating alternative markets and marketing times, these two gains will provide several dollars per hundredweight in risk protection that the average producer does not have.

Other risk protection alternatives. Production efficiency and good buying and selling techniques reduce risk and increase profit at the same time. The following steps for risk protection usually do not increase profit, and some may decrease profit. Each manager must decide if the risk protection these strategies provide is worth the cost of the action.

- Implement big decisions in small steps over time (i.e., spread sales of crops and livestock, buy land a little at a time, construct buildings over a period of years).
- Calculate cash flows for a range of price and yield possibilities before making long-term commitments for land, buildings, or machinery.
- Keep cash flow and profit records up-to-date so that problems can be detected at once.
- Contract or hedge when prices are favorable, but be aware of the reverse risk of contracting more than is produced and having to fill a contract with commodities that have a higher price than the contract.
- Arrange for debt repayment periods to be as long as allowable by credit institutions. In some cases, loans allow "waiving" or delaying principal payments during adverse conditions.
- Time debt repayments to coincide with sales. Credit institutions often allow more flexibility in time of payments than is used by borrowers.
- Stay in a liquid financial position. This essentially means exercising careful control of borrowing for resources that must be paid for more quickly than they are depleted and also exercising caution about the purchase of resources that would sell for substantially less than they cost.
- Reduce the percentage and amount borrowed. Avoid overextension in debts for land and buildings at high interest rates.
- Maintain a credit or cash reserve equal to one or two years of debt payments.
- Diversify by producing more than one type of crop and/or livestock.
- Select stable enterprises.
- Use low-investment production systems rather than high-investment systems.
- Crop-share rather than rent for cash.
- Lease rather than buy.
- Do some work for a guaranteed wage, such as custom work.
- Find a partner with money, land, or machinery to exchange for labor and management.
- Minimize production risk by having adequate amounts of labor, machinery, and supplies to get jobs done well and on time.
- Carry comprehensive insurance for buildings, crops, livestock, machinery, liability, lives of people important to the business, etc.
- Maintain a high level of maintenance on machinery, equipment, and buildings.
- Have employee policies that minimize the chances of employees' leaving the business.

GOOD DECISIONS DO NOT ENSURE GOOD RESULTS

A good decision is one that is most likely to attain the desired income, risk, and other objectives of the manager. The fact that an event is most likely, however, does not mean the event will occur. Managers who make good decisions are more likely to have good results than are managers who do not make good decisions. However, sometimes good decisions will have bad results. This is why an important ingredient of management is the ability to evaluate, control, and tolerate risk and uncertainty.

DISCUSSION QUESTIONS

1. What are the sources of risk in farming?
2. Why is it necessary that all managers have some tolerance for risk? Is it possible to be a manager if you dislike risk?
3. Does the risk tolerance of a manager affect the organization of the farm? How?
4. What are some different risk-income goals that managers might have?
5. Can a manager reduce risk by studying changes that are occurring in the environment? Give examples.
6. How can a manager calculate *expected returns* from a decision and *outcomes* from a decision?
7. What is a decision tree? How can it be helpful for making management decisions in an uncertain environment?
8. What strategies can a manager use to reduce risk?
9. Is there a cost to reducing farm business risk? Explain.
10. Will good decisions always have good results? Why?

RELATED READINGS

ANDERSON, JOCK, R., JOHN L. DILLON and BRIAN HARDAKER. *Agricultural Decision Analysis,* chaps. 5–7. Ames, Iowa: Iowa State University Press, 1977.

BARRY, PETER J., and DONALD R. FRASER. "Risk Management in Primary Agricultural Production: Methods, Distribution, Rewards, and Structural Implications," *American Journal of Agricultural Economics,* 58 (1976): 286–295.

HALTER, ALBERT N., and GERALD W. DEAN. "Decisions under Uncertainty with Research Applications." Cincinnati: South-Western Publishing Co., 1971.

KADLEC, JOHN E. "Guidelines for Farm Decision Making in a Period of Uncertainty," Purdue University Cooperative Extension Service EC 456, West Lafayette, Ind., 1978.

NELSON, GENE A., GEORGE L. CASLER and ODELL WALKER. *Making Farm Decisions in a Risky World: A Guidebook.* Oregon State University Agricultural Extension Service, Corvallis, Ore., 1978.

PENSON, JOHN B., JR., and DAVID A. LINS. *Agricultural Finance: An Introduction to Micro and Macro Concepts,* chaps. 6–7. Englewood Cliffs, N.J.: Prentice-Hall, 1980.

Risk Management in Agriculture, edited by Peter J. Barry. Ames, Iowa: Iowa State University Press, 1984.

WESTON, J. FRED, and EUGENE F. BRIGHAM. *Essentials of Managerial Finance.* (9th ed.), chaps. 14–15. Hinsdale, Ill.: The Dryden Press, 1982.

Farm Financial Records

5

Farm records are important. They are essential for reporting and documenting income taxes, they are important for making management decisions, they are important for obtaining credit, they are helpful in checking whether the business is operating according to plans, and they are useful for determining if the farm can compete with other similar farms.

The details of records may make them look complicated, but the basic elements of records are simple. Once these elements are understood, farm records are simple.

Why do farm record systems often fail? Some fail because farmers do not use the records they keep and consequently lose enthusiasm. Others fail because the system is not understood by the farmer and each entry is a frustration. Still others fail because record entries are neglected for months at a time, resulting in loss of accuracy and usefulness.

Farmers should identify their specific needs for information from records and then select a record system to meet these needs. They should learn this system thoroughly and discipline themselves to follow the planned system.

The present chapter focuses on records for measuring the financial strength of the business. Chapter 6 will focus on the use of records for making management decisions, obtaining credit, and reporting income taxes. It will also present some helpful guidelines for keeping records.

BALANCE SHEETS

One of the most important indicators of financial progress of a farm business or of an individual is the balance sheet, sometimes called a net worth statement or a financial statement. The balance sheet is a listing, on a particular date, of all the assets (what is owned), and their value, all the liabilities (the amount that is owed), and the difference between assets and liabilities, which is net worth (the amount that is owned after payment of debts).

Assets and liabilities are listed according to whether they are current, intermediate, or long term (Figure 5.1). Current assets are cash and other resources that are expected to be realized in cash, sold, or used up within one year. Current liabilities are debts expected to be paid within one year. Intermediate assets are resources that are expected to last from one to ten years, and intermediate liabilities are debts to be paid back within one to ten years. Long-term assets and liabilities are those that last for more than ten years.

FINANCIAL STATEMENT
(Agricultural)

☐ Individual
☐ Partnership

Phone: 432-6318

By:
Name Kirk and Susan Henly

Address R.R. #2 Ockley Center

To:

Date of Statement

ASSETS		LIABILITIES	
CURRENT ASSETS		**CURRENT LIABILITIES (Due within 12 Months)**	
Cash	$100.00	Notes Due this Bank • *secured*	
Crops or Feed on Hand (Schedule F)		• *unsecured*	
Livestock Held for Sale (Schedule D)		Notes to Others • *secured* (include CCC loans)	
Marketable Bonds and Securities (Schedule C)		• *unsecured*	
Accounts Receivable		Accounts Payable (gas, feed, repairs, vet, etc.)	
Notes Receivable			
Cash Invested in Growing Crops (Schedule F)		Portion Intermediate and Long Term Debt	
Other Current Assets		Due within 12 Months	
		Taxes • *Income, Real and Personal*	
		Rent	
		Other Debts Due within 12 Months	
TOTAL—Current Assets	$100.00	TOTAL—Current Liabilities	
INTERMEDIATE TERM ASSETS		**INTERMEDIATE TERM LIABILITIES**	
Cash Value Life Insurance (Schedule B)		Portion of loans of more than 12 Months on:	
Machinery, Equipment, Cars, Trucks (Schedule G)	$1600.00	• *Machinery and Equipment*	
		Automobile	$200.0
Breeding Stock (Schedule E)			
Securities (not readily marketable) (Schedule C)		• *Breeding Stock*	
Household Furnishings and Equipment			
Other Intermediate Assets		• *Life Insurance* (Schedule B)	
		• *Household Furnishings and Equipment*	
		Lease Payments Due Beyond 1 Year	
		Other Intermediate Term Liabilities	
TOTAL—Intermediate Assets	$1600.00	TOTAL—Intermediate Liabilities	$200
LONG TERM OR FIXED ASSETS		**LONG TERM LIABILITIES**	
Farm Real Estate (Schedule A)		Real Estate Mortgages (Schedule A) • *Except*	
		that portion listed under Current Liabilities	
Other Real Estate (Schedule A)		TOTAL—Long Term Liabilities	
		TOTAL LIABILITIES	$200.0
TOTAL—Fixed Assets		PRESENT NET WORTH	$1500.
TOTAL ASSETS	$1700.00	TOTAL LIABILITIES & NET WORTH	$1700.

SCHEDULE A—*Real Estate—Owned or Rented*

Title Held By	Description (County, Twp., Etc.)	Acres	Year Purch.	Present Value	Mortgage	Date D
Owned				$	$	
Rented			Type Lease		Expires	

For purpose of securing credit from time to time this statement is furnished and is certified to be true and correct. I (or We) agree to notify said bank promptly of any material change he

Date January 2 , 19 76

Signature Kirk Henley

Witness Sadie Hood

Signature Susan Henley

Figure 5.1 Financial statement, Kirk and Susan Henly. Courtesy of Continental Illinois National Bank and Trust Company of Chicago.

1. Marital Status ☐ Married ☐ Separated						5. Insurance on Machinery, Equipment and Livestock $ —				

1. Marital Status ☐ Married ☐ Separated
☐ Unmarried (including single, divorced, and widowed)

(Do not complete if this is an application for individual unsecured credit not primarily for agricultural purposes unless you reside in a community property state or property upon which you are relying as a basis for repayment of the credit requested is located in a community property state).

2. Ages of Dependents   **No dependents**
3. Insurance on Crops $
4. Insurance on Buildings (Fire, Ext. Cov.) $

If a Partnership Give Detail: Name Partners

5. Insurance on Machinery, Equipment and Livestock $ —
6. List Contingent Liabilities   —
7. Your Age **22**   Physical Condition **Excellent**
8. Have you been involved in bankruptcy?   Yes **(No)**
9. Defendant in suits or legal actions or judgments outstanding?   Yes **(No)**
10. Do you carry health, accident, or hospital insurance?   **(Yes)** No
11. Liability Insurance Coverage **$300,000**

Addresses   Per Cent Interest

SCHEDULE B—Life Insurance (include credit life)

Insurance Company	Beneficiary	Face Value	Cash Value	Amt. Borrowed	Due	From Whom
Hamilton Life	Susan Henley	$50,000	—	—	—	—

SCHEDULE C—Bonds and Securities (in your name)

No. of Shares or Par Value Bonds	Description	Market Value
	TOTAL	

SCHEDULE D—Livestock Held for Sale

Number	Description	Wt.	Price	Value
	TOTAL			

SCHEDULE E—Breeding Stock

Number	Description	Age	Wt.	Price	Value
	TOTAL				

SCHEDULE F—Crops or Feed on Hand or Growing (your share only)

Crop or Feed	Amt. on Hand Bu. or Tons	Total Value	Acres in Crops Owned	Acres in Crops Rented	Cash Invested in Crop
TOTALS					

SCHEDULE G—Machinery and Equipment

No.	Make	Kind	Model	Year	Description	Value
		Tractor				
		Combine				
		C. Picker				
		Planter				
		Plow				
		Disc.				
		Cult.				
		Drill				
		Man. Sp.				
		Wagon				
		For. Harv.				
		Mower				
		Baler				
		Rake				
		Sprayer				
		Elev.				
		Gr. Dryer				
I	Ford	Auto	Mustang	1971	2 Dr.	$1,600
		Truck				
		Lvstk. Eq.				
		Misc.				
					TOTAL	

Current assets are usually valued at market value or cost of production. Finished products in inventory (bales of cotton, hundredweights of rice, bushels of soybeans, finished cattle, and so on) should be valued at *sale or market value minus marketing costs*. Products in process (growing wheat, growing cattle, and so on) should be valued at either *cost of the product* as of the date of the inventory or at *market value* if there is a competitive market for such products. Growing wheat would likely be valued at cost, but growing cattle might be valued at feeder cattle market price. Intermediate and long-term assets are recorded on the balance sheet at their initial cost less accumulated depreciation or at their replacement cost minus accumulated depreciation when replacement cost is greatly different from the initial cost. (Depreciation is discussed later in the chapter.) Land is generally recorded at market value.

A series of balance sheets over time will show trends in the financial worth of a business or individual. On farms where one individual or family is involved, the business and personal balance sheets are often the same. When businesses are owned or operated by several persons, the business and each person may have separate balance sheets.

Kirk and Susan Henly graduated from college in January 1976. When Kirk and Susan graduated, their financial statement was very simple: They had $100 in the bank and an automobile worth $1,600. They owed $200 on their automobile and had a net worth of $1,500 (Figure 5.1).

Kirk and Susan had a strong desire to farm. They were able to locate a 200-acre farm to rent on the share basis and to obtain an FmHA loan to provide capital to get started. The Henlys did a good job, and as a result, their farm business and income grew.

The Henlys' farm organization and growth over the years is listed below:

1976: 200 acres share-rented
   • 100 acres corn
   • 100 acres beans
   24 sows, share basis
   Susan worked at a local grain elevator

Farm Operating Profit[1]	$8,000
Nonfarm Income	7,200

1977: Increased sows to 48

Farm Operating Profit:	$10,000
Nonfarm Income	7,500

1978: Rented additional 200 acres, share basis
    Purchased 100 acres

Farm Operating Profit	$20,000
Nonfarm Income	8,000

[1]Returns to unpaid factors—operators' time (labor and management) and equity—are discussed in detail later in this chapter.

1979: Added 50 sows on the farm that was share-rented in 1976
         Susan quit her job and the Henlys started a family
         Hired one person

Farm Operating Profit	$21,657
Increase in Land Value	20,000
Nonfarm Income	5,000

1980: Cash-rented an additional 200 acres
   • 100 acres corn on owned land
   • 400 acres corn on share-rented land
   • 200 acres soybeans on cash-rented land
   • 98 sows farrow-to-finish on share basis

Farm Operating Profit	$23,000
Increase in Land Value	20,000

Kirk and Susan Henly's annual balance sheet summaries from January 1, 1976, through January 1, 1981, are shown in Figure 5.2.

Factors Affecting Net Worth Change

Kirk and Susan's net worth increased from $1,500 on January 1, 1976, to $94,540 on January 1, 1981. This increase in net worth was due to:

- Doing a good job of farming and making a good farm profit for the type of operation
- Susan's off-farm income
- Keeping living costs low
- Keeping income taxes low by expanding while reporting on the cash tax basis [2]
- Purchasing land and other assets that increased in value.

Another potential source of net worth gain is gifts received from others. This was not a source that increased the Henlys' net worth.

Net worth can grow slowly or even decrease if farm and nonfarm incomes are low or negative, if income taxes are high, if living expenditures are high, if gifts are made to others, or if assets do not increase or even decrease in value.

Uses of the Balance Sheet

It is useful for a manager to observe the sources of changes in the net worth for each period (see Figure 5.3). By summarizing the source of net worth change, the manager can determine why net worth is increasing or decreasing. This information, along

[2] If in the future the inventory is reduced through sales, income taxes might be required on this delayed income (see Chapter 22). If the Henlys expect to reduce their inventory, the expected income tax should be listed as a liability, and net worth would decrease.

	Jan. 1, 1976	Jan. 1, 1977	Jan. 1, 1978	Jan. 1, 1979	Jan. 1, 1980	Jan. 1, 1981
Assets						
Current						
Cash	100	500	1,000	1,000	1,000	2,000
Crop inventory		15,000	15,500	73,200	72,875	59,540
Livestock inventory		4,000	8,000	8,750	18,750	16,000
Supplies		400	400	600	840	1,000
Intermediate						
Machinery	1,600	31,000	27,000	53,000	44,700	90,000
Breeding stock		1,200	1,000	950	750	1,000
Furniture		1,000	1,500	2,000	2,500	3,000
Long-term						
Land				150,000	170,000	190,000
Total assets	1,700	53,100	54,400	289,500	311,415	362,540
Liabilities						
Current						
Production loans		12,000	16,000	62,000	60,000	55,000
Intermediate						
Machinery and breeding stock loan	200	32,000	20,000	50,000	45,000	80,000
Long-term						
Land mortgage				140,000	137,000	133,000
Total liabilities	200	44,000	36,000	252,000	242,000	268,000
Net worth	1,500	9,100	18,400	37,500	69,415	94,540

Figure 5.2   Balance sheet summaries, Kirk and Susan Henly, 1976–1981.

with a farm record analysis explained in the next chapter, can be helpful in making operational decisions. Knowledge of the assets, liabilities, and net worth is also important for making investment decisions. A balance sheet is requested by most lenders prior to making a farm loan. Debt-asset ratios are discussed in Chapter 7.

Finally, if net worth is increasing, it can be a very satisfying experience for the manager to prepare a balance sheet each year and to observe the net worth change over time.

Prepare a personal balance sheet as of this date. Decide on a day each year that you will make a new balance sheet. Keep a file of all of your balance sheets.

1. Factors increasing net worth

    Farm operating profit   _____

    Non-farm income   _____

    Gains from increase
      in durable asset value due to inflation
      (land, buildings, etc.)   _____

    Gifts received   _____

    Total increasing factors   _____

2. Factors decreasing net worth

    Family living cost   _____

    Income taxes   _____

    Farm operating loss   _____

    Nonfarm income loss   _____

    Decrease in durable
      asset value due to deflation _____

    Gifts to others   _____

    Total decreasing factors   _____

3. Change in net worth
    (1 − 2)   _____

Figure 5.3 Sources of changes in net worth.

RECORDS FOR MEASURING FARM PROFIT

There are several measures of farm earnings, each of which provides unique information to the manager.

Farm Operating Profit or Income Statement

One of the most useful measures of farm earnings is farm operating profit, often referred to as the income statement. Farm operating profit is usually the return to operator's (and family's) labor and management and the equity (net worth) that the operator has invested in the business.[3] Farm operating profit is receipts minus expenses plus inventory increase, or minus inventory decrease.

[3] Another way of considering farm operating profit is the return to unpaid factors of production: the operator and the operator's family usually do not receive a direct payment for labor, management, and equity.

$$\text{Farm operating profit} = (\text{Receipts} - \text{expenses}) + \text{Inventory increase}$$
$$or - \text{Inventory decrease}$$

Farm operating profit is computed for a particular time period, usually one year, and is determined by three records elements: *receipts, expenses,* and *inventories* (Figure 5.4).

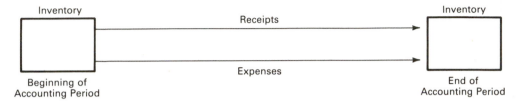

Figure 5.4 Basic elements of farm records.

The receipts and expenses are a series of transactions that occur during the accounting period. The inventory is a listing of farm products and production resources (excluding durable assets) on hand and their value on a particular date.

If the ending inventory is greater than the beginning inventory, this indicates an increase in value and is similar to a receipt; it is *added* to income. If ending inventory is less than beginning inventory, this indicates a decrease in value and is similar to an expense; it is *subtracted* from income.

Receipts. Receipts should be from farm production items only (corn, soybeans, wheat, milk, etc.).

- Gifts from others should be *excluded.*
- Money borrowed for the farm business should be *excluded.*
- Off-farm income should be *excluded.*
- If capital items are sold at a higher price than they were valued because they were depreciated too rapidly, the gain above book value should be *included.*
- Products sold but for which payment is yet to be received should be *included.*

Expenses. Expenses should be for farm production items and depreciation only.

- Family living and other personal expenditures should be *excluded.*
- Principal payments on debts should be *excluded.*
- Purchase of capital items should *excluded.*
- Interest payments on farm debts should be *included.*
- If capital items are sold at a lower price than they were valued because they were depreciated too slowly, the loss below book value should be *included.*

- Production items purchased but not paid for should be *included.*
- Depreciation of capital items should be *included.*

Inventory.   Inventory may be taken from the balance sheet. Both the quantity and value should be listed.

- Farm products, such as corn, soybeans, wheat, rice, and cotton, are *included.*
- Farm products in process, such as growing wheat and feeder cattle, should be *included.*
- Current production resources, such as feed, fertilizer, and supplies, should be *included.*
- Raised breeding stock should be *included.*
- Durable assets, such as buildings, machinery, equipment, and land, should be *excluded.*
- Purchased breeding stock should be *excluded.*
- Personal items, such as furniture, should be *excluded.*
- Accounts receivable and payable are accounted for in receipts and expenses and are therefore *excluded* from inventory.
- Finished products in inventory (bales of cotton, hundredweights of rice, bushels of soybeans, finished cattle, etc.) should be valued at *sale or market value minus marketing costs.*
- Products in process (growing wheat, growing cattle, etc.) should be valued at either *cost of the product* as of the date of the inventory or at *market value* if there is a competitive market for such products. Growing wheat would likely be valued at cost, but growing cattle might be valued at feeder cattle market price.

Depreciation.   Depreciation is the procedure used for allocating the cost of a durable asset, or factor of production, over the years or accounting periods in which it is used. There is no need to depreciate inputs such as feed or fertilizer because these inputs are used and charged as expenses in a single accounting period. But some inputs, such as buildings and machinery, last for several accounting periods. Each period should be charged for the amount of the resource used during that period.

From an income tax standpoint, it may be desirable to depreciate an asset as fast as the law allows because rapid depreciation reduces current taxable income and income taxes. If the "real" rate of depreciation is different from the most desirable from a tax standpoint, the manager should keep two depreciation records, one to compute farm earnings and the other to report taxes.

Three depreciation methods are illustrated. The first method is a procedure generally used for determining depreciation to calculate farm earnings. The second and third methods are those used for determining depreciation for income tax purposes.

1. Straight-line method (farm business management option)

$$\text{Depreciation} = \frac{\text{Original cost} - \text{Trade-in or salvage value}}{\text{Years of life}}$$

2. Accelerated cost recovery system (ACRS)
   Depreciation is a percentage of original cost specified by the Internal Revenue Service for various types of property.
3. Straight-line method (tax option)

$$\text{Depreciation} = \frac{\text{Original cost}}{\text{Years of life}}$$

As an example, assume that a new tractor purchased for $25,000 has an estimated life expectancy of ten years. Assume also that it will have a trade-in or salvage value of $5,000. The tractor will decline in value by nearly an equal amount each year. From a business standpoint, the most logical way to depreciate the tractor is with the straight-line method.

$$\text{Annual depreciation} = \frac{\$25,000 - \$5,000}{10} = \$2,000$$

The straight-line method of depreciation results in a $2,000 depreciation each year. Each accounting period is charged $2,000 for the tractor used during that period.

From a business management standpoint, managers should be as accurate as possible in estimating depreciation for the life of each durable item. But from a tax standpoint, managers may wish to delay taxes by maximizing current depreciation, which will reduce current income and income tax.

For maximizing current depreciation, the ACRS method should be used. Depreciable assets used by farmers are classified in one of four periods: three-year, five-year, ten-year, and fifteen-year.[4]

- *Three-year property* includes autos, pick ups, light-duty trucks (less than 13,000 pounds), swine used for breeding, race horses over two years of age, and other horses over twelve years of age.
- *Five-year property* includes agricultural machinery and equipment, heavy-duty trucks, cattle used for breeding or dairy, sheep, goats, and horses (other than racehorses) less than twelve years of age. This category also includes depreciable personal property eligible for investment credit, such as fences, grain bins, silos, drainage tile, feed bunks, paved yards, and wells, as well as single-purpose agricultural and horticultural structures.
- *Ten-year property* is not common in agriculture. One example is a mobile home used as a farm office or for housing hired labor.

---

[4] Tax laws and regulations change. Some of the specifics in this section may have changed, but the general principles are applicable.

- *Fifteen-year real property* includes general-purpose barns, machinery sheds, and rental houses. Cost recovery is not allowed on land or a personal residence.

Recovery period classes are mutually exclusive. Property defined as belonging in one class cannot be treated as being in another.

The percentage depreciation for each of the classifications of property is defined by the Internal Revenue Service (Tables 5.1 and 5.2).

TABLE 5.1 Percent Recovery Deduction by Year for Recovery Class of Personal Property

Recovery Year	Recovery Period Class of Personal Property		
	3-year	5-year	10-year
1	25%	15%	8%
2	38	22	14
3	37	21	12
4	—	21	10
5	—	21	10
6	—	—	10
7	—	—	9
8	—	—	9
9	—	—	9
10	—	—	9

TABLE 5.2 ACRS Cost Recovery Percentages by Month and Year for 15-Year Real Property[a]

Recovery Year	Month of Tax Year in Which Asset Is First Placed in Service											
	1	2	3	4	5	6	7	8	9	10	11	12
1	12%	11%	10%	9%	8%	7%	6%	5%	4%	3%	2%	1%
2	10	10	11	11	11	11	11	11	11	11	11	12
3	9	9	9	9	10	10	10	10	10	10	10	10
4	8	8	8	8	8	8	9	9	9	9	9	9
5	7	7	7	7	7	7	8	8	8	8	8	8
6	6	6	6	6	7	7	7	7	7	7	7	7
7	6	6	6	6	6	6	6	6	6	6	6	6
8	6	6	6	6	6	6	5	6	6	6	6	6
9	6	6	6	6	5	6	5	5	5	6	6	6
10	5	6	5	6	5	5	5	5	5	5	6	5
11	5	5	5	5	5	5	5	5	5	5	5	5
12	5	5	5	5	5	5	5	5	5	5	5	5
13	5	5	5	5	5	5	5	5	5	5	5	5
14	5	5	5	5	5	5	5	5	5	5	5	5
15	5	5	5	5	5	5	5	5	5	5	5	5
16	—	—	1	1	2	2	3	3	4	4	4	5

[a]This table does not apply to low-income housing property.

Under the ACRS method, the $25,000 tractor would be in the five-year category and depreciation would be:

Year	Percent	Initial Cost	Depreciation
1	15	$25,000	$3,750
2	22	25,000	5,500
3	21	25,000	5,250
4	21	25,000	5,250
5	21	25,000	5,250

Managers who choose to use the straight-line method for tax purposes must use one of three time lengths for each period and must ignore salvage value.

Recovery Period Category	Depreciation Periods (Years)
3-year personal property	3, 5, or 12
5-year personal property	5, 12, or 25
10-year personal property	10, 25, or 35
15-year real property	15, 35, or 45

For tax purposes, farmers have the option of treating up to $7,500 ($10,000 in 1986 and later) of capital investment per year as an expense.[5]

Farm operating profit: Kirk and Susan Henly example.   In 1979 the Henlys' operation included:

- 400 acres share-rented 50–50, half corn and half soybeans
- 100 acres owned, all in corn
- 98 sows, farrow-to-finish, 50–50 share

Following is a summary of the Henlys' inventory, depreciation, receipts, and expenses, for 1979, based on Figures 5.5, 5.6 and 5.7.

Cash Receipts	$110,833
Inventory Increase	9,915
Total	$120,748
Cash Expenses	$ 99,091
Farm Operating Profit	$21,657

[5] Investment tax credit is not available for capital assets treated as expenses. See Chapter 22 for an explanation of investment tax credit.

Henly Farm, 1979

Inventory

Livestock (not including purchased breeding stock), grain, hay, supplies, etc.

Item	First of Year			End of Year		
	No.	Value per Unit	Total Value	No.	Value per Unit	Total Value
Beef cattle						
Total						
Dairy cattle						
Total						
Hogs ½ sows ½ growing pigs	50 200	$150 50	$3,750 5,000	98 380	$150 60	$ 7,350 11,400
Total			$8,750			$18,750
Sheep						
Total						

Item	First of Year			End of Year		
	Tons, Bushels, Bales	Price per Unit	Total Value	Tons, Bushels, Bales	Price per Unit	Total Value
Grain Soybeans Corn	7,700 12,000	$6.00 2.25	$46,200 27,000	7,700 11,000	$6.25 2.25	$48,125 24,750
Total			$73,200			$72,875
Forage						
Total						
Supplies ½ supplement	5 tons	$240	$600	7 tons	$240	$840
Total			$600			$840
TOTAL			$82,550			$92,465

Figure 5.5 1979 Beginning and ending inventory, Henly farm.

Total Farm Profit

Lenders are interested in farm operating profit and trends in operating profit over time. Total farm profit includes not only operating profit but also changes in the value of durable assets (usually land) due to inflation or deflation.

Depreciation Schedule
Kirk and Susan Henly

Buildings, improvements, equipment, machinery, purchased breeding stock

Item	Date Acquired	Cost	Salvage Value	Value at Start of Year	Depreciation Method	Depreciation Useful Life	Depreciation This Year (1979)	Value at End of Year (1979)
Permanent buildings								
Total								
Improvements								
Total								
Equipment								
Total								
Machinery								
1 tractor	3/1/76	$12,000	$2,000	$ 9,000	SL[a]	10 yrs.	$1,000	$ 8,000
1 tractor	3/12/78	15,000	2,000	13,700	SL	10 yrs.	1,300	12,400
Plow, disk planter, field cultivator, cultivator	3/12/78	18,000	3,000	15,000	SL	5 yrs.	3,000	12,000
Combine	8/17/78	18,300	3,300	15,300	SL	5 yrs.	3,000	12,300
Total				$53,000			8,300	$44,700
Purchased breeding stock								
4 boars	10/1/78	$1,000		$950	SL	5 yrs.	$200	$750
Total				$950			200	$750
TOTAL				$53,950			$8,500	$45,450

[a]Straight line

Figure 5.6 Depreciation schedule, Kirk and Susan Henly, 1979.

Farm Receipts

$\frac{1}{2}$ 798 hogs avg. $96.76 ea.	$ 38,609
$\frac{1}{2}$ 7,480 bu. soybeans @ $6.03	45,104
12,000 bu. corn @ $2.26	27,120
Total	$110,833

Farm Expenses

Fertilizer and lime	9,438
Herbicide and insecticide	4,830
Seed	3,710
Fuel	7,718
Repairs	3,923
Feed supplement	15,925
Veterinary and medicinal	686
Insurance	1,580
Taxes: Real estate and personal property	1,531
Utilities	2,040
Supplies	1,312
Hired labor	12,000
Interest	23,580
Miscellaneous	2,318
Depreciation	8,500
Total	$99,091

Figure 5.7 Farm receipt and expense summary for Kirk and Susan Henly, 1979.

Total farm profit = farm operating profit + increase in value of durable assets due to inflation

or

− decrease in value of durable assets due to deflation

Changes in durable asset value due to depreciation have already been considered in farm operating profit; therefore depreciation is not a factor in farm operating profit adjustment.

For the Henlys:

Total farm profit = $21,657 + $20,000 (land value increase) = $41,657

Total farm profit tells managers how much their time and equity money have been earning. This is the best figure to compare to income from an off-farm job and earnings from investment of equity in other alternatives.

Kirk Henly had an opportunity to work as a farm manager for a seed producer for $20,000 per year. He thought he could earn 10% on his 1979 average net worth (excluding household furnishings) of $51,208 or $5,121. Thus he compared $25,121 ($20,000 labor and management returns plus $5,121 capital return) to his total farm profit. This comparison demonstrated that farming was the Henlys' best alternative before income taxes.

Total farm profit is really the *bottom line*. This is what the business is making before taxes.

Rate Earned on Equity

Farm profit is the return to the unpaid factors of production, usually the operator's labor, management, and equity. Operating return to equity can be figured by subtracting the value of unpaid operator and family time from farm operating profit and dividing this by average equity and multiplying by 100.

$$\frac{\text{Operating return}}{\text{to equity}} = \frac{\text{Farm operating profit} - \begin{array}{c}\text{Value of unpaid operator}\\\text{and family time}\end{array}}{(\text{Beginning equity} + \text{Ending equity}) \div 2} \times 100$$

The Henly operating return to equity in 1979 was:

$$\text{Operating Return to Equity} = \frac{\$21,657 - \$20,000}{(\$35,500 + \$66,915) \div 2} = \frac{\$1,657}{\$51,208} = 3.2\%$$

$$\text{Total return to equity} = \frac{\text{Total farm profit} - \begin{array}{c}\text{Value of unpaid operator}\\\text{and family time}\end{array}}{(\text{Beginning equity} + \text{Ending equity}) \div 2} \times 100$$

For the Henlys:

$$\text{TRE} = \frac{\$41,657 - \$20,000}{(\$35,500 + \$66,915) \div 2} \quad \frac{\$21,657}{\$51,208} = 42.3\%$$

Total return to equity is a useful indicator to the manager of whether or not his capital is returning as much in the farm business as it could in other alternatives. Lenders are often interested in both operating and total return to equity.

Return to Labor and Management

An assumed interest on equity can be subtracted from farm profit to determine return to labor and management:

$$\frac{\text{Operating return to}}{\text{labor and management}} = \frac{\text{Farm operating profit} - (\text{Interest rate}}{\times \text{ Average equity})}$$

The Henly operating return to labor and management in 1979 was:

$$\frac{\text{Operating return to labor}}{\text{and management}} = \$21,657 - (0.10 \times \$51,208) = \$16,536$$

$$\frac{\text{Total return to labor}}{\text{and management}} = \frac{\text{Total farm profit} - (\text{Interest rate}}{\times \text{ Average equity})}$$

For the Henlys:

> Total return to labor
> and management   = $41,657 − $5,121 = $36,536

Total return to labor and management is useful to the operator for making a comparison with salaries in other job alternatives.

ENTERPRISE ACCOUNTS

The returns to a particular crop or livestock enterprise can be determined in the same way that the returns to the total farm are figured. For enterprise accounts, each enterprise would have records that make it a separate component of the total business.

$$\frac{\text{Enterprise}}{\text{operating profit}} = \frac{\text{Enterprise}}{\text{receipts}} - \frac{\text{Enterprise}}{\text{expenses}} \pm \frac{\text{Enterprise}}{\text{inventory change}}$$

The concept of enterprise accounts is simple. However, keeping enterprise accounts is more complex than keeping total farm accounts for four reasons:

1. Receipts must be kept separately.
2. Expenses must be kept separately.
3. Transfers from one enterprise to the other must be recorded.
4. Certain resources are used by more than one enterprise, so decisions must be made regarding how costs for these resources should be allocated.

Transfers from One Enterprise to Another

Feed.   Crops produced are often the major farm product, and feed is usually the major livestock input. It is therefore important to keep accurate crop production and crop utilization records.

In cases where there is only one livestock enterprise, feed consumption can be determined by:

1. Beginning inventory _____
   Production   _____
   Purchase   _____
       Total   _____
2. Ending inventory   _____
   Sales   _____
       Total   _____
3. Total feed fed (1 − 2)   _____

In cases where there are two or more livestock enterprises, separate feed storage bins might be used for each enterprise. If there is more than one enterprise and feed cannot be stored separately, it may be necessary to weigh feed prior to feeding. Since feed is the major input for all livestock enterprises, an accurate record is essential even when one does not keep enterprise accounts.

Livestock waste.   Livestock provide manure for the crop enterprise. Crop machinery may be used to haul this waste, the value of which should be credited to the livestock and charged to the crops. The machinery costs associated with waste hauling should be charged to livestock.

Salvage feeds.   Crop residues are sometimes utilized by livestock, but these salvage feeds would not be used if livestock were not raised. In such cases, the cropping enterprise should not be credited, but fencing and other costs associated with using salvage feeds should be charged to livestock.

Other transfers.   Transfers such as feeder calves to the feed lot may also present problems. It is desirable to price transfer items as near market value as possible.

Resources Used by More Than One Enterprise

Buildings, machinery, and equipment.   Buildings and machinery often are used by more than one enterprise. If the machine or building was purchased for major use by more than one enterprise, costs for that item should be allocated according to the percentage used. For example, if a tractor is purchased to be used for corn planting and moving livestock equipment and the tractor is used half the time for each purpose, costs should be budgeted 50–50 (assuming similar operating costs). If, however, a machine or building is purchased for a given enterprise and used part-time by another enterprise, only operating costs for the time used by the secondary enterprise should be charged. For instance, if a farmer purchases a large tractor for the crop enterprise but uses it some for moving livestock equipment, only operating costs (fuel, oil, repair) should be charged to livestock. This is true because the farmer would not have purchased the tractor if it had not been for the cropping enterprise.

Labor.   Detailed labor records can be used to allocate labor among enterprises. One can allocate labor by computing the productive man-work units (PMWU) for each enterprise and allocating labor costs according to the percentage each enterprise uses of total farm PMWUs. (See Chapter 6). Also, one might make weekly or monthly judgments about the use of labor.

Overhead.   With regard to such overhead costs as telephone and accounting, some managers make judgments about how such costs should be allocated among enterprises, while other managers allocate overhead costs on the basis of gross income received from each enterprise or on the basis of labor used in each enterprise.

Still other managers keep overhead costs in a separate account and do not attempt to allocate them.

Receipts and Expenses

Most receipts and expenses can be easily assigned to a particular enterprise. Some expenses, such as hired labor, may need to be allocated on the basis of detailed records or at the discretion of the manager.

Use of Enterprise Accounts

Enterprise accounts are very useful for identifying areas of needed management improvement and for planning farm organization and expansion. It is useful for a manager to know cost per hundredweight of milk, per box of oranges, per ton of asparagus, and per quart of strawberries. It is also beneficial to know the components of total cost, such as labor, machinery, and fertilizer.

SUMMARY

You should make up a balance sheet for yourself at least once each year. Keep the balance sheets on file so that you can observe your change in net worth from year to year. It is also useful to determine the sources of change in net worth.

Each year (or other accounting period), you should figure farm operating profit and total farm profit. You will need a record of receipts, expenses, and beginning and ending inventories to calculate farm profit. It is useful management information to divide operating and total farm profit into the returns to equity and the returns to labor and management.

Enterprise accounts are helpful for improving management. They require only the same three elements as total farm records (receipts, expenses, and inventories) for the particular enterprises for which accounts are being kept.

Chapter 6 deals with the use of farm records and some additional kinds of records designed for improving management, controlling the farm business, securing credit, and reporting taxes. Record-keeping systems and methods are also presented.

DISCUSSION QUESTIONS

1. What is a balance sheet?
2. What factors determine the change in net worth from one year to the next?
3. Prepare a change in net worth analysis (Figure 5.3) for the Henlys for 1979 (assumptions will be required for income tax and family living expense).
4. How might a farm business have a negative operating profit but an increasing net worth in a particular year? What implications would this situation have for the long-term welfare of the business?

5. What are the three basic elements of farm financial records?

6. How should inventory be valued? When should inventories be taken?

7. What is the purpose of depreciating an asset?

8. What is the difference between farm business management depreciation and tax management depreciation? When is it advisable for a manager to keep two different depreciation listings?

9. How is farm operating profit calculated? How is total farm profit calculated?

10. Farm profit is the return to which resources? How can the return to these individual resources be determined?

11. What record elements are needed to keep farm enterprise accounts? Why are enterprise accounts more difficult to keep than total farm accounts?

RELATED READINGS

See readings listed for Chapter 6.

Farm Records
and Their Use

6

In Chapter 5 records for measuring financial progress and farm profit were discussed. This chapter concentrates on the use of records for improving the management of the farm, securing credit, and reporting income taxes. The chapter concludes with some guidelines for the selection of a record-keeping system.

RECORDS FOR COMPARATIVE ANALYSIS

Comparative farm business analysis is a procedure for evaluating a farm business on the basis of how it compares to similar farms. Comparative analysis can be useful for finding ways to increase farm profit. It can be helpful for identifying farm strengths and weaknesses, enabling the manager to organize the farm to capitalize on strengths and to minimize losses due to weaknesses. Comparative analysis can be helpful to a farm management consultant for identifying areas of the business that should be carefully examined. A comparison with other farms can also be stimulating; competition often increases interest and enthusiasm for doing a better job. Professional managers may find comparative analysis to be an effective tool for motivating resident farm managers and operators.

A comparison with other farms may not be totally relevant because each farm is unique with respect to goals, resources, and management strengths and weaknesses. Managers must carefully analyze their own situation before undertaking changes on the basis of a comparative farm analysis.

Farms that are better than average in key areas make above-average incomes. Comparative analysis can be used to evaluate the following key factors that affect profit:

1. Size and volume
2. Crop efficiency
3. Livestock efficiency
4. Labor efficiency
5. Machinery efficiency
6. Prices paid for inputs
7. Prices received for products

Enterprise combination and production systems are also important factors affecting farm profit. However, because the unique resources of each farm and the abilities of each manager are so important in determining the best organization and production systems, comparative analysis is of limited usefulness for evaluating these factors.

Comparative business analysis requires detailed and accurate information about the farm being analyzed and similar data for a group of similar kinds of farms. Because of year-to-year variability in crop yields and livestock production due to weather and disease, it is desirable to make comparisons for each year for at least a three-year period.

To make a good comparative analysis of a farm, a manager must:

1. Know the key factors affecting farm profit.
2. Know appropriate measures of key factors affecting profit. These measures will be presented in this chapter.
3. Identify acceptable standards for key factors. For comparative analysis, these standards are usually the level of key factors observed on similar farms, but the standards might also be obtained from research experiments, extension publications, and the manager's understanding of desirable business goals.
4. Compare the key factors for the farm being analyzed to appropriate standards.

It should be kept in mind that measures and standards are only general indicators or guidelines for the key factors affecting farm profit. Measures do not evaluate perfectly the key factors, and the standards are not always the best level of performance. So, having found areas to evaluate with these general indicators, the manager then must use management experience and a knowledge of decision-making principles to determine the best course of action. In the following sections key factors, standards, and measures are explained and subsequently illustrated using a case farm.

Earnings Comparisons

Income comparisons are useful for determining *where* a farm business stands relative to other farms but not *why* earnings are high or low. Farm earnings for comparative business analysis differ somewhat from the measures of earnings already presented in Chapter 5. Three of the measures of earnings—farm income, labor income, and rate earned on investment—are explained below. They are good overall indicators of management effectiveness.

Farm income. *Farm income* is the return to the operator's labor and management and all of the capital in the business, including borrowed capital and farms leased from others. It is computed the same way as farm operating profit in Chapter 5, with the following exceptions:

1. *Interest on debt is omitted from expenses.* Differences from farm to farm in the amount of debt and associated interest expense result in differences in farm in-

come not caused by key farm management factors. Elimination of farm-to-farm interest variation gives a better picture of the effect of management factors on earnings. Therefore, earnings are adjusted as if there were no debt on the farm, and interest on debt is omitted.

2. *Family labor other than that of the operator is charged as an expense.* Earnings comparisons would not be meaningful if farms had different amounts of unpaid labor. To keep the unpaid labor input consistent among farms, a charge is made for labor other than the operator's.

3. *Rented land and buildings are converted to the same basis as owned land and buildings.* Cash rents are omitted, taxes on rented land are included, and the landlord's share of receipts and expenses are included. The purpose of this adjustment is to put the earnings of various farms on the basis of yields, prices, and costs rather than on the basis of the types of rental arrangements.

   As is true for computing farm operating profit, *the value of durable assets is not changed for inflation or deflation* from the beginning to the end of the accounting period, so farm income is operating income. Regular depreciation of assets is included, and variations in the inventory value of crops, livestock, and supplies are considered.

Farm income is often separated into the return to labor and management and the return to capital.

Labor income.   Labor income is the return to the operator's labor and management. It is calculated by subtracting interest on investment from farm income.

Labor income = Farm income − (Interest rate[1] × Average farm investment[2])

Rate earned on investment.   This is the return to all of the capital invested in the business, including borrowed money and farms leased from others. It is calculated by subtracting the value of the operator's time from farm income and dividing the remainder by average investment and multiplying by 100.

$$\text{Rate earned on investment} = \frac{\text{Farm income} - \text{Value of operator's time}[3]}{\text{Average investment}[2]} \times 100$$

Following is an earnings' evaluation for the Herman Jerkum farm.

Herman Jerkum is a dairy farmer in a northern state. Herman's uncle gave him a dairy farm several years ago, and Herman has been satisfied with his

---

[1]Use the same rate of interest as is used for computing labor income of comparative farms.

[2](Beginning investment plus ending investment) ÷ 2.

[3]Use the same procedure for determining the value of operator's time as is used for comparative farms. The value of the operator's time is usually established at the rate that could be obtained by the operator in the best alternative other than the farm.

income and has no farm debt. Herman's net cash income (cash receipts minus cash expenses) was $18,035 last year. This is as much as most of his friends in town have been making.

Last week Herman attended a farm management seminar and has wondered if he might do better. Herman has asked us to evaluate his farm business and give him advice about how his income might be increased. Because Herman has been involved with a state record project, he is able to provide us with detailed information about his farm and groups of similar farms. Table 6.1 is from a real farm record summary.

Herman's earnings are low compared to even the least profitable group of similar farms. He is able to make an acceptable income only by living from the return to his capital and by spending some of the capital. The returns to his labor are negative. This means that if he had invested in bonds or another good alternative instead of having the money in the farm, he would make more money with no work! Our job is to help Herman find out why his income is so low.

TABLE 6.1   Earnings

| | | 40 Dairy Farms Similar to Herman Jerkum's | |
Measure of Earnings	Herman Jerkum	Least Profitable 20 Farms	Most Profitable 20 Farms
Farm income	$ 9,500	$19,133	$83,429
Labor income	− 20,196	− 10,894	40,343
Rate earned on investment	− 1%	− 0.5%	8%

Size and Volume Comparisons

Size and volume of business are among the most significant factors affecting farm profit. A brief discussion of measures of size will be followed by an analysis of Herman Jerkum's farm. For setting size standards, see Chapter 13.

Productive man work units. A PMWU is the average amount of crop and livestock production accomplished in a 10-hour day on a typical farm. Total PMWUs measure size in terms of typical labor requirements. Productive man work units for various enterprises are shown in Figure 6.1. PMWUs are one of the best measures of size and volume.

Acres in major crops or group of crops refers to the total number of acres in the most important crop or group of crops. It is a good indicator of total size on farms that specialize in the production of a crop or group of crops and where livestock are unimportant. An example would be acres of corn and soybeans in a cash grain area. This measure is a useful indicator of size on any farm with a significant land base.

Crop	Your Acres	PMWU per Acre	Total PMWU	Livestock	Number of Units	PMWU per Unit	Total PMWU
Corn		0.5		Dairy cow unit		7.0	
Wheat		0.3		Beef cow unit		0.8	
Oats		0.3		Feeder cattle/month		0.04	
Soybeans		0.4		Sow, 2 litters to market		4.4	
Grain sorghum		0.6		Sow, 2 litters to weaning		2.6	
Alfalfa hay		0.9		Purchased feeder pig		0.1	
Clover hay		0.6		Ewe and lamb		0.5	
Corn silage		1.0		Feeder lamb		0.1	
Grass silage		1.0		Hens, commercial flock (1,000)		9.0	
Corn (sweet or pop)		1.5		Hens, farm flock (1,000)		26.0	
Cantaloupe		10.0		Contract pullets to 20 weeks (1,000)		51.2	
Potatoes		6.0		Turkeys (1,000)		11.0	
Tobacco		40.0		Contract broilers (1,000)		0.6	
Tomatoes		10.0					
Watermelons		6.0					
Total crops	xxxxx	xxxxx		Total livestock	xxxxx	xxxxx	
Total for your farm							
Total per person							

Figure 6.1 Productive man work units (number of 10-hour days) for various crops and livestock. *Source:* Farm Planning and Financial Management, ID-68. Cooperative Extension Service, Purdue University, West Lafayette, Ind., 1980.

Total number of important livestock is a useful measure of size on farms specializing in the production of one class of livestock when cash crops are not important. Examples would be dairy farms in New England and beef-cow ranches in the West.

Capital invested is a good indicator of the fixed plant size.

Number of man equivalents (number of persons employed) is an indicator of farm labor and management input. It is calculated by determining the total months of operator, family, and hired labor divided by 12.

As is apparent from Table 6.2, Herman's size of business is very similar to the least profitable farms and substantially smaller than the most profitable farms. Increasing size should be considered as one possibility for increasing profit. It would be helpful for Herman to read Chapter 13 as he considers this possibility.

Crop Efficiency Comparisons

Technical efficiency is output per unit of input. *Crop yields* are usually good indicators of crop efficiency and profit because most of the variation in yields among farms with similar soils and similar weather is the result of management practices rather than differences in the amounts of inputs. High-yielding crops are planted on time, disease is controlled, weeds are controlled, the correct seed and fertilizer are used, and the crops are harvested on time. Seed, fertilizer, planting, harvesting, and many other costs are about the same for correct or incorrect choices. Making the correct choice is a matter of knowing what to do, being willing to do it, and having the organizational skills to get the correct things done at the opportune time. Thus a comparison of yields with other farms that have similar soils and weather is a good measure of crop efficiency.

The *crop yield index* indicates the percentage of crop yields on one farm as com-

TABLE 6.2 Size Analysis

| | | 40 Dairy Farms Similar to Herman Jerkum's | |
Measure of Size	Herman Jerkum	Least Profitable 20 Farms	Most Profitable 20 Farms
PMWU	878	867	1,332
Tillable acres	276	293	492
Acres in:			
Corn	178	160	260
Soybeans	0	65	87
Hay	58	53	102
Number of cows	78	77	113
Number of man equivalents	1.85	2.09	3.20
Total capital investment	$679,049	$654,642	$858,903

pared to the average of similar farms. A crop yield index of 110 on a Kansas wheat farm would mean that wheat yields on that farm are 10% above the average of farms in the same area with similar soils. When more than one crop is raised, the crop yield index is computed as a weighted average and the index indicates the percentage above or below the average for all crops.

A word of caution: If high crop yields are obtained with the use of extremely high levels of inputs (fertilizer, labor, machinery), they may not result in higher profits. A manager should consider costs of inputs in relation to yield as discussed in Chapter 3.

Costs per bushel or ton or *net returns per bushel, ton, or acre* are the best indicators of crop efficiency. Enterprise accounts are needed to secure this information.

According to Table 6.3, Herman's crop yields are 15% above average! It is likely that crops are contributing substantial profit to the business. Herman's earnings difficulties are probably due to some problem other than crop efficiency. Having excellent crop management skills, he should consider expanding crops to capitalize on his expertise in this part of the business.

Livestock Efficiency Comparisons

Production per animal—pounds of milk per cow; rate of gain on cattle, hogs, or feeder lambs; percent calf crop; eggs per hen—is a good indicator of livestock efficiency for the same reason crop yields are an indicator of crop efficiency. The increased output per animal is largely due to good management practices rather than more inputs. The amount of money spent on breeding livestock, feed, buildings, labor, and so on is generally similar regardless of the output per animal. Thus farms with livestock that show more output per animal are usually more profitable than farms with lower output per animal.

Livestock receipts per animal are similar to production per animal, but sale price of livestock and livestock products is considered as well as amount of production.

Livestock receipts per dollar of feed fed refers to the total value of receipts from livestock divided by the total value of all feed fed. This shows returns above feed costs available to pay for labor, buildings, utilities, veterinary services, medicine, and

TABLE 6.3   Crop Efficiency Analysis

Measure of Crop Efficiency	Herman Jerkum	40 Dairy Farms Similar to Herman Jerkum's	
		Least Profitable 20 Farms	Most Profitable 20 Farms
Corn yield/bu./acre	122	101	110
Hay yield/ton/acre	4.3	4.0	4.3
Crop yield index	115	95	105

other costs and to provide profit. Livestock receipts per dollar of feed fed is affected by feed fed per unit of output, price paid for feed, and price received for livestock or livestock products. Because feed is the most important single input in livestock production, profit on livestock farms is closely associated with livestock receipts per dollar of feed fed.

The *livestock efficiency index* is the percentage of one farm's livestock receipts per dollar of feed fed as compared to similar farms. It is much like the crop efficiency index.

Cost per unit of production and *net returns per unit of production* are the best indicators of livestock efficiency, but enterprise accounts are required for calculating these indicators.

As is obvious from Table 6.4, Herman has a major problem with his dairy herd. Production per cow is much lower than on other farms. This is probably one of the reasons he is getting only $1.02 in receipts for each dollar of feed fed. Herman has only 2 cents above each dollar of feed cost to pay for buildings, labor, veterinary costs, interest, supplies, and other nonfeed costs. His dairy herd is losing a great deal of money. Herman's livestock efficiency index is only 65, indicating that Herman is only 65% as efficient as similar dairy farms. It appears that Herman must make major adjustments in his dairy herd management or get out of the dairy enterprise.

Labor Efficiency Comparisons

Productive man work units per person is the sum of productive man work units for all enterprises divided by the man equivalents.[4] It is an indicator of the amount of production per person employed.

Labor cost per productive man work unit is the total labor cost, including a labor charge for hired labor, the operator and operator's family, and the labor portion of custom work (usually one-fourth of the total custom charge), divided by total PMWUs. Labor cost per PMWU is an indicator of labor cost per unit of production.

TABLE 6.4 Livestock Efficiency Analysis

| | | 40 Dairy Farms Similar to Herman Jerkum's | |
Measure of Livestock Efficiency	Herman Jerkum	Least Profitable 20 Farms	Most Profitable 20 Farms
Pounds milk sold/ cow	10,526	11,188	13,500
Receipts per dollar feed fed	$1.02	$1.47	$1.69
Livestock efficiency index	65	93	107

[4]Man equivalents is the total number of months of labor from all sources (operator, family, hired) divided by 12.

TABLE 6.5 Labor Efficiency

Measure of Labor Efficiency	Herman Jerkum	40 Dairy Farms Similar to Herman Jerkum's	
		Least Profitable 20 Farms	Most Profitable 20 Farms
Productive man work units per man	474	300	375
Cost per productive man work unit	$33.68	$47.38	$43.22

It is clear from Table 6.5 that Herman Jerkum has a very high labor efficiency as indicated by the production per person, 474 PMWUs compared to 300 for the least profitable farms and 375 for the most profitable farms. Also, Herman's cost per PMWU is low, $33.68 versus $47.38 for the least profitable farms and $43.22 for the most profitable farms.

High labor efficiency and low labor cost usually increase farm profit. However, if an operator attempts to do too much, important jobs may not get done on time, and crop or livestock efficiency may suffer. In light of Herman's low livestock efficiency, he should examine whether or not he has sufficient labor to care adequately for his cows.

Machinery Efficiency Comparisons

Machinery investment per tillable acre should be high enough to get the job done on time but not so high that costs offset gains in production. Total machinery investment is divided by tillable acres to calculate machinery investment per acre.

Machinery and power cost per tillable acre is another indicator of whether the appropriate amount of machinery is on hand and is also a measure of the cost of crop production. Total machinery and power cost includes (1) fuel, oil, and grease, (2) machinery repairs, (3) machinery depreciation, (4) interest, taxes, insurance, and storage, and (5) the machinery part of custom hire, usually three-fourths of the custom-hire cost.

As Table 6.6 indicates, Herman's machinery investment of $175 per acre is higher than both the most profitable ($133/acre) and the least profitable ($129/acre) similar farms. Also, Herman's machinery cost per acre is $49 higher than that of the most profitable farms.

There are several possible reasons for Herman's high machinery cost that should be evaluated when we visit the farm to collect more information. Herman may have too much machinery for his acreage and may have made mistakes in the size and type of machinery purchased. He may have all new equipment while the other similar farms have older equipment. If this is true, Herman's interest and depreciation costs would be higher compared to others. If the farm labor supply is low, Herman may

TABLE 6.6 Machinery Efficiency

Measure of Labor Efficiency	Herman Jerkum	40 Dairy Farms Similar to Herman Jerkum's	
		Least Profitable 20 Farms	Most Profitable 20 Farms
Machinery investment per tillable acre	$175	$129	$133
Power and machinery cost per tillable acre	124	91	75

have purchased large machinery to substitute for labor. Finally, because Herman's crop yields are exceptionally good, he may be achieving these yields as a result of having large machinery that enhances timeliness.

Reducing machinery costs may be a way of improving profit and should be evaluated in more depth during our farm visit.

Comparisons of Prices Paid for Resources and Prices Received for Products

Prices paid for inputs are difficult to measure because of farm-to-farm differences in the kind of inputs used. Different varieties and brands of seed, different fertilizer analyses, and other factors make comparative analysis difficult.

Products sold tend to be more uniform, and price comparisons can be useful if data are available. The average price received by one farm for rice, cotton, corn, soybeans, hogs, cattle, eggs, and milk compared to the price received by other similar farms can be an indicator of the effectiveness of marketing.

Data were not available on the price received for products sold from the records for farms similar to Herman Jerkum's.

Summary

From the comparative business analysis it appears that Herman Jerkum must improve the efficiency of his dairy herd or eliminate it. Herman should consider whether or not he has sufficient labor to be efficient with his dairy operation. He appears to be very good with crops and should consider expanding his crop acreage. Herman's machinery costs appear to be high. He should evaluate the possibility of reducing the amount of machinery or spreading the use of his machinery over more acres by expanding the cropping enterprise or doing some custom work.

It is desirable to observe a comparative analysis each year for at least a three-year period. Such an analysis gives the manager the opportunity to assess the consistency of strong and weak points. Also, several years' records can be used to determine if progress is being made in correcting weaknesses.

RECORDS FOR FARM BUSINESS CONTROL

The purpose of farm business control is to determine if the farm business is operating according to plans. Effective control involves:

1. Identifying the important factors to be controlled
2. Establishing appropriate levels, standards, or goals for the factors being controlled
3. Comparing the actual level of selected factors to the standard or goals
4. Taking action to correct undesirable deviations between the actual situation and the standard.

Comparative farm business analysis is a type of control. The control factors (presented in the preceding section) are the measures of income, size, efficiency, and prices. The goals or standards are the levels of the key profit factors attained by similar farms. In addition to the comparative analysis, other types of control may be useful to an operator and are discussed in the sections that follow.

Cash Flow

Cash flow projections and control are essential for farms that need substantial amounts of borrowed capital and are useful on all farms for planning and control. A cash-flow projection is a chronological listing of all cash income (farm operating, farm capital, and nonfarm) and of all expenses (farm operating, farm capital, and nonfarm). Records of actual cash receipts and expenses are compared to projected cash receipts and expenses monthly, quarterly, or at other specified times. Reasons for variations between projected and actual receipts and expenses should be determined.

It is imperative that farms with tight financial situations keep their cash flows updated as conditions change. The Henlys (discussed in Chapter 5) used the cash flow shown in Figure 6.2 at the start of their first year of operation. Later, as weather and prices were more favorable than expected, the Henlys revised their cash flow (Figure 6.3). The revised cash flow showed loan repayment to be more rapid than initially projected, and this improved cash-flow situation enabled the Henlys to expand sooner than they had anticipated. In their revised cash-flow budget, the Henlys projected a year-end debt of $33,030, some $6,300 less than the $39,330 in the original budget. By keeping the cash flow updated, a manager can adjust the farm to the optimum organization for the amount of money available. Also, the lender can be advised early of faster or slower loan-repayment expectations. Several computer models have been developed to aid in projecting cash flows.

Enterprise and Resource Management Control

A manager may have plans for certain practices to be followed to obtain efficient farm production. The practices and the dates or circumstances under which they

CASH FLOW STATEMENT

Name _____ Henly Farm, Year, 1976 _____

50-50 rental
100 acres corn, 100 acres soybeans
24 sows, nonfarm job

OPERATING INCOME Months:	Jan.–Mar.	Apr.–June	July–Sept.	Oct.–Dec.
1. Crops				$10,500
2. Livestock				9,600
3. Livestock products				
4. Government payments				
5.				
6. Total operating income				$20,100
CAPITAL SALES				
7. Livestock (dairy, breeding)				
8. Machinery				
9.				
10. Total capital sales				
NONFARM INCOME				
11. Wages	$1,800	$1,800	$1,800	$1,800
12.				
13. Total nonfarm income	$1,800	$1,800	$1,800	$1,800
OPERATING EXPENSES				
14. Hired labor				
15. Repairs and maintenance	$250	$250	$250	$250
16. Rent and leases				
17. Feed purchased	500	1,000	2,000	1,100
18. Feeder stock purchased				
19. Seed and plants		1,000		
20. Chemicals				
21. Fertilizer and lime		2,500		
22. Custom hire				
23. Supplies	150	150	150	150
24. Breeding fees				
25. Veterinary and medicine	20	20	90	90
26. Gas, fuel, and oil	100	800	300	700
27. Utilities	200	200	200	200
28. Taxes (property)				
29. Insurance	300			
30. Miscellaneous	300	300	300	300
31.				
32. Total operating expenses	$1,820	$6,220	$3,290	$2,790
CAPITAL EXPENDITURES				
33. Livestock (dairy, breeding)	$1,500			
34. Machinery	40,000			
35.				
36. Total capital expenditures	$41,500			
OTHER EXPENDITURES				
37. Family and nonfarm business	$1,500	$1,500	$1,500	$1,500
38. Prior years' debt—Principal payment				
39. Prior years' debt—Interest payment				
CASH FLOW SUMMARY				
40. Beginning bank balance	$100	$0	$0	$0
41. Total income (6 + 10 + 3)	1,800	1,800	1,800	21,900
42. Total expenditures (32 + 36 + 37 + 38 + 39)	44,820	7,720	4,790	4,290
43. Cash difference (40 + 41 − 42)	−42,920	−5,920	−2,990	17,610
44. Borrowing necessary	42,920	5,920	2,990	
45. Current year's debt—Principal payment				12,500
46. Current year's debt—Interest payment				4,500
47. Ending bank balance	0	0	0	610
48. Current year's outstanding debt	42,920	48,840	51,830	39,330
49. Total outstanding debt	42,920	48,840	51,830	39,330

Figure 6.2 Beginning cash flow, Kirk and Susan Henly.

CASH FLOW STATEMENT

50-50 rental
100 acres corn, 100 acres soybeans
24 sows, nonfarm job

Name _____ Henly Farm Year 1976—Revised _____

OPERATING INCOME Months:	Jan.–Mar.	Apr.–June	July–Sept.	Oct.–Dec.
1. Crops				$14,000
2. Livestock				12,480
3. Livestock products				
4. Government payments				
5.				
6. Total operating income				$26,480
CAPITAL SALES				
7. Livestock (dairy, breeding)				
8. Machinery				
9.				
10. Total capital sales				
NONFARM INCOME				
11. Wages	$1,800	$1,800	$1,800	$1,800
12.				
13. Total nonfarm income	$1,800	$1,800	$1,800	$1,800
OPERATING EXPENSES				
14. Hired labor				
15. Repairs and maintenance	$250	$250	$250	$250
16. Rent and leases				
17. Feed purchased	500	1,000	2,000	1,100
18. Feeder stock purchased				
19. Seed and plants		1,000		
20. Chemicals				
21. Fertilizer and lime		2,500		
22. Custom hire				
23. Supplies	150	150	150	150
24. Breeding fees				
25. Veterinary and medicine	20	20	90	90
26. Gas, fuel, and oil	100	800	300	700
27. Utilities	200	200	200	200
28. Taxes (property)				
29. Insurance	300			
30. Miscellaneous	300	300	300	300
31.				
32. Total operating expenses	$1,820	$6,220	$3,290	$2,790
CAPITAL EXPENDITURES				
33. Livestock (dairy, breeding)	$1,500			
34. Machinery	40,000			
35.				
36. Total capital expenditures	$41,500			
OTHER EXPENDITURES				
37. Family and nonfarm business	$1,500	$1,500	$1,500	$1,500
38. Prior years' debt—Principal payment				
39. Prior years' debt—Interest payment				
CASH FLOW SUMMARY				
40. Beginning bank balance	$100	$0	$0	$0
41. Total income (6 + 10 + 3)	1,800	1,800	1,800	28,280
42. Total expenditures (32 + 36 + 37 + 38 + 39)	44,820	7,720	4,790	4,290
43. Cash difference (40 + 41 − 42)	−42,900	−5,920	−2,990	23,990
44. Borrowing necessary	42,920	5,920	2,990	
45. Current year's debt—Principal payment				18,800
46. Current year's debt—Interest payment				4,500
47. Ending bank balance	0	0	0	690
48. Current year's outstanding debt	42,920	48,840	51,830	33,030
49. Total outstanding debt	42,920	48,840	51,830	33,030

Figure 6.3 Revised cash flow, Kirk and Susan Henly.

should be performed could be incorporated into a control system, a formal way of checking to be sure that these jobs are done at the desired times. For example, a control system for a corn enterprise might include the following:

Activity	Target Time
Decide on fertilizer	August
Fertilize and fall plow	October–November
Decide on seed variety	December
Order seed	December
Decide on chemicals	December
Order chemicals	December
Forward contract one-fourth of crop when prices appear favorable	January–April
Have seed and chemicals delivered	February
Start planting	Soil temperature 55°F but not later than April 25
Finish planting	May 10
Rotary hoe	2 weeks after planting
Cultivate	4 weeks after planting
Check for insects	Each month of growing season
Start harvest	Crop moisture 26% but not later than October 10
Finish harvest	November 20
Plan marketing of three-fourths of crop	November–August

Similar control systems may be developed for all crop and livestock enterprises, labor management, and machinery management.

Many experienced farmers with one- or two-person farms use an "unwritten" control system that they remember and apply each day. These unwritten control systems help keep overhead time at a minimum. However, as a farm becomes larger and more people are involved, the business becomes more complex, and it is then helpful to adopt a written enterprise and resource control system.

> Choose an enterprise or input and develop a control system for it. Indicate (1) the important points you will check, (2) the standard or level of attainment, (3) how you will obtain information to determine if the plan is operating according to the standard chosen, and (4) what steps should be taken if your business is not operating according to plans.

PRODUCTION RECORDS

Detailed production records can be helpful to managers by providing information that enables them to make better decisions.

Crop Records

It is useful to have a farm map. Aerial photos are often available from the local ASCS office. Copies of aerial photographs provide an excellent place to record crop practices and yields (Figure 6.4). The following kinds of crop information should be recorded either on maps or in record books:

1. Soil map showing soil type, slope, drainage outlets
2. Tile map showing location, size, and installation date of all tile
3. Soil-test maps or records
4. Annual map or record for each field showing:
   - Type of crop
   - Date planted
   - Seed variety
   - Population

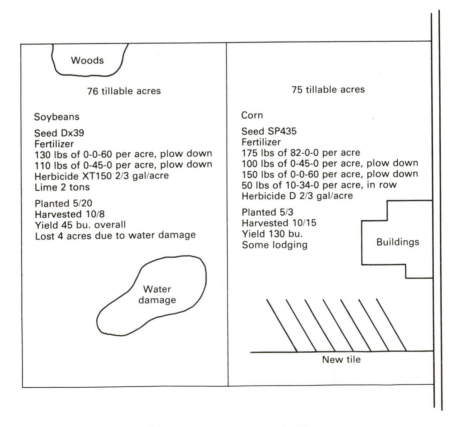

Figure 6.4 Farm Crop Record, 1984.

- Type of herbicide
- Weed problems, kinds of weeds
- Disease problems
- Type and amount of fertilizer
- Date and amount of lime application
- Date and amount of water application
- Harvest date
- Crop yield.

Livestock Records

Livestock records tend to be more detailed and complex than crop records. The most desirable amount of detail will depend on how the manager uses the records. Keeping records that do not aid in decision making will not make money.

A livestock producer should know the amount and kind of feed consumed, the cost of the feed, and the resulting output or product. Information about health and breeding is especially helpful. Numerous livestock records are available from livestock specialists in state extension offices. Some record items kept for livestock are shown in Figure 6.5.

Labor Records

Farm labor records may be kept by enterprise or operation to provide such information as:

- Labor requirements throughout the year
- Labor requirements of each enterprise
- Labor requirements of each operation
- Return per hour from various enterprises and operations.

Additional information about labor can be found in Chapter 21.

Machinery Records

Individual machinery expense records can be kept as a supplement to overall cost records. Individual machinery records enable the operator to be informed about:

1. Repair costs and rate of breakdown for different kinds and makes of machinery
2. Costs of different operations
3. Times to service machines
4. The condition of machines and whether or not they are ready for operation.

Feeder Livestock: Record for Each Lot or Pen

1. Purchased animals
    Date purchased
    Weight purchased
    Price
    Quality
    Seller

2. Feed
    Kind of feed
    Amount of feed

3. Veterinary and health
    Deaths and cause
    Treatments by kind

4. Sales
    Date sold
    Weight
    Grade
    Price
    Quality (might include carcass data)
    Purchaser

Breeding Livestock

1. Individual Records on Dams and Sires
    Birth date
    Sire
    Dam
    Weight at various ages
    Number, weight, and birth date of offspring
    Rate of gain or production of offspring
    Productivity of the animal for various periods
    Health record

2. Feed
    Kind of feed
    Amount of feed

3. Sales—Animal or Products
    Date sold
    Weight
    Price
    Purchaser

Figure 6.5 Livestock record information.

Farm Experiment Records

Because management and other resources are unique to each farm, a manager is likely to find that comparisons on his or her own farm of different seed varieties, fertilizers, and tillage are very useful.

Mike Babb found that fall plowing of heavy soil resulted in a 10-bushel yield increase over spring plowing and a 15-bushel yield increase over spring or fall chiseling. On lighter ground, Mike found that chiseling resulted in a slightly better yield than either fall or spring plowing, and it reduced erosion.

Mike's neighbor plants test plots with different seed corn hybrids and has found differences among hybrids of as much as 40 bushels per acre. Mike and his neighbor have scales so that they can collect accurate yield information, and they agree that their scales are among their most important farm equipment.

Mike and his neighbor both keep good records of the results of their experiments.

RECORDS FOR TAXES

Farmers must keep records to report and sometimes substantiate their income tax declarations. For many farmers, federal income tax has become a major item of expense. To minimize taxes for a given level of income and to minimize frustration and concern should farm records be audited by the Internal Revenue Service, records should be accurate and well documented. Many farmers do an inadequate job of tax management; they fail to record expenses (especially those paid in cash), they fail to classify qualifying receipts for capital gains income, and they fail to take full advantage of such provisions of the law as investment credit. Tax management strategies are discussed in Chapter 22.

Reporting Methods

Income taxes may be reported using the *cash method* or the *accrual method*. For the cash method, only transactions for which payment has been actually or constructively received or made are reported. For the accrual method, all transactions are reported, whether or not payment has been made or received. Change in inventory also is considered in the accrual method. The cash method is used by most farmers because it (1) reduces current income taxes on growing farms (inventory increases with size, but the value is not reported as a receipt), (2) provides more flexibility in reporting farm income (income can be more easily shifted between years), and (3) does not require inventory records. The *Farmers Tax Guide,* Department of the Treasury Internal Revenue Service Publication No. 225, is a good, detailed reference for farm tax record needs. Following is a summary of some of the key elements of tax records.

Cash Receipts and Expenses

Tax reporting forms are good references for devising or selecting a record for taxes. For cash-method reporting, the following records are needed:

1. Receipts
   - Ordinary: corn, wheat, market hogs, etc.
   - Capital gains: raised breeding stock
2. Sale capital items: tractor, buildings, farm land, etc.
3. Expenses
   - Ordinary: fertilizer, feed, interest, etc.
4. List of capital items: price paid, date acquired, investment tax credit, and depreciation method and rate.

For the accrual method of tax reporting, operating inventories are required in addition to the records required for the cash method. Most record requirements for taxes can be met with records kept for measuring farm earnings. Some additional needs are the capital gains receipts, investment credit, taxes withheld for labor, and possibly a different depreciation schedule if more rapid depreciation is used for taxes.

RECORDS FOR SECURING CREDIT

Lenders are much more likely to provide financial support to businesses that have demonstrated good and growing earnings as well as growth in net worth. Earnings and net worth growth must be validated with appropriate records. For instance, balance sheets for the past three years will show the net worth change as well as debt in relation to assets. Farm operating profit and total farm profit show earnings and earning trends. Balance sheets and income records (discussed in Chapter 5) are the two main types of records of interest to lenders. Information about comparative analysis and the efficiency of the business (discussed earlier in this chapter) will be of interest to certain lenders.

Good records are a definite help for obtaining needed credit. Guidelines for securing credit are explained in Chapter 7.

RECORD-KEEPING SYSTEMS AND GUIDELINES

Use Available Record Systems

Many universities, extension services, financial institutions, and other commercial organizations have well-designed record-keeping systems for measuring earnings for farm business analysis and for income tax purposes. It is better to choose one of these systems than to fail to keep records. However, the best approach is first to decide what information is needed from the farm record system for managing the business, obtaining credit, and reporting taxes. Then select or develop a record-keeping system that serves these needs. By following this approach, you will better understand the results obtained.

> Develop and outline a record and control system for a farm. Specify the type of farm for which you will develop a record system. Specifically list the types of records you would use for management, credit, and taxes.

Use Comparative Analysis

If possible, join a group of producers whose farms and interests are similar to yours and keep or even develop a record system with them. By cooperating, not only will you benefit from the good ideas of others, but you will also be more likely to enjoy your record analysis. Most important, you will know where you stand in relation to others. Agriculture is a competitive business. Only those who are above average in key management areas will make good financial returns.

Keep a Separate Checking Account

Keep a separate checking account for the farm business or for parts of the farm business that you would like to evaluate individually. Deposit *all* receipts from the farm in that account. Pay *all* bills from that account. Clearly label all transfers for family living and other nonfarm expenditures. Try to make living and nonfarm transfers at specific times so that they are easily identified. This farm bank account will serve as a good cross-check for the record system.

Have a Specific Procedure

Set a specific time for updating records (Monday morning, Saturday afternoon, Wednesday evening, etc.). Pick a time that has the least schedule conflicts. Have a "system" of labeled boxes, spindles, envelopes, folders, and file dividers to fit your needs. An example of some categories:

1. Bills to be paid
2. Paid bills (to be posted)
3. Posted bills (by month)[5]
4. Accounts receivable
5. Receipts (to be posted)
6. Posted receipts (by month)[5]

If much labor is hired, it is recommended that a separate record be kept for each individual. A simple system is to insert an extra sheet in your account book with columns for the following information:

- Date
- Name
- Time worked
- Gross pay
- Social Security tax withheld
- Income tax withheld

---

[5]Posted bills and receipts may also be filed according to kind of item, such as crops, livestock, machinery, and equipment.

SUMMARY

Records are a helpful management tool. They can tell an operator how farm earnings compare to those of similar farms and can give insight into ways to improve earnings. Records can help keep a business operating according to plans. Crop and livestock production records can help increase efficiency by providing valuable information about the effect of various production practices. Good records are a necessity for reporting income taxes and are a tremendous help for obtaining credit.

Decide *which* records can be of use to you. Develop or choose a record system that meets the needs you have identified. Have a plan for keeping records up-to-date and for making maximum use of the records information.

DISCUSSION QUESTIONS

1. What is comparative farm business analysis?
2. Can comparative farm business analysis be directly applied or is further analysis required?
3. Explain the differences between farm operating profit and farm income. Why is farm income most appropriate for comparative business analysis and farm operating profit most useful for measuring the earnings of the business?
4. List the key factors affecting profit that can be validly evaluated in comparative farm business analysis?
5. Why is it important for a farm operator to use comparative analysis of farm records?
6. Comparative analysis should be based on at least three years' records when possible. Why?
7. What is a record control system? What are the most important types of farm business control systems and how are they used?
8. Is it necessary to keep production records? What kinds of production records are most important?
9. What types of records are needed for income taxes?
10. What types of records are needed for securing credit?
11. Explain how a checking account may be used as a means of checking the accuracy of farm records.
12. Design a complete farm record system for a farm with which you are familiar.

RELATED READINGS

AMERICAN BANKERS ASSOCIATION. *Agricultural Credit Analysis Handbook*. Washington, D.C.: American Bankers Association, 1975.

BAKER, TIMOTHY G., and JOHN R. BRAKE. *Cash Flow Analysis of the Farm Business,* Agricultural Experiment Station Extension Bulletin E-911. East Lansing, Mich.: Michigan State University, 1977.

BARRY, PETER J., JOHN A. HOPKIN and C. B. BAKER. *Financial Management in Agriculture* (3rd ed.). Danville, Ill.: Interstate Publishers, 1983.

CARSON, ED, and JEAN W. BAUER. *Your Family and Home Filing System*. West Lafayette, Ind.: Purdue University Cooperative Extension Service, 1982.

Farmers Tax Guide, 1983. Internal Revenue Service, Department of the Treasury, Washington, D.C. 1983.

FREY, THOMAS L., and D. KLINEFELTER. "Coordinated Financial Statements of Agriculture," (2nd ed.). Skokie, Ill.: Century Communications, 1982.

FREY, THOMAS L., and A. GENE NELSON. "You and Your Balance Sheet," Skokie, Ill.: Agri Business Publications, 1983.

FREY, THOMAS L., AND A. GENE NELSON. "You and Your Income Statement," Skokie, Ill.: Agri Business Publications, 1983.

JAMES, SYDNEY C., and EVERETT STONEBERG. *Farm Accounting and Business Analysis*. (2nd ed.). Ames, Ia.: Iowa State University Press, 1979.

LEE, WARREN F., MICHAEL D. BOEHLJE, AARON G. NELSON, and WILLIAM G. MURRAY. *Agriculture Finance*. (7th ed.). Ames, Ia.: Iowa State University Press, 1980.

NELSON, A. GENE, and THOMAS L. FREY. "You and Your Cash Flow," Skokie, Ill.: Agri Business Publications, 1983.

PENSON, JOHN B., JR., and DAVID A. LINS. *Agricultural Finance: An Introduction to Micro and Macro Concepts*. Englewood Cliffs, N.J.: Prentice-Hall, 1980.

WESTON, J. FRED, and EUGENE F. BRIGHAM. *Essentials of Managerial Finances*. (6th ed.). Hinsdale, Ill.: Dryden Press, 1982.

Financial Management
Guidelines for Farming

7

Capital investments required for competitive-size commercial farms range from $250,000 to $2,000,000, depending on the type of enterprise (Table 7.1). It takes more capital to farm than can be saved from most jobs, and capital requirements in the future are likely to increase faster than a person could save money from a salaried job. Farming has one of the highest requirements of capital per person of any type of business. Because of this, it is important that farm managers have a good understanding of strategies for gaining control of capital. Concepts about gaining control of capital, borrowing and repayment of money, and sources of credit are presented in this chapter.

GUIDELINES FOR GAINING CONTROL OF CAPITAL FOR FARMING

Keep Level of Efficiency High

By doing an outstanding job with their farm operations, managers open at least three doors to increased capital availability. First, a well-managed farm is more likely to generate sufficient net earnings so that money remains after living expenses are paid to reinvest in the farm. Second, financial institutions are more likely to loan money to a farm manager who has demonstrated good farm earnings for the size and type of operation. Finally, operators who do a good job are much more likely to be able to rent land and buildings from owners in their community.

Many people and institutions have money to invest. They are looking for safe investments that bring high returns, and the desired safety and returns can be attained by investing the capital with good managers. Capital gravitates toward managers who do a good job with crop and livestock efficiency and with total management.

Invest Early

Money invested in a business early in life, with the earnings from that investment remaining in the business, will grow to a relatively large sum even when the percentage return is "average."

Bill Marconi is graduating from college at the end of May. He plans to farm, but the farm he has rented will not be available until next year. Bill is considering two

TABLE 7.1 Capital Investments and Incomes on Indiana Farms Grouped by Type of Enterprise, 1975–1981[a]

Item	Hog	Dairy	Crop	Crop-Hog
Number of farms	30	41	61	20
Capital investment per farm				
Land and improvements[b]	$644,532	$467,129	$1,248,007	$ 896,322
Machinery and equipment[b]	68,668	53,805	82,423	74,472
Feed, grain, and supplies	91,657	48,974	145,289	112,299
Livestock	92,828	91,588	23,005	63,428
Total	$897,685	$661,496	$1,498,724	$1,146,521
Number of persons per farm	2.4	2.3	2.1	2.2
Investment per person	$386,752	$287,607	$713,678	$542,075
Number of tillable acres	502	400	861	710
Labor income	$22,963	$17,956	$22,327	$26,445
Rate earned on investment	5.5	5.3	4.8	5.0

[a]Purdue Farm Account Keepers.

[b]Book values, typically about 75% of actual market value.

alternatives for the time between June 1 and January 1 when he moves to the farm: He will either take a trip to see the country or get a job and invest the money in the farm. If Bill takes a job rather than travel, his job earnings and reduced travel expenses will result in $10,000 he could invest in his farm business. Bill figures he can make an 8% return above inflation and taxes on the invested money. If he invests $10,000, he would leave both the investment and its return in the farm. Bill calculates the growth over a forty-year period on the invested $10,000 as follows:

Today	$ 10,000
10 years	21,580
20 years	46,610
30 years	100,630
40 years	217,250

The $10,000 would grow 21.7 times in forty years provided Bill can make an 8% real return!

Of course, in making this decision Bill must consider all of his goals, not just money. But to attain the goal of net worth accumulation, a manager should invest early and should keep the investment growing by being efficient.

Following are some ways to obtain money to invest early:

Watch consumption slippage.   Money saved by keeping living costs low through more careful shopping and/or lower living standards can be invested in the business to generate income over time.

Delay and reduce income taxes.   There are strategies for legally reducing and delaying income taxes (see Chapter 22). Money from delayed or reduced income tax can be invested in the business to accumulate net worth. If $10,000 in tax payment can be delayed for the life of the business, that $10,000 could be used as the base for generating $217,250, as shown earlier.

Get your spouse to work in the farm business or in a nonfarm job.   If a spouse saves hired labor on the farm or contributes money to the business from a nonfarm job, this savings or contribution can be used for investment capital for net worth growth. Actually, this is another reduced-standard-of-living alternative. Rather than spending time contributing to the quality of life within the home, time is devoted to generating net worth for the business. This alternative must be weighed in light of all goals.

Get big enough soon enough.   Beginning farmers often increase farm size rapidly to the point at which earnings are sufficient for the desired living standard. If size of the business stops at this point, there will be no income for investment in the farm business. It is therefore important to grow quickly to the size at which earnings are higher than living standards so that money will be available for investment in the farm for net worth growth.

Janet Wilsey expects to make $40 per acre farmed for her labor and management. Janet would like to have $16,000 per year for living expenses, so it will take 400 acres to provide this amount. If she rents only 400 acres, money will not be available for growth. But if Janet can rent 600 acres, she will have $8,000 to add to the business each year. The return on annual investment can be reinvested, and net worth will increase rapidly. Janet might also increase net worth with a livestock enterprise.

Choose enterprises and production methods that use less capital. Limited capital can restrict size and also restrict the ability to generate earnings above living costs. It is almost like the "chicken or the egg" question. To accumulate net worth, farms should grow quickly to a size at which earnings are greater than living costs. But it takes capital and net worth to attain that size.

There are wide ranges in capital required per unit of production. Operators can choose new or used machinery, high-investment automated or low-investment high-labor livestock buildings. Machines can be purchased or custom-hired. It is important for a manager with a low net worth to select enterprises and production systems that permit the attainment of high volume. Initially these will often be low-investment production systems. The choice of enterprises and production systems is discussed in Chapters 9, 10, 11, 16, and 17.

Leasing.   Leasing can be a way to gain control of land, machinery, and even buildings that a manager does not have borrowing power to purchase. Renting land is discussed in Chapter 15 and leasing machinery in Chapter 16.

Partnership. A partnership with family or nonfamily farmers who have substantial amounts of capital but need labor and management is often a good way to gain control of needed resources. Partnership arrangements are discussed in Chapter 19.

BORROWING CAPITAL

Capital requirements for farming are so great that most farm businesses must operate with some level of borrowed capital. "How much should I borrow?" is a question often asked by farmers. The key considerations for answering that question follow.

The Amount Needed for the Business to Survive

A certain minimum size of business is needed for the farm to generate sufficient income to support the operator (see Chapter 13). If one does not own or cannot lease needed resources, the remaining alternative is to borrow and purchase. Even though an operator and the rest of the family would prefer not to increase borrowing, the choice may be either to increase borrowing and remain in the farming business or not increase borrowing and change to another occupation. Many farmers face this choice, and some borrow more than they prefer in order to remain in the business they like best. Other farmers choose to give up farming or take another job in addition to farming because the level of debt required is not acceptable to them.

The level of risk varies with many factors (discussed in Chapter 4) as well as with the amount of money borrowed. Hence, with a particular risk tolerance, a manager can find trade-offs between the amount borrowed and the choice of enterprises, production systems, and other management practices. If a manager finds it necessary to borrow more money than preferred from a risk standpoint (in order to secure needed resources to attain income goals), it is possible to make adjustments in the farm organization to compensate for borrowing risk.

Carl and Doris Burvicek were able to buy a Mississippi Delta farm on contract with a small down payment. They also secured a large operating loan. The Burviceks had only 20% equity in their total business. Because this debt load resulted in far more risk than Carl and Doris preferred, they took steps to reduce risk. They diversified by raising cotton, rice, soybeans, and wheat rather than a single crop. They contracted the sale of some of their crops in advance for a specific price. They wrote a clause in their land-purchase contract that enabled them to adjust the amount of contract payment to the yield and price level. Carl and Doris did not purchase expensive new machinery. Being a good mechanic, Carl purchased used machinery off-season and put it in good operating condition during the winter. The Burviceks kept living costs to a minimum; they purchased used furniture and drove old automobiles. Farming was important enough to the Burviceks that they were willing to accept more risk and inconvenience than was their preference in order to be in the farming business.

Risk Tolerance and Other Goals

Once farmers have increased size and net worth sufficiently to generate an income higher than required for living, they have the "luxury" of selecting the level of debt that is in line with their income preference and risk tolerance.

The amount of debt that is "best" is likely to change over time. A young farmer is often forced to have a high debt in order to farm. In many cases, people who have little to lose do not hesitate to take big risks because the chance for gain is great while the chance for loss is small. But as managers accumulate money, they often become increasingly concerned about protecting what they have rather than making more. This is because they have more to lose, and the satisfaction from additional money is no longer as great.

Age, health, number of children, interests of children, economic events, and many other factors are likely to change a manager's desire for income and tolerance for risk. Consequently, the "best" amount of risk is likely to change over time.

Rate of Return on Investment

The greater the payoff from an investment, the greater the amount a manager can borrow for a given level of risk. In fact, it is the rate of return on the investment that determines if borrowing is profitable.

For example, a manager who has $10,000 and invests it at 15% will earn $1,500 per year. Borrowing an additional $40,000 at 10% interest and investing the total at 15%, the manager will earn $7,500 minus $4,000 interest, or $3,500 (Table 7.2). The

TABLE 7.2   Borrowing or Leverage: Does It Pay?

	Earn 15%	Earn 10%	Earn 5%
No borrowing: Invest own $10,000			
Invest	$10,000	$10,000	$10,000
Earn	1,500	1,000	500
Ending capital	$11,500	$11,000	$10,500
Using borrowing as leverage: Invest own $10,000, borrow $40,000 at 10% interest			
Invest	$50,000	$50,000	$50,000
Earn	7,500	5,000	2,500
Less interest cost (10%)	−4,000	−4,000	−4,000
Net return	$ 3,500	$ 1,000	−$ 1,500
Rate earned on equity	35%	7%	−15%
Ending capital	$13,500	$11,000	$ 8,500
Gain (or Loss) from leverage	$ 2,000	0	($ 2,000)

gain from borrowing is $2,000. If, however, the return from the investment turns out to be 5% there will be a loss of $2,000 from borrowing rather than a gain.

Adding to owned capital with borrowed capital for an investment is sometimes called *leverage*. That is probably a good name: If properly used, the additional borrowed capital can help the manager control a larger investment just as a lever helps to move a large object. But if the end of the lever is not carefully handled, it can fly free and injure the manager. The higher the expected return in relation to the interest rate, the safer that borrowing or leverage is likely to be.

The return to borrowed money is likely to be high:

- If the level of management is high in the areas where the money is to be invested. It is desirable to have this high management level verified with demonstrated performance and a comparative business analysis (Chapter 6).
- If the investment makes use of an existing fixed resource. For example, if an operator has only 150 days' work with the existing operation, investment in a crop or livestock enterprise that uses the remaining labor and management is likely to pay a high return because it uses fixed labor and management. Investments that result in the use of salvage feeds are likely to pay a high rate of return because feed is a major component of livestock costs, and cheap feed with at least average management will almost assure a profit. Unused buildings and equipment can also help make returns high.
- If economies of size exist (see Chapter 13).
- If the inflation rate is high relative to interest. The return to investment, especially in durable assets, is likely to be high in a period of low real interest rates.[1] In a period of high real interest rates, the opposite is true.

Ability to Repay

A farm manager asked a banker, "How much money will you loan me?" The banker responded, "We will loan as much as you can repay." Development of a cash-flow budget as discussed in Chapter 6 is very important for determining the amount of borrowing that is feasible.

Cash flow is likely to be favorable when money is invested in resources that are quickly converted to products. Seed, fertilizer, feed, and operating resources are soon converted to crop and livestock products that can be sold, thus providing cash for repayment of loans.

Machinery lasts for several production periods and usually must be paid for more quickly than it wears out. A typical machine life is ten years, and a typical machinery loan is five years. Farmers purchasing machinery are forced to invest some of their equity in machinery. For this reason, machinery loans are more difficult to repay than loans on operating resources. Because buildings last longer than

---

[1] Real interest rate is the difference between interest rate paid and the inflation rate.

machinery, building loans are even more difficult to repay. Usually the most difficult loan of all to repay is one on land, because land never wears out.

Some managers use refinancing as a strategy to reduce the cash-flow problems associated with borrowing for machinery, buildings, or land. This strategy works especially well in a period of inflation.

> Dan Schultz bought a full line of new equipment at a cost of $120,000 when he expanded his farm and needed bigger machinery. He financed his machinery on a five-year note with 20% down and $20,000 principal plus interest due each year. After two years Dan had a $60,000 note and his machinery was appraised at $100,000. Because of the $40,000 equity and the fact that the machinery still had an eight-year life remaining, a competing banker was willing to give Dan a five-year note on the $60,000 with only a $12,000 principal payment required each year. This improved Dan's current cash flow by $8,000.

Some strategies that could improve cash flow are:

- Reduce living costs.
- Refinance fixed assets for a longer period, thus reducing principal payments (as illustrated in the above example).
- Sell assets that have a high principal requirement in relation to returns, such as land.
- Expand in areas that use mainly operating resources in relation to durable resources, such as rental land.
- Do some work for pay, such as custom work or a nonfarm job.
- Delay replacement of depreciable resources.

Cash-flow budgets should be developed and kept current as conditions change. Cash-flow budgets will be quite helpful to the manager in deciding how much debt can be carried.

Debt Ratios

Risk tolerance, earning potential of the investment, ability to repay the loan, and other factors previously discussed in this chapter are more important for deciding how much to borrow than are financial ratios. Nevertheless, ratios are useful to managers and are often considered by financial institutions to judge the credit risk of a potential borrower. Debt ratios should be viewed in light of the type of farm and farm organization, the management skill and character of the borrower, and interest rates, inflation, and other economic conditions. Some commonly used ratios are:

Percent debt = (Liabilities ÷ Assets) × 100

Lenders prefer 50% debt or less, but 75% to 80% or even more may be acceptable if other factors about the borrower are favorable.

$$\text{Current ratio} = \text{Current assets} \div \text{Current liabilities}$$

To avoid financial difficulties, a current ratio of 1.0 or above is required, and 1.5 to 2.0 is preferred by lenders.

$$\text{Asset to liability ratio} = \text{Total assets} \div \text{Total liabilities}$$

This ratio is similar to percent debt; 2.0 is preferred, but a ratio as low as 1.3 may be acceptable to lenders under certain circumstances.

$$\text{Debt-to-net-worth ratio} = \text{Total liabilities} \div \text{Net worth}$$

This ratio provides similar insight as provided by percent debt and asset-to-liability ratios. Although 1.0 or less is preferred, a ratio as high as 2.5 may be acceptable to the lender in some cases.

SECURING CREDIT

Knowledge of what creditors look for in making loans and of alternative credit sources and their characteristics can be invaluable to someone seeking credit. In the remainder of this chapter strategies for obtaining credit are explained, and characteristics of various credit sources are given.

Strategies for Improving the Likelihood of Obtaining Loans

Have a plan.   The one most important principle for obtaining credit is to have a plan. When requesting a loan, indicate *why* the loan is needed, the *amount* needed, *when* it is needed, *how much* it will earn, and *how* it will be repaid. This information is especially effective if the figures in the plan can be backed up with performance data from records. A sophisticated analysis using modern planning techniques may be helpful for gaining the lender's confidence. Each lender has information forms for evaluating loans. These forms usually include a net worth statement, an income statement, and a cash-flow projection. Secure copies of these beforehand and be prepared to supply information requested by the lender.

"Customize" your request.   Fit your loan request to the preferences of the lending institution, but don't lose control of management. Know what type of loan the lender likes to make, and define your request as near to the lender's preference as possible while still being accurate.

A manager wanted to expand by purchasing land. He found that the financial institutions he was dealing with preferred to finance bare tillable land with no natural obstructions. The manager had no objection to purchasing this type of land, so he devoted his energy toward finding the type of farm to buy that would be most appealing to the lending agency.

Develop a good credit image.   Each borrower develops a credit image over time. This is the general impression that lenders have about how good a risk a particular person is likely to be and whether this is a good type of borrower to have as a client. Credit images can be improved by the following practices:

Be prompt in paying obligations. Past performance in making payments is a key ingredient of one's credit image.

Minimize surprises. If the plan you have established for repaying a loan changes because of adverse weather, adverse prices, or other factors, keep your lender informed. Above all, be honest with the lender.

Jim McNeil borrowed money to increase his cattle feeding. Jim purchased a group of 300 feeders that unfortunately had a disease. Forty-three animals died, and the remainder did not do well. Jim was operating with tight finances, and unless something good happened to offset the bad, he would not be able to meet his debt payments. Jim was reluctant to tell his lender; no one likes to admit that one's plan is not working. Instead, Jim hoped that prices would increase sufficiently to offset the death loss, but this did not occur. Jim received a letter from his loan representative indicating that his loan payment was due. Jim did not have all the needed money. Finally, he told his lender what had happened. His loan representative then had to explain to others in the lending institution that Jim could not pay his loan in full. This was embarrassing to the loan representative. Jim had seriously hurt his credit image.

Joe Beltzer borrowed from the same loan representative for expanding his cropping program. Weather was not good, and spring planting was delayed. Joe saw his lender and advised her of the late planting. Later, a portion of the crops flooded out. Again he told his lender. Joe's lender advised others in her institution about Joe's problems. One month before his note was due, Joe brought a revised plan to the lender showing how much he would fall short of full payment and how he planned to make up the balance due. Joe's credit image was not hurt by adverse conditions because he kept his lender advised and avoided disappointing surprises. A good principle to follow in personal relations is to keep persons informed and to avoid a big surprise about an adverse change in circumstances.

Get to know your lender on a personal basis. If your lender knows you as an individual, understands your goals, and appreciates your management skill as well as your character, your credit image will be enhanced.

Start with small loan requests and build your image. Lending institutions are more cautious the greater the size of the loan. It is easier to obtain credit if a manager starts with relatively small loans, makes payments on time, and increases loan requests each year as a good credit image grows.

The Lender as Adviser

People who lend money have the ability to influence the decisions and actions of farmers. Sometimes this influence is exercised through a suggestion. In some cases, certain management practices may be required as a condition of the loan.

Many lenders have experience and can provide helpful information to borrowers. However, the goals of the lender are often quite different from the goals of the borrower, and a manager must take this into account when considering the counsel of the lender. Whereas the borrower's major goal is usually increased income, the lender's main goal is the security of the loan. Income and security may conflict as goals. Also, many lenders tend to be conservative; this is one reason they have taken salaried jobs from a credit institution rather than going into business for themselves.

Managers should listen carefully to lenders and incorporate their ideas when they fit the desired strategy, but borrowers should recognize that not all of a lender's advice will fit their specific situation. And lenders, like managers, vary tremendously in their ability. Some may give excellent advice because they know farming and understand the manager's goals; they also may have the wisdom to present their counsel with the objective of meeting the farmer's needs. Other lenders may not have an understanding of either farming or the manager.

Sources of Credit

Characteristics of credit sources vary from community to community depending on the individuals associated with the financial institutions. Following are some generalizations about credit institutions.

Farmers Home Administration (FmHA).   FmHA provides real estate loans, intermediate credit for machinery, and operating loans to low-resource operators. Interest rates for limited resource loans are usually lower than those of other financial institutions. Loans can be secured up to 100% of the value of the collateral offered for the loan. This is an excellent source of credit for starting farmers. The two biggest disadvantages of FmHA are that fund availability varies according to federal government allocations and that there may be long delays in obtaining financing. Because of low interest rates, the demand is usually greater than the amount of funds available. The ability to tolerate delay and frustration often determines who will obtain the available money. Persistence and patience may pay, but you also have to consider the costs of waiting.

FmHA allocates disaster loans. If a disaster area is declared because of weather, this often results in low-interest funds being made available. It is generally profitable for managers to take advantage of disaster loans. If you hear that your area has been declared a disaster area, check on the implications of that designation for low-interest loans for yourself.

Production Credit Association (PCA).   Production Credit makes intermediate (for machinery and breeding livestock) and operating loans to commercial farmers. They tend to place emphasis on cash flow and ability to repay the loan rather than on collateral alone, although collateral does help. Interest rates are usually competitive with those of commercial banks. Effective interest rates of PCA are higher than the rate charged because of stock purchase requirements.

After becoming established, a farmer who has obtained operating and/or intermediate loans through FmHA would typically transfer to Production Credit or a commercial bank. There is no upper limit on the amount that PCA can loan. PCA does not require liquidation of loans for operating purposes. Many farms "roll over" their inventory but do not liquidate it unless they go out of business. For example, a dairy farmer has a feed and cow inventory on a continuous basis. Production Credit recognizes this continuing inventory and provides financial support for it on a continuing basis.

Commercial banks.   Commercial banks generally provide operating, intermediate, and real estate loans, although types of credit will vary from bank to bank. Operating and intermediate are the most typical loans because of limited loan length and the speed of repayment required for real estate loans.

Commercial banks tend to require collateral in addition to favorable cash flow and repayment ability. Country banks have a limit on the amount of the line of credit they can extend. Sometimes smaller local commercial banks participate with larger regional banks to package larger loans. Bankers sometimes vary the interest rate according to the risk of the loan. There may be a number of banks in a geographic area, permitting a manager to select a bank that has a loan representative who fits the characteristics desired by the borrower.

Federal Land Banks.   Federal Land Banks loan money for land purchases. They consider cash flow as well as collateral and continuity of management. Federal Land Bank loans are long-term, requiring little principal payment in early years. Interest rates are variable during the term of the loan, depending on the cost of money, and are competitive with other land finance agencies. There is no prepayment penalty. Federal Land Banks require stock purchases; this increases the effective interest rate above the stated rate.

Insurance companies.   Many insurance companies finance farmland purchases, and some companies finance farm building investments. Insurance company loans for land purchase vary among companies but tend to be long-term with low principal payments. Interest rates are usually competitive with those of other lending institutions.

Land contracts.   Land contracts are agreements between a seller and a buyer that require a specified number of payments of principal and interest at specified times. Once the conditions of the contract are met, title of the farm is transferred to the buyer. The land contract provides a means for the buyer to finance the farm. At one time land contracts became popular because in many cases land could be purchased with a low down payment of only 10% to 20%, sometimes even less. The amount down is at the discretion of the seller, but many sellers accept a low down payment. In recent years the down payment percentage of both Federal Land Bank and insurance companies has decreased, and the land contract has become more of an advantage to the seller than to the buyer. Sellers often gain an income tax advantage by spreading the sale of a farm over several years.

Since the contract is often a benefit to sellers, a buyer who is willing to purchase on contract may be able to negotiate a favorable land price or interest rate. The purchaser must be cautious (and the seller, too) about the terms of the contract. Such factors as possession, sale of part of the property, improvement of the property, maximum repayment, responsibility for various expenses, and the option to reduce or skip principal payments in unfavorable years should be carefully considered and then discussed with a qualified person who prepares the contract.

One issue in a contract that is of special concern to the buyer is the payment terms. Because land-contract sellers are often near retirement age, they may not want long contracts. A ten-year contract is typical. If the principal is paid in ten yearly payments, the purchaser may have difficulty meeting cash-flow demands. In the case of small purchases on farms with substantial equity or cash reserves, this cash-flow demand may not present a problem, but it could result in difficulties for the starting or highly leveraged farmer.

If there are limits on prepayment of a contract, it may be difficult to use equity gained through principal payments and land value increases as collateral for additional borrowing. Thus the contract equity is "trapped" until the contract is completely paid.

In summary, a land contract can provide advantages for both the buyer and the seller, but terms vary greatly depending on the conditions specified. If these conditions are not carefully thought through in advance, they can create problems in the future for the buyer and/or the seller. Land contracts require more care, consideration, and study than do Federal Land Bank, insurance company, or commercial bank mortgages.

Dealer credit.   Dealer credit is often available from farm suppliers for operating capital (seed, fertilizer, feed) or machinery and equipment. Dealer credit tends to be variable. In times of tight competition for the farmer's business, some dealers will offer favorable credit terms to gain customers. While it may be profitable for a farmer to take advantage of these credit terms, the farmer should not depend on the permanent availability of these favorable terms. If the competitive situation changes, credit may change. Some dealers have specific credit plans. Typically, the interest charge is greater than for loans from commercial banks or Production Credit.

Individuals.   Farmers are sometimes able to obtain a loan from individuals who are willing to charge a lower interest rate than that of commercial institutions. Even at the lower rate, these individuals can obtain higher interest than a bank savings account would pay. There are three main disadvantages of borrowing from individuals: (1) Situations change, and the lender may not be willing to loan money on a continuous basis; (2) there is usually a low upper limit on the amount they will lend; and (3) borrowing from an individual does little to enhance one's credit image.

Competition tends to keep interest rates fairly close among lenders, but they may vary on a given loan at a particular time. It pays to shop for credit, but a manager must be careful not to switch lenders too frequently because this might jeopardize availability of credit. In most cases, availability of credit is more important than a small difference in interest rate.

Managers of modern farms must be knowledgeable about financial management. They must be able to project their capital needs, find sources of capital, and service debts. Capital requirements per farm and per person in farming will continue to increase, and capital management will be even more important in the future.

Make a plan of the amount and kind of capital needed for a farm that is of interest to you. What sources would you suggest for obtaining this capital?

Obtain a credit application from a local finance agency (bank, PCA, FmHA) and complete this application for a case farm (year 1 of the Henly case in Chapter 5 could be used). Visit with a lender about your loan request and present the completed form. Ask the lender what he or she looks for when loaning money.

DISCUSSION QUESTIONS

1. How much capital is required for different kinds of commercial farms in your area, for the total farm and per full-time person?
2. What are the sources of capital requirements determined in question 1?
3. To get started in farming by renting land, how many dollars minimum would you need to borrow?
4. What is the best source of borrowed capital for a starting farmer?
5. What is meant by the statement "Keep efficiency level high"? How can the efficiency level be measured?
6. How does a high level of efficiency help a manager gain control of capital?
7. Why is it important to invest early? What are some ways of obtaining money in order to make early investments?
8. What factors determine how much a manager should borrow?

9. Which of the following debts would be easiest to repay and which would be most difficult (a) in a period of rapid inflation and relatively low interest rates and (b) in a period of stable prices and relatively higher interest rates? Why?

   • Land mortgage
   • Building debt
   • Machinery note
   • Operating loan

10. When are returns to investment likely to be high?
11. What steps can a manager take to improve the cash-flow situation?
12. List six or seven sources of credit for agricultural borrowers. What types of purchases would most likely be financed by each of the institutions listed?
13. What practices can a manager follow that will be helpful in securing credit?
14. What are some advantages and disadvantages of obtaining management advice from a lender?
15. How valuable are financial ratios for making borrowing decisions? Would the ratios need to be different for the purchase of land, buildings, machinery, and operating capital? Why?

RELATED READINGS

AMERICAN BANKERS ASSOCIATION. *Agricultural Lending: Sources of Funds.* Washington, D.C.: Agricultural Bankers Division, 1976.

LEE, WARREN F., MICHAEL D. BOEHLJE, AARON G. NELSON, and WILLIAM G. MURRAY. *Agricultural Finance* (7th ed.). Ames, Ia.: Iowa State University Press, 1980.

MELTON, JAMES O. "Agricultural Lending by Life Insurance Companies," *Agricultural Finance Review,* 37 (1977).

PENSON, JOHN B., JR., and DAVID A. LINS. *Agricultural Finance: An Introduction to Micro and Macro Concepts,* chaps. 19–22. Englewood Cliffs, N.J: Prentice-Hall, 1980.

SCHNEEBERGER, KENNETH C., and DONALD D. OSBORN. *Financial Planning in Agriculture.* Danville, Ill.: The Interstate Publishers, Inc., 1977.

Also, see Related Readings, Chapter 6.

Decision-Making Methods

8

Factors to consider in developing a strategy or plan for the farm business were discussed in Chapter 2. Principles for making farm management decisions were presented in Chapters 3 and 4. Farm accounting and financial management procedures and considerations were covered in Chapters 5, 6, and 7. This chapter focuses on quantifying and integrating the concepts in the first seven chapters and provides procedures for making decisions that are discussed in Chapters 9–22.

MODELS FOR FARM DECISION MAKING

A model is an abstract representation of a real situation or, in other words, a small imitation of the real thing. Architects sometimes build small model houses and make sketches before building a house. The architect's purpose in building a model house is to predict the effect of a decision and action before taking action. It is easier and cheaper to make changes in the model than to make changes in the finished house.

Similarly, business managers may develop models for actions they are considering. In this case, the model is usually on paper and shows the costs, returns, capital requirements, labor requirements, and other factors for a particular decision and action. A farmer may wish to use a model to explore the effect on income, cash flow, investments, and net worth of such changes as size, enterprise combination, building system, amount of labor, and prices.

Business models have been made through hand budgeting for many years. Computers and advanced mathematical methods allow the consideration of more aspects of a decision and more alternative plans. The computer allows models to be much more useful and more realistic, especially for complex decisions.

However, one must remember that models are abstractions. They are not the real thing but are only imitations. The way to find exactly how a decision will affect the business is to take action. Taking action, however, can be expensive and time-consuming, and if the same action is taken by the same business at various times, different complexities might occur each time. Nevertheless, business models have proved useful for predicting the outcome of decisions.

Another method of predicting the effect of a decision is to observe the impact of the proposed action on another business that has already taken a similar action. This is fast and inexpensive, but farm businesses are unique. Capital, labor, and management situations differ greatly among farms, consequently, the same action may have different results for each farm.

As stated, the effect of a decision can be determined by trying it, observing someone else who has already tried it, or by developing a model. All of these approaches should be used to some extent. The use of the model is becoming more important because of the growing complexity and size of farms and because more realistic models are being developed as computers become more efficient and economical.

In applying a model for decision making, the manager should follow these steps:

1. Carefully identify the decision.
2. Specify all of the factors that affect the decision and how these factors are related.
3. Collect needed information about the important factors affecting the decision.
4. Make a complete analysis.
5. Decide.
6. Act.
7. Evaluate the outcome.

BUDGETING

Budgeting is an analytical tool used by farmers to evaluate certain farm changes or to project farm income and cash flow. Budgeting was used in Chapter 3 for applying principles for decision making. A more comprehensive discussion of budgeting and some additional examples are presented here.

Three main kinds of budgets are: partial budgets, total budgets, and cash-flow budgets.

Partial Budgets

Partial budgets are used to make decisions for only a segment of the farm operation, such as "Should some cows be culled?" "Should an additional 80 acres be rented?" and "Should a larger tractor be purchased?" The following format is commonly used for partial budgets.

Partial Budget for _____ Farm		
Decision being evaluated _____		
A. 1. Additional receipts	$ _____	
2. Reduced costs	_____	
3. Subtotal (1 + 2)		$ _____
B. 1. Additional costs	$ _____	
2. Reduced receipts	_____	
3. Subtotal (1 + 2)		_____
C. Net income change (A3 − B3)		$ _____

When budgeting several changes in the farm business, it is desirable to prepare a budget for each change rather than including all changes in one budget. If several changes are included in one budget, it is not possible to determine the effect of each change. This same principle is true for computerized budgets as well as for hand budgets.

When budgeting the impact of a particular decision on income, a knowledge of the principles discussed in Chapter 3 is helpful in arriving at the best estimate of what will happen when changes are made. Budgets are used to integrate costs and returns information and to determine effects of changes on farm income. The following illustrations are typical farm decisions. These examples demonstrate how partial budgeting can be used and how fixed and variable costs should be handled.

Case 1: Should I discontinue my poultry sideline?   An important factor in the interpretation of farm records for use in management decisions is recognizing the difference between fixed and variable costs. The following situation illustrates what this distinction meant to the Triple D Farm.

The principal enterprise was a fifty-cow dairy with home-grown replacements. The farm also had a 5,000-bird market-egg flock. The farm was at capacity insofar as land and building resources were concerned. The labor force consisted of a father and son who were fully employed. Year-end analysis of the poultry enterprise account produced the figures in Table 8.1. Based on these records, the family concluded that they should discontinue the poultry enterprise because it had an annual loss of $3,175. The family asked a farm management extension agent to counsel them.

The agent examined the poultry enterprise account with the family. He suggested that they recalculate the costs and returns from this enterprise, using only the actual cash expenditures that would be reduced if the enterprise were dropped. He

TABLE 8.1 Enterprise Account: Total Costs and Returns for 5,000-Bird Market-Egg Flock, Triple D Farm

Returns		
Eggs	$55,000	
Cull hens	1,575	
Total income		$56,575
Costs		
Feed	$33,400	
Replacement pullets	11,750	
Repairs, power, and fuel	1,100	
Interest, depreciation, tax on buildings and equipment	6,250	
Supplies	750	
Operators' labor (1,300 hours)	6,500	
Total costs		$59,750
Gain (or Loss)		($ 3,175)

pointed out that the labor was a fixed cost to the total business: Any labor saved from discontinuing poultry could not be profitably employed elsewhere on the farm, since the dairy unit was at capacity for the existing buildings. He also pointed out that building taxes, depreciation, and interest costs would not be reduced if the poultry enterprise were discontinued.

Following the agent's advice, the family recalculated the costs and returns from the poultry flock, eliminating the fixed costs of labor and of building and equipment ownership. Their figures appear in Table 8.2.

The partial budget, which included variable costs only, indicated that instead of losing $3,175 per year, the family in fact was earning $9,575 as a payment toward fixed buildings, equipment, labor, and management. While this return is less than the family would like to receive, it is much better than no return at all, which would be the result if the poultry enterprise were discontinued.

This case illustrates the need for proper classification of costs for farm decision making.

Case 2: Should we dispose of two low-producing cows?   Would an operator be better off selling two low-producing cows and concentrating time and effort on the remaining higher producers? This was the situation: Farm milk records indicated a herd average of 13,500 pounds per cow. The operator wanted to sell two cows producing only 10,500 pounds of milk because he thought they didn't pay. Table 8.3 shows what would happen to costs and returns if they were sold.

TABLE 8.2   Partial Budget for Triple D Farm

Decision being evaluated:			
Should we keep the 5,000-bird market-egg flock?			
A. 1. Additional revenue			
Eggs		$55,000	
Cull hens		1,575	
2. Reduced costs		0	
3. Subtotal (1 + 2)			$56,575
B. 1. Additional costs			
Feed		$33,400	
Replacement pullets		11,750	
Repairs, power, and fuel		1,100	
Supplies		750	
2. Reduced revenue		0	
3. Subtotal (1 + 2)			47,000
C. Return to buildings, labor, and management			
if hens are kept			$ 9,575
Decision: Keep the laying flock because income will be $9,575 greater with the flock than without it.			

TABLE 8.3 Partial Budget for Triple D Farm

Decision being evaluated: Should we sell two low-producing cows?

A.	1. Additional receipts		
	Hay sold: 7 tons at $55.00	$ 385.00	
	2. Reduced costs		
	Corn: 160 bushels at $3.00	480.00	
	Purchased feed	364.00	
	Veterinary and medicine	75.00	
	Interest, supplies, and misc.	72.00	
		$ 991.00	
	3. Subtotal (1 + 2)		$1,376.00
B.	1. Added costs	0	
	2. Reduced returns		
	Milk: 21,000 pounds at $13.00	$2,730.00	
	Calves: 2 at $50.00	100.00	
	3. Subtotal (1 + 2)		$2,830.00
C.	Gain (or loss) if cows are sold		($1,454.00)

Decision: Keep the cows because income will decrease $1,454 if they are sold.

Perhaps an even better alternative would be to replace the two low producers with higher-producing cows. This alternative should be budgeted for Triple D Farm. Partial budgeting is useful for numerous farm decisions. Other examples are: used versus new machinery, more hired labor or labor-saving equipment investments, invest in farm grain storage or rent storage at the elevator—to name but a few.

Budgeting Annual Costs of Depreciable Resources

Capital resources are used in more than one production period. Their cost should therefore be assigned to the production periods in which they are used (Chapter 5). The best measure of the profitability of a capital resource investment is increase in net worth over the total planning period (see "Capital Investment Decision," Chapter 3). But for a partial budget, a manager may wish to make an estimate of costs and returns for a single year.

The costs associated with depreciable capital items are depreciation, interest, taxes, insurance, and repairs. One procedure for estimating costs for each year of the production period for a partial budget is to calculate depreciation, interest, insurance, taxes, and repair costs as follows:

1. Determine depreciation and interest cost per year in the following way:

   $AC = (TD \times Ain) + iSV$

   AC = Annual average cost of depreciation and interest for the planning period in current dollars.

TD = Total depreciation for the planning period. Initial cost[1] of the capital item minus the salvage value. The salvage value should be expressed in terms of current price level.

Ain = Percentage of TD which represents annual cost of interest and depreciation for interest rate i and number of years n (from Appendix A).

i = Real interest rate. The approximate real interest rate can be calculated by subtracting the inflation rate from the market interest rate.[2] The real interest is used so that costs are on the basis of the current price level. The market interest rate usually is determined not only by the current supply and demand of capital, but also anticipated rate of inflation or deflation (change of the value of capital in the future).

SV = Salvage value of the capital item at the end of the planning period in current dollars. Interest is charged on the salvage value as a cost because it represents part of the inventory during the planning period.

For example, assume a tractor costs $50,000 and is expected to be used ten years. A similar ten-year-old tractor would have a value today of $10,000. Assume also that the market interest rate is 13% and inflation is expected to be 5% for the ten-year period that the tractor will be used. Real interest rate is 8%. Thus:

TD = $50,000 (cost) − $10,000 (salvage value) = $40,000

Ain = .1490 (i is 8% and n is 10 years) (from table in Appendix A)

AC = ($40,000 × .1490) + (.08 × $10,000)

AC = $5,960 + $800 = $6,760.

2. Insurance and taxes may be estimated as a percentage of initial cost and considered to be uniform for the planning period. For the tractor in the example above assume insurance is .5% and taxes 1%. Then,

Taxes and insurance = 1.5% of $50,000 = $750 per year

3. Repair costs may be estimated as a percentage of initial investment over the entire planning period for buildings and equipment and a cost per hour of use for farm machinery (see Chapters 16 and 17).

The advantages of using the above procedure for calculating the annual cost of capital resources are that the procedure is relatively easy to figure, it accounts for changes in the price level, and it is a close approximation of the actual costs.

Total Farm Budgets

Total farm budgets are prepared to provide analyses for decisions that have a major impact on the total farm or when a new plan is being developed for the total farm.

---

[1] Initial cost of capital items which qualify for investment credit should be reduced by the amount of the credit or by the amount that tax will be reduced with the credit (see Chapter 22).

[2] The exact value of $i = \left(\dfrac{1 + \text{interest rate charged}}{1 + \text{inflation rate}} \right) - 1$

Receipts, costs, and farm profit for the current situation should be budgeted first. The same calculations should then be made for the alternative farm plans and differences observed.

Total farm budgeting involves observing the effect of changes in such factors as the following:

- Acres of various kinds of crops
- Numbers of different kinds of livestock
- Size in acres or number of livestock
- Investments in land, building, machinery, and equipment
- Hiring additional labor.

If budgets are prepared for more than one alternative farm plan, it is desirable to have a budget format that is easy to manipulate. One such format is the block budget. The block budgeting procedure involves these steps:

1. Prepare a return above direct cost budget for one unit of each enterprise to be considered.
   a. Calculate returns for one unit of each enterprise.
   b. Calculate direct costs for one unit of each enterprise. Direct costs, which are almost always variable, are generally associated with an enterprise at a constant rate per unit. Direct costs for crops include seed, fertilizer, chemicals, fuel, repairs, and interest on operating capital and stored grain.
   c. Subtract direct costs from returns to determine returns over direct costs per unit.
2. Multiply returns over direct costs by the number of units of each enterprise to determine total farm return over direct costs.
3. Determine costs of indirect resources associated with the total farm rather than per unit of enterprise. Indirect resources include labor; depreciation, interest, taxes, and insurance on buildings, machinery, and equipment; land maintenance; and miscellaneous farm overhead costs. Indirect costs may be either fixed or variable.
4. Subtract indirect costs from returns over direct costs to determine net returns to the farm business.

Generally, in preparing budgets for additional alternative farm plans, only steps 2, 3, and 4 need to be done because step 1 usually remains the same. Thus block budgeting simplifies the budgeting process.

Here is how Arny Russell is using block budgets to decide what crops to grow and whether he should rent all or part of 400 acres that are available in his area. Arny owns and farms 600 acres on which he usually plants half corn and half soybeans, and he has no livestock. First, Arny developed a budget of direct costs per acre for the

TABLE 8.4   Returns, Direct Costs, and Income over Direct Costs for Corn, Soybeans, and Wheat, Arny Russell Farm

		Corn	Soybeans	Wheat
A.	Returns			
	Yield per acre	115 bu.	35 bu.	50 bu.
	Price	× $2.75	× $6.50	× $3.75
		$316.25	$227.50	$187.50
B.	Direct costs per acre			
	Fertilizer and lime	$ 56.00	$ 25.00	$ 36.00
	Seed and chemicals	25.00	23.00	13.00
	Machine operation and drying	45.00	28.00	22.00
	Interest on operating capital, stored grain, and miscellaneous	14.50	11.00	9.50
C.	Total direct costs	$140.50	$ 87.00	$ 80.50
D.	Income over direct costs	$175.75	$140.50	$107.00

crops he would consider planting (Table 8.4) by following step 1 (listed earlier). Then Arny followed steps 2, 3, and 4 to develop farm profit estimates for three farm organization alternatives (Table 8.5).

He usually plants half corn and half soybeans, so he considered that organization in his first budget (Table 8.5). Projected farm operating profit is $51,875. In budget 2, Arny decided to budget all corn. All other costs would remain the same except storage. If Arny plants all corn rather than half corn and half beans, he will need 20,000 bushels more storage because corn yields more than beans. Arny figures rental of that storage will cost about $6,000. Machinery, labor, and other costs will remain the same. It was easy for Arny to prepare the second budget because the block budgets remained the same and costs and returns only needed to be multiplied by different acreages. The all-corn budget showed an operating profit increase from $51,875 to $56,450. Arny preferred half corn and half beans to all corn because it spreads risk and labor demands. Also, if all corn is planted every year, yields might eventually decline. So Arny decided that even though all corn showed a $4,575 higher income, he would plant half corn and half beans.

Next, Arny budgeted renting 400 more acres and increasing corn and soybeans to 500 acres each. Cash rent for the added land would be $100 per acre. Also, more machinery would be needed, and hired help would be required. While the budget for renting land is more complex than changing only the acreage of corn and soybeans, it is still much easier to prepare using the block budgets. Arny's results showed that profit would decrease to $44,125 if the 400 acres were rented (budget 3, Table 8.5). If Arny had not taken time to prepare budgets, he might have rented the ground and had more work, more risk, and less profit.

Additional budgets for crops, livestock, and the total farm are presented in Chapters 10, 11, and 12.

Budgeting is one tool that a farm manager must understand and be able to ap-

TABLE 8.5   Total Farm Budgets for Three Alternatives, Using Block Budgets, Arny Russell Farm

		Budget 1 Present 600 Acres 300 Corn 300 Soybeans	Budget 2 Present 600 Acres All Corn No Soybeans	Budget 3 Present 600 Acres Rent 400 Acres 500 Corn 500 Soybeans
A.	Receipts[a]			
	1. Corn	$ 94,875	$189,750	$158,125
	2. Soybeans	68,250	0	113,750
	3. Total	$163,125	$189,750	$271,875
B.	Direct costs[a]			
	1. Corn	$ 42,150	$ 84,300	$ 70,250
	2. Soybeans	26,100	0	43,500
	3. Total	$ 68,250	$ 84,300	$113,750
C.	Income over direct costs (A – B)	$ 94,875	$105,450	$158,125
D.	Indirect costs			
	1. Machinery[b]	$ 24,000	$ 24,000	$ 35,000
	2. Storage[c]	10,000	16,000	$ 20,000
	3. Land taxes	6,000	6,000	6,000
	4. Hired labor	2,000	2,000	12,000
	5. Building[b] machine storage	1,000	1,000	1,000
	6. Cash rent	0	0	40,000
	7. Total	$ 43,000	$ 49,000	$114,000
E.	Farm Operating Profit (C – D)	$ 51,875	$ 56,450	$ 44,125

[a]From Table 8.4, multiplied by acres of each crop.

[b]Depreciation, interest, insurance, and taxes.

[c]Drying, handling, and storage facilities depreciation, interest, insurance, and taxes.

ply to all types of farm decisions. The farm manager must also know the sources and be able to organize information needed for various budgets.

Cash Flow

In the foregoing discussion of total and partial budgets, the question "Will it pay?" was answered for several case situations. From a business management standpoint, the answer to "Will it pay?" must be yes before a manager should proceed. But the manager must also be able to answer yes to the question "Can I pay for it?" before proceeding. The first question involves profit; the second, cash flow. Cash flow becomes a consideration when money is borrowed to implement a decision, especially when it is borrowed for land, buildings, or equipment. Cash-flow budgets were discussed in Chapter 6.

LINEAR PROGRAMMING

Linear programming has become a widely used tool for making farm management decisions regarding what products to produce, what system of production to use, and how much to produce. It, like budgeting, is aimed at finding the "best" or most profitable organization for a particular farm.

Linear programming has three advantages over the budgeting technique. First, it ensures that the combination of products or enterprises selected is the most profitable possible from the alternatives considered, given the set of input-output relationships and resource restrictions. Second, with the linear programming method it is possible to consider many more alternative organizations than would be feasible with budgeting. Third, linear programming provides information that is not available from budgeting: *Shadow prices* show the amount that an additional unit of a limiting resource would increase gross income, and *penalty costs* show the loss in net income that would occur if one unit of an enterprise not included in the "best" organization were added to that organization.

Linear programming is a mathematical method for choosing the best combination of activities to maximize or minimize an objective subject to limitations or constraints. In farm management, the *activities* are usually crop or livestock enterprises and systems of production, the *objectives* are maximizing income or minimizing cost, and the *limitations* are land, labor, capital, management, and other resources.

A California ranch developed a linear program to help decide the combination of crops that should be grown. The ranch managers started with a simple situation and then progressed with the addition of a large number of enterprises and constraints to make the linear programming model as realistic as possible for their situation. Following is the procedure used to develop the initial ranch plan.

Four kinds of information are needed to develop a linear programming farm plan:

1. Limiting resources must be specified.
2. Enterprises or production systems must be identified.
3. The amount of each limiting resource used by each enterprise must be determined.
4. Returns to each enterprise above variable costs must be calculated.

For the ranch, the above is outlined in Table 8.6. To find a linear programming solution, the information is arranged as shown in Table 8.7.

The linear programming solution, with an objective of maximizing profit, resulted in the following information:

1. Most profitable combination of crops:

TABLE 8.6 Information Needed for a Linear Programming Plan

Limiting Resources

10,000 acres of land

    400 field hands, maximum 2,500 hours per person

      10 irrigation workers, maximum 2,500 hours per person

      25 tractor drivers, maximum 2,500 hours per person

Crops, use of limiting resources, and return above variable costs per acre

1. Strawberries
Field hand labor	1,430 hours
Irrigation labor	13 hours
Tractor labor	9.4 hours
Returns per acre above variable costs	$6,746

2. Asparagus
Field hand labor	223 hours
Irrigation labor	2.8 hours
Tractor labor	3.9 hours
Returns per acre above variable costs	$1,321

3. Sweet corn
Field hand labor	45 hours
Irrigation labor	1.7 hours
Tractor labor	20.2 hours
Returns per acre above variable costs	$ 532

4. Celery
Field hand labor	360 hours
Irrigation labor	2.6 hours
Tractor labor	13.7 hours
Returns per acre above variable costs	$1,024

5. Rent out land $ 100

TABLE 8.7 Layout of Linear Programming Information

Limiting Resource	Amount of Limiting Resource[a]		Enterprises				
			Strawberries	Asparagus	Sweet Corn	Celery	Rent Out
Land	10,000 acres	≥	1	1	1	1	1
Field labor	1,000,000 hours	≥	1,430	233	45	360	0
Irrigation labor	25,000 hours	≥	13.0	2.8	1.7	2.6	0
Tractor labor	62,500 hours	≥	9.4	3.9	20.2	13.7	0
Returns above variable costs			$6,746	$1,321	$532	$1024	$100

[a] Resources required by all enterprises must not exceed the amount available.

	Acres
Strawberries	0
Asparagus	3,455
Sweet corn	4,282
Celery	0
Rent out	2,263

2. Returns to land and labor: $7,080,311

3. Profit decreases by the following amounts if one acre of crops not in the "optimum plan" are included in the farm plan:

Strawberries	$ 701
Celery	$1,040

4. One more unit of limiting resources would increase *gross* income by the following amounts:

Farm labor (1 hour)	$ 5.07
Tractor drivers (1 hour)	$10.09

5. Returns per acre would have the following impact on acres of various crops grown:

If returns to asparagus decreased to $1,209 per acre, asparagus would start to be replaced by strawberries.

If the returns to sweet corn decreased below $296 per acre, the acreage would be reduced.

The results of this linear program indicate that asparagus and sweet corn are the most profitable crops, the labor supply is exhausted before all of the land is used, and the break-even wage that could be paid for an additional hour of labor is $5.07 for field help and $10.09 for tractor drivers.

The manager should first consider if more labor could be hired for less than the amounts shown. If it could, the plan should be rerun with more labor included.

If more labor cannot be hired at wages below the break-even level, the manager should proceed to grow the amount of sweet corn and asparagus in the plan and to rent out 2,253 acres.

Linear programming computer programs enable a manager to obtain a program solution by systematically listing the information as shown in Table 8.7.

Many farm management models for making a variety of decisions are based on linear programming.

FARM MANAGEMENT SIMULATION

Simulation is the use of models to explore what would happen to selected farm business aspects, such as income, under different circumstances. Farm management simulation includes the use of all total or partial business models. Budgeting and linear programming are special cases of simulation.

Some models have been developed to make it easier for a farm manager to simulate the impact of certain decisions, price changes, and production changes. Many of these models are computerized. Managers can make such choices as crop combination; livestock enterprise selection; size; investment in land, buildings and machinery; production practices; and other factors. After each choice, the impact of the choice on income, cash flow, and farm resource requirements is determined. This provides the manager with insight into the impact of various decisions. The manager can also explore the impact of changing prices, yields, and livestock production. Some of the models are designed to generate normal production variation and seasonal and cyclical price variations.

COMPUTERS FOR FARM MANAGEMENT

Computers can be used to aid the manager in keeping records, securing information, budgeting, projecting cash flow, and making numerous plans and management decisions. Computers do calculations much more quickly than can be done by hand, they store and organize large amounts of information, and they can help solve complex problems that would be impractical to solve by hand computations. Computer use in agriculture will increase in the future because farms are becoming larger and more complex, computer prices are declining, new uses for computers are evolving, and more and more people understand how to use computers.

While farms may not need a computer to survive, a computer can help a capable manager to have more timely, accurate information and to be better able to analyze the consequences of numerous farm decisions.

How to Get Computer Services

Willard Steckland has been using a computer in his farm business since 1975. Some of Willard's experiences may be helpful to you.

In 1975 Willard attended a computer workshop offered by his extension service and found that he could use the computer to do farm planning. At the workshop Willard provided information about his farm in an "input" form. After his farm data were processed by the computer, Willard received "output," or results. He learned how to interpret the output at the workshop. Willard has continued to use the farm planning model over the years whenever he has had a major decision to make, such as machinery purchases, building investment, land rental or purchase, and livestock expansion.

Willard did not have to buy a computer or write a program, and the fees charged ($20 for each run) were small in relation to the cost of owning a computer. Willard used several financial management and enterprise planning models on a fee basis. Also, he joined a computerized record-keeping service that required that he submit data on computer forms. From the service he received a record summary and a comparative record analysis.

In 1978 Willard read about *programmable calculators* and purchased one to do small budgeting jobs. Programmable calculators are similar to pocket calculators, but they have more memory and use small instruction chips that direct the calculator to make computations to complete the desired analyses. With the programmable calculator Willard could quickly determine payoff to different enterprises and rate of return to farm capital investments. However, since the programmable calculator had very limited data storage and computational ability, for larger problems Willard continued to use programs available through his extension service.

In 1981 Willard's state extension service introduced a computer system that placed a computer in each county extension office. The computer could be used to make certain decisions, such as how much to pay for land, how much to pay for feeder cattle, and how to market grain, to name a few. Willard often went to the county extension office to do an analysis for a particular decision. This saved him time as he did not have to wait for his results, and he frequently made several computer runs as he observed the results of each run.

As more programs became available, Willard learned that he must be selective due to a "learning cost" associated with becoming familiar with each program. It takes time and effort to learn the kind of analysis the model makes, the input needed, and the meaning of the output. Experts with commercial farm management firms and the extension service advised Willard about which programs were most relevant for his farm and taught him how to use selected programs.

Three years ago Willard became interested in a *home farm computer*. He talked with his extension specialist, a representative of a farm management service that offered consultation regarding computers, and numerous computer hardware and software vendors. Willard was advised that in purchasing a home farm computer, his first step should be deciding how the computer would be used. What jobs would the computer do? How much time would this save? What additional information would be available? What is the value of this additional information? In other words, what is the return to the ownership of a computer? Initially, Willard thought he could use the home farm computer to do all the analyses he had been doing through the computer services. He found that a computer system that costs $8,000 (the amount of money he would be willing to invest) would lack the capacity to handle the large farm-planning programs. After a careful study, Willard ascertained that his main uses of the computer would be those listed in Table 8.8.

While the listing of computer uses did not provide a dollar value of return to the

TABLE 8.8   Uses, Advantages, and Disadvantages of a Home Farm Computer, Willard Steckland Farm

Use	Advantages over Present System	Disadvantages Compared to Present System
A. Keep farm records in computer	1. Records can be summarized at any time.	1. Computer use would require more time to enter data.
	2. Records can be tailored to the farm.	2. Willard would need to purchase or write a suitable program.
	3. Records would be completely confidential	
B. Cash-flow projections	1. Records can be updated quickly.	1. Need to purchase or write a program.
	2. Results will help operator keep the lender advised.	2. Takes time to enter data in computer.
C. Cattle enterprise records and analyses	1. Can determine performance and profitability of each lot of cattle.	1. Must purchase or write program.
	2. Forecasts break-even price before purchase.	2. Takes time to secure needed data and to do analyses.
	3. Computes least-cost feed mix for cattle.	
	4. Estimates optimum selling weight.	
	5. Determines maximum to pay for feeder cattle.	
D. Crop enterprise records and analyses	1. Determines cost of production per acre and per unit of production.	1. Willard must purchase or write a program.
	2. Stores information about past practices and yields by field, such as seed variety, fertilizer, and chemical use.	2. Must input detailed data and take time to do various analyses.
	3. Budgets profit per acre with varying prices.	
	4. Calculates break-even rental rates.	
	5. Calculates maximum payment for land purchases.	

computer, it did give Willard an understanding of the benefits of owning a home farm computer.

The next question is "What are the costs?" Three costs were identified:

	(Annual Cost)
1. Ownership cost of the computer: depreciation, interest, repairs, and taxes (25% of investment of $5,000)	$1,250
2. Depreciation of software ($3,000 over five years)	600
3. Extra time required to operate and learn to use computer (200 hours per year at $5.00 per hour)	1,000
Total	$2,850

The question Willard must answer is "Are the benefits to owning a home farm computer worth $2,850 per year?" Judging that the returns would justify the expenditure, he decided to purchase a home farm computer.

Software.   The second step in purchasing a home farm computer is to determine what software (programs or instructions for the computer) is available and which computers the software will fit. Computer programs are the limiting factors to computer use at the present time. You should first determine what software is available to do the kinds of things you want done, then choose a computer that is compatible with the software you plan to use. Two types of general programs usually come with a small computer. The *operating system* tells the computer what to do, and a second program, the *compiler* or *interpreter,* translates a third type of program, *the applications program* (which usually does not come with the computer), so that it can be used by the computer. Most small home farm computer users are concerned mainly with the *applications programs* or *software.* It is important to know if the operating system and the interpreter come with the computer or must be purchased separately. It is also important to determine kinds of applications software that will fit the operating system. Computer programs such as the ones listed for Willard's farm are all application programs.

In addition to purchasing an existing applications program, it is possible to write one's own program or modify an existing program. Of course this requires substantial programming skill and time and is likely to be undertaken by only a few individuals with special interests and skills in computer programming. Spread sheets and data base management software are available and are easily adapted for solving numerous management problems.

Another alternative is to contract with others to write the desired applications programs. This is normally too costly for a single farm business, but a group of farmers with similar needs might share in the cost of a contracted program.

Willard was able to obtain software to meet his needs from commercial agencies and his state extension service. Fortunately, all of the software he found was written in the same computer language.

Hardware.   The next step for Willard was to choose a computer. He talked with several computer vendors about the advantages of various computer hardware (the computer and accompanying equipment) components and read numerous publications. A brief summary of what Willard learned follows. Keep in mind, however, that if you are choosing a computer to purchase, a more extensive study than is presented in this book is recommended.

The computer consists of five main parts: (1) The central processing unit (CPU), (2) the main memory (RAM and ROM), (3) the secondary memory, (4) the input device(s), and (5) the output device(s) (see Figure 8.1).

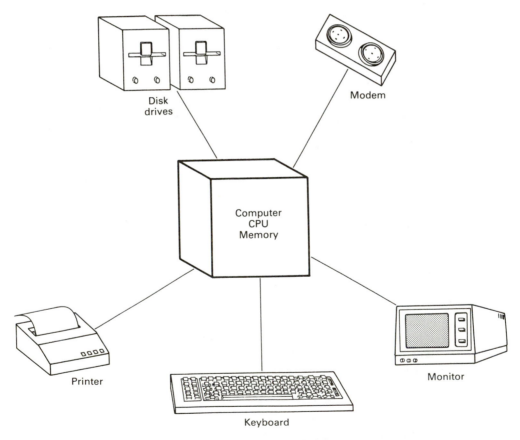

Figure 8.1 Hardware components of a typical farm computer system.

The central processing unit (CPU) is the brain of the computer. It controls the movement of information and the automatic computations called for by the program. It does all of the arithmetic called for by the program or instructions.

In addition to the CPU, two different memories are included in the main part of the computer. The "read-only memory" (ROM) contains frequently used instructions for the computer, which are generally provided by the manufacturer. The user does not have access to the ROM. The size of the ROM and the instructions included in the memory are important because they affect the amount of memory required in the random-access memory (RAM) that is available to the user. The random-access memory includes both instructions and information for processing. Since the size of the RAM is limited and because all information in the RAM is lost when power is turned off, instructions for the RAM are generally stored on secondary memory devices such as disks, cards, or tapes.

All memory is measured in units of kilobytes, or 1,024 characters, represented by the letter K. Thus a computer with a 32K system of RAM would have 32 times 1,024, or 32,768, memory cells available for holding information. The larger the memory, the greater the number of things that can be done with the computer. Typically, home farm computers should contain at least 64K, and even 128K may be needed. In most computer systems, the memory can be expanded with supplemental memory units. It is important to consider the amount of RAM storage. Unfortunately, in comparing computers, the number of RAM K will vary with the construction of the CPU and with the instructions and size of the ROM. Nevertheless, units of K of the RAM is a useful guideline.

Input and output.   A *keyboard* is the typical input device. There should be a separate numeric ten-key pad for convenience. The key device and spacing should feel comfortable to you. A movable keyboard attached to the computer with a cable will provide more flexibility.

A *screen monitor* provides a way for a user to view input, receive output, and interact with the computer. The screen should be a minimum of eighty characters wide and should hold a minimum of twenty-three lines. There is little advantage to a color unit except for video games. Some computers use a standard television set as the monitor. A TV is not as satisfactory because the characters are not as sharp as they are on a specialized monitor and less information can be displayed.

A *printer* is needed in addition to the monitor in order to have output in a form that can be shown to others, such as a prospective lender.

A *disk drive* allows the input of stored information from soft "floppy" or hard disks. Different programs and information can be kept on each disk, thus allowing a substantial amount of supplemental computer storage. Some units are cassette-tape drivers, but they are not as reliable. The floppy disk is most popular.

Finally, a *modem* allows a computer to send and receive information over the telephone. The computer can be coupled to other computers and other sources of information, greatly expanding its capacity.

Purchase now? There are two disadvantages to purchasing a home farm computer now: In the future greater amounts of high-quality software will be available, and computers and software are likely to improve and become less expensive. The advantage of purchasing a computer now is that the manager's skill and understanding about using the computer will improve over time. Since there is much to be learned by all persons involved when a computer is introduced into farm business, the sooner learning begins, the sooner the computer becomes a productive tool for the farm.

Farms likely to find the computer a useful tool are farms that have a person who is "computer-and-management-oriented." Also, farms with numerous financial transactions and complex records are likely to find a computer useful. Examples include a vegetable farm with many crops and enterprise accounts for each; a dairy farm with individual cow records; a seed farm with lists of customers, seed orders, amounts paid, and balances due; and a purebred livestock farm with records of performance of various bloodlines including bloodlines purchased by each customer in the past.

Although a home computer can help with data filing, recall of information, and analysis, it will not answer the questions "What records should I keep?" and "What analyses should I pursue?" Unquestionably, though, the computer is a useful tool in the hands of a knowledgeable, competent manager.

METHODS AND MANAGEMENT

The decision-making methods described in this chapter can make excellent managers even more effective. These methods do not replace good management, of course, but they enable the manager to be more efficient at compiling data and making comprehensive analyses. The manager must still make accurate judgments about such things as possible production alternatives, physical relationships between input and output, and prices. Unless combined with good management judgments about alternatives, production relationships, and prices, the results of models are useless at best and can be misleading.

DISCUSSION QUESTIONS

1. What is a model? What is the purpose of using a model for farm management?
2. List three ways to determine the effect of a decision and action and give the advantages and disadvantages of each.
3. What are the steps in applying a model for decision making?
4. What are the components of a partial budget? Develop a partial budget for a decision on a case farm.
5. What is the advantage of block budgets for evaluating different farm organizations? Use block budgeting to compare two organization alternatives for a farm.

6. What important questions will partial and total farm budgets answer?
7. What question will a cash-flow budget answer?
8. What types of decisions can linear programming help a manager make?
9. Give the advantages of linear programming over budgeting.
10. What kinds of information are needed for linear programming?
11. Why is the use of computers for farm management likely to increase in the future?
12. What are the best alternatives in your area for obtaining computer services for farm management?
13. What is the most important consideration in purchasing a home farm computer?
14. List the components of a home farm computer and give the desirable characteristics of each component.
15. Give some advantages of purchasing a home farm computer now. What types of farms are most likely to benefit from the immediate purchase of a computer?
16. Will applying sophisticated management methods make a manager successful? Why or why not?

RELATED READINGS

BROCKINGTON, N. R. *Computer Modelling in Agriculture.* Oxford: Oxford University Press, 1979.

COOK, THOMAS M., and ROBERT A. RUSSELL. *Introduction to Management Science* (2nd ed.). Englewood Cliffs, N.J.: Prentice-Hall, 1981.

DOBBINS, CRAIG L., and ROBERT C. SUTER. *A Microcomputer for the Farm Family?* West Lafayette, Ind.: Purdue University, Cooperative Extension Service, 1981.

HEADY, EARL O. *Economic Models and Quantitative Methods for Decisions and Planning in Agriculture.* Ames, Ia.: Iowa State University Press, 1971.

"On-Farm Computer Use." Proceedings of a conference at Purdue University Agricultural Extension Service, West Lafayette, Ind., November 1983.

SONKA, STEVEN T. *Computers in Farming.* New York: McGraw-Hill, 1983.

Introduction to Farm
Strategy Decisions

9

An approach for developing a farm strategy or plan is presented briefly in this chapter. This approach is a more structured application of the principles discussed in Chapter 2. It is an outline of the general farm planning procedures presented in subsequent chapters. Chapter 10 deals with planning crops for a farm business and Chapter 11 with livestock planning.

In developing a farm strategy or plan, the manager must determine:

1. The operating environment
2. Goals of the owners and managers
3. Management strengths and weaknesses
4. Physical resources available.

THE OPERATING ENVIRONMENT

The operating environment creates economic advantages in the production and marketing of some products and economic disadvantages in the production and marketing of other products. Managers who have profit as a major goal must either choose crop and livestock enterprises that have an advantage in their geographic area or move to a geographic area where the products in which they have interest have an advantage.

An extreme example of a mismatch between the environment and management preference would be an operator located in the Midwest who desires to raise cotton. Cotton will not mature under Midwest climatic conditions. Another extreme example is an operator who likes dairy and produces milk in a remote area that is so far from a market that transportation costs push total costs above price.

Subtle environmental differences may give an advantage to one enterprise over another in a particular geographic area and make it difficult to produce the disadvantaged product economically in that area. Some areas have a labor surplus, hence lower labor costs, resulting in an advantage in labor-intensive enterprises. Factors such as climate, soil, markets, transportation costs, and resource costs give one area a comparative advantage over another area in the production of certain crops and livestock.

Consideration of the operating environment leads to the first planning step.

Planning Step 1

Determine the crop and livestock enterprises that will have comparative advantages in the future in your geographic area or *identify the geographic area that will have a comparative advantage in the future in the enterprises you plan to pursue.*

There are several good ways to identify enterprises that have comparative advantages:

- Observe what the most prosperous farmers in your area have been raising.
- Study the long-term history of farm profits for different types of farms in your area.
- Budget costs and returns of various enterprises.
- Project future changes in the environment that could affect the relative profitability of different crops and livestock.

> Make a listing in order of greatest advantage of the crops and livestock that can be grown in your area. Remember that the crops that have the greatest advantage may not be those that have the highest production per acre compared to other areas. This is because some areas have few alternatives while others have many. The yield of wheat per acre is higher in the Corn Belt than in the Plains, but wheat is a good alternative in the Plains because it is generally the best possibility. In the Corn Belt, corn usually makes more money than wheat.

PHYSICAL RESOURCES

Planning Step 2

Inventory the physical resources available—land, buildings, machinery, and labor—and determine which crop, livestock, and production systems will pay the highest return to these resources.

Land is discussed in Chapters 10, 14, and 15, buildings in Chapters 11 and 17, and machinery in Chapters 10 and 16.

> Prepare budgets of costs and returns for the crop and livestock enterprises that are most likely to be profitable in your geographic area and on your farm.

MANAGEMENT SKILLS AND GOALS

In preparation for the next step, assess the skills of the persons who will be involved with the management and operation of the farm and inventory the goals of the managers and owners as outlined in Chapter 2. Then proceed with step 3.

Planning Step 3

List enterprises, production systems, size and growth rates, marketing practices, financial practices, and other strategy characteristics that fit the abilities and goals of the managers, owners, and operators.

The abilities and preferences of the persons involved must be considered along with the operating environment and the resources available.

LIMITING RESOURCES

Typically, one or more resources (land, labor, capital, management) are most limiting in keeping a manager from obtaining stated goals. Understanding the limiting resources and their impact on the most desirable farm organization is an important planning step.

Planning Step 4

Identify your most limiting resources, considering both management and physical resources, plan ways to secure more of the limiting resources, and identify enterprises with low requirements of limiting resources.

Louie Caldwill was two years out of high school and wanted to start farming. Louie's father, who worked in town, owned 180 acres that he was willing to rent to Louie. Louie figured he needed another 200 acres and a set of machinery to have an operation large enough to provide his desired level of income. He identified his most limiting resources as land, capital, and management experience. Louie formed a cooperative arrangement with an older neighbor, John Brown, who was known to be one of the top farmers in the area. Having no sons or daughters, John's most limiting resource was labor. Louie traded his labor for machinery use and management counsel from John. By eliminating fixed machinery costs, Louie was able to make a satisfactory income on the 180 acres that he rented from his father. As his skill improved he was able to rent land from others in the community.

Because Louie had a sizable land base and a good profit record, lending institutions were more willing to loan him money. After he had farmed for ten years, capital and land were no longer his most limiting factors; these became labor and the ability to supervise labor. Louie began using larger machinery and automated livestock systems to cut labor requirements, and he improved his labor management skills.

Managers must continually adjust their businesses to changes in the most limiting factors of production and marketing.

THE FARM STRATEGY

Planning Step 5

Identify alternative enterprises, production systems, marketing systems, and size and growth rates that:

1. *Have a high comparative advantage in your geographic area.*
2. *Have a high comparative advantage with your physical resources.*
3. *Fit management skills.*
4. *Fit owner, manager, and operator goals.*
5. *Use small amounts of the most limiting resources.*

COMPREHENSIVE ANALYSIS

Planning Step 6

Collect accurate resource, production, and price information.
Use the appropriate methods of projecting income and cash flow for various alternatives (as discussed in Chapter 8).

DECISION AND ACTION

Planning Step 7

Make decisions on the basis of steps 1 through 6 and put your plan into action.

ADJUSTING STRATEGY

Planning Step 8

Adjust your strategy as changes occur in the environment, management skills, goals, and resources.
One of the most important jobs of a manager is to monitor changes in the environment and to determine the implications of these changes for the farm strategy. The manager must be able to sort short-run changes from long-run changes. For example, because of the cattle cycle, one can observe several-year periods during which cattle are profitable and alternating periods when they are unprofitable. The percep-

tive manager expects this variation in profit over time. The inexperienced manager may quit production after cattle have been unprofitable for a number of years and start only after they have been profitable for a while. Inexperienced managers who get in and out of business are often in or out at the wrong times simply because they do not understand the long-term price movements of cattle.

Managers must distinguish short-run changes, such as the cattle cycle, from long-run trends in the profitability of enterprises, such as the shift away from draft horses when the tractor was introduced.

In developing a strategy or plan for the farm, you must consider all of the factors presented in this chapter. If few of the physical resources of the farm are fixed (assets are largely in the form of cash rather than land or buildings), then management is the resource around which the farm should be planned. If, on the other hand, there are large amounts of fixed land and buildings, management is still a critical factor, but physical resources become a more important consideration because the payoff to variable resources is great in situations where they are added to a large amount of fixed resources.

Because land is usually the most important physical resource, cropping system decisions will be discussed first (Chapter 10), followed by livestock decisions and crop-livestock decisions (Chapter 11). Subsequent chapters deal with budgeting returns to the total farm (Chapter 12), size and growth (Chapter 13), investments and resource acquisition (Chapters 14, 15, 16, and 17), and marketing strategy (Chapter 18).

DISCUSSION QUESTIONS

1. List the four key factors that determine the "best" farm strategy or plan.

2. Which of the factors listed for question 1 is most important? Why?

3. As the factors change, what effect does this have on the "best" farm plan or strategy?

4. What are the eight steps to developing a farm strategy or plan?

RELATED READINGS

BARNARD, C. S., and J. S. NIR. *Farm Planning and Control.* London: Cambridge University Press, 1973.

CASTLE, EMERY N., MANNING H. BECKER, AND FREDRICK J. SMITH. *Farm Business Management: The Decision-Making Process* (2nd ed.), chap. 10. New York: Macmillan, 1962.

"Farm Planning and Financial Management," ID-68. Purdue University, Cooperative Extension Service, West Lafayette, Ind., 1980.

FORSTER, D. LYNN, and BERNARD L. ERVEN. *Foundations for Managing the Farm Business,* chap. 8. Columbus, O.: Grid Publishing, 1981.

HARSH, STEPHEN B., LARRY J. CONNOR and GERALD D. SCHWAB. *Managing the Farm Business,* chaps. 9–10. Englewood Cliffs, N.J.: Prentice-Hall, 1981.

MISSOURI FARM MANAGEMENT STAFF. *Missouri Farm Planning Handbook,* Manual 75. Columbia, MO.: University of Missouri—Columbia, 1981.

THOMAS, KENNETH, R. N. WEIGLE, and RICHARD HAWKINS. *Where Do I Want to Be?* North Central Regional Extension Publication 34–3. Madison, Wis.: University of Wisconsin Extension, 1973.

Cropping Decisions

10

The profitability of the cropping enterprise is determined by the types of crops produced, the system or methods of production, the level of technical efficiency (output from given input), volume produced, prices paid for resources, and prices received for crops sold.

The profitability of different crops, production systems, technical practices, and marketing methods varies greatly with geographic location and resources of particular farms. Unfortunately, it is not possible to present examples and illustrations that are appropriate for each person who reads this book. To make the illustrations relevant for you, identify one or more case farms with which you are familiar and follow the same procedures with those farms as are used with the examples presented. Perhaps you can work with a group in which each person selects a different type of farm to plan. Each of you can exchange information and discuss results after planning is completed.

The examples presented in this chapter should be helpful in making applications to your case farm situation.

CHOICE OF CROPS

Climate, general soil type, and markets affect the profitability of crops that can be grown in a particular geographic area. Similarly, the most profitable crop combination for a particular farm is affected by the specific soil types and slopes, field layout, drainage, and water supply, as well as by management skill, labor supply, capital availability, and market access.

Much of the land in the United States is suited only to grazing (Table 10.1). The keys to profit are efficiency of production and marketing or use of production. Since pasture can be marketed only through livestock, farm profit is usually as closely related to livestock management ability as to crop management ability on farms that are mostly suited to grazing.

On cropland that is suitable for growing more than one alternative crop, the following procedure should be used to develop a cropping plan. An example will be given to illustrate each of the four steps in the procedure.

TABLE 10.1   Land Use in the United States

Land Use	Million of Acres	Percent
Grazing land	700	36.7
Commercial forestry land	484	25.4
Agricultural land		
Crops	409	21.5
Pastured cropland	69	3.6
Nonproducing (farmsteads, etc.)	45	2.4
Public recreation areas	46	2.4
Land for cities of 25,000 or more	17	0.9
Land for transportation	25	1.3
Reservoirs, water management, wildlife	24	1.3
Mineral production, deserts, swamps, miscellaneous	85	4.5
Total	1,904	100.0

Source: Farm Planning and Financial Management, Table C–1, p. 17 (West Lafayette, Ind.: Purdue University, Cooperative Extension Service, 1980).

Step 1: Inventory Land Resources

Collect information about:

1. Land overview
   - Total acres
   - Tillable acres
   - Cropland
   - Pastureland
   - Woods
   - Roads, farmstead, irrigation ditches, waste, other
2. Soil characteristics
   - Soil type, location, acres
   - Expected crop yield and yield variability for each soil type with different levels of management
   - Slope
   - Degree of erosion
   - Moisture-holding capacity
   - Internal drainage
   - Surface drainage
   - Native vegetation
   - Soil nutrient levels (soil test)

3. Background
   - Cropping history
   - Historic crop yields
   - Stones, weeds, problems
4. Drainage
   - Drainage outlets
   - Tile size
   - Wet areas, areas of crop loss in wet years
5. Farm layout
   - Size and shape of fields
   - Location of improvements, fences, erosion-control devices, irrigation
   - Streams, natural barriers
6. Irrigation
   - Water availability
   - Ditches, wells, and equipment
   - Water quality.

Bill and Mary Christian, who own an accounting and tax advisory service in Boston, Massachusetts, inherited a 730-acre farm in Fountain County, Indiana. Because the Christians live over 1,000 miles from the farm and because they have not kept up on agricultural management practices, they have hired Brad Aid as their farm manager. Brad manages several farms in the area of the Christian farm. For 5% of the owners' gross income, Brad has agreed to develop a good plan for the farm and to find an operator who can implement the plan. He will check to see that the plan is carried out correctly and that the soil, tile, buildings, and other improvements are maintained. Also, Brad will keep records for the farm and send quarterly reports to the Christians indicating receipts, expenses, and the progress of crops, livestock, and improvement projects on the farm.

Brad's first step was to secure information for planning the cropping program. This information includes:

- Soil map
- Field layout
- Drainage
- Soil test.

Brad obtained a soil map from the local Soil Conservation Service (Figure 10.1). The Soil Conservation Service is a U.S. Department of Agriculture organization that provides soil, drainage, erosion-control, and other information to farmer cooperators without charge. The soil map shows the type, slope, and erosion of farm soils, information essential for planning the intensity of the cropping program and for projecting yields and costs. Once managers know the soil type, they can determine moisture-holding capacity, natural drainage, and native fertility. The soil map,

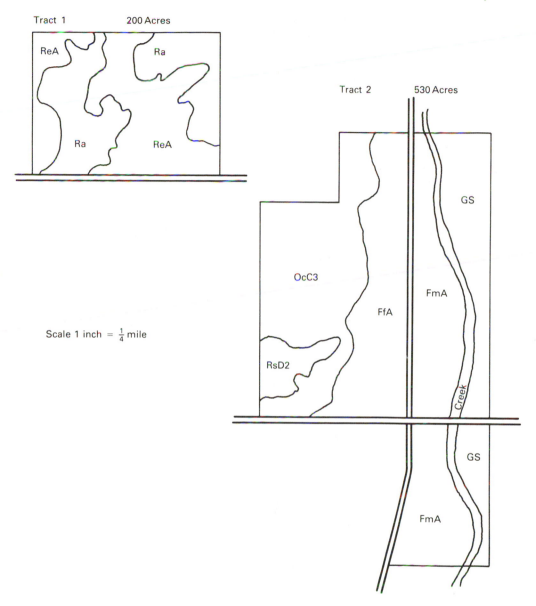

Figure 10.1 Soil maps of the Christian farm, Fountain County, Indiana.

along with information about drainage outlets, farm tile, soil tests, and past yields, enables managers to project yields and resource requirements.

The soil map (Figure 10.1, Table 10.2) shows that tract 1 is highly productive land with little susceptibility to erosion and with good moisture-holding capacity. With excellent management, yields of 130 to 140 bushels of corn, 45 to 50 bushels of

TABLE 10.2 Characteristics of Soils on the Christian Farm

Key	Soil Type	Texture	Soil Color	Natural Drainage	Available Water to 40 In.	Wind Erosion Potential	Water Erosion Potential	Expected Yield with Outstanding Management			
								Corn (bu.)	Soybeans (bu.)	Wheat (bu.)	Hay (tons)
FmA	Fox loam 0%–2% slope	Stratified sand and gravel	Brownish	Good	5–6 in.	Moderate	Slight	90	32	41	2.9
FfA	Fox fine sandy loam 0%–2% slope	Stratified sand and gravel	Brownish	Good	5–6 in.	Moderate	Slight	90	32	41	2.9
GS	Genesee silt loam 0%–2% slope	Silt loam	Brownish	Good	to 8 in.	Slight	None	120	42	48	3.9
OcC3	Ockley silt loam 6%–12% slope	Stratified sand and gravel	Brownish	Good	6–7 in.	Slight	Severe	95	33	43	3.0
Ra	Ragsdale silty clay loam	Silty clay loam	Dark	Poor	to 8 in.	Slight	None	140	50	60	5.0
ReA	Reesville silt loam 0%–2% slope	Silt loam	Grayish	Rather poor	to 8 in.	Slight	None	130	45	50	4.4
RsD2	Russell silt loam 12%–18% slope	Silt loam	Brownish	Good	6–7 in.	Slight	Severe	90	32	41	2.9

soybeans, 50 to 60 bushels of wheat, and 4.5 to 5 tons of hay per acre can be expected. The field map shows that there are no natural obstructions, so large machinery can easily be operated across the 200 acres in tract 1 (Figure 10.2). The field map, prepared from an aerial photo obtained from the Agricultural Stabilization and Conservation County Office, was updated by Brad as to the location of fences and other added details.

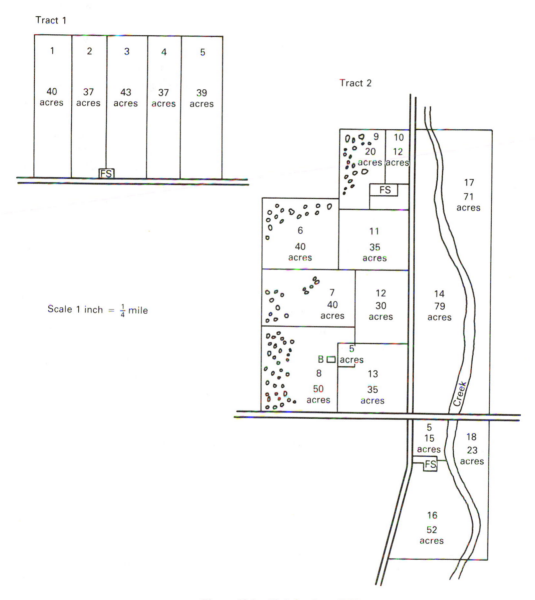

Figure 10.2   Christian farm field maps.

One remaining consideration is drainage. The soil is silty clay loam with poor internal drainage and needs substantial tile. The big question is "Is there a good drainage outlet?" If a good outlet exists, a farm can be drained by adding tile. But if a good drainage outlet is not available, drainage improvement can be costly or even impossible. The county engineer's office showed an excellent drainage outlet. According to Soil Conservation Service District Manager Martin Williams, the drainage outlet for the Christian farm is a 12-inch tile that has adequate capacity to service tract 1. Also, the Christians reported that their family had tiled various wet areas over the years and did not encounter difficulties in finding a good outlet. Since there is no map of existing tile, one of Brad's jobs will be to locate as much of the existing tile as possible and then determine if additional tile is needed. Because the Soil Conservation Office helped the Christian family plan some of their drainage projects in the past, they have some sketches of proposed tile locations. An analysis of the payoff to drainage is presented in Chapter 14.

The second tract of the Christian farm is another story. The soils are quite variable. There is some productive bottom land along the creek, Genesee soil (Figure 10.1, Table 10.2), but it floods one out of every four years on the average. The second bottom of Fox soil is droughty. The Fox soil has 15 to 24 inches of loam topsoil underlaid with gravel. It is excellent wheat and hay ground, but corn yields vary from 40 to 140 bushels and soybean yields from 10 to 40 bushels per acre, depending on the amount of rainfall. West of the Fox is some sloping and eroded Ockley soil, which is a transition to the upland Reesville and Ragsdale productive soils. The Ockley is sloping and eroded and cannot support row crops.

Drainage is not a problem. Most of tract 2 is underlaid with gravel and has little need for tile. There is good surface drainage, as most of tract 2 slopes toward the creek. Reduced and variable yields due to the low moisure-holding capacity of Fox and Ockley is a problem. Brad Aid will need to budget the payoff to irrigation on these soils (see Chapter 14).

There are some woods along the creek and on the west side of the farm. The forest has limited commercial value. Brad will need to consider whether it will be profitable to clear the woods (see Chapter 14). Two gullies on the Ockley soil are too deep to cross with machinery.

Brad Aid took complete soil tests and summarized the results on a coded map (Figures 10.3 through 10.5). These tests will help Brad develop the optimum fertilizer plan for the farm. The plan will be presented later in this chapter.

Step 2: Group Soils

Land should be divided into sections that have similar slopes and on which yields of crops and costs of crop production are similar. Grouping of soils enables the manager to determine the most profitable crop combination for each soil group. The manager can then develop a farm plan with highest profit potential and acceptable erosion levels for each soil group. A crop rotation developed for each soil group is

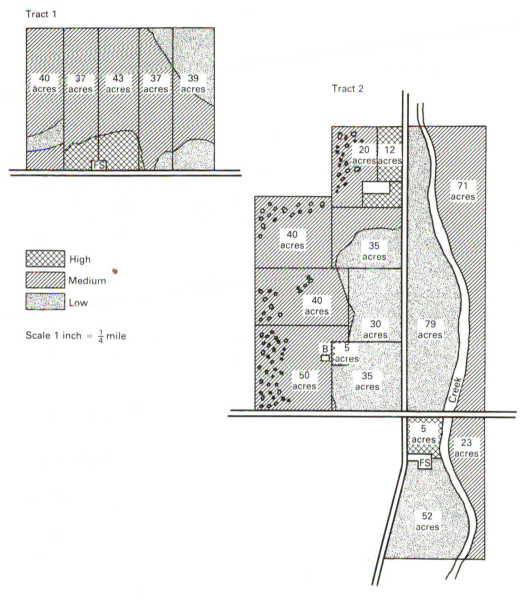

Figure 10.3 Christian farm soil test maps for potash.

likely to result in higher total farm profit and less soil erosion than would be possible if the same cropping system were used on the entire farm.

Also, cost, yield, and profit projections are likely to be more accurate when they are forecast for each group of similar soils. On some farms, of course, all soils are similar and soil grouping is unnecessary. There is the practical consideration of

Tract 1

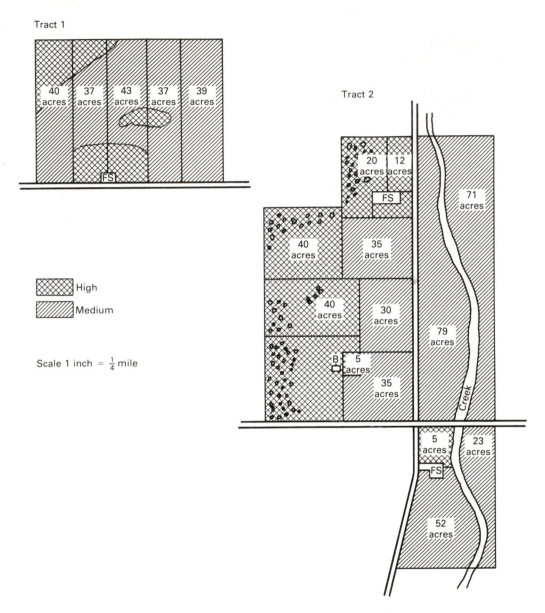

Figure 10.4 Christian farm soil test maps for phosphate.

keeping the number of soil groups low so that the farm plan does not become overly complicated and fields do not become too small.

Brad Aid included all of tract 1 of the Christian farm in the same soil group (Figure 10.10). Although the crop yields are significantly different on Reesville and Ragsdale soils (Table 10.1), Brad judged that the relative profitability of different

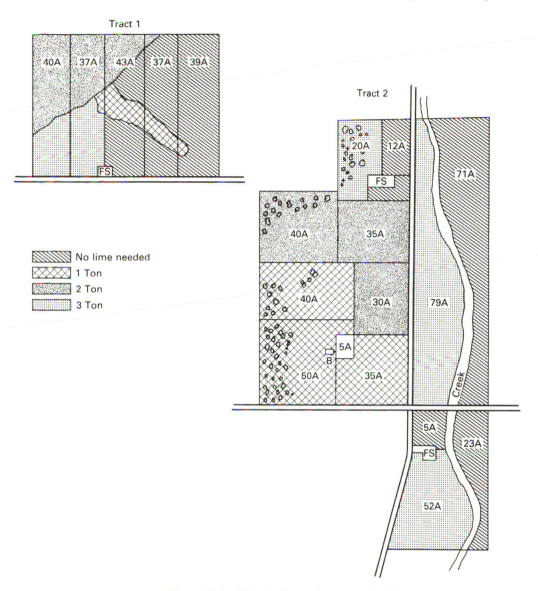

Figure 10.5 Christian farm soil test maps for lime.

crops would be similar and that erosion would not be a problem on either of the two soil types. Also, because of the location of the different soils, it would be difficult to plan them separately. Brad judged that there is 50% Reesville soil and 50% Ragsdale soil, so he developed cost and yield budgets based on an average of the two soils.

Tract 2 is a quite different situation. The Genesee creek-bottom soil that Brad included in soil group 2 is productive, but the costs and returns budgets need to consider the risk of flooding. Crops are lost one year out of four. The Fox soils in group 3

Figure 10.6   Christian Farm Soil Group 1

Figure 10.7   Christian Farm Soil Group 2

Figure 10.8   Christian Farm Soil Group 3

Figure 10.9   Christian Farm Soil Group 4

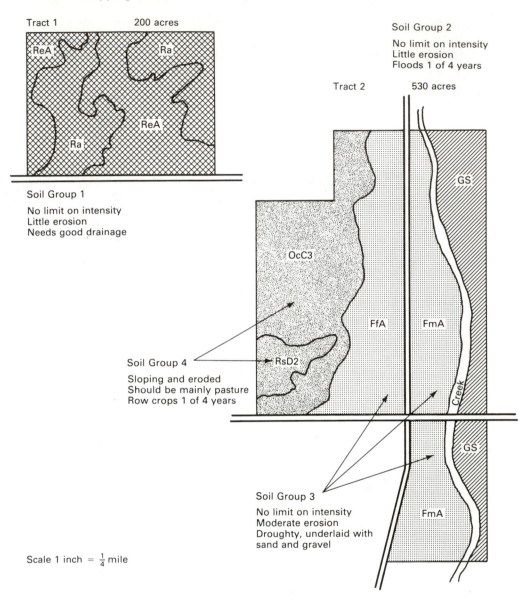

Figure 10.10 Soil grouping for budgeting returns and planning the cropping system.

have the potential for relatively higher yields of wheat and alfalfa compared to corn and beans than do soils in groups 1 and 2. Group 3 soils are more droughty and result in greater yield variability. Irrigation might be profitable on the Fox soils. Group 4 soils are sloping and susceptible to erosion. If these soils are planted to row crops more than one of four years, there will be substantial erosion.

Step 3: Estimate Costs and Returns

After the soils are divided into similar groups, costs, returns, and profit figures are calculated for different crops and crop rotations for each soil group.

Information about the profitability of each crop and crop rotation, along with an appraisal of the likely effect on soil erosion and soil structure, is the basis for choosing a cropping plan for the farm. There are five basic components for estimating profitability: (1) Crops and crop rotations that may be profitable and do not cause excessive soil erosion and structure problems should be identified. (2) Yields and (3) prices must be estimated for various crops and crop rotations to enable the manager to project gross returns. (4) Inputs required and (5) cost of input information are needed to allow the manager to calculate cost per acre. Following is an explanation and an illustration of estimating costs and returns.

Crops to be considered.   Prepare budgets for alternative crops and crop rotations that are profitable, control erosion, and meet the goals of the owners, managers, and operators. Budgeted crops should be suited to the soil and other resources of the farm, to markets available, and to the climatic conditions. The crops also should have a comparative advantage relative to other geographic areas.

Brad Aid judged that corn, soybeans, wheat, oats, and alfalfa-grass-hay should be considered for the Christian farm. Specialty crops such as strawberries, melons, and green beans also can be profitable in the farm's geographic area. But Brad did not consider these crops because he had no special markets at which to sell them nor an operator with experience in growing specialty crops. Specialty crops are profitable only for a limited number of managers who have both the skills to produce them and the capability to locate good markets for them.

Brad therefore decided to develop budgets only for the crops commonly produced by commercial farmers in the area: corn, soybeans, wheat, oats, and alfalfa.

Estimating returns.   Returns are determined by yields and prices received. Yields depend on:

1. The soil characteristics of the particular farm (step 1)
2. Climatic conditions of the area: rainfall, temperature, and length of day
3. The weather conditions of the particular year and season
4. The interaction among crops. Continuous cropping sometimes results in a buildup of disease and a decline in yield. A rotation may result in higher yields for all crops (Table 10.3).
5. The management and operation of the farm and technical practices used.

It is more difficult to forecast yields than to forecast resource inputs because yields are affected by unpredictable factors such as weather, disease, and insects.

To estimate yields, collect information about the soil, past crop history of the

TABLE 10.3 Corn and Soybean Yields in a Crop-Herbicide Rotation Experiment, 1966–1975, Urbana, Illinois

	Yield (bu./acre)
Continuous corn	124.3
Corn-corn-soybeans (1st year corn)	133.2
Corn-corn-soybeans (2nd year corn)	131.3
Soybeans (in corn-corn-soybeans rotation)	52.3
Corn-soybeans-wheat	135.9
Soybeans (in corn-soybeans-wheat rotation)	54.0
Continuous soybeans	47.4

Source: Farm Planning and Financial Management, Table C-6A, p. 21 (West Lafayette, Ind.: Purdue University, Cooperative Extension Service, 1980).

farm, and crop yields on similar soils of other farms in the area. The judgment of professional agronomists and of farm managers with the state extension service or commercial organizations can be helpful for estimating crop yields.

Prices received.   Product prices are difficult to forecast for the following reasons:

1. Local, national, and world supplies are dependent on the weather and have a major impact on prices.
2. U.S. farm policy and decisions of other governments affect demand. Actions by government and institutions are difficult to predict.
3. Small changes in supply have a great effect on prices.

To estimate crop prices, one must know long-term price trends and relationships as well as the current price outlook. It is desirable to become acquainted with the farm marketing and farm management extension and research specialists in the state. Also, consider subscribing to a commercial commodity price-outlook service.

In developing a cropping program for the farm, a manager should be most concerned with long-run price relationships and trends, which are the basis for estimating what prices are likely to average over a period of time. The long-term cropping program then should be modified or adjusted to capitalize on the short-term price situation. Brad's yield and price forecasts appear in section A of Tables 10.4 through 10.9.

Estimating costs.   Costs are determined by the amounts of resources used (fertilizer, seed, herbicide, insecticide, machinery, labor, storage, land, management) and the price per unit of resources. One good way to estimate quantities of

TABLE 10.4   Estimated Costs and Returns Per Acre for Various Crops, Christian Farm Soil Group 1: Ragsdale and Reesville

	Rotation Corn	Continuous Corn	First Year Soybeans	Second Year Soybeans
A. Returns per acre				
1. Yield per acre	140	130	45	42
2. Price per bushel/ton	$ 3.00	$ 3.00	$ 7.00	$ 7.00
3. Gross returns	$420.00	$390.00	$315.00	$294.00
B. Costs per acre				
4. Fertilizer and lime	$ 65.00	$ 69.00	$ 28.00	$ 28.00
5. Seed	17.00	17.00	12.00	12.00
6. Chemicals	13.00	18.00	15.00	15.00
7. Machine operation[1]	44.00	42.50	26.00	26.00
8. Miscellaneous and interest on operating capital and stored grain	31.80	30.60	23.60	22.80
9. Total direct costs[2]	$170.80	$177.10	$104.60	$103.80
10. Labor	$ 30.00	$ 30.00	$ 26.25	$ 26.25
11. Management	10.00	10.00	10.00	10.00
12. Machine ownership costs[3]	50.00	50.00	44.00	44.00
13. Storage ownership costs[4]	32.20	29.90	10.40	9.70
14. Land tax and maintenance[5]	15.00	15.00	15.00	15.00
15. Other land charge[5]	100.00	100.00	100.00	100.00
16. Total costs	$408.00	$412.00	$310.25	$308.75
C. Profitability[6]				
17. Net returns (3 minus 16)	$ 12.00	− $ 22.00	$ 4.75	− $ 14.75
18. Return to land investment (17 plus 15)	$112.00	$ 78.00	$104.75	$ 85.25

[1]Includes fuel and repairs for machinery operation and crop drying.

[2]For an explanation of direct costs and their use in simplifying budgeting see Total Farm Budgets in Chapter 8.

[3]Includes depreciation, interest, taxes and insurance on machinery.

[4]Includes cost of storage and handling facilities for corn and soybeans. Wheat, oats and hay are sold at or near harvest time.

[5]The total of lines 14 and 15 is an approximation of land rental rates.

[6]Returns are from operating and do not include increases or decreases in capital asset value due to inflation or deflation.

resources needed is on the basis of quantities previously used as shown in past farm records. Also, the extension service usually publishes farm planning data that provide estimates of resource requirements and resource prices for various crops in different geographic areas. This planning information is sometimes developed for specific soil types. Several commercial agencies also publish resource requirement and cost information.

The best price sources are price bids from farm supply businesses for specified resource quantities at a specified time and place of delivery. Since the manager can control the amounts of resources used and information about prices can be specifically determined, it is possible to forecast production costs more accurately than returns.

Budgeting net returns per acre.[1]   Brad Aid secured as much information as possible about past yields and studied the yield projections for various soil types (Table 10.1). He considered the farm soil tests (Figures 10.3 through 10.5) and took into account yields he had been able to obtain with his management system on farms with similar soils. On the basis of all of these considerations, as well as yield information published in extension, research, and farm records summaries, Brad estimated the average yields shown in Tables 10.4 through 10.9.

To project crop prices, Brad studied world, national, and local supply and demand conditions for each crop. He considered present and future government programs and talked with extension and commercial price analysts to secure their judgments about prices. On the basis of all of his study, Brad projected the price averages shown in Tables 10.4 through 10.9. The average prices and yields allowed Brad to calculate an average gross return for each crop.

In projecting costs, Brad planned the amount of resources that would be used on various crops. To make resource-use plans, Brad relied on his experience on similar farms, extension planning information, published record summaries for similar farms, and the economic principles discussed in Chapter 3. Brad then estimated the future prices of resources based on the lowest prices available from suppliers in the area. He used the quantity and price estimates to determine cost per acre for various crops (Tables 10.4 through 10.9).

The return and cost estimates are the basis for choosing the most profitable cropping program and estimating income from the cropping program.

Measuring profitability.   The manager's objective should be to maximize net returns to fixed and limiting resources (Chapters 3 and 8). If there are no fixed resources, net returns per acre (returns after all costs) should be used as a measure of profit (line 17, Tables 10.4 through 10.9). If land is fixed, the operating returns to land investment should be used as a profit measure (line 18). If the operator's labor and management are fixed, returns to labor and management should be used as a measure of crop profitability. And if land, labor, and management are fixed, returns

[1] Net returns is for operating and does not include increases or decreases in the value of capital assets due to inflation or deflation (see Chapter 5).

TABLE 10.5 Estimated Costs and Returns Per Acre for Various Crops, Christian Farm Soil Group 1: Ragsdale and Reesville

		Wheat	Oats	Alfalfa-Grass-Hay
A.	Returns per acre			
	1. Yield per acre	60	90	5
	2. Price per bushel/ton	$ 3.75	$ 1.80	$ 70.00
	3. Gross returns	$225.00	$162.00	$350.00
B.	Costs per acre			
	4. Fertilizer and lime	$ 45.00	$ 35.00	$ 50.00
	5. Seed	13.50	10.00	15.00
	6. Chemicals	0	0	6.00
	7. Machine operation[1]	20.00	20.00	35.00
	8. Miscellaneous and interest on operating capital and stored grain	10.00	8.00	10.00
	9. Total direct costs[2]	$ 88.50	$ 73.00	$116.00
	10. Labor	$ 22.50	$ 22.50	$ 60.00
	11. Management	8.00	8.00	10.00
	12. Machine ownership costs[3]	40.00	40.00	65.00
	13. Storage ownership costs[4]	5.00	5.00	15.00
	14. Land tax and maintenance[5]	15.00	15.00	15.00
	15. Other land charge[5]	100.00	100.00	100.00
	16. Total costs	$279.00	$263.50	$381.00
C.	Profitability[6]			
	17. Net returns (3 minus 16)	−$ 54.00	−$101.50	−$ 31.00
	18. Return to land investment (17 plus 15)	$ 46.00	−$ 1.50	$ 69.00

[1]Includes fuel and repairs for machinery operation and crop drying.

[2]For an explanation of direct costs and their use in simplifying budgeting see Total Farm Budgets in Chapter 8.

[3]Includes depreciation, interest, taxes and insurance on machinery.

[4]Includes cost of storage and handling facilities for corn and soybeans. Wheat, oats and hay are sold at or near harvest time.

[5]The total of lines 14 and 15 is an approximation of land rental rates.

[6]Returns are from operating and do not include increases or decreases in capital asset value due to inflation or deflation.

TABLE 10.6   Estimated Costs and Returns Per Acre for Various Crops, Christian Farm Soil Group 2: Genesee

	Continuous Corn
A. Returns per acre	
1. Yield per acre	100
2. Price per bushel/ton	$ 3.00
3. Gross returns	$300.00
B. Costs per acre	
4. Fertilizer and lime	$ 43.00
5. Seed	12.00
6. Chemicals	14.00
7. Machine operation[1]	39.00
8. Miscellaneous and interest on operating capital and stored grain	24.00
9. Total direct costs[2]	$132.00
10. Labor	$ 30.00
11. Management	10.00
12. Machine ownership costs[3]	45.00
13. Storage ownership costs[4]	23.00
14. Land tax and maintenance[5]	8.00
15. Other land charge[5]	50.00
16. Total costs	$298.00
C. Profitability[6]	
17. Net returns, (3 minus 16)	$ 2.00
18. Return to land investment (17 plus 15)	$ 52.00

[1]Includes fuel and repairs for machinery operation and crop drying.

[2]For an explanation of direct costs and their use in simplifying budgeting see Total Farm Budgets in Chapter 8.

[3]Includes depreciation, interest, taxes and insurance on machinery.

[4]Includes cost of storage and handling facilities for corn and soybeans. Wheat, oats and hay are sold at or near harvest time.

[5]The total of lines 14 and 15 is an approximation of land rental rates.

[6]Returns are from operating and do not include increases or decreases in capital asset value due to inflation or deflation.

to all of these should be used. When the return to a resource is computed, the cost of that resource is excluded.

    Because land is a fixed resource to the Christians while other resources are variable, Brad Aid used operating returns to land investment as a measure of profitability for the Christian farm. If the Christians ever consider selling the farm and investing the money in other alternatives, the returns that the money would make in the other

TABLE 10.7 Estimated Costs and Returns Per Acre for Various Crops, Christian Farm
Soil Group 3: Fox Loam and Sandy Loam

		Rotation Corn	Continuous Corn	First Year Soybeans	Second Year Soybeans
A.	Return per acre				
	1. Yield per acre	90	84	34	31
	2. Price per bushel/ton	$ 3.00	$ 3.00	$ 7.00	$ 7.00
	3. Gross returns	$270.00	$252.00	$238.00	$217.00
B.	Costs per acre				
	4. Fertilizer and lime	$ 40.00	$ 43.00	$ 19.00	$ 19.00
	5. Seed	12.00	12.00	10.00	10.00
	6. Chemicals	8.00	13.00	8.00	8.00
	7. Machine operation[1]	35.00	35.00	24.00	24.00
	8. Miscellaneous and interest on operating captial and stored grain	21.80	21.10	17.50	16.70
	9. Total direct costs[2]	$116.80	$124.10	$ 78.50	$ 77.70
	10. Labor	$ 30.00	$ 30.00	$ 26.25	$ 26.25
	11. Management	10.00	10.00	10.00	10.00
	12. Machine ownership costs[3]	40.00	40.00	35.00	35.00
	13. Storage ownership costs[4]	20.70	19.30	8.00	7.30
	14. Land tax and maintenance[5]	6.00	6.00	6.00	6.00
	15. Other land charge[5]	44.00	44.00	44.00	44.00
	16. Total costs	$267.50	$273.40	$207.75	$206.25
C.	Profitability[6]				
	17. Net returns (3 minus 16)	$ 2.50	−$ 21.40	$ 30.25	$ 10.75
	22. Return to land investment (17 plus 15)	$ 46.50	$ 22.60	$ 74.25	$ 54.75

[1]Includes fuel and repairs for machinery operation and crop drying.

[2]For an explanation of direct costs and their use in simplifying budgeting see Total Farm Budgets in Chapter 8.

[3]Includes depreciation, interest, taxes and insurance on machinery.

[4]Includes cost of storage and handling facilities for corn and soybeans. Wheat, oats and hay are sold at or near harvest time.

[5]The total of lines 14 and 15 is an approximation of land rental rates.

[6]Returns are from operating and do not include increases or decreases in capital asset value due to inflation or deflation.

TABLE 10.8 Estimated Costs and Returns Per Acre for Various Crops, Christian Farm Soil Group 3: Fox Loam and Sandy Loam

		Wheat	Oats	Alfalfa-Grass-Hay
A.	Returns per acre			
	1. Yield per acre	53	70	3.5
	2. Price per bushel/ton	$ 3.75	$ 1.80	$ 70.00
	3. Gross returns	$198.75	$126.00	$245.00
B.	Costs per acre			
	4. Fertilizer and lime	$ 40.00	$ 28.00	$ 40.00
	5. Seed	13.00	10.00	13.00
	6. Chemicals	0	0	6.00
	7. Machine operation[1]	20.00	17.00	30.00
	8. Miscellaneous and interest on operating capital and stored grain	10.00	8.00	9.00
	9. Total direct costs[2]	$ 83.00	$ 63.00	$ 98.00
	10. Labor	$ 22.50	$ 22.50	$ 40.00
	11. Management	8.00	8.00	10.00
	12. Machine ownership costs[2]	40.00	40.00	50.00
	13. Storage ownership costs[4]	5.00	5.00	10.00
	14. Land tax and maintenance[5]	6.00	6.00	6.00
	18. Other land charge[5]	44.00	44.00	44.00
	16. Total costs	$208.50	$188.50	$258.00
C.	Profitability[6]			
	17. Net returns (3 minus 16)	−$ 9.75	−$ 62.50	−$ 13.00
	22. Return to land investment (17 plus 15)	$ 34.25	−$ 18.50	$ 31.00

[1]Includes fuel and repairs for machinery operation and crop drying.

[2]For an explanation of direct costs and their use in simplifying budgeting see Total Farm Budgets in Chapter 8.

[3]Includes depreciation, interest, taxes and insurance on machinery.

[4]Includes cost of storage and handling facilities for corn and soybeans. Wheat, oats and hay are sold at or near harvest time.

[5]The total of lines 14 and 15 is an approximation of land rental rates.

[6]Returns are from operating and do not include increases or decreases in capital asset value due to inflation or deflation.

TABLE 10.9   Estimated Costs and Returns Per Acre for Permanent Pasture, Christian Farm
Soil Group 4: Ockley and Russell Soils, Sloping 6%–18%

		Permanent Alfalfa-Grass-Hay
A.	Returns per acre	
	1. Yield per acre	3
	2. Price per ton	$ 70.00
	3. Gross returns	$210.00
B.	Costs per acre	
	4. Fertilizer and lime	$ 30.00
	5. Seed	12.00
	6. Chemicals	5.00
	7. Machine operation[1]	20.00
	8. Miscellaneous and interest on operating capital and stored grain	8.00
	9. Total direct costs[2]	$ 75.00
	10. Labor	$ 40.00
	11. Management	10.00
	12. Machine ownership costs[3]	38.00
	13. Storage ownership costs[4]	8.00
	14. Land tax and maintenance[5]	6.00
	15. Other land charge[5]	30.00
	16. Total costs	$207.00
C.	Profitability[6]	
	20. Net returns (3 minus 16)	$ 3.00
	18. Return to land investment (17 plus 15)	$ 33.00

[1]Includes fuel and repairs for machinery operation and crop drying.

[2]For an explanation of direct costs and their use in simplifying budgeting see Total Farm Budgets in Chapter 8.

[3]Includes depreciation, interest, taxes and insurance on machinery.

[4]Includes cost of storage and handling facilities for corn and soybeans. Wheat, oats and hay are sold at or near harvest time.

[5]The total of lines 14 and 15 is an approximation of land rental rates.

[6]Returns are from operating and do not include increases or decreases in capital asset value due to inflation or deflation.

alternatives should be included as a cost of land. Expected change in land values would also need to be considered (see Chapter 14).

Step 4: Select the Cropping Program

Select a cropping program that:

1. Meets income and other goals of the owner, manager, and operator.
2. Includes a high proportion of high-profit crops.
3. Takes advantage of complementarity among crops.
4. Keeps soil erosion low and maintains soil structure.
5. Stretches the limiting resources.
6. Tends to have the most uniform requirements of labor and machinery throughout the year and from year to year.
7. Produces crops for which adequate markets are available.

Goals of the owner, manager, and operator.   Brad discussed goals with the Christians and found that their highest-priority goal was to keep the farm in good condition. They wanted to keep soil fertility high, maintain and improve drainage, keep erosion at a low level, and keep the property neat by clipping weeds and painting buildings when needed. The Christians also wanted the farm to make money and thought it should have an operating return of at least 4% on the current market value of their investment. Another goal of the Christians was that any farm improvements must pay their own way from a cash-flow standpoint and not be subsidized from the Christians' nonfarm income. Finally, the Christians would appreciate tax advantages that might result from the operation of the farm.

Keeping in mind the Christians' goals, the farm itself, and the surrounding area, Brad decided to hire an operator, purchase machinery, and direct-operate the farm. Direct operation would serve a threefold purpose. First, it would give Brad full control over the farm, which would assure him that he could meet the Christians' requirements for maintaining the soil and keeping the farm neat. Second, direct operation rather than cash or share rental would provide the Christians' tax advantages of investment credit, rapid depreciation of machinery, and delay of taxes on inventory buildup. Finally, Brad figured that net returns would be somewhat higher with direct operation.

Profitability.   Selected crop rotations that meet the seven criteria listed under step 4 should be budgeted for each soil group. A cropping program that meets all seven criteria should then be selected for the total farm.

Soil Group 1: Ragsdale and Reesville Silt Loam (196 Tillable Acres). Brad Aid calculated that on the 196 tillable acres of highly productive soil group 1, rotation corn and rotation soybeans resulted in the highest net returns per acre (Table 10.4, line 17) and the highest returns to land per acre (line 18). Because the land is level and has only a slight susceptibility to erosion, Brad judged that continuous row crops would not cause soil problems. Continuous corn is one possibility, but it is not as profitable as rotating corn and soybeans. Continuous beans were judged to be undesirable because of disease problems that often occur when beans are raised year after year on the same ground. Wheat and alfalfa-grass are not needed to reduce soil erosion or soil structure problems on this soil group.

A rotation of corn and soybeans has another advantage over continuous cropping in that it spreads labor and machinery use over more days of the year. It is usually feasible to harvest soybeans earlier than corn. Soybeans can be planted slightly later than corn with less yield loss.

So the crop choice for soil group 1 is obvious: a corn-soybean rotation, with half corn and half beans.

Net returns/acre: Rotation corn	$ 12.00
Net returns/acre: Rotation soybeans	4.75
Net returns/acre	$ 16.75 ÷ 2 acres = $ 8.38
Returns to land investment/acre[a]	$216.75 ÷ 2 acres = $ 108.38
Net returns to 196 tillable acres	$ 8.38 × 196 = $ 1,642.48
Returns to land, 196 Tillable Acres	$108.38 × 196 = $21,242.48

[a]Operating returns

Soil Group 2: Genesee Soil (94 Tillable Acres). Brad decided that continuous corn is the only feasible crop on the bottom ground that can be expected to flood in some years. Since this land is on a small stream, the water rises and falls quickly. Corn can withstand the flooding much better than soybeans. There would be serious problems in growing hay on this land because flooding would cover the hay with dirt and at times ruin cut hay. Brad reduced his estimate of corn yield to account for flood losses, as it is expected that there will be occasional years when no crop is harvested due to flood loss.

If Brad establishes a livestock program, continuous pasture would be an alternative for this soil group. The return to pasture depends on the manager's ability with livestock.

Net returns/acre: Continuous corn	$ 2.00
Returns to land investment/acre[a]:	
Continuous corn	52.00
Net returns to 94 tillable acres	$2.00 × 94 = $188.00
Returns to land, 94 tillable acres	$52.00 × 94 = $4,888.00

[a]Operating returns

Soil Group 3: Fox Loam and Sandy Loam (288 Tillable Acres). This soil group is composed of land that has little slope (less than 3%). Fox soil is underlaid with gravel and is droughty. Yields are highly variable. Wind erosion can be a problem if land remains bare over the winter.

Brad budgeted three rotations that he thought would be profitable and would prevent soil erosion.

Rotation 1: Corn-Soybeans-Wheat-Alfalfa

Net Returns/Acre		Operating Returns to Land Investment/Acre	
Corn	$ 2.50	Corn	$ 46.50
Soybeans	30.25	Soybeans	74.25
Wheat	− 9.75	Wheat	34.25
Alfalfa	−13.00	Alfalfa	31.00
	$10 ÷ 4 = $2.50		$186.00 ÷ 4 = $46.50

Rotation 2: Corn-Soybeans-Wheat

Net Returns/Acre		Operating Returns to Land Investment/Acre	
Corn	$ 2.50	Corn	$ 46.50
Soybeans	30.25	Soybeans	74.25
Wheat	− 9.75	Wheat	34.25
	$23.00 ÷ 3 = $7.67		$155.00 ÷ 3 = $51.67

Rotation 3: Corn-Soybeans-Cover

Net Returns/Acre		Operating Returns to Land Investment/Acre	
Corn	$ 2.50	Corn	$ 46.50
Soybeans	30.25	Soybeans	74.25
Cover	−20.00	Cover	−20.00
	$12.75 ÷ 2 = $6.38		$100.75 ÷ 2 = $50.38

Although Brad would like to consider a rotation of corn and soybeans, which would likely be profitable, he ruled out this alternative because of possible wind erosion that could occur during the winter after soybeans. This disadvantage could be eliminated with the use of a winter cover crop after the beans (rotation 3).

Brad decided to follow rotation 2. The budget for it showed a slightly higher return than rotation 3 and the corn-beans-wheat rotation would spread the use of labor and machinery. Also, Brad reasoned that rotation 2 would result in less erosion than rotation 3, and if a livestock operation is added, rotation 2 will provide straw and fall pasture from the legume-grass mixture that is seeded with the wheat.

Brad calculated returns to soil group 3 as follows:

Net returns to 288 tillable acres	$7.67 × 288 = $2,208.96
Returns to land investment[a]	$51.67 × 288 = $14,880.96

[a]Operating returns

Soil Group 4: Ockley and Russell Silt Loams (6%–18% Slope, Eroded, 83 Tillable Acres) Because of the substantial slope and present erosion, Brad decided that soil group 4 should remain in continuous alfalfa-grass-hay or pasture.

From the budget in Table 10.9 for soil group 4, budgeted net returns per acre is $3.00 and returns to land per acre is $33.00. Net returns to the 83 acres would be 3.00 × 83 = $249.00 and returns to land would be $33.00 × 83 = $2,739.00.

Brad then budgeted net returns to the cropping program and operating returns to land investment for the total farm:

Soil Group	Tillable Acres	Net Return/Acre	Total Net Returns
Net returns			
1	196	$ 8.38	$ 1,642.48
2	94	2.00	188.00
3	288	7.67	2,208.96
4	83	3.00	249.00
			$ 4,288.44
Returns to land			
1	196	$108.38	$21,242.48
2	94	52.00	4,888.00
3	288	51.67	14,880.96
4	83	33.00	2,739.00
			$43,750.44

Brad showed the crop budgets to the Christians, explaining to them that they could expect to make a return to land of $43,750 per year from the proposed cropping program. Brad pointed out that because of the acreage of droughty land plus the land subject to flooding, returns were likely to be quite variable. Since the risk on Genesee soil is flooding and the risk on Fox soil is drought, it is most unlikely (although it could happen) that both of these would be below average in a single year.

With their present financial situation, the Christians need not be concerned about the amount of income variability. But if they borrow money to expand the business, the income variability can affect their ability to make loan payments on time. Managers must keep debt at a lower level on farms that are subject to greater income variability than on farms that have less variability in income.

Brad had completed one important part of his plan, choice of crops. Next he turned to making a plan that would enable him to achieve the yield, price, and cost figures in his budgets.

CROP PRODUCTION DECISIONS

Earnings from crops on farms with similar resources vary widely (Table 10.10). One main reason for this variation in income is differences in efficiency, that is, the amount of production from given resources. The best measure of crop efficiency on farms with similar soils in the same geographical area is yield.

The reason that farms with higher yields make more money from crops is that a significant amount of yield differences are due to the *kind of resources used and the way in which they are used* rather than from the use of more resources.

It is possible, of course, to reduce income by increasing yield through the addition of large amounts of costly resources (see Chapter 3). But much of the time, yield variations are the result of management rather than the amount of physical input.

> Have you ever seen two farms side by side with similar soils and kinds of crops but wide differences in production per acre? Watch for these differences. The land, labor, and machinery costs per acre for the high- and low-yielding farms are often about the same, and there is usually little difference in the amounts of other resources used. The differences are in the kinds of resources used and in the way in which they are used.

Some things that a manager can do to obtain high crop yields are discussed in this section.

TABLE 10.10 Relationship Between Corn Yields and Labor Incomes, 166 Farms, Indiana Farm Accounts, 1980.

Corn Yield Per Acre		Number of Farms	Acres of Cropland	Percent Land in Corn	Labor Incomes
Range	Average				
30 – 85	68	33	619	61	$ 24,719
87 –100	94	33	674	62	29,730
100 –111	106	34	694	56	33,896
111 –125	118	33	680	54	61,893
125 –153	138	33	694	56	66,548
Average	105	166	672	58	$ 43,282

Source: Indiana Farm Account Keepers. R. C. Suter. Department of Agricultural Economics, Purdue University, West Lafayette, Ind., 1984.

Kind and Amount of Fertilizer

To make decisions about the kind and amount of fertilizer to use, the manager should follow the principle of adding fertilizer as long as the cost of a unit of fertilizer is less than the value of the additional crop gained from adding the unit of fertilizer. To make this decision, the manager needs information about the price of fertilizer, the price of the crop, and the relationship between the amount of fertilizer used and yields (see Chapter 3).

To obtain high profits from the cropping enterprise, managers must be able to predict the relationship between the amount and kind of fertilizer used and yield and be able to obtain greater than average yield increases from a given amount of fertilizer. To accomplish this, managers may use several sources of information. Soil tests by universities or commercial services with fertilization recommendations can be helpful. Knowledge about fertilizer requirements of the crops to be grown is useful, as are plant tissue tests. Other good sources of information are fertilizer test plots on the farm, the study of university experiments, consultation with professional agronomists from an extension or commercial service, and exchange of information with other farmers. Finally, managers must have the ability to integrate the information from all of these sources for their particular farm and circumstances.

Brad Aid developed the fertilization plan for soil group 1 on the Christian farm (Figure 10.11) after studying soil types and soil tests and observing university fertilizer experiment data. He took into account yields obtained on other farms in the area with various amounts of fertilizer, and he considered the cost of the fertilizer and the price of the crops.

Seed Varieties

Varieties of seed have a major impact on yields. Many agricultural experiment stations publish yield data for different seed varieties (Figure 10.12). These reports illustrate the importance of knowing which varieties to plant. Managers who know which seed varieties result in the highest yields can increase yields substantially simply by choosing the correct variety. Sometimes seed sales representatives can be helpful in selecting the best variety for a particular farm. On the other hand, sales representatives may not know which varieties are best, their company may not have the best varieties, or they may be trying to dispose of seed they have not been able to sell.

There is a strong relationship between soil type, weather conditions, and yield of specific varieties. Many top crop farmers believe it is important to have seed variety trials on their farm. They may plant 10 acres each of several varieties in a test field to determine which varieties yield best.

Seed varieties affect not only yield but also such factors as lodging, disease resistance, insect resistance, and plant size. It is important, therefore, to secure information about characteristics associated with different seed varieties for your soils and growing conditions.

Soil Group 1: Reesville = Ragsdale Soil, 196 Tillable Acres

Field	Crop	Past Yields	Yield Goal	Soil Test	Fertilization Plan for 1984
1	Corn	133 bu./acre	140 bu.	Potash: Med. Phosphate: Med. Lime: Needs 2–3 tons	**Corn**
2	Soybeans	43 bu./acre	45 bu.	Potash: Med. Phosphate: Med. Lime:	

Corn fertilization plan:

1. Spread 2–3 tons lime per acre depending on soil test.
2. Broadcast 200 lbs. of 0-0-60 per area (300 lbs. on the 6 acres with low test).
3. Broadcast 100 lbs. 0-45-0 per acre.
4. 50 lbs. 8-32-0 in row.
5. 220 lbs. 82-0-0 before planting.

1-2 tons on 15 acres, no lime on other

Soybeans

1. Spread 1-2 tons lime on 15 acres where needed.
2. Broadcast 100 lbs. of 00-60 and 100 lbs. of 0-45-0 per acre.

Past Field Layout

Tract 1

1	2	3	4	5
40 acres	37 acres	43 acres	37 acres	39 acres

FS

Future Field Layout

1	2
98 acres	98 acres

FS

Figure 10.11 Fertilizer plan for the Christian farm.

Plant Population

A uniform plant stand and the optimum population of plants per acre are important for attaining high yields (Figure 10.13). A good stand is the result of (1) tillage that puts the soil in proper condition so that seeds are most likely to grow, (2) proper setting of the planter so that seeds are distributed at desired spacing and depth and are properly covered, (3) a planter in good condition that is not likely to malfunction, (4) good seed germination, (5) adequate soil moisture, and (6) the manager's ability to consider the important variables affecting population and to follow necessary practices to attain a good stand.

> Determine the best population for various crops in your area for different types of soils. The level of management, soil type, fertility level, and other factors affect the population that will result in the highest yields.

Northern Loams and Clay Loams, High Population and Fertility.

Data in this table may generally be used as a guide to the performance of these hybrids on loams and clay loams at high population and fertility in the shaded area. In 1982, the Wanatah test was planted at the rate of 26,550 seeds per acre May 3 and harvested October 12. A June soil test indicated 47 pounds P and 190 pounds K. The Auburn test was planted at the rate of 26,550 seeds per acre May 23, but the experiment was lost due to excessive rain in June.

Northern Loams and Clay Loams (High Population and Fertility), Three-Year Averages.

Brand-hybrid *	Acre yield	Water at harvest	Broken or lodged plants	Stand
	bu.	%	%	%
1980-82, AVERAGE OF 3 EXPERIMENTS				
Adler 30X (Sx)	179	23.6	4	94
Cargill 967 (Sx)	177	26.0	11	95
Campbell C-99 (Sx)	177	26.9	8	95
CFS W4000 (Sx)	173	24.1	5	90
AgriGold A6475 (Sx)	171	24.4	5	95
P-A-G SX351 (Sx)	170	26.8	8	92
Bo-Jac 452 (Sx)	167	23.7	7	92
Asgrow RX777 (Sx)	167	23.8	8	87
Jacobi CX56 (Sx)	165	24.2	6	92
Lynks LX4315 (Sx)	163	23.4	4	86
Dennis 25 (Sx)	159	23.6	4	91
Lowe 380 (Sx)	158	25.7	6	91
Gold Tag 3006 (Sx)	157	23.7	6	90
Lowe 511 (Sx)	157	29.3	5	85
Beck 60X (Sx)	155	23.5	6	91
Golden Har. H2500 (Sx)	155	23.9	5	93
Rupp XR1780 (Sx)	155	23.8	9	91
DeKalb XL56 (MSx)	153	23.6	8	92
AgriGold A6450 (Sx)	152	22.2	4	91
Gold Tag 2006 (Sx)	150	21.5	8	90
DeKalb XL23 (Sx)	150	21.8	6	94
Paymaster 8201 (Sx)	149	24.9	6	88
Cargill 921 (Sx)	146	24.3	8	95
Beck 40X (Sx)	145	20.3	8	92
Prairie Str. SX33 (Sx)	145	20.8	4	90
Funk G-4435 (MSx)	144	23.5	5	94
MCA 5858 (Sx)	143	19.9	22	91
Golden Har. H2448 (Sx)	142	21.2	9	92
P-A-G SX397 (Sx)	140	23.2	9	87
Dennis 6 (Sx)	138	21.2	8	90
Supercrost 2396 (Sx)	134	20.2	8	92
Sohigro 39 (Sx)	133	21.2	14	92
Bailey SX222 (Sx)	129	20.1	13	90
	---	-----	---	---
Average	154	23.4	7	91
BLSD	13	0.9	NS	6

* (Sx) Indicates a single cross.
  (MSx) Indicates a modified single cross.

Figure 10.12 Sample information about the relationship between seed varieties and yield. *Source:* Purdue University Agricultural Experiment Station Bulletin No. 396, December 1982.

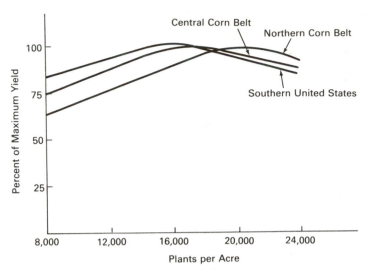

Figure 10.13 Approximate yield curves of different corn plant populations. *Source:* Modern Corn Production, 1975.

Weed Control

Weeds compete for plant nutrients and moisture. It is only logical that weeds reduce yields. Yet you can observe wide variation in weed control. Managers with high-yielding, high-profit crop enterprises control weeds with tillage practices and chemicals.

Design weed-control practices for a farm in your area.

Insect and Disease Control

Various insects attack plants and reduce yields. Chemicals, seed varieties, and crop rotations are the three most common methods operators use to control insects and plant disease. Rotation of crops rather than continuous cropping may reduce insect and disease problems and therefore chemical costs. In some areas of the country, scouting services are available to help operators detect and solve disease and insect problems.

Date of Planting and Harvesting

For many crops, yields are closely related to the date of planting and harvesting (Figure 10.14, Table 10.11). For example, in some areas, corn yields decrease about 1 bushel per acre for each day corn is planted after May 10 and 2 bushels per day after May 25. If an operator's average planting date is May 20, yield will usually be 10

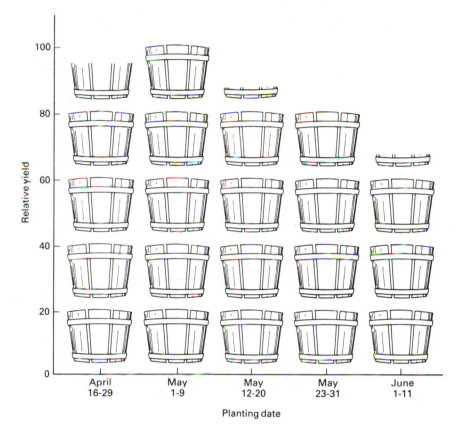

Figure 10.14   Ten-year average yield at Lansing, Michigan. *Source:* Samuel R. Aldrich, Walter O. Scott, and Earl R. Leng, *Modern Corn Production,* 2nd ed. (Champaign, Ill.: A & L Publications, 1975).

bushels per acre less than if corn was planted by May 10. If the corn price is $3.00 per bushel, this would mean a decrease in returns of $30.00 per acre. Costs per acre are not likely to change much as the planting date changes. If costs are $5.00 per acre less with late planting, the loss of profit per acre would be $25.00. On a 500-acre farm, this would be a $12,500 reduction in profit due to the single factor of late corn planting.

TABLE 10.11   Average Field Losses of Corn in Tests in Illinois, Indiana, Iowa, and Nebraska over Several Seasons. (Source: V.W. Davis, USDA)

	October	November	December
Machine loss	4.6%	7.0%	11.8%
Total loss	5.0%	8.4%	18.4%

Similarly, field losses of corn can be expected to increase as the fall progresses (Table 10.11). As timeliness declines, the loss of yield becomes greater for both planting and harvesting.

Timely planting and harvesting can be accomplished by having:

1. Adequate machinery to get the job done on time
2. Machinery in good condition and ready when the weather is suitable
3. Seed, fuel, fertilizer, labor, and other resources on hand when needed
4. Labor and management willing to operate long hours when the weather is favorable and with flexibility to adapt to a schedule that is affected by the weather, machinery breakdowns, and labor availability
5. Management that is aware that timeliness is critical and may mean the difference between profit and loss in the cropping enterprise.

Tillage Practices

Tillage practices can affect not only yield but also machinery cost, labor cost, soil erosion, soil structure, and timeliness. The "best" tillage system depends on the soil type, soil slope, farm size, capital, labor, and the manager.

Plowing requires the most power, is the slowest operation, and is often a bottleneck to getting work done on time. For this reason many farmers plow in the fall. Yet fall plowing can result in substantial amounts of wind and water soil erosion. To minimize erosion but still get soil prepared in the fall, some farmers have changed to fall chiseling and no-till planting. Plowing or chiseling can result in different yields depending on the soil type. You should be aware of the impact of various tillage practices on costs and yields for your area.

The following factors should be considered in selecting a farm tillage system:

1. Seed germination and plant population, weed control, and insect control are affected by the tillage system. Be sure that the system you use does not result in plant-population, weed, or insect problems.
2. The tillage system often affects timeliness and the amount of machinery needed. It is not always true that fewer tillage operations require less machinery and result in greater timeliness.
3. The tillage system affects soil erosion and the intensity with which land can be farmed without erosion and structure problems. Chiseling rather than plowing, planting across slopes, and spring rather than fall plowing reduce erosion. Substituting tillage practices to minimize erosion for a rotation that minimizes erosion should be considered.

> Read experiment results and discuss tillage practices with agronomists and successful farmers in your area. Then develop a tillage-system plan for your farm.

PRODUCTION SYSTEM

Selection of the optimum size and kind of machinery is discussed in Chapter 16.

BUYING AND SELLING

While the producers of most farm products cannot greatly influence the price of the things they purchase or sell at a particular place and time, they can affect prices of resources and products by their choices of *time and place of purchases and sales.* Even a small change in the purchase price of resources or the sale price of products can have a tremendous impact on profit (see Chapter 18).

The next step is to plan a profitable livestock system. This is discussed in Chapter 11.

DISCUSSION QUESTIONS

1. What steps are involved in choosing the best crops to grow?
2. List the steps involved in taking a land inventory?
3. What is the purpose of grouping soils? What are some principles for grouping?
4. Determine the costs and returns of various crops in your area. Calculate the returns to selected crop rotations.
5. Should a manager budget net returns, returns to labor and management, returns to land, or a combination of these? Which returns budgets are appropriate for different situations?
6. What are the most important factors to consider when selecting a cropping program for a farm?
7. Give some reasons why earnings on crop farms may vary widely.
8. What significant technical practices cause variation in earnings in your area?
9. How much influence does buying and selling have on crop enterprise profit?

RELATED READINGS

ALDRICH, SAMUEL R., WALTER D. SCOTT, and EARL R. LONG. *Modern Corn Production,* 2d ed. Cincinnati: Farm Quarterly, 1978.

CASTLE, EMERY N., MANNING H. BECKER, and FREDERICK J. SMITH. *Farm Business Management,* (2nd ed.), chap. 11. New York: The Macmillan Company, 1972.

Farm Planning and Financial Management, Cooperative Extension Service ID-68, Purdue University, West Lafayette, Ind.: 1980.

HERBST, J. H. *Farm Management Principles, Budgets, Plans,* (6th ed.), chap. 5. Champaign, Ill.: Stripes Publishing Co., 1983.

Livestock Decisions

11

SHOULD I RAISE LIVESTOCK?

Livestock is highly profitable in situations where excellent livestock-production management ability is available or where fixed or salvage resources are available (crop residue, pasture, labor, buildings, or management that would not be used if livestock were not raised). Raising livestock usually requires less capital to employ an operator and also provides a more favorable cash flow than does crop farming with owned land. Livestock production provides the opportunity for delaying taxes through rapid depreciation and through accumulation of income in growing inventories and the decreasing of taxes with investment credit and capital gains. Livestock prices and profits are cyclical. Livestock usually requires more continuous attention and more decisions per unit of income and investment than crops.

The checklist in Table 11.1 will be helpful in deciding whether or not you should keep livestock. Complete it for a farm with which you are familiar.

If you have above-average livestock management ability or fixed resources that

TABLE 11.1 Should I Raise Livestock?

Yes	No	
———	———	1. Do I need or want to make more income and am I willing to work with livestock to obtain it?
		2. Do I have any free or low-cost fixed resources?
———	———	a. Feed
———	———	b. Labor and management
———	———	c. Buildings and equipment
———	———	3. Am I willing to contribute the continuous attention that livestock requires?
———	———	4. Am I at least average in ability with livestock?
———	———	5. Do I need a better cash-flow situation?
———	———	6. Do I need investment credit, depreciation, capital gains?
———	———	7. Am I short of capital?
———	———	8. Am I short of land?
———	———	9. Do I enjoy working with livestock?
———	———	10. Am I willing to make a long-term commitment?
———	———	11. Am I willing to accept the risks of price fluctuations and disease?

can only be sold through livestock, and if you are willing to make a long-term commitment, it is likely that livestock will make money for you.

Christian Farm

Brad Aid (see Chapter 10) used the checklist to determine if he should plan livestock for the Christian farm. The completed checklist (Table 11.2) showed that livestock could be advantageous on the Christian farm. Brad Aid concluded that livestock should be considered because he believes he can make money by using the permanent pasture, existing buildings, and the operator's labor and management during the times of the year that the operator is not involved with crop work. Brad also believes that the livestock business will likely have some income tax advantages for the Christians.

Raising livestock will require Brad to hire an operator with livestock management interest and skill. It is more difficult to find a manager who has both crop and livestock management ability than to find an operator to produce crops only. Live-

TABLE 11.2   Should I Raise Livestock? Christian Farm

Yes	No	
✔	____	1. Do I need or want to make more income and am I willing to work with livestock to obtain it?
		2. Do I have any free or low-cost fixed resources?
✔	____	a. Feed
✔	____	b. Labor and management
✔	____	c. Buildings and equipment
____	____	3. Am I willing to contribute the continuous attention that livestock requires?[a]
____	____	4. Am I at least average in ability with livestock?[a]
____	✔	5. Do I need a better cash-flow situation?
✔	____	6. Do I need investment credit, depreciation, capital gains?
____	✔	7. Am I short of capital?
____	✔	8. Am I short of land?
____	____	9. Do I enjoy working with livestock?[a]
✔	____	10. Am I willing to make a long-term commitment?
✔	____	11. Am I willing to accept the risks of price fluctuations and disease?

[a]If Brad decides to raise livestock, he would need to hire an operator who could answer yes to questions 3, 4, and 9.

stock will require additional investment in inventory, equipment, and perhaps buildings and will also make management of the farm more difficult for Brad. Having determined that livestock would likely be profitable, Brad and the Christians then proceeded to evaluate various kinds and amounts of livestock and the systems of production.

PLANNING KIND, AMOUNT, AND SYSTEM OF PRODUCTION

The best livestock system for you is the one that fits your unique resources and the markets available in your area.

Livestock can play either of two major roles in the farm business:

1. Livestock provides a way to sell fixed or salvage resources that could not be sold without livestock.
2. Livestock stands as an independent enterprise using mainly resources that could be sold or must be purchased.

The trend has been toward role 2, but there is still a need for livestock for role 1 in many farm businesses. In role 1 the amounts of salvage or fixed feed, labor, and buildings are the critical factors that determine the best livestock system. Generally, role 1 livestock enterprises are smaller and do not gain all of the economies of size (see Chapter 13). The manager must therefore secure purchased resources at a competitive cost and must find good markets for livestock.

Management ability, least-cost size, and availability of markets are the critical factors that determine success in role 2 livestock enterprises. The following are steps for planning a livestock enterprise for *either* role. The Christians' farm example relates mainly to role 1.

Step 1

Inventory your management ability, physical resources, goals, and personal preferences and compare these to the requirements of different kinds of livestock and systems of production.

Management.   Research and farm-record summaries consistently show wide ranges in cost of producing livestock and profit from livestock production (Table 11.3). The low-cost third of livestock producers make money with livestock most of the time (Figure 11.1). Average livestock producers make money when prices are high, lose money when prices are low, and on the average receive modest returns to their labor and investment. The high-cost third of livestock producers make money only when prices are at the highest point of the price cycle but lose money most of the time. High-price periods encourage inefficient producers to stay in business, but their resources are often exhausted during the low-price part of the cycle. Some farmers

TABLE 11.3 Differences in Net Farm Income Resulting from Variations in Livestock Production Efficiency, Marketing, and Purchasing, 1981

Type Farm	Livestock Receipts per Dollar Feed Fed	Net Farm Income	Units of Livestock	Value of Feed Fed	Farm Income Difference Due to Difference in Livestock Receipts per Dollar Feed Fed
High-profit 50% Large hog farms (12 farms)	$1.78	$140,681	337 sows	$244,812	
					$71,742
Low-Profit 50% Large hog farms (11 farms)	$1.47	−$5,232	318 sows	$218,042	
High-profit 50% Large dairy farms (11 farms)	$1.65	$81,705	117 cows	$154,991	
					$33,533
Low-profit 50% Large dairy farms (11 farms)	$1.42	$3,358	116 cows	$136,597	

Source: Cooperative Extension Service Farm Business Summaries EC–250 and EC–251, Purdue University 1981.

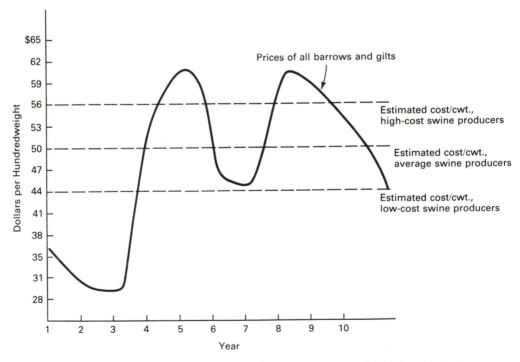

Figure 11.1 Prices of all barrows and gilts, estimated production costs per hundredweight of pork for average, high-cost, and low-cost swine producers.

who raise crops and livestock subsidize livestock losses with crop profits without knowing they are doing so because they keep inadequate records.

Livestock tends to be a highly profitable business for those in the upper third of production efficiency.

High levels of all aspects of management—production, buying and selling—are desirable. To be successful, different levels of production, buying, and selling management are required by different types of livestock (Table 11.4).

How do your management skills fit the requirements of livestock enterprises in Table 11.4? Rate your ability in the table below.

Production	Selling	Buying

Managers with operations large enough to require more than one person may hire operators to provide needed management in production, buying, or selling. Different production systems require different kinds of management. Though there is a wide range in types of production systems, there tends to be two general types:

1. High-investment, low-labor systems in which livestock is confined and feed and waste handling are partially or totally automated.
2. Lower-investment systems in which more labor is involved in feeding and handling livestock and disposing of livestock waste. These systems are often (but not always) associated with pasture production.

Table 11.5 shows management characteristics that best fit each system. How does your management ability fit the requirements of the high-investment versus the low-investment system?

TABLE 11.4   Level of Management Required by Various Kinds of Livestock

Livestock Enterprise	Type of Management Required		
	Production	Selling	Buying
Swine, farrow to finish	High	Medium	Medium
Buy feeder pigs	Medium	High	High
Dairy cattle	High	Low	Medium
Beef cows	Medium	High	Medium
Beef feeders	Medium	High	High
Laying hens	High	High	Medium
Ewes	High	High	Medium
Feeder lambs	High	High	High
Broilers	High	High	High
Turkeys	High	High	High

TABLE 11.5   Management Requirements of Livestock Production Systems

Management Characteristics	Type of Production System	
	High Investment, Low Labor	Low Investment, High Labor
Short on experience		✔
Good mechanical ability	✔	
Can supervise and manage labor		✔
Top production management	✔	

When selecting an operator for the Christian farm, Brad will look for someone who can manage the type of livestock system dictated by salvage feed, existing buildings, capital availability, and income goals.

Feed.   Some kinds of forages are difficult to sell except through livestock. On the Christian farm (see Chapter 10), the permanent meadow and woods pasture are likely to have much greater return through a well-managed livestock enterprise than through rental of pasture. Some hay could be baled and sold, but on half of the permanent meadow acres hay cannot be harvested because of rough topography and trees.

Substantial cornstalks and wheat-interseeding crop residues could also provide feed for livestock. In years when the bottom land floods early in the season, a second planting of corn would be susceptible to an early frost. It would be desirable to have the option of converting this corn to silage and feeding it to livestock.

In addition to the free or low-cost feeds on the Christian farm, there are substantial amounts of corn and hay that could be sold or fed to livestock. When market crops are fed to livestock on the farm, reduced transportation and marketing costs provide a slight competitive advantage over a livestock unit that must purchase all of its feed.

Brad inventoried crop production of the Christian farm (Table 11.6) and secured information about the feed requirements of various types of livestock (Table 11.7). The latter table shows the quantities of grain and forage required. Beef cows can consume low-quality forage without adverse effects. Dairy cows require high-quality forage, but feeder cattle can utilize either high-quality or low-quality forage, depending on the type of cattle and their stage of feeding.

> Inventory the crops available for feeding livestock on your farm. Identify those crops that will not have a market if they are not fed to livestock.

Labor.   In some cases, livestock may be kept to utilize labor that remains after the cropping system has had its claim. The use of surplus labor with livestock has become less important than in the past. Capital costs have increased relative to

TABLE 11.6   Crops Produced That Could Be Fed to Livestock, Christian Farm

Crop	Acres	Average Yield/Acre	Total Production
Corn	286	90–140 bu.	31,760 bu.
Cornstalks[a]	150.0	0.3 ton[b]	45 tons
Wheat/interseeding[a]	96.0	1.0 ton[b]	96 tons
Hay or pasture	41.5	3.0 tons[b]	125 tons
Permanent pasture[a]	41.5	3.0 tons[b]	125 tons
Woods pasture[a]	35.0	1.0 ton[b]	35 tons

[a]No other market if not fed to livestock.
[b]Hay equivalent.

labor, and the use of small amounts of labor is not as important as it once was. Also, the high-investment livestock production systems must be operated at nearly full capacity throughout the year to reduce building costs per unit of production. Continuous, uniform livestock production does not fit neatly with the use of surplus crop labor.

Nevertheless, livestock does provide the opportunity to use surplus labor. Even with high-investment production systems, some jobs (such as building and equipment maintenance and repair) can be scheduled when crop labor requirements are low.

For greatest efficiency, persons involved in livestock production should possess both labor and management skills to some extent. Workers must be able to detect and solve problems such as broken waterers, poorly adjusted feeders, and improperly set fans. With moderate-size livestock enterprises, the operator must be able to handle both animal husbandry and mechanical problems. On larger farms on which several people work, animal husbandry jobs may be separated from the equipment maintenance jobs, and there may be some jobs for unskilled workers.

Labor is required on a continuous basis for livestock production because livestock must be observed, fed, and watered each day. For this reason, livestock farms require two persons. It is possible for one operator to work 365 days a year for a short period while the livestock program is being initiated, but usually an operator would prefer completing this phase quickly and expanding to a two-person farm that would allow the operator some time away from the farm. The importance of a livestock unit's being a two-person farm was emphasized by a dairy farmer who said, "The only difference between being in jail and having a one-operator dairy farm is that in jail you don't have to milk the cows."

A two-person operation provides insurance in case one person becomes ill or is injured. Some jobs can be done more efficiently by two persons than by one. It is generally advantageous for a livestock farm to have at least two full-time workers.

Brad is considering hiring two full-time workers on the Christian farm. Two people will be needed for crops during the planting and harvesting seasons. Since Brad is considering keeping livestock to use salvage feed, the livestock enterprise can

TABLE 11.7 Feed and Labor Requirements for Various Livestock Enterprises

Livestock Enterprise	Feed Requirement			Labor Requirement		Capital per Hour of Labor
	Corn Equivalent	Hay Equivalent	Purchased Feed	Direct	Total	
	(bu.)	(tons)	(lbs.)	(hrs.)	(hrs.)	
Sow, feeder pigs sold						
High investment ($2\frac{1}{3}$ litters)	65	—	1,380	16	21	$ 57
Low investment (2 litters)	60	.25	1,130	20	26	35
Finishing 100 purchased pigs						
High investment	930	—	10,400	60	80	107
Low investment	960	—	10,650	75	100	59
Sow, 1 litter, farrow to finish	100	1.00	1,050	12	16	51
Sow, farrow to finish						
High investment ($2\frac{1}{3}$ litters)	230	—	2,960	24	32	77
Low investment (2 litters)	203	.25	2,500	33	44	37
Pasture (2 litters)	202	1.40	2,350	36	47	42
1,000 laying hens (12 ¼-mo. cycle)						
Farm flock (5,000–10,000)	—	—	80,000	232	250	29
Owned, semiautomated (15,000–20,000)	—	—	80,000	72	90	91
Contract, semiautomated (15,000–20,000)	—	—	—	72	85	82
Owned, fully automated (50,000 +)	—	—	80,000	42	60	144
1,000 pullets, owned	—	—	14,000	9	12	214
1,000 pullets, contract	—	—	—	9	12	177
1,000 broilers, owned	—	—	7,800	5	6	115
1,000 broilers, contract	—	—	—	5	6	98
Tom turkeys, owned						
Range-reared (5,000 +)	—	—	60,000	100	110	39
Confinement (10,000 +)	—	—	60,000	50	60	90
Dairy cow (13,500 lbs. milk)						
Pasture	134	6.25	1,400	54	75	62
Dry lot	162	3.50	1,500	50	65	68
Dairy heifer	21	5.50	380	16	21	56
Dairy bull calf to feeder size	12	1.00	245	9	12	41
Veal calf	—	—	405	5	6	30
Feeder calf						
Steer	60	—	450	3	4	258
Heifer	50	—	390	2	3	281
Steer, grown out	—	1.65	165	2	3	207
Feeder steer, yearling						
High forage	41	—	190	1.5	2	283
High grain	47	—	130	1.5	2	273
Beef cow, calf sold	6	6.00	125	5	8	167
Beef cow, calf fed out	47	6.00	430	7	12	169
Ewe and lamb	4.5	1.00	15	4	5	30
Feeder lamb	2.5	0.10	15	0.8	1	32

Source: Farm Planning and Financial Management, rev. ed. (West Lafayette, Ind.: Purdue University, Cooperative Extension Service, 1980).

be planned to use labor not claimed by the cropping enterprise. A two-person operation would avoid the problem of finding part-time help during planting and harvesting and would also provide insurance in case one of the operators becomes incapacitated or decides to move to another job.

Brad listed the amount of permanent labor available in each month of the year and estimated the amount of labor required for crops (Tables 11.8 and 11.9). The difference between permanent labor available and crop labor requirements is surplus labor, which is available for livestock.

Brad estimates there will be a labor surplus above crop requirements of about 2,447 hours per year. He plans to provide two weeks of vacation time for each operator. This would leave approximately 2,247 hours that could be "sold" through livestock. During months of heavy crop-labor requirements, some part-time help could be used, or Brad could plan a livestock program that does not use much labor during these months. Approximately one-third of the total livestock labor requirement consists of general planning and overhead, jobs that need not be done in a specific month. The remaining two-thirds is direct labor.

Capital.   The amount of capital required for raising livestock is generally lower than the amount of capital required for farming owned land (Table 11.10). Also, there is a wide range in capital requirements of different livestock production systems. Because rental land is limited and capital requirements for purchased land are substantial, raising livestock often provides an opportunity to start farming with limited capital.

TABLE 11.8   Direct Crop-Labor Requirements, Christian Farm

Month	Labor Required (Hours per Acre)					
	Corn	Soybeans	Wheat	Straw	Hay	Pasture
January	—	—	—	—	—	—
February	—	—	—	—	—	—
March	0.1	—	—	—	—	—
April	0.4	0.3	—	—	0.1	0.1
May	0.8	0.8	—	—	1.5	—
June	0.2	0.2	—	—	1.8	0.1
July	—	—	1.5	1.5	1.6	—
August	—	—	—	1.5	1.0	0.1
September	—	0.7	0.7	—	1.0	—
October	0.8	0.5	0.3	—	—	—
November	0.5	—	—	—	—	—
December	0.2	—	—	—	—	—
Overhead and planning (any month)	1.0	1.0	0.5	—	1.0	—
Total hours	4.0	3.5	3.0	3.0	8.0	0.3

TABLE 11.9 Permanent Labor Available, Crop Use, and Surplus for Livestock, Christian Farm

Month	Total Hours Permanent Labor Available[a]	Direct Crop Labor[b]	Indirect Crop Labor[b]	Total Crop Labor	Available for Livestock Production and Vacation
January	400–500	—	150	150	250
February	400–500	—	150	150	250
March	400–500	29	122	151	249
April	400–500	182	—	182	218
May	400–500	448	—	448	52
June	400–500	175	—	175	230
July	400–500	354	—	354	143
August	400–500	190	—	190	225
September	400–500	245	—	245	219
October	400–500	356	—	356	144
November	400–500	144	50	194	225
December	400–500	58	100	158	242
Total hours	5,2000	2,181	572	2,753	2,447

[a]Two workers, average 50 hours per week; will work up to 60 hours in any one week but total hours for the year is based on 50 hours per week for 52 weeks minus 2 weeks' vacation.

[b]Labor for 288 acres corn, 194 acres soybeans, 96 acres wheat and straw, 41.5 acres each for hay and pasture.

It is easier to pay for low-investment livestock facilities than for land or high-investment facilities. Therefore, in addition to needing less capital for a full-time job, the starting farmer will find it easier to repay loans needed for low-investment livestock facilities.

The Christians are willing to invest money in livestock as long as it will pay a reasonable return over time and does not require them to subsidize the farm from their nonfarm income. Since there is currently no debt on the farm, the Christians can use land as collateral for borrowing money for livestock investments. Brad Aid can use excess cash from the crops to subsidize the livestock operation, which may have a negative cash flow when it is getting started.

Brad secured information about livestock investments for different kinds of livestock and systems of production (Tables 11.11 through 11.13). This investment information enabled Brad to determine capital needs for the livestock operation. After securing information about terms of financing, Brad can prepare an interest and principal repayment schedule, which will be an important part of his cash-flow projection.

Other considerations. *Penalty for stopping production or selling the farm.* For the livestock enterprise to be profitable, it is usually necessary for the operator to

TABLE 11.10   Capital Requirements to Employ a
Person Full-Time

Enterprise	Capital Investment to Provide Full-Time Job
Dairy	$ 195,000
Feeder cattle	825,000
Beef cows, calf sold	500,000
Ewe and lamb	90,000
Feeder lamb	96,000
Rent land 50–50	180,000
Cash-rent land	270,000
Operate owned land	1,380,000
Sows, farrow to finish	170,000
Sows, sell feeder pigs	140,000
Finishing feeder pigs	250,000
Laying hens	400,000
Broilers	345,000
Turkeys	200,000

Source: Adapted from *Farm Planning and Financial Management,* rev. ed., Tables 4, 5, and 6. (West Lafayette, Ind.: Purdue University, Cooperative Extension Service, 1980).

raise livestock over a long period of time. It is difficult to make money without a long-term commitment because most of the investment in livestock buildings and equipment can be recovered only by raising livestock. As a general rule, it is not possible to sell livestock buildings for more than 40 cents per dollar of original investment, even when buildings are in good condition. There are two major reasons why buildings are difficult to sell:

1. Livestock buildings are often located near the home and farm crop storage, and it is not practical to sell one part of the farmstead without selling the entire farmstead.
2. Persons who would like to own livestock buildings generally have a specific preference regarding the type of buildings and the geographic location. It would be unusual that there would be enough individuals with a preference for a particular set of buildings to provide a strong market.

Consequently, farmers who make major investments in livestock buildings and equipment should plan to operate the livestock enterprise until the investment has been used. The lowest penalty for stopping exists among livestock and systems of production that require the least investment in buildings and equipment. The follow-

TABLE 11.11 Capital Requirements for Various Swine Enterprises

| Production System | Capital per Animal Unit | | | | | Capital to Employ One Person Full-Time |
| | Operating Capital | | Equipment | Buildings | Total | |
	Production Inventory	Breeding Livestock				
Sow, feeder pigs sold						
High investment	$ 80	$205	$ 495	$ 410	$1,190	$170,000
Low investment	67	205	295	330	900	104,000
Finishing pigs (per 100 pigs fed/year)						
High investment	2,295	—	3,020	3,260	8,575	322,000
Low investment	2,330	—	1,330	2,250	5,910	177,000
Sow, 1 litter, farrow to finish	120	140	345	215	820	154,000
Sow, farrow to finish						
High investment	440	205	1,030	800	2,475	232,000
Low investment	380	210	505	535	1,630	111,000
Pasture	370	215	910	485	1,980	126,000

Source: Farm Planning and Financial Management, rev. ed. (West Lafayette, Ind.: Purdue University, Cooperative Extension Service, 1980).

TABLE 11.12 Capital Requirements for Various Poultry Enterprises

	Capital per 1000–Bird Unit					Capital to Employ One Person Full-Time
	Supplement, Etc.	Livestock	Equipment	Building	Total	
1,000 laying hens						
Farm flock (5,000–10,000)	—	$1,150	$3,000	$3,000	$7,150	$ 86,000
Owned, semiautomated (15,000–20,000)	—	1,150	3,600	3,400	8,150	272,000
Contract, semiautomated (15,000–20,000)	—	—	3,600	3,400	7,000	247,000
Owned, fully automated (50,000 +)	—	1,150	4,250	3,250	8,650	432,000
1,000 pullets, owned	$ 301	183	1,065	1,021	2,570	642,000
1,000 pullets, contract	38	—	1,065	1,021	2,124	531,000
1,000 broilers, owned	71	35	235	350	691	345,500
1,000 broilers, contract	3	—	235	350	588	294,000
1,000 tom turkeys, owned						
Range rearing (10,000 +)	1,200	399	1,240	1,500	4,339	118,000
Confinement (10,000 +)	1,200	399	775	3,000	5,374	269,000

Source: Farm Planning and Financial Management, rev. ed. (West Lafayette, Ind.: Purdue University, Cooperative Extension Service, 1980).

TABLE 11.13 Capital Requirements for Ruminant Species

	Capital per Animal Unit						Capital to Employ One Person Full-Time
	Operating Capital						
Production System	Feed	Supplement, Etc.	Livestock	Equipment	Buildings	Total	
Dairy cow, 13,500 lbs. milk							
Pasture (40–50 cows)	$104	—	$1,750	$1,300	$1,475	$4,637	$185,000
Drylot (60–70 cows)	146	—	1,750	1,120	1,430	4,446	206,000
Dairy heifer	169	72	250	162	520	1,173	268,000
Dairy bull calf to feeder size	22	31	82	75	290	500	125,000
Feeder calf							
Steer	98	39	364	153	377	1,031	780,000
Heifer	70	29	262	144	338	843	849,000
Yearling steer							
High-forage ration	36	12	251	81	188	566	854,000
High-grain ration	31	10	238	81	188	546	820,000
Grow-out cattle	33	20	312	81	175	621	621,000
Beef-cow, calf sold	93	28	1,050	67	97	1,335	500,000
Beef cow, calf fed out	156	53	1,285	175	357	2,026	508,000
Ewe and lamb	26	12	72	18	22	150	90,000
Feeder lamb	3	1	20	3	5	32	96,000
Veal calf	—	28	30	66	54	178	89,000

Source: Farm Planning and Financial Management, rev. ed. (West Lafayette, Ind.: Purdue University, Cooperative Extension Service, 1980).

ing is a ranking of livestock enterprises and systems of production according to their penalty for stopping production, from lowest to highest.

Enterprise	System of Production
Beef cows or ewe flock	Extensive, uses existing buildings and lots
Feeder pigs and feeder cattle	Low-investment facilities, uses existing buildings
Turkeys, pullets	Pasture system
Dairy	Automated, new buildings and equipment
Farrow-to-finish sows	Automated, new buildings and equipment
Poultry	Automated
Feeder cattle, hogs	Automated

Risk. Because of price cycles and disease problems, livestock production can be a risky business. Incomes of swine, beef, and poultry farms fluctuate widely from year to year, mainly due to price cycles (Figure 11.2). Milk prices are regulated through a government support system, so price swings are of a lesser magnitude and dairy farm incomes fluctuate less from year to year than income of other types of

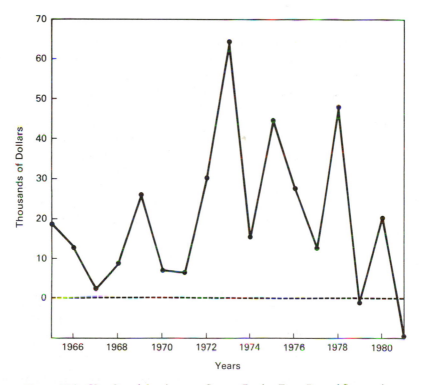

Figure 11.2   Hog farm labor income. *Source:* Purdue Farm Record Summaries.

farms. Risk is especially great on farms that specialize in livestock but do not produce their own feed.

Markets. Market availability for livestock and livestock products varies throughout the United States and also within states. It is crucial to take market availability into consideration when choosing a livestock system for your farm.

What prices are received in your area relative to other areas of the country for the following livestock and livestock products?

Livestock or Livestock Product	Average Price in Your Area for 19——	Comparison with the Major Markets in:	
Cattle	_____	_____	_____
Feeder cattle	_____	_____	_____
Milk	_____	_____	_____
Pork	_____	_____	_____
Broilers	_____	_____	_____
Turkeys	_____	_____	_____
Eggs	_____	_____	_____
Lamb	_____	_____	_____
Wool	_____	_____	_____

Considering the price and cost of production differences in your chart, do you have a relative advantage or disadvantage in producing any of the products?

One good indicator of how competitive product and input markets are for a given livestock enterprise in a chosen geographical area is the amount of that particular type of livestock being produced. If a substantial amount of a particular type of livestock is being produced in your area, it is likely that this type of livestock has a comparative advantage. Conversely, if you observe very little of a particular kind of livestock, be sure to analyze product price, input cost, and typical animal performance in your area compared to others before initiating such an enterprise.

The value of fixed or salvage resources. Many farms have resources such as management, labor, feed, buildings, or equipment that cannot be sold or rented but can be used by livestock. These salvage resources can reduce the cost of livestock production by the amounts shown in the following table and provide for excellent profit opportunities.

Fixed or Salvage Resources	Possible Decrease in Production Costs[1]
Pasture and crop residue	20%–30%
Labor and management	5%–25%
Buildings and equipment	5%–25%

[1]Range in cost reduction is due to difference in resource requirements by type of livestock and system of production.

Even with average management, salvage or fixed resources can usually be profitably sold through livestock. The importance that these resources should have in determining the livestock system depends on their value. The value of fixed resources in the livestock program is determined by the approximate value of inputs they could replace or substitute for if all resources for livestock production are purchased.

Bill Ramirez, who operates a 1,000-acre crop farm, has 13 acres of pasture in the corner of one of his fields. He estimates that the permanent pasture will yield 2 tons of hay equivalent per acre. If rented, this amount of pasture would cost about $40 per acre. Since he has been unable to find anyone in the area to rent the pasture, it must be sold through livestock if it is to be sold. Bill decided not to raise livestock, however, because in his judgment the $520 is not sufficient to offset the management requirements of a small livestock enterprise. Instead, Bill is concentrating his effort on crops. He reasons that the gain from doing a better job on crops will be greater than the gain from using the $520 worth of pasture.

If Bill's farm had been smaller—say, 320 acres—he would likely have had surplus labor and management as well as pasture. In this case, he probably could increase profit by adding a forage-consuming livestock enterprise.

Brad Aid evaluated the fixed and salvage resources on the Christian farm as follows:

45 tons cornstalks at	$ 5/ton	$ 225
96 tons wheat/interseeding at	$10/ton	960
125 tons permanent pasture at	$20/ton	2,500
35 tons woods pasture at	$15/ton	525
500 hours labor[a] at	$ 5/hour	2,500
Barns and existing fence and equipment—annual use value		2,500
Total		$9,210

[a] Table 11.9 shows 2,447 hours of surplus labor based on the hiring of two persons. If livestock were not raised, a second person would be replaced with part-time help and only 500 hours of labor would be unused.

Brad judged that the sale of salvage resources through livestock would likely be profitable. In situations like that of the Christian farm, livestock would make it desirable to hire an additional full-time operator. Brad reasoned that the additional full-time person would have better crop and livestock skills than part-time help, and the improved labor quality would more than offset the effect on crops of competition from the livestock enterprise. In this case, crop efficiency would be as good or better with livestock than it would be without livestock.

Step 2

Choose livestock alternatives that are most likely to be profitable. When considering livestock alternatives, answer the following questions about each.

1. Will it use most of the fixed resources available?
2. Will it be competitive with other geographic areas in terms of resource costs and markets?
3. Will it fit the management skills of the operator?
4. Will it fit the goals and preferences of the owner and operator?
5. Will it fit the capital availability, cash flow, and risk-bearing ability of the farm?
6. Will it use salable feed produced on the farm?
7. Will it gain most of the economies of size (see Chapter 13)?
8. Will it be of sufficient size to generate the income desired?

Brad Aid observed that the highest-value fixed resource is forage. He could use beef cows, feeder cattle, dairy cows, ewes, or lambs to consume the salvage forage. He ruled out sheep and lambs because of difficulty in finding operators skilled in either enterprise and because of his own limited experience with sheep. He also eliminated dairy because a dairy herd would require a great deal of additional investment in buildings and equipment, and there would be a high penalty for stopping production.

Brad decided to consider three beef alternatives:

1. Beef cows, calves sold
2. Beef cows, cows raised
3. Purchased feeder cattle, two groups per year.

After planning sufficient cattle to use all of the salvage forage, Brad then considered keeping additional livestock in order to use labor, buildings, and salable feed. These included:

1. Feeder pigs purchased and fed out
2. Swine, farrow to finish.

Broilers, laying hens, or turkeys were not taken into consideration for two reasons: limited market access and lack of management experience with these enterprises.

Step 3

Budget resource use, costs, and returns of selected livestock alternatives. It is usually most profitable first to choose a livestock enterprise that will use the most valuable fixed salvage resource. After that enterprise has had its claim, livestock should be added to use remaining fixed resources. If management can efficiently handle even more livestock, and if more income is desired, additional livestock should be kept. It is usually desirable to budget two or more livestock alternatives to determine which is most profitable.

Brad Aid developed his first alternative livestock system in the following way:

1. Beef cows (calves sold at 450 pounds) were chosen as the forage consuming live-stock in alternative 1.

2. The number of beef cows required to consume salvage forage was calculated:

$$\frac{301 \text{ tons available (Table 11.6)}}{4.5 \text{ tons}^3/\text{cow (Table 11.7)}} = 67 \text{ cows}$$

3. Feed, labor, and capital required were figured and compared to availability (Table 11.14). As Brad previously calculated, 67 beef cows would use all of the salvage forage. They also would require 100.5 tons of hay and 402 bushels of corn. There would still be 1,711 hours of fixed labor available after the beef cows had had their claim. The Christians would have to invest $78,487 in cattle and feed inventory and $3,988 in equipment. Two of the barns would be used for the beef cows, two remaining being available for other possible enterprises.

4. Low-investment farrow-to-finish swine were planned to use the surplus labor and the two remaining barns.

5. Labor being the most valuable remaining fixed resource, the number of sows that could be kept with the labor available was determined:

$$\frac{1,711 \text{ hours}}{44 \text{ hours/sow and 2 litters}} = 39 \text{ sows}$$

6. Finally, the resources needed for the total alternative 1 livestock program were calculated (Table 11.15). It was found that these requirements would be:

- 8,319 bushels of corn, leaving for sale 23,441 of the 31,760 bushels produced.
- 100.5 tons of salable hay and 311 tons of hay equivalent in the form of pasture. Since there are only 301 tons of salvage pasture available, 10.5 tons of forage that could be used for hay will be added to pasture, increasing total hay requirements to 111 tons. Total hay production is 125 tons, so 14 tons would be available either for sale or for storage to build an inventory to be used in an unfavorable crop year.

---

[3]1.5 tons of hay are excluded from total forage needs because salvage feed would not be used to meet this requirement.

TABLE 11.14 Livestock Resource Requirement Worksheet

Column number	1	2	3	4	5	6	7	8
		Feed Requirements[a]				Labor Require-ment[a]	Capital Requirements[b]	
Livestock Enterprise	No. of units on your farm	Corn equiv.	Corn silage	Hay	Silage pasture		Livestock and feed	Building and equipment
		bu.	tons	tons	tons	hours	$	$
Beef Cows: Calves sold at 450 lbs.	67	402		100.5	301.5	536	78,457	10,988
1. Total required		402		100.5	301.5	536	78,457	10,988
2. Total fixed or salvage resources		0		0	301	2247	0	7,000
3. Salable or purchased resources needed (−) or surplus (+) of fixed resources (2−1)		−402		−100.5	−.5	1711	−78,457	−3,988

[a]Table 11.7
[b]Tables 11.11 and 11.13

TABLE 11.15 Livestock Resource Requirement Worksheet

Column number	1	2	3	4	5	6	7	8
		Feed Requirements[a]				Labor Require-ment[a]	Capital Requirements[b]	
Livestock Enterprise	No. of units on your farm	Corn equiv.	Corn silage	Hay	Silage pasture		Livestock and feed	Building and equipment
		bu.	tons	tons	tons	hours	$	$
Beef cows: Calves sold at 450 lbs.	67	402		100.5	301.5	536	78,457	10,988
Sows, farrow to finish	39	7917			10	1711	23,010	40,560
1. Total required		8319		100.5	311.5	2252	101,467	51,548
2. Total fixed or salvage resources		0		0	301	500	0	14,000
3. Salable or purchased resources needed (−) or surplus (+) of fixed resources (2-1)		−8319		−100.5	−10.5	−1752	−101,467	−$37,548

[a]Table 11.7
[b]Tables 11.11 and 11.13

Labor required was about equal to the 2,247 hours of fixed permanent labor available. Brad scheduled farrowing during the months of December, February, June, and August because farrowing is the highest labor-requirement period for the swine enterprise and a substantial amount of labor is available in those months. Cows will calve in March, when there are 249 hours of permanent labor available for live-stock. Some part-time labor may be needed during planting and harvest to be sure that both crops and livestock are handled efficiently.

Brad's proposed livestock program makes possible the sale of fixed forage, labor, and buildings that could not be sold in any other way and should result in high returns to the fixed resources. Brad budgeted returns above all costs except fixed resources (Table 11.16). He estimated that returns to labor and fixed resources for the beef cows would be $57.67 per cow, or $3863.89 for 67 cows. This figured to be $7.21 per hour of labor.

The Christian farm profit from the cow herd was hindered somewhat because valuable high-quality hay was fed to the cows, and beef cows do not pay good returns to high-value feed. However, this disadvantage was more than overcome by the use of fixed pasture, labor, and barns. Swine, dairy, beef feeders, sheep, and lambs all pay higher returns to high-quality forage than beef cows; it would be wise, therefore, for Brad to budget returns to one or more of these enterprises.

Returns to fixed resources and labor from raising swine were budgeted to be $304.79 per sow, or $11,886.81 to the swine enterprise (Table 11.17).

Returns to fixed resources for both beef and swine would be:

Beef cows	$ 3,863.89
Swine	11,886.81
Total	$15,750.70
Minus 1752 hours labor at $5.00 per hour and 10.5 ton pasture at $20.00 per ton	8,970.00
Return to fixed resources	$ 6,780.70

If livestock were expanded beyond fixed resources, labor, pasture, and buildings would have to be budgeted at full cost.

The next question Brad Aid must answer is "Should the beef cow and swine enterprise be expanded? If beef cows are expanded, it would be necessary to hire more labor and build additional barns. Also, the need for more hay and pasture would result in reduced crop sales. Thus, beef cow costs would increase by the following amount per cow:

Labor	$40.00
Overhead	15.67
Pasture	35.00
Total	$90.67

TABLE 11.16 Income and Costs for Beef Cow Herd Per Cow (Herd Size Under 100 Cows)

Item	Good Commercial Farms		Christian Farm	
A. Income				
1. Market animals	3.15 cwt. at $75.00	$236.25	3.15 cwt. at $75.00	$236.25
2. Cull breeding stock	2.00 cwt. at $45.00	$ 90.00	2.00 cwt. at $45.00	$ 90.00
3. Gross Income		$326.25		$326.25
B. Direct costs				
1. Feed				
a. Corn	6 bu. at $ 3.00	$ 18.00	6 bu. at $ 3.00	$ 18.00
b. Hay	1.5 tons at $30.00	45.00	1.5 tons at $52.00	78.00
c. Pasture	3.5 tons at $10.00	35.00	Fixed	0.00
d. Salvage roughage	1.0 tons at $ 0.00	0.00	Fixed	0.00
e. Protein supplements, salt, minerals	125 lbs. at $ 0.14	17.50	125 lbs. at $ 0.14	17.50
f. Total feed		$115.50		$113.50
2. Veterinary and medicine		7.50		7.50
3. Breeding		10.00		10.00
4. Marketing		6.25		6.25
5. Power, fuel, and equipment repair		8.50		8.50
6. Miscellaneous (bedding, supplies)		5.00		5.00
7. Total direct costs		$152.75		$150.75
8. Income over direct cost		173.50		175.50
C. Overhead expense				
1. Investment overhead		$133.50		$117.83
2. Total labor	8 hrs. at $ 5.00	40.00	Fixed	0.00
3. Total overhead		$173.50		$117.83
D. Total expense		$326.25		$268.58
E. Summary				
1. Net return to management		$ 0.00		$ 57.67
2. Net return to labor and management				
a. Total		40.00		57.67
b. Per hour		5.00		7.21

TABLE 11.17 Income and Costs for Farrow-to-Finish Hog Production—Confinement Systems [a]

Item	Good Commercial Farms			Christian Farm		
A. Income						
1. Market animals	31.900 cwt. at $51.00		$1,627.00	31.900 cwt. at $51.00		$1,627.00
2. Breeders	2.125 cwt. at $44.00		$ 93.50	2.125 cwt. at $44.00		$ 93.50
3. Gross income			$1,720.50			$1,720.50
B. Direct costs						
1. Feed						
a. Corn	203 bu. at $ 3.00		$ 609.00	203 bu. at $ 3.00		$ 609.00
b. Pasture (hay equivalent)	$\frac{1}{4}$ ton at $30.00		7.50	$\frac{1}{4}$ ton at $30.00		7.50
c. Purchased feed	2,500 lbs. at $ 0.16		400.00	2,500 lbs.at $ 0.16		400.00
d. Total feed			$1,016.50			$1,016.50
2. Veterinary and medicine			25.00			25.00
3. Boar depreciation			15.00			15.00
4. Marketing			31.00			31.00
5. Power, fuel, and equipment repair			60.00			60.00
6. Miscellaneous (bedding, supplies)			26.00			26.00
7. Total direct costs			$1,173.50			$1,173.50
8. Income over direct cost			$547.00			547.00
C. Overhead expense						
1. Investment overhead			$269.00	Fixed		$242.21
2. Total labor	44 hrs. at $ 5.00		220.00			0.00
3. Total overhead			$ 489.00			$ 242.21
D. Total expense			$1,662.50			$1,415.71
E. Summary						
1. Net return to management			$ 58.00			$ 304.79
2. Returns to labor and management						
a. Total			278.00			304.79
b. Per hour			6.32			6.93

[a]Low investment facilities; per sow and 2 litters fed out.

Since beef cows were returning only $57.67 per cow while costs would increase $90.67 per cow, additional beef cows would lose $33.00 each.

Expanding the swine enterprise further would require an additional $246.79 per sow over the previous budget. The budgeted return was $304.79 per sow, so an increased cost of $246.79 would result in reducing net returns to $58.00 per added sow. In the judgment of Brad and the Christians, $58.00 would not be adequate to warrant the additional investment necessary for a swine enterprise larger than 39 sows. Therefore, it was decided that livestock alternative 1 would be 67 beef cows and 39 sows. If used, this livestock program would increase the Christians' farm's net returns by $6,780.70 per year.

Additional alternatives should be considered. A logical possibility is the substitution of different types of beef-feeding enterprises for the beef cows.

Develop one other livestock alternative for the Christian farm and budget the resource use and net income from this alternative.

Step 4

Choose a livestock system. On the basis of budgets prepared in step 3, choose a livestock system that adds the most to profits and other farm goals.

Step 5

Integrate the crop and livestock systems. The added livestock system may require changes in the cropping system to provide needed resources. For example, a swine enterprise may require straw and a place to spread manure during the cropping season. Hence, it may be desirable to plant some wheat on a farm that was previously devoted to continuous row crops. The manager must carefully budget changes in profit to the crop operation to be sure that the loss from changing crops is adequately offset by the profits from livestock.

The budgeting procedure for role 2 livestock enterprises is the same as was used for the Christian farm, but there would be fewer fixed or salvage resources with low value.

In summary, livestock can be a profitable addition to the farm business, especially if outstanding livestock-management ability is available or if fixed resources can be used.

Income budgets for the total farm are discussed in Chapter 12.

DISCUSSION QUESTIONS

1. What are the important factors that determine whether or not a manager should raise livestock?

2. What are two different roles that livestock might play in a farm business? Which role requires the higher level of livestock-management ability?

3. What are the steps for planning a livestock enterprise for a farm business?

4. How much impact does the level of management have on the profitability of livestock? Secure some farm-record summary data for your area that will illustrate the effect of management differences.

5. Discuss the production, marketing, and buying management requirements for different kinds of livestock.

6. Under what farm circumstances do low-investment livestock production systems fit? High-investment systems?

7. What are the most important fixed resources that might be sold through livestock? Why are these resources fixed? How do fixed resources affect the profitability of the livestock enterprise?

8. Does livestock require more or less capital to provide a full-time job than farming owned land? Than farming rented land? How much capital is required to provide a full-time job with various kinds of livestock?

9. Why is continuity so important with a livestock enterprise? Which kinds of livestock and systems of production have the least penalty for stopping production? Which have the highest?

10. Are livestock-farm incomes more or less variable than crop-farm incomes? Which kinds of livestock farms have the greatest variability? The lowest variability?

11. Which kind of livestock has the most competitive markets in your area? Explain.

12. List the important considerations for changing a livestock program for a farm.

13. What kinds of returns per unit and per full-time worker do various kinds of livestock usually pay in your area?

14. How might the selection of a livestock program affect the cropping program?

RELATED READINGS

"Farm Planning and Financial Management", ID-68. Purdue University, Cooperative Extension Service. West Lafayette, Ind., 1980.

HARSH, STEPHEN B., LARRY J. CONNOR, and GERALD D. SCHWAB. *Managing the Farm Business,* chaps. 9–10. Englewood Cliffs, N.J.: Prentice-Hall, 1981.

HEDGES, TRIMBLE R. *Farm Management Decisions,* chaps. 15–17. Englewood Cliffs, N.J.: Prentice-Hall, 1963.

HERBST, J. H. *Farm Management Principles, Budgets, Plans,* (6th ed.) chap. 6–7. Champaign, Ill.: Stipes Publishing Company, 1983.

KAY, RONALD D. *Farm Management,* chaps. 4–5. New York: McGraw-Hill, 1981.

MISSOURI FARM MANAGEMENT STAFF. *Missouri Farm Planning Handbook,* Manual 75. Columbia, Mo.: University of Missouri—Columbia, 1981.

Total Farm Budgeting

12

Budgets for planning cropping and livestock programs were presented in the two preceding chapters. In this chapter these crop and livestock budgets are integrated into a total farm budget for the Christian farm. The procedure is similar to the one used for block budgeting in Chapter 8. Budget forms that will be helpful in preparing total farm budgets are presented.

Brad Aid budgeted farm profit, cash flow, capital investment, and capital borrowing needs for the Christian farm. The procedures and forms discussed here were helpful to Brad for making his estimates.

> Study the procedure that Brad used and follow this procedure to estimate farm profit and cash flow for a farm with which you are familiar.

PROCEDURE

Brad used six worksheets to calculate profit, cash flow, investment, and borrowing required on the Christian farm.

1. On worksheet 1 (Figure 12.1) Brad listed (from Chapter 10):
   a. Acres of each crop on each soil type
   b. Average yields
   c. Amount of production
   d. Income over direct cost per acre.
   He then calculated income over direct cost for each crop on each soil in column 5 and totaled these on line 21.

2. On worksheet 2 (Figure 12.2) Brad listed (from Chapter 11):
   a. Feed requirements
   b. Labor requirements
   c. Capital requirements
   d. Income over direct cost per unit.
   Next Brad calculated total requirements for feed, labor, and capital and total income over direct costs (line 1). Note that salable feed is included as a cost to livestock because it is counted as a receipt to crops.

Worksheet I. Cropping System

Crop	1 Acres[a]	2 Average yield[a]	3 Production	4 Income over direct cost[b] Per acre[b]	5 Income over direct cost[b] Total (1x4)
1. Corn — Ragsdale and Reesville soil	98	140 bu.	13,720 bu.	$ 249.20	$34,421.60
2. Soybeans — Ragsdale and Reesville soil	98	45 bu.	4,410 bu.	210.40	20,619.20
3. Corn — Genesee soil	94	100 bu.	9,400 bu.	168.00	15,792.00
4. Corn — Fox soil	96	90 bu.	8,640 bu.	153.20	14,707.20
5. Soybeans — Fox soil	96	34 bu.	3,264 bu.	159.50	15,312.00
6. Wheat — Fox soil	96	53 bu.	5,088 bu.	115.75	11,112.00
7. Straw — Fox soil	96	1 ton	96 tons	Bedding[c]	—
8. Hay — Ockley and Russell soil	41.5	3 tons	125 tons	135.00	5,602.50
9. Pasture — Ockley and Russell soil	41.5	3 tons	125 tons	Salvage[d]	—
10. Woods pasture	35	1 ton	35 tons	Salvage[d]	—
11. Wheat interseeding	96	1 ton	96 tons	Salvage[d]	—
12. Corn stalks	150	0.3	45 tons	Salvage[d]	—
13.					
14.					
15.					
16.					
17.					
18.					
19.					
20. Woods, waste, and farmstead	34.0				
21. Total	730.0				$107,566.50

[a]See Chapter 10.

[b]See Tables 10.4–10.9, line 3 minus line 9. Also refer to block budgeting in Chapter 8.

[c]Livestock charged for cost of raking, baling and transporting straw.

[d]Cost of fertilizing, seeding, and maintaining salvage feed acreage assumed equal to the reduction in fertilizer costs resulting from the use of livestock waste.

Figure 12.1 Worksheet 1: Cropping system.

3. On worksheet 3 (Figure 12.3) Brad listed all of the capital items the farm would have after it is in operation, and he summarized assets, debts, and net worth on a balance sheet.

4. Brad computed on worksheet 4 (Figure 12.4) annual interest and principal payments for money borrowed to add machinery, livestock, and equipment to the Christian farm.

5. On worksheet 5 (Figure 12.5) Brad computed operating returns and total returns by drawing information from worksheets 1 through 4.

6. Brad computed cash flow on worksheet 6 (Figure 12.6).

Worksheet 2: Livesock System

Column number	1	2	3	4	5	6	7	8	9	10	11
Livestock enterprise	Number of Units on Your Farm	Feed Requirements[a]				Labor[a] (hours)	Capital Requirements[b]			Income over Direct Cost/Unit[c]	Total Income over Direct Cost
		Corn Equiv. (bu.)	Corn Silage (tons)	Hay (tons)	Salvage Pasture (tons)		Livestock and Feed	Building	Equipment		
Beef cows: calves sold	67	402		101	301.5	536	$78,457	$6,499	$4,489	$175.50	$11,758.50
Sows, farrow to finish	39	7,917			10.0	1,716	23,010	20,865	19,695	547.00	21,333.00
1. Total		8,319		100.5	311.5	2,252	$101,467	$27,364	$24,184		$33,091.50
2. Total resources available		31,760		125	301.0			$14,000			
3. Resources needed (−) or surplus (+)		23,441		24.0	−10.5		−$101,467	−$13,364	−$24,184		

aTable 11.7
bTables 11.11 and 11.13
cTables 11.16 and 11.17

Figure 12.2 Worksheet 2: Livestock system.

Worksheet 3: Projected Investment and Balance Sheet after Plan is in Operation

A. Beginning investment

1. Field machinery and equipment ($ _300_ /tillable acre)	$185,850
2. Livestock equipment (Worksheet 2, col. 9, line 3)	24,184
3. Total machinery and equipment (lines 1 + 2)	$ 210,034
4. Improvements (buildings, fences, etc.)	
a. Existing[a]	$50,000
b. Additions Worksheet 2, col. 8, line 3	13,364
5. Land (owned, excluding improvements) 730 acres at $1,300	949,000
6. Capital for livestock and feed (Worksheet 2, col. 7, line 3)	101,467
7. Total investment (lines 3 + 4a + 4b + 5 + 6)	$1,323,865

B. Balance sheet

Assets (total value of what you own)

1. Current (cash, feed, market livestock, etc.)	$31,117
2. Intermediate (machinery, equipment, breeding livestock)	280,384
3. Long-term (land, buildings)	1,012,364
4. Total (lines 1 + 2 + 3)	$1,323,865

Liabilities (total amount you owe)

5. Current (operating loans)	$31,117
6. Intermediate (1-10 years)	293,748
7. Long-term (11 + years)	0
8. Total (lines 5 + 6 + 7)	$324,865
9. Net worth (line 4 − line 8)	$999,000

[a]For an owner operator the farmhouse is not included but for the Christian farm, since it is a labor benefit, the farmhouse is included.

Figure 12.3   Worksheet 3: Projected investment and balance sheet after plan is in operation.

FARM PROFIT

Brad projects an annual operating profit of $25,894 and a total profit of $65,610 (worksheet 5). Operating return on investment would be 4.4% and total return 7.4% before income tax (worksheet 5). Brad projects a positive cash flow of $18,814 before income tax (worksheet 6).

INVESTMENT AND DEBT

Brad estimated total capital investment to be $1,323,865 (worksheet 3). The Christians own the farm debt-free but would have to borrow money for operating capital, machinery, livestock equipment, and added livestock buildings. Brad has projected

Worksheet 4: Interest and Debt Principal Repayment.

A. Existing debt		Amount Outstanding	Average Annual Interest	Average Annual Principal Payment
Type of Loan				
1. Current (operating)		$ 0	$	
2. Intermediate (1–9 years)		0		
3. Long-term (10 + years)		0		
4. Total		$ 0	$	$

	1 Amount of Loan	2 Rate	3 Average Amount	4 Years to Repay	5 Annual Principal Payment
B. Additional debt		Annual Interest[a]			
Type of Loan					
5. Current (operating)	$ 31,117	10%	$ 3,111.70		
6. Intermediate (1–9 years)	293,748	10%	29,374.80	8	$ 36,719 (col. 1 ÷ col. 4)
7. Long-term (10 + years)		%			
8. Total (lines 5 + 6 + 7)			$ 32,486.50		$ 36,719
9. Total: existing + additional (line 4 + line 8)			$ 32,486.50		$ 36,719

[a]Interest rate should be multiplied by average amount of loan for planning period for which budget is preprared. In this case, Brad evaluated the plan the first year of operation and calculated interest for the initial amount of the loan.

Figure 12.4 Worksheet 4: Interest and principal repayment.

that $31,117 operating capital will be required on a continuing basis for livestock, plus an additional $293,748 for machinery, equipment, and buildings (worksheet 3). The principal on the operating capital can be renewed each year and need not be repaid. The other items must be repaid over eight years, with 10% of the principal due each year (worksheet 5). Crop operating capital requirements will be for less than one year. The interest cost for these loans has been included as a direct cost for crops.

INCOME VARIABILITY

It is sometimes desirable to project farm earnings for a range of prices and yields rather than the average alone. This gives the owner, operator, and manager insight into the range of income that might be available from the farm. Also, this kind of analysis can be helpful for determining if cash-flow problems are likely to be encountered.

Table 12.1 presents an analysis of returns to the Christian farm with cash receipts 10% higher than projected and 10% lower than projected.

A 10% change in prices or yields would change farm profit by $23,302. The im-

A. Income over Direct Costs

    1. Crops
      (Worksheet 1, col. 5, line 21) $107,566.50

    2. Livestock
      (Worksheet 2, col. 11, line 1)   33,091.50

    3. Total
      (lines 1 + 2) $ 140,658.00

B. Other cash costs and net cash income

    4. Hired labor and management $ 35,000

    5. Cash rent   0

    6. Land property tax and land maintenance   7,935

    7. Insurance
      (0.5% of Worksheet 3, part A, lines 3 + 4 + 6)   1,874

    8. Building repairs
      (2% of Worksheet 3, part A, line 4)   1,267

    9. Building and inventory property tax
      (1% of Worksheet 3, part A, lines 3 + 4 + 6)   3,749

    10. Miscellaneous
      (2% of line 3)   2,813

    11. Interest
      (Worksheet 4, line 9)   32,487

    12. Total other
      (lines 4 + 5 + 6 + 7 + 8 + 9 + 10 + 11)   85,125

    13. Net cash income
      (line 3 − line 12) $ 55,533

C. Depreciation

    14. Buildings
      (7% of Worksheet 3, part A, lines 4a and 4b) $ 4,435

    15. Machinery
      (12% of Worksheet 3, part A, line 3)   25,204

    16. Total depreciation
      (line 14 + 15) $ 29,639

D. Estimated change in farm value

    17. Annual change in farm value
      (estimated to be +3 % of total farm assets) $ 39,716

E. Returns (before tax)

	Operating Returns	Total Returns
18. Return to operator and labor and equity (line 13 − line 16)	$ 25,894	$ 65,610
19. Operator labor and management charge[a]	0	0
20. Return to equity (line 18 + line 19)	$ 25,894	$ 65,610
21. Rate earned on equity (line 20 ÷ Worksheet 3, part B, line 9)	2.6%	6.6%
22. Return to total investment (lines 11 + 18)	$ 58,381	$ 98,097
23. Rate earned on total investment (line 22 ÷ Worksheet 3, part A, line 7)	4.4%	7.4%
24. Return to operators labor (line 18 − ___% of worksheet 3, part B, line 9)	—	

[a]In this situation labor and management are cash costs on line 4.

Figure 12.5 Worksheet 5: Projected income.

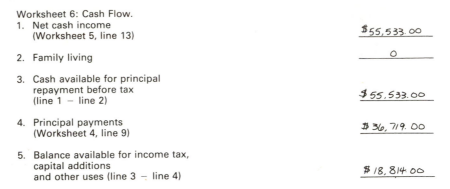

Worksheet 6: Cash Flow.
1. Net cash income
   (Worksheet 5, line 13) $55,533.00

2. Family living   0

3. Cash available for principal
   repayment before tax
   (line 1 — line 2) $55,533.00

4. Principal payments
   (Worksheet 4, line 9) $36,719.00

5. Balance available for income tax,
   capital additions
   and other uses (line 3 — line 4) $18,814.00

Figure 12.6 Worksheet 6: Projected Cash flow.

TABLE 12.1 Christian Farm Sales

Product	Amount	Price	Gross Returns
Corn	23,441 bu.	$ 3.00	$ 70,323
Soybeans	7,674 bu.	7.00	53,718
Wheat	5,088 bu.	3.75	19,080
Hay	13.5 tons	70.00	945
Cattle			
Cull cows	134 cwt.	45.00	6,030
Calves	211 cwt.	75.00	15,825
Hogs			
Cull sows	83 cwt.	44.00	3,652
Hogs	1,244 cwt.	51.00	63,444
Total returns, average prices			$233,017
Prices or production 10% above average			$256,319
Prices or production 10% below average			$209,715

pact of this $23,302 change on farm profit, return on investment, and cash flow is calculated in Table 12.2.

Brad reviewed with the Christians the impact of varying prices and yields on income and cash flow. This analysis was helpful because it warned the Christians about possible income variations before they occurred, thus enabling Brad to keep their confidence in bad years when farm income was below Brad's long-term average budget. The Christians were now aware that there could be a negative cash flow of −$4,488 even if prices or production fell to 10% below average. After reviewing the farm and budget plans, the Christians and Brad Aid agreed that the plan, as presented should be implemented.

TABLE 12.2   Impact of 10% Variation in Prices or Production, Christian Farm

	Average Prices	Prices or Production 10% Below Average	Prices or Production 10% Above Average
Net operating income	25,894	2,592	49,196
(a) Return to total investment (operating)	$58,381	$35,079	$81,683
(b) Rate earned on total investment (operating)	4.4%	2.6%	6.2%
Balance available for income taxes, capital additions, and other uses	$18,814	−$ 4,488	$42,116

COMPUTER PROGRAM FOR BUDGETING AND FARM PLANNING

Computer budgets are especially useful for projecting farm income and cash flow and can eliminate many of the hand calculations followed in preparing the Christian budgets.[1]

DISCUSSION QUESTIONS

1. What is income over direct cost? Give examples for both crops and livestock.
2. What are indirect costs? Give examples.
3. Compute profit and cash flow for a hypothetical farm.
4. How would profit and cash flow vary in a good or bad year? Budget the variability.

RELATED READINGS

CASTLE, EMERY N., MANNING H. BECKER, and FREDRICK J. SMITH. *Farm Business Management,* chap. 5. New York: Macmillan Company, 1972.

FORSTER, LYNN D., and BERNARD L. ERVEN. *Foundations for Managing the Farm Business,* chaps. 5–7. Columbus, Ohio: Grid Publishing Company, 1981.

HERBST, J. H. *Farm Management Principles, Budgets, Plans,* chap. 4. Champaign, Ill.: Stipes Publishing Co., 1983.

KAY, RONALD D. *Farm Management: Planning, Control, and Implementation,* chaps. 5–6. New York: McGraw-Hill, 1981.

OSBORN, DONALD D., and KENNETH C. SCHNEEBERGER. *Modern Agricultural Management,* chap. 12. Reston, Va.: Reston Publishing Co., 1983.

[1]One such model is Farm Business and Financial Management Long Range Average Plan, Model C-4 (West Lafayette, Ind.: Department of Agricultural Economics, Purdue University).

How Big Should
the Farm Business Be?

13

SIZE AND PROFIT

Farm size and growth decisions are some of the most important decisions that farmers make. Profits usually increase as the size of a small farm is increased because modern equipment ownership or fixed costs are spread over more units, the operator's labor and management are more fully used, resources are purchased for lower prices, products are sold for higher prices, and profit per unit is multiplied by more units. However, if a small farm is losing money, an increase in farm size may multiply a loss per unit times more units. The greater the volume, the larger the loss. These negative profit margins are often caused by low production efficiency or adverse economic conditions.

Some farmers can make money on a small or moderate-size unit, but when they expand, efficiency declines, costs increase, and profit decreases. For growth to be profitable, production efficiency must first be attained and then maintained as size is increased.

A study of dairy farmers near Louisville, Kentucky, shows the typical relationship found with efficiency, size, and profit (Figure 13.1, Table 13.1). When all costs were considered (including a payment for the operators' labor and interest on investment), the large efficient farms made more money than small efficient farms. But the large least efficient farms lost more money than the small least efficient farms.

TABLE 13.1 Returns to Management with Different-Size Dairy Herds and Three Levels of Management (Louisville Milkshed)

Number of cows	Returns to Management (Total Receipts Minus Total Costs)		
	Least Efficient Producers	Average Producers	Most Efficient Producers
20	−$ 5,769	−$3,780	$ 8,037
30	− 5,067	− 1,161	14,529
40	− 6,210	− 369	19,803
50	− 8,514	− 1,104	24,348
60	− 11,325	− 1,650	27,984
70	− 14,874	− 5,037	30,414

Source: "Factors Affecting Cost of Producing Grade A Milk in the Louisville Milkshed," Research Bulletin No. 767 (Lafayette, Ind.: Purdue University Agricultural Experiment Station, November 1963). Costs and returns have been updated.

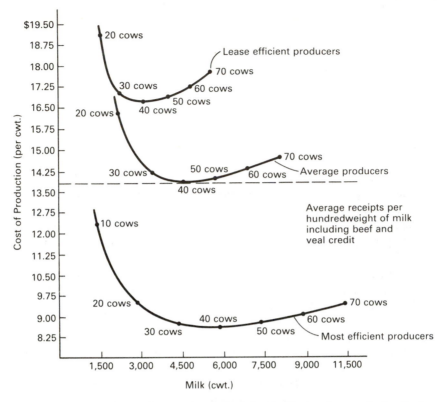

Figure 13.1 Average cost per hundredweight of milk at various production levels and herd sizes: most efficient, average, and least efficient producers, Louisville milkshed.

FACTORS THAT DETERMINE THE "BEST" SIZE

1. Goals

Two young farmers were discussing their goals. One said, "I would like to make a comfortable living farming, but I also would like to have plenty of time to become involved in community activities, to sit by the fire in the winter, and to take vacations and do things with my family." The other farmer said, "I would like to see how far I can take this business—I plan to increase size as long as I can make money." If everything except goals is the same for these two farmers, their "best" sizes would be different. Although increasing size may generate more profit, it often results in greater risk, stress, and income variability, less cash for personal use, and less time for doing things outside of the farm business. However, once a farmer achieves a desired size and business growth stops, more cash and leisure time may be available on a large farm than on a small one.

2. Management Ability

If management skill is not above average, increasing farm size may result in less profit. On a one-operator farm, it is crucial to have the skill to produce crops and/or livestock efficiently. It is also necessary to have the ability to gain control of resources, and it is helpful to have the know-how to purchase resources at below-average prices and to market crops and livestock at above-average prices. As size increases beyond one operator, workers with livestock and crop-production skills may be hired. Buying and selling ability may be hired as well. The key abilities on larger units are people management, financial management, resource acquisition, and business strategy development. Some operators can be very successful when working by themselves, but, as they add more workers, they may not have the personnel and financial management skills to be successful.

> Art Adams and Bill Brown had similar farm and family situations. They each provided nearly all the labor and management for their 320-acre crop-livestock farms. They each owned 160 acres (with an $80,000 mortgage) and rented 160 acres. They were 38 years old and had been farming over fifteen years. Adams and Brown borrowed heavily to get their farms to their present stages, but they now were only about 33% in debt, compared to 80% when they started farming. They each had a net worth of about $200,000, compared to $10,000 when they started farming. Their children were in high school, and they had relatively high family living expenses.
>
> Adams and Brown both thought that this would be an appropriate time to expand their crops and livestock.
>
> Art Adams rented an additional 320 acres, hired another employee, and doubled his cattle-feeding enterprise. Art was better with crops than with livestock, so he hired someone who was good with cattle. The employee was also good at buying and selling cattle, which was one of Art's weak points. Art Adams developed a systematic plan and was able to obtain sufficient credit. He was skillful at supervising people, and the new assistant operator enjoyed working for Art. The Adams farm income increased 75%.
>
> Bill Brown observed Art's expansion and decided to follow suit. Bill lacked skill in acquiring resources, but he managed to rent an additional 320 acres. It was not very productive land, and he paid a high price for rent. When Bill asked for credit, he did not have a well-developed plan and was able to obtain only two-thirds of the amount he needed. He hired an assistant operator who was good with crops but not interested in cattle. Bill liked crops too. Both Bill and the assistant operator wanted to work on crops. The cattle enterprise, which had been doubled, was neglected. Bill had difficulty in assigning jobs to his assistant. Labor efficiency was low, and the assistant operator was frustrated. Bill did not have enough money to buy needed equipment, and some of the crops were planted late. Bill did not enjoy working with an assistant. After two years, farm income was less than half of what it had been before Bill expanded.

Both Adams and Brown had the ability to manage one-operator units. Adams had the ability to expand, but Brown did not.

3. Living Cost per Unit of Production

Many farms have difficulty increasing net worth because family living expense consumes the farm earnings. These farms can often increase net worth much faster if they can find some way to increase the business size beyond that required to generate a satisfactory living income.

For example, a crop farmer has a gross income of $300 per acre, costs of $250 per acre, and family living expenses of $10,000 per year. As long as the farm is only 200 acres, the farmer cannot generate net worth. As acreage increases, annual net worth increases rapidly (Table 13.2).

4. Size-Cost-Profit Relationships

Fixed and indivisible resources.   Entering the farming business or starting a particular enterprise may require a large input of certain resources. Average production costs are usually reduced if these fixed or "lumpy" resources are spread over many units.

Operators may decide that if they are going to farm, they must spend all their time on the farm. Labor and management costs per unit of production decline until they are fully employed. Likewise, tractors, buildings, and other durables have the same total fixed cost regardless of the extent to which they are needed. Fixed cost per unit of production declines until they are fully used.

Larger machines, buildings, and equipment.   Larger machines, buildings, and equipment may result in lower production costs per unit because they save labor and management. Studies of crop field machinery have shown that larger machinery results in about the same machinery cost per acre as does small machinery *if it is operated the same number of hours*. Since the large machinery covers more acres per hour and there is only one operator on both large and small machinery, labor cost per acre is less with larger machinery. But to operate large machinery the

TABLE 13.2   Net Worth Increase with Different-Size Crop Farms (Hypothetical)

Acres	Gross Income per Acre	Cost per Acre	Total Net Income	Family Living Expenses	Annual Net Worth Change before Taxes
200	$300	$250	$10,000	$10,000	$ 0
300	300	240	18,000	10,000	8,000
400	300	230	28,000	10,000	18,000
800	300	230	56,000	10,000	46,000
1,000	300	230	70,000	10,000	60,000

same number of hours as small machinery, size or volume must be increased. Farmers who can attain the larger size with big machinery have a lower cost per acre because of reduced labor costs.

Much of crop and livestock mechanization results in lower costs for larger operations.

Prices of resources and products.   Even though farmers generally have little control over the price they pay for inputs or the prices they receive for products, larger farms can often buy and sell at slightly more advantageous prices. These small differences can have a major effect on profits. Crop-farm summaries for a Midwestern state showed a return to the operators' labor and management of 25 cents per bushel of corn. A 10% decrease in prices paid for inputs because of volume purchases would increase profit by 10 cents per bushel. A 5% increase in selling price (because large volumes attract more buyers) would result in an increase of 15 cents per bushel. These small percentage gains from buying and selling would result in doubled returns (from 25 cents to 50 cents per bushel) to the operators' labor and management.

Smaller farms can sometimes gain buying and selling advantages through cooperating and grouping the purchases and sales of several farms.

5. Tax Considerations

Farmers who operate growing farms can delay paying income taxes, especially if they report on the cash basis.

> Paul and Betty Burtz farm 500 acres and have a taxable income of $25,000 per year. They have set a goal of renting 100 additional acres each year for the next several years. For each 100 acres added, expenses are increased for the year the land is rented, but the crops are sold the following year. Costs are $250 per acre, or $25,000 for each added 100 acres. As long as the Burtzes' taxable income is $25,000, it is entirely offset by the "growth" expenses, and no income tax is paid.
>
> Of course, when they stop growing, income on the larger unit will be higher than for the smaller acreage. Income taxes will be higher too. In the meantime, they have the use of delayed tax money for their farm operation.

6. Price Level

During periods of relatively high and rising farm-product prices, large farms generally make much higher incomes than do small farms. During times of more stable or declining farm-product prices, farms that can control costs through crop and livestock efficiency make high returns.

Farms that are large and have high efficiency make good incomes most of the time (Table 13.3). Size and volume are most beneficial when farm-product prices are high relative to costs.

TABLE 13.3 Comparison of Swine-Enterprise Profit for Various Sizes and Efficiency Levels

Enterprise Size, No. 220 lb. Hogs Produced	Feed Cost (per cwt. gain)	Other Costs (per cwt. gain)	Total Cost (per cwt. gain)	Hog Price	Profit (per cwt.)	Total Profit
A. Big but not good; 3,000 hogs produced	$33.00	$17.00	$50.00	$55.00	$ 5.00	$33,000
				50.00	0	0
				45.00	− 5.00	−$33,000
B. Small but good; 700 hogs produced	28.00	15.00	43.00	55.00	12.00	18,480
				50.00	7.00	10,780
				45.00	2.00	3,080
C. Big and good; 3,000 hogs produced	28.00	15.00	43.00	55.00	12.00	79,200
				50.00	7.00	46,200
				45.00	2.00	13,200

7. Inflation and Interest

The relationship between interest rate and inflation is important to farms operating with substantial amounts of borrowed capital, especially because the capital requirement for farming is large. During the 1970s, the inflation rate was nearly as high as the interest rate. The value of farm assets purchased with borrowed money often increased faster than interest costs. Thus the ownership of land, buildings, and machinery was often "free." Beginning in the 1980s, interest became much higher than inflation. As a result, the cost of owning land, buildings, and machinery increased, while the value of these assets declined. Rapid growth tended to be highly profitable during the early 1970s and highly unprofitable during the early 1980s.

HOW BIG?

Minimum Size

Ivan Itus read in a farm magazine that it is necessary to operate 600 acres in his area in order to be competitive. Yet Ivan is making a good living on 80 acres. Ivan has three characteristics that were not considered in the article.

First, Ivan's living costs are low. He enjoys living on the farm so much that he is willing to forego trading cars often and taking expensive vacations. He is talented and can repair most equipment and appliances. He and his wife have a garden to help reduce food costs. Their children are grown and live away from home.

Second, Ivan enjoys farm work so much that he is willing to accept a lower wage. Ivan receives about half as much per hour of work as he would make in an off-farm job, but he works more hours and pays less in taxes. Finally, Ivan owns his 80 acres, including his house. He has no house or land rental payments. Ivan and his wife are able to save money each year after living expenses even though they farm only 80 acres and have a small livestock enterprise.

In contrast, Pete Begin and his wife Sally are starting farming and have rented a 300-acre unit. Pete has no capital, but his father cosigned notes to help him get started.

In budgeting, Pete determined that he can make $40 per acre, or $12,000 per year after all costs. Pete and Sally's friends are making over $18,000 in nonfarm jobs. Both Pete and Sally would like to live at a level comparable to that of their friends. Also, they would like to save money to become independent from Pete's father. The Begins must have a larger unit to cover their living and savings needs, and the 600 acres in the magazine article is probably correct for them.

Farmers who have land and buildings that are completely or nearly debt-free, who are willing to work for a low wage, and who keep living costs down can get along on a small unit.

Farmers who would like an income comparable to that of workers in nonfarm jobs and who must rent their land and buildings or who are heavily in debt for their farm must be at least large enough to gain most of the economies of size. Beyond this, they should be of such a size that profit per unit is multiplied by sufficient units to generate the income needed for living, debt payment, savings, and business growth.

The size of enterprise and farm needed to gain most of the economies of size varies by the individual situation and region and tends to change (usually increase) over time. Enterprise sizes in the Midwest, where most of the economies are gained, are shown in Table 13.4 and may be used for comparison.

Maximum Size

The maximum size of a farm depends largely on goals, management ability, and risk tolerance.

A young man who was starting to farm with few resources set a goal of owning and operating 1,000 acres. He was interested in the income, but he also wanted to achieve this size as a personal accomplishment. He first expanded his rental acreage and then began purchasing land. Land values increased, and his net worth increased rapidly. He could have operated 200 owned and 400 rented acres with a relatively high income and low risk. However, his original goal was so important to him that he continued to buy land with high indebtedness and substantial risk.

During this expansion he was able to keep crop yields relatively high and costs low. He worked long days and spent a minimum amount of money on family living

TABLE 13.4 Size-Cost Relationships for Midwest Farm Enterprises[a]

Enterprise	Size at Which Most Economies Are Gained	Near Minimum-Cost Size	Your Present Size	Size Being Considered
Sows, farrow to finish				
High investment	100	200	—————	—————
Low investment	45	90	—————	—————
Dairy cows	45	200	—————	—————
Beef cows	300[b]	600[b]	—————	—————
Feeder cattle fed per year	300	1,500	—————	—————
Feeder pigs fed per year	1,500	4,500	—————	—————
Crop acres	500	1,200	—————	—————
Employees	1–2	2–3	—————	—————
Productive man-work units	300–600	600–1,000	—————	—————

[a]Sizes are based on the judgments of the author and several farm management extension specialists. Economies of size are affected by the particular farm situation, the people and resources involved, changing technology, and markets for inputs and farm products. These relationships should be adapted for the individual farm situation, geographic area, and changes in technology and market conditions.

[b]If low cost feed is available, any size enterprise that uses the low cost feed is economical.

in the early years. In a period of high interest rates and declining farm-product prices, he had serious financial difficulties. Nevertheless, this farmer is satisfied because he is pursuing the goals he desires and he has the management skills to handle a large operation and the ability to carry the tremendous risk associated with adverse prices or weather. To him, achieving his goal is worth the risk of bankruptcy.

Most operators would not have the desire or ability to manage such a rapidly growing and highly levered farm.

Return to the operator for managing large farms has been increasing (Figure 13.2). The combination of technology, trained people, product prices, and input costs may have resulted in this higher payoff to larger farms.

There is a size for each operator, however, beyond which efficiency declines, costs increase, and income declines. It *is* possible for a farm to be too big.

Optimum Size and Rate of Growth

The "best" size of a farm is one that best serves the goals of the operator and best fits the operator's abilities. It is usually important to be large enough so that economies of size are gained, costs are competitive, and earnings provide a comfortable income for the family. It is possible to grow so large that efficiencies are lost and profit declines. It is possible to grow so fast with borrowed money that the risk of bankruptcy becomes high.

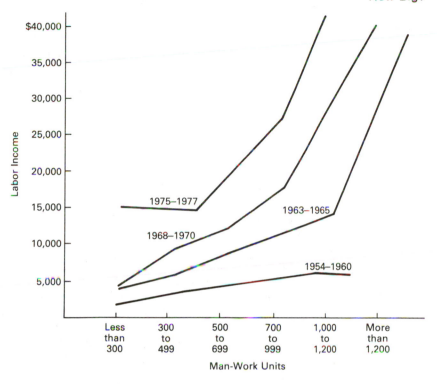

Figure 13.2 Relationship between size of farm measured in man-work units and labor income. *Source:* Indiana Farm Account Keepers, Department of Agricultural Economics, Purdue University, West Lafayette, Indiana.

As new technologies evolve, the size at which most of the economies are gained becomes larger. It is therefore necessary for farms to grow in order to maintain real income.

During a period of rapid growth, efficiency often declines until the operator can get all of the bugs out of the new system of operation and get on top of the more complex larger unit. It is desirable to have some excess cash reserves during a growth period.

An outstanding livestock producer doubled the size of his operation. The new buildings he built did not operate well during the initial expansion period. The buildings had to be modified to improve livestock performance. Breeding stock saved for the expansion was not of as good quality as the usual standard. As a result of these problems and other management factors, costs of production increased drastically the first year after expansion, but by the third year efficiency and costs were back to pre-expansion standards. Thus, during an expansion period, it is wise to have some financial reserve in savings or borrowing capacity to cover unexpected operating and investment costs.

HOW TO GROW

Growth is most likely to be profitable in enterprises where excellent management has been demonstrated. Operators who have been consistently above average in livestock efficiency but below average in crop efficiency, for example, should probably grow by increasing livestock. Areas of growth should capitalize on management strengths such as buying ability, marketing skills, and personnel and financial management know-how.

Growth in enterprises that more fully utilize fixed resources is likely to be profitable if the fixed resources are an important part of the cost of production of that enterprise. Suppose an operator has large amounts of low-quality forage with no market. There is likely to be a high return to selling this forage through beef cows because the forage is "free" and because forage makes up about 50% of total cost in the beef-cow enterprise.

Growth is likely to be more profitable in enterprises in which increased size will result in reduced cost per unit of production. For example, an operator has two enterprises, A and B, with 60 units of A and 200 units of B. The least-cost size of A is 60, and the least-cost size of B is 400. It would likely be more profitable to expand B rather than A because profit per unit will increase with B but not with A.

Growth is more advantageous in enterprises that fit available capital and labor resources and have a comparative advantage in the geographic area.

A balance of size in two or more enterprises usually reduces risks. Methods for controlling risk are discussed in Chapter 4.

Growth by purchasing land, renting land, improving land, and adding buildings is discussed in Chapters 14 through 17.

DISCUSSION QUESTIONS

1. Do large farms make more money than small farms? Explain.
2. How does each of the following factors affect the "best" farm size for a particular operator?
   - Goals
   - Management ability
   - Living cost
   - Size-cost relationship
   - Taxes
   - Price level
   - Inflation and interest
3. What is the minimum farm size for an operator with fixed resources? For an operator without fixed resources?
4. List and explain the factors that determine the "best" size for a manager.
5. Under what circumstances is it most likely to be profitable to increase size?
6. What usually happens to production efficiency when farm size increases? Why?
7. What are the important considerations for deciding which enterprises should be expanded?

RELATED READINGS

Economic Growth of the Agricultural Firm, Technical Bulletin No. 86. Pullman, Wash.: Washington State University, 1977.

"Economies of Size Studies," The Center for Agricultural and Rural Development. Ames, Iowa: Iowa State University, 1983.

HARSH, STEPHEN B., LARRY J. CONNER, and GERALD D. SCHWAB. *Managing the Farm Business,* chap. 15. Englewood Cliffs, N.J.: Prentice-Hall, 1981.

HEADY, EARL O., YIE-LARD CHAN, and STEVEN SONKA. *Farm Size and Cost Functions in Relation to Machinery Technology.* The Center for Agricultural and Rural Development (Ames, Ia.: Iowa State University, 1976.)

MILLER, T. A., G. E. RODEWALD, and R. G. McELROY. Economies of Size in U.S. Field Crop Farming, AER-472, U.S.D.A., ERS, 1981.

SOSNICK, S. H. "The Relation of Labor Costs to Farm Size," *Farm-Size Relationship with Emphasis on California,* chap. 7. California Agricultural Experiment Station, Giannini Foundation Project Report, 1980.

STANTON, B. F. "Perspectives on Farm Size," American Journal of Agricultural Economics, 60, 727–37, 1978.

Buying and
Improving Land

14

WHY BUY LAND?

Control and Expansion

In most areas of the United States, land is difficult to rent. Share-rental land is scarce. Cash-rental land is expensive, and cash rents have tended to increase over time. One way to gain control of land is to purchase it.

> In 1970 Otto Bayh was paying $40.00 per acre cash rent for corn and soybean ground near London, Ohio. The 160 acres adjoining Otto's rented farm was for sale for $600 per acre. The interest rate would have been 8%, or $48.00 per acre, and land taxes $5.00 per acre. After adding $10.00 per acre for land maintenance (tile, etc.), the total annual cost of purchasing the land would have been $63.00 per acre. Reasoning that he could save $23.00 per acre by renting rather than buying ($40.00 versus $63.00), Otto did not purchase the farm. In 1984 the son of the woman who owned Otto's rental farm decided to farm, and the landlady rented the farm to her son. This left Otto less land to farm and decreased income.

Production Efficiency

It takes an investment of both time and money to bring land up to its most profitable level of productivity. Improvement of fertility level, erosion control, drainage, and weed control often must take place over a period of years. Operators of rented land sometimes do not make improvements because they are not sure how long they will be able to rent the farm. Landlords may not be willing to make investments in improvements because they are short of capital or are not knowledgeable about potential benefits. Operators have more control in making improvements on owned land than on rented land.

Base of Operation

The profit from livestock production is due mainly to managerial skill (see Chapter 11). On a share-rental farm, the operator divides the return to management skill with the landlord. Because buildings are often low-investment and obsolete on rented farms, an operator may be contributing outstanding skill and substantial labor while the landlord may be contributing only average production facilities. Hence, someone with exceptional skill in livestock management can usually profit by having full ownership of the livestock enterprise. This may be achieved by purchasing a land parcel of sufficient size for raising livestock.

Some lenders in a community may be more likely to provide financial support to operators who own at least a portion of the land they farm.

Expectation of Increased Land Earnings and Land Price

Land prices and per-acre earnings from land increased almost continuously from 1933 to 1981 (Table 14.1). In the United States, land prices more than tripled from 1970 to 1981, and land prices in the Corn Belt more than quadrupled during this same period. Earnings from Corn Belt land tripled during the 1970–1981 period.

The main cost of owning land is interest on the land investment. Once land is purchased, interest cost per acre does not increase with fixed-interest loans but can increase with variable-interest loans. Many managers have purchased land because of the expectation that land values and earnings will increase while the costs of owning land will remain relatively constant.

Tax Considerations

The costs of land ownership (interest, taxes, maintenance) are often higher than returns (cash rent, landlord's share of crops) at the time the land is purchased. If a farmer is paying income taxes, the current cost of newly purchased land can reduce taxable income and, consequently, taxes. If land values increase, this gain remains untaxed until the land is sold and then is taxed at a lower rate as a capital gain (see Chapter 22). Thus, a part of the early years' costs is offset by reduced income taxes. Of course, if land values and future earnings do not increase, it would be more profitable to pay the taxes than to buy the land. But if one expects earnings and land values to increase, it may be possible to divert some current potential tax money into the purchase of land.

> Harry Bloufier purchased 400 acres in 1958 for $400 per acre. The farm is now completely paid off, and the 400 acres return $100 per acre to land and $50 per acre to Harry's labor and management. Harry's taxable income of $60,000 puts him in a high tax bracket. Harry's daughter, Marie, has graduated from high school and is considering farming after she completes four years in agriculture at the state university. The Bloufier farm may need to be expanded if she returns. A parcel of 200 acres near the Bloufier farm is for sale for $2,000 per acre. The $400,000 farm can be financed at 10% interest ($40,000 per year). Harry has budgeted most likely returns to be $100 per acre ($20,000). The big question is whether he should buy now or wait to see if Marie will return to the farm. If he decides to buy now, Harry will lose $20,000 ($20,000 return minus

TABLE 14.1 Farm Real Estate: Index Numbers of Average Value per Acre, Indiana and U.S.A., 1912–1983[a] (1977 = 100)

Year	U.S.A. (48 states)	Indiana	Year	U.S.A. (48 states)	Indiana
1912	7.9	6.6	1949	14.4	12.1
1913	8.1	6.9			
1914	8.4	7.0	1950	14.1	12.0
1915	8.4	6.9	1951	16.3	14.3
1916	8.9	7.6	1952	17.9	15.7
1917	9.6	7.9	1953	18.2	16.1
1918	10.6	8.8	1954	18.0	15.9
1919	11.6	9.3	1955	18.7	16.9
			1956	19.4	17.7
1920	14.1	11.1	1957	20.6	19.1
1921	13.1	10.1	1958	21.7	19.9
1922	11.4	8.2	1959	23.3	20.9
1923	11.1	7.9			
1924	10.7	7.4	1960	24.2	21.4
1925	10.4	7.0	1961	24.6	20.6
1926	10.2	6.5	1962	25.9	21.1
1927	9.7	6.0	1963	27.2	22.0
1928	9.6	5.7	1964	29.0	23.6
1929	9.5	5.7	1965	30.6	25.1
			1966	33.0	28.8
1930	9.3	5.5	1967	35.4	31.2
1931	8.4	4.9	1968	37.8	32.9
1932	7.0	4.1	1969	34.9	33.2
1933	5.7	3.6			
1934	6.0	3.9			
1935	6.2	4.1	1970	41.5	32.3
1936	6.5	4.5	1971	43.3	33.9
1937	6.7	4.8	1972	46.9	35.2
1938	6.8	5.0	1973	53.0	40.8
1939	6.7	5.0	1974	66.1	50.2
			1975	75.2	62.5
1940	6.7	5.1	1976	85.5	75.9
1941	6.7	5.3	1977	100.0	100.0
1942	7.3	6.0	1978	109.1	112.4
1943	8.0	6.7	1979	125.4	129.6
1944	9.1	7.7			
1945	10.1	8.5	1980	144.9	149.5
1946	11.4	9.9	1981	158.3	160.9
1947	12.8	10.8	1982	157.0	140.0
1948	13.8	11.8	1983	148.0	122.0

[a]All farm real estate with improvements as of March 1 (1912–1975), Feb. 1 (1976–1981), April 1 (1983).

Source: Farm Real Estate Market Developments. Compiled by J. H. Atkinson, Department of Agricultural Economics, Purdue University, West Lafayette, Ind.

$40,000 interest) per year. Can such a purchase make economic sense? Yes, *if* land earnings and prices increase.

First, nearly half of Harry's loss would be offset by reduced income tax. There would be a $20,000 operating loss each year, but income taxes will be reduced approximately $9,000 thus reducing the loss after taxes to about $11,000 (see Chapter 22). To offset this loss and the estimated 20% capital gains tax he will pay when he sells the farm, Harry would need an annual land-price increase of approximately $14,000 ($70.00 per acre).

Other Advantages

Other reasons for buying land include the following:

- Some investors consider land a relatively secure investment because there is a fixed supply and an increasing demand. There is some validity to this argument, but we must also remember that it is possible to create substitutes for land such as intensive cropping, land improvements, hydroponics, and high-rise apartments.
- Many people enjoy owning land and gain greater personal satisfaction from land ownership than would result from any other type of investment.
- Land is a farm asset that can usually be sold at a higher price relative to initial cost than can depreciable property such as buildings or equipment.
- Land located near or adjoining an existing farm may come up for sale only once in a lifetime. The convenience of having the farm concentrated may make that unit more valuable to farmers operating near it.

DISADVANTAGES OF OWNING LAND

Are there any disadvantages to owning land? Yes, there are three important disadvantages.

Low Operating Returns

Because land ownership has the many advantages presented earlier, prices are often bid up to the point that current operating returns are low. If you have limited capital and must borrow most of the money to buy land, it may be difficult to make the interest and principal payments.

Paul and Mary Hartsell started farming in central Iowa on a 420-acre crop and cattle farm rented on a 50-50 crop-livestock basis. Their farm income averaged about $23,400 per year. Wanting to own a farm of their own, Paul and Mary lived conservatively and saved $10,000 per year. But the price of farms was going up faster than the amount they could save. When a 300-acre farm came up for sale, Paul and Mary reasoned that if they waited to buy the farm, they might never be able to buy one. Using their savings for a down payment, they purchased the farm for $2,000 per acre, a total of $600,000. Interest cost at 10.5% was $210 per acre. Other expenditures were $7.00 per acre for taxes and $40.00 for principal, bringing the total annual cash outlay to $257 per acre. The land was returning about $120 per acre. Paul and Mary needed $257 cost minus $120 return times 300 acres, or $41,100 per year, to subsidize the purchase of the new farm. The Hartsells' earnings from the rented farm fell $31,100 short of providing the needed subsidy for the purchase of the new farm.

After two years of farming the purchased unit, Paul and Mary had exhausted all sources of credit and could no longer make debt payments. They were forced by their lenders to sell the farm at an unfavorable time when the selling price was $100 per acre less than they paid for it. Their losses included $30,000 on the purchase and sale of the farm plus an additional $58,200 operating loss ($29,100 per year). The Hartsells' total loss on the purchased farm was $88,200. It will take them several years to recover losses that could have been avoided had they prepared a cash-flow budget before buying the unit (see Chapter 6).

Declining Prices

Another disadvantage to purchasing land is risk associated with declining land prices. Land prices increased from 1933 to 1981. This could lead one to believe that land prices must always increase. However, from 1920 to 1933 land prices declined each year; in 1934 they were less than half the 1920 prices. Land prices also decreased in most areas of the United States in 1981 and 1982. During the 1920s, early 1930s, and early 1980s many farmers went bankrupt because they could not make land mortgage payments with declining prices for agricultural products.

Capital Requirements

The capital requirement per hour of labor is much greater for purchased land than for livestock or rental land. For example, assume approximately 400 hours of labor are required to operate a $200,000, 100-acre tract; investment per hour of labor is $500 for land ($200,000 ÷ 400) plus machinery and operating investment. An investment of $200,000 in livestock would provide a half- to full-time job (1,250 to 2,500 hours of work) depending on the kind of livestock and system of production. Therefore, investment per hour of labor in livestock is only $80 to $160. The high capital requirement of owning land is a disadvantage to a person with limited capital.

In summary, purchasing land usually results in a tighter cash-flow situation and increased risk; nevertheless, the purchase of land has helped many farmers to accumulate net worth. There are several reasons why a land purchase might be an aid to net worth accumulation: Land price has often appreciated; land purchase forces savings to meet mortgage payments; owned land may be more productive than rented land; purchase of land may result in more acres farmed; and land purchase usually reduces income taxes. On the other hand, purchase of land just before a major price decline has caused numerous farmers to have financial difficulty and even to go bankrupt. Also, purchase of land can restrict farm growth by requiring so much subsidy that money is not available for expansion with livestock or land rental.

HOW TO PURCHASE LAND DESPITE LOW NET WORTH

Land ownership has many advantages for a farmer, but it is difficult to pay for land unless purchased land can be subsidized with income from other sources. How can a person with a low net worth afford the down payment and mortgage payments? The following are some ways that can help such a person buy land without encountering cash-flow problems:

1. In addition to purchasing a farm, rent land and buildings on the crop- and livestock-share basis. The share-rental basis reduces risk as well as the amount of operating capital needed relative to a cash lease.

   Rick Schultz, who farms south of Minneapolis, figured that in 1980 it took about 3 acres of share-rented land to subsidize the purchase of 1 acre. Income from livestock can also be used to subsidize land purchases.

2. In the case of a married couple, one person might work off the farm if the farm business is not large enough to provide productive work for two people. Off-farm income could be used to pay for a purchased farm.

3. Secure FmHA financing. This could reduce the amount of down payment and provide mortgage money at a lower rate of interest (see Chapter 7).

4. Purchase only small parcels of land. When equity in purchased land reaches a certain level as a result of debt repayment or inflation, the land frequently pays for itself.[1] At this point another small unit could be purchased. Over time these small land parcels accumulate into a significant land holding. If land is for sale in units that are larger than you can afford, find a partner to share the purchase or purchase the total unit and sell the part that you cannot afford.

WHEN TO BUY LAND

Buying a farm is a major decision because the investment is so great. The payments continue for a long time. Timing of the purchase is crucial. Many who purchased land in 1946 or 1972 were able to pay off the mortgages quickly because of relatively

---

[1] The percentage equity received in order for a farm to pay for itself varies with economic conditions and geographic location. You must prepare a budget to determine equity required before a subsidy is unnecessary.

high farm-product prices. On the other hand, many who purchased farms during the 1920s or early 1980s lost their farms. Long-term farm-product price changes are often caused by unpredictable events such as weather, government decisions, and economic conditions. Even managers with some expertise in forecasting prices should recognize that there is a great deal of uncertainty involved.

Perhaps, then, even more important than the price are the answers to these questions: How does land ownership fit with the long range goals of the business? Can I pay for land even when faced with adverse weather and prices? How much risk am I willing to accept in order to own land?

WHAT TO LOOK FOR IN BUYING A FARM

Information presented in Chapters 10, 11, and 12 can help you determine the likely earnings of a farm that you may wish to purchase. To estimate earnings, the most important data to collect include:

1. The number of tillable acres. The acreage can usually be figured from an ASCS farm map with the use of a planometer. Tillable acres are often fewer than expected because of roads, farmstead, ditches, and fences.
2. Soil type and productivity (see Chapter 10).
3. Drainage outlet. Some farms lack an adequate drainage outlet. This causes crop yields to suffer, and it may be costly or impossible to correct the problem.
4. Natural field boundaries. There are economies to the use of large machinery, and large machinery can be more easily used in large fields with few natural obstructions or barriers.
5. Potential for irrigation. Is there an economic water source? Are fields arranged so that irrigation is feasible?
6. Suitability of buildings for various types of livestock.

If you are considering purchasing a farm in an area where you have operated for a long time, you are already familiar with markets, weather, labor availability, tax rates, capital availability, and other factors. But if you are considering a farm in an area with which you are not completely familiar, study the checklist presented in Table 14.2.

Marshall and Ann Johnson owned 160 acres in Illinois and wanted to expand their farm. Unfortunately, no rental land was available, and land was selling for about $2,400 per acre. Marshall heard that excellent land in the Mississippi River Delta was selling for $800 per acre. He visited several farms that were for sale in Mississippi, Arkansas, and Louisiana. The farms were level and black; in fact, this area had much Illinois soil that had washed down the river and was deposited there when the river overflowed.

TABLE 14.2   Things to Consider before Buying a Farm

Farm size	Accessibility
Acreage: total, tillable	Off-farm opportunities
Cropland: excellent, above average, average,	Farmstead
below average, poor	Site and/or location
Pastureland	Arrangement
Woods: waste, other	Dwellings
Farmstead: total	Condition and appearance
Soil types and characteristics	Number of rooms: down, up
Acreage of each	Dimensions, type of structure
Productivity rating	General arrangement
Parent material	Foundation, basement
Predominate slope	Siding, roof
Degree of erosion	Heating system, conveniences
Drought resistance	Floors, other features
Lime content, depth	Built-in equipment
Texture, clay content	Farm buildings
Internal drainage	Number, present use
Surface drainage	Dimensions, square feet
Native vegetation	Foundations, floors, roofs
Stones, weeds, problems	Companion equipment
Climate	Flexibility of use
Rainfall, annual, growing season	Remodeling possibilities, costs
Frost-free dates	Water supply
Length of growing season	Location
Temperatures, monthly	Buildings, pastures
Drought, tornado, hail, flood	Irrigation, spraying
Productive capacity of land	Other physical features
Cropping history	Timber
Fertility	Orchards
Crops yields	Special improvements
Carrying capacity for livestock	Community characteristics
Range or pasture acreage	Types of farming in area
Animal unit carrying capacity	Quality of farms
Roughage consumed per animal unit	Tenure patterns
Concentrate consumed per animal unit	Type of neighbors
Farm layout	Schools, churches
Farmstead location in relation to rest of	Customs, traditions
farm	Residential opportunities
Location of improvements: fences,	Marketing facilities and services
gates, erosion-control practices,	Elevators and grain markets
irrigation	Livestock yards
Size and shape of fields	Milk market
Location points of entry	Fruit and vegetable markets
Convenience in farming	Other
Location	Tax district
Distance to trading centers	Zoning regulations
Kinds of roads	Assessments, taxes

Source: Dr. R. C. Suter, Department of Agricultural Economics, Purdue University.

Marshall and Ann were able to sell their 160-acre Illinois farm for $2,400 per acre and buy 480 acres in the Mississippi Delta north of Vicksburg, Mississippi. The 480 acres in Mississippi were valued at the same price as the 160 acres in Illinois, and this was the size farm the Johnsons wanted. The first year there was little rain for six weeks after the soybeans were planted, and soybean yield on the total farm was only 10 bushels per acre, one-third of the expected yield. The second year there were heavy rains all spring, and overflow from the river resulted in the Johnson farm being under water until June. Although Marshall planted some soybeans in July, he lost his wheat. Due to late planting, the bean yield was only 15 bushels per acre and thus lost money. Marshall found weather conditions in the Mississippi Delta to be far more variable than in Illinois. There was a reason that land in the delta was priced at only one-third the price of land in Illinois. Not being prepared to assume so much risk, the Johnsons moved back to Illinois after three years. The two moves cost them a great deal of net worth growth.

When considering a move to a new area, be sure you understand the climate, living conditions, soil, markets, and other factors before making your decision.

WHERE TO BUY LAND

There are better buys on land in some geographic areas than in others. This results from a variety of local factors, such as the following:

1. Weather. An area that has had two or more years of poorer-than-normal weather is likely to have lower-priced land than other geographic areas.
2. Age of farmers in the community. A community where the average age is high is likely to have more retirements, resulting in an increased amount of land coming on the market.
3. Local farmer attitude toward growth. In areas where farmers have very competitive attitudes regarding growth and acquisition of land, an increased demand for land is reflected in increased prices. On the other hand, in areas where interest in growth is lacking, relatively lower land prices might prevail.
4. Recent changes not yet accounted for in land price. Perhaps a new market has been established or a new crop discovered for an area. Sometimes improvements made in an area are slow to be reflected in the price of land.
5. Management skill of local farmers. In areas where management skill is superior, land prices are likely to be relatively higher than in areas where the management skill of farmers is average or below average.
6. Amount of speculation. Some people count an increase in land value as part of their earnings, thus encouraging land prices to increase even more. Similarly, when land prices decrease, people hesitate to buy, thinking they may find a more favorable price later. This encourages land prices to continue downward.

There are differences in speculative activity in different geographic areas. Sooner or later, however, land prices will be determined by earnings rather than change in value.

7. Development activity. Sometimes the demand for land for houses and shopping centers spills over to agricultural land in the area. From a land-speculation standpoint, it may be desirable to own land in such an area, but from an agricultural-earnings standpoint, it may be difficult to pay for development land.

Changing conditions in different geographic areas over time cause the price of land to change. But there is often a lag between the change in conditions and the change in land price. Managers who buy early when they identify situations where land price is below equilibrium can profit from their actions. Land accumulated in this way can later be consolidated through trades that enable managers to delay capital gains tax until the farmland is sold.

For many years development land was priced higher than agricultural land around a large city. In the period from 1973 to 1975, worldwide food shortages resulting from unfavorable weather caused agricultural-product and land prices to soar. At the same time a deep recession caused the prices of development land to decline. This was the situation when Lin Ky began to search for land. Lin found that development land was cheaper than farmland in his area. Much of the development land needed cleaning up. Some had been cash-rented with little supervision, and the nutrient content of the soil had been depleted. Other development land had not been farmed and brush had grown up. Most farmers did not consider the possibility of purchasing the development land for farming. Lin, however, bought the land $200 per acre below local farmland prices. He spent $100 per acre on clearing and fertilization. His land investment, after improvements, was $100 per acre less than the market price of agricultural land in the area.

While you may save money through purchases of land in selected areas, you should also keep in mind that in most cases there are good reasons for differences in price among areas.

FACTORS AFFECTING LAND PRICES AND RETURNS

Change in land values[2] and earnings is critically important to the land-buying decision. Following is an explanation of some of the factors that affect land prices.

---

[2]The term land value as used here is the same as market value or price.

Earnings

Land price is closely related to rate of return to land and farm operating earnings (Figures 14.1 and 14.2). Whenever returns have increased, buyers have tended to bid up the price of land. On the other hand, when returns have fallen, land prices have tended to decline or to remain stable until earnings increase. Average rate of return on investment varies among geographic areas and from farm to farm. It may change over time. For many years it has been about 4% in the Midwest. One might ask, "Why are returns so low, often below interest rates?" Land returns are low most likely because of expectations that land earnings and land prices will increase and because of the desire to control land.

The return to land per acre is determined by the price and cost structure for agricultural commodities. It is important for farm managers to evaluate and project cost of production and domestic and foreign demand for agricultural products when making judgments about land price. Government farm programs also affect farm earnings.

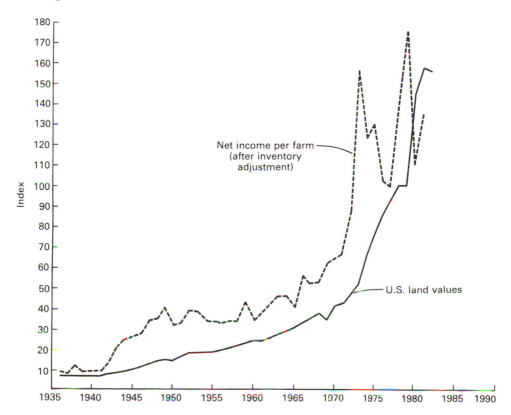

Figure 14.1 U.S. land values and net income per farm (1977 = 100). *Source:* USDA, Economic Indicators of the Farm Sector; State Income and Balance Sheet Statistics, 1981.

Figure 14.2   Percent return on total investment, Indiana farm record cooperators, and percent change in Indiana farm land values.

General Price Level

Land prices and the returns to land are associated with changes in the general price level. As the price of nonfood items increases, food becomes a relatively better buy.

Land Demand for Expansion

The development of larger machinery has enabled each operator to farm more acres. New machinery, weed and insect control, communications, and other technologies change the size-cost relationship and consequently increase the demand for land. Such technological changes have been especially rapid during the past two decades. Should the rate of evolution of these technologies decline, the increase in demand for land would diminish.

Interest Rates

Since interest is the major cost of owning land, interest rates are inversely related to returns and value of land per acre.

Rate of Change in Land Values

If land prices increase year after year, buyers may include the anticipated increase as a return to land and bid more for land, causing an even larger increase in land prices. This "bull" psychology often continues until land returns decline as a result of such things as droughts or low commodity prices. Eventually, with reduced operating returns, land prices are likely to decline. If the decline continues for a period of years, the anticipation of continued declines in land values and returns may result in an even greater weakness in the land market.

Risk and Uncertainty

Risk and uncertainty are costs to producers, and as they increase, land prices tend to decrease. As economic or climatic risk changes, land values are likely to change conversely. In some instances, government programs reduce risk and uncertainty.

Production-Increasing Technologies

New seed varieties, weed control, and other technologies have increased yields greatly during the past forty years. These technologies, combined with a possible guaranteed price through government programs, could have an upward effect on land values. Because of the inelastic demand for many farm commodities, the increased production resulting from the technologies would have a negative effect on farm-product prices and land values in the absence of government price supports.

Return on Other Investments

As returns to alternative investments (stocks, bonds, housing) increase relative to land returns, one would expect this to have a downward effect on land prices. The opposite would be expected as land returns increase relative to other investment returns.

By projecting factors affecting land prices, managers can forecast land-value changes. Operating returns and land-value changes are key factors in the land-purchase decision.

ANALYZING LAND PURCHASES

Decisions about buying land should be based on the return on investment over time (Will it pay even better than other alternatives?) and cash flow over time (Can I pay for it?).

To answer the question "How much will this land return?" one needs to estimate the following information *for the time period for which the decision is being made:*

1. Production of each crop each year
2. Price of each crop each year
3. Resources needed each year
4. Price of resources each year
5. Income tax rate
6. Capital gains tax rate
7. Initial purchase price of the farm
8. Value of the farm at the end of the period.

To answer the question "Can I pay for it?" the purchaser not only prepares estimates of items 1 through 8 above but also of:

- Interest and principal payments
- Cash availability from other farm and nonfarm sources.

Because the estimations will vary over time, the computations of rate of return and present value are complex. The methods presented in Chapter 3 for making capital investment decisions apply to land purchases. A method for making a hand budget computation of rate of return and cash flow is presented for only a single year. The computations should be continued for the length of the planning period. Then, a computer model that determines maximum bid price is discussed. Both of these methods should be helpful to a manager in determining whether or not a specific land purchase will pay and can be paid for. The two methods will be illustrated with a case example.

Olie Allen has an opportunity to purchase 205 acres near his home farm for $2,000 per acre. Olie has asked for advice on whether or not to purchase.

Land Purchase Budget

First, we help Olie develop some background information on the 205 acres, indicating the number of tillable acres, soil type and slope, drainage, field size, crop yield potential, and crop yield variability in part A of Figure 14.3. Next, we make an estimate of net income excluding interest on land investment in part B.1. (Refer to Chapter 10 for detailed procedures.)

In Section B.2 we adjust the asking price of the farm for improvements that need to be made to obtain the returns shown in B1 and for tax benefits from investment credit. Of course, if taxable income is zero, tax benefits cannot be used to offset tax due and should be omitted.

In Section B.3 we determine the operating return on total investment to be 5.5%, which Olie would receive if he purchased the farm. Olie expects land values to increase 4% per year, so in Section B.4 we calculate total return on the land to be 9.5%.

A. Background Information and Sources.

1. Total acres in sale tract .... _205_

2. Tillable acres in sale tract .... _190_

3. Characteristics of nontillable land .... _____

   a. Can it be cleared? (cost/acre) .... _____

   b. Residential or development value .... _____

   c. Forest or pasture value .... _____

   d. Waste, roads, buildings, etc. .... _15_

4. What soil types and yield potential?(soil map)
   Fincastle, Brookston, Crosby   130 bu. corn, 40 bu. Soybeans

5. What slope, erosion, intensity potential? (soil map)
   Most 0%-3%, Little erosion

6. Is there a good drainage outlet? Drainage of the farm?
   Good outlet, needs $5,000 tile
   SCS, county engineer, and drainage records.

7. Are fields large enough for the efficient use of large machinery?
   Yes, all in two large fields

8. How variable is the yield on different soil types?

   Not highly variable

B. How Much Will It Pay?

1 Land Use (Crop)	2 Tillable Acres	3 Gross Return per Acre[a]	4 Cost per Acre[b]	5 Net Returns per Acre	6 Total Net Returns (2 × 5)
corn	190	130 × $3 $390	$272	$118	$22,420
1. Total operating returns					$22,420

Returns per acre = $\dfrac{\text{Total returns}}{\text{Total acres}}$ = $\dfrac{\$22,420}{205}$ = $109.37

[a]If adding this farm unit results in higher selling prices, reflect this in gross return.
[b]Include all costs except interest on land. If adding this unit results in reduced machinery and labor costs for the added land, reflect this in cost calculations.

Figure 14.3   Land purchase evaluation budget.

B2. Adjusted Price

   a. Price paid $2,000 × 205 acres $410,000

   b. Improvements needed to attain income in B.1
      (land clearing, tile, etc.)   5,000

   c. Investment credit on tile, fences, and
      specialized buildings   5,000

   d. Adjusted price (a + b − c) $410,000

B3. Operating Return on Total Investment before Tax

$$\frac{\text{Operating income (B.1)}}{\text{Adjusted price (B.2)}} \times 100 = \text{Percent operating return on total investment before tax}$$

$$\frac{\$22,420}{\$410,000} \times 100 = \underline{\hspace{0.5cm} 5.5\% \hspace{0.5cm}}$$

B4. Total Return on Total Investment before Tax

   a. Expected annual total change in value
      (increase or decrease) +4% $16,400

   b. Total operating return (B.1)   22,420

   c. Total Returns (a + b) $38,820

$$\frac{\text{Total return (B.4c)}}{\text{Adjusted price (B.2)}} \times 100 = \text{Percent total return on total investment before tax}$$

$$\frac{\$38,820}{\$40,000} \times 100 = \underline{\hspace{0.5cm} 9.5\% \hspace{0.5cm}}$$

B5. Operating Return on Equity before Tax

   a. Total farm value $410,000

   b. Total debt on farm   307,500

   c. Equity (a − b) $102,500

   d. Net operating returns (B.1)   22,420

   e. Annual land interest payments (10% interest)   30,750

   f. Net operating return after interest
      paid on land (d − e)   −$8,330

$$\frac{\begin{array}{c}\text{Net operating return after}\\ \text{interest paid on land (f)}\\ \hline \text{Equity (c)}\end{array}} \times 100 = \text{Net operating return on equity before tax}$$

$$\frac{-\$8,330}{\$102,500} \times 100 = \underline{\hspace{0.5cm} -8.1\% \hspace{0.5cm}}$$

B6. Total Return on Equity before Tax

   a. Net operating return after interest
      paid on land (B.5f)   −$8,330

   b. Expected annual total change in value (B.4a)   16,400

Figure 14.3   (continued)

c. Total return to equity before tax (a + b) $8,070

$$\frac{\text{Total return to equity before tax (c)}}{\text{Equity (B.5c)}} \times 100 = \text{Total percent return to equity before tax}$$

$$\frac{\$8,070}{\$102,500} \times 100 = \underline{\hspace{0.5cm} 7.9\% \hspace{0.5cm}}$$

B7. Some Tax Considerations

   a. The increase in land value is not taxed until the land is sold, and then it is taxed as a capital gain if it has been held for more than one year.

   b. If a substantial percentage is borrowed, operating profit is negative and income taxes could be reduced.

   c. Clearing land can be deducted as an ordinary expense up to the smaller of $5,000 or 25% of net income. The land value increase resulting from clearing is a capital gain.

B8. Net Worth Change as a Result of Land Purchase If Farm Is Sold at End of Year

a. Operating return (B.5f)		$ −8,330
b. Land value increase (B.4a)		16,400
c. Income tax reduction: 35% of operating loss (B.8a)		2,916
d. Capital gains tax: 14% of land value in increase		−2,296
e. Net worth change (a + b + c + d)		$ 8,690

C. Can I Pay for It?

1. Total operating income (B.1)	$22,420
2. Annual payments	
Interest (B.5e)	$30,750
Principal	1,870
Total[c]	$32,620
3. Change in income tax a. Net operating income (B.1)	$22,420
b. Interest (B.5e)	30,750
c. Taxable income (a − b)	−$8,330
d. Tax change (c × tax rate 35 %)[d]	−$2,916

4. Net cash flow

Operating income (1)	−	Annual interest and principal payment (2)	±	Change in income tax (3d)	=	Net cash flow
$22,420	−	$32,620	+	$ 2,916	=	−$ 7,284

[c]Principal and interest amortized over a 30-year repayment period.
[d]Tax rate will depend on individual circumstances.

Figure 14.3 (continued)

The previously calculated returns assume no debt. However, if Olie purchases the farm, he plans to put only $102,500 down and to borrow $307,500 at 10% interest. We calculate in Section B.5 that operating returns to the farm after interest payments would be −$8,330, or −8.1% on Olie's $102,500 equity.

If we add the expected increase in land value, Olie's return to equity increases to 7.9% (Section B.6). The computations to this point are before taxes. Olie can capitalize substantially on the income tax benefits listed in Section B.7. If the farm were sold at the end of one year, Olie's net worth from owning the farm would increase by approximately $8,690. This figure needs to be compared to estimates of net-worth change if the equity capital ($102,500) were used in other alternatives.

Finally, we help Olie check his cash flow. Annual principal and interest payments are $32,620. Operating returns will be $22,420 (B.1). Being an established operator with a high income, Olie's income taxes are substantial. His taxes would be reduced by 35% of the $8,330 operating loss (C.3). When operating income and tax reductions are subtracted from annual principal and interest payments, Olie will have an annual cash deficit of $7,284, which must be made up from other sources of farm or nonfarm income (C.4).

The preceding analysis was done for the first year only. It gives insight but can be misleading, especially if earnings change over time. The budget and investment analysis procedure discussed in Chapter 3 should be completed for the entire planning period.

> Locate a farm that is for sale in your area and make the same analysis that we made for Olie.

Maximum Bid Price Computer Model

The maximum bid price computer program, illustrated in Figure 14.4, is another method of analyzing the impact of a land purchase.

To obtain an estimate of the return to land and cash flow over a period of time, Olie decided to run the purchase through the maximum bid price computer model. He had to provide the ten input items shown in Figure 14.4. Olie judged the market price of land in his area to be $2,000 (1). He indicated a desire to make at least 10% on his investment after taxes (2). Olie transferred the net returns per acre from Part B.1 (Figure 14.3) of the land budget (3). He estimated that because of inflation and world demand for food, earnings from land would increase about 3% per year (4). He planned to pay 25% down (5) and to have a mortgage interest rate of 10% (6) for a thirty-year loan (7). Olie expects land prices to increase 4% per year (8). Olie would like to evaluate this purchase for a fifteen-year period (9), and he is in the 35% income tax bracket (10).

Computer results. The computer results show that with the input specified by Olie, he could afford to pay $1,790 per acre, substantially below the $2,000 asking

MAXIMUM BID PRICE CALCULATION
for: OLIE JOHNSON

Input data:

1) Average price of comparable parcels	$2,000 per acre
2) Desired after tax return on capital	10.0%
3) Return to hand before income taxes	$109.37 per acre/year
4) Rate of change in return to land	3.0%
5) Purchase price down payment	25.0%
6) Mortgage interest rate	10.00%
7) Mortgage repayment period	30 years
8) Land value rate of change	4.0% per year
9) Planning horizon	15 years
10) Marginal income tax rate	35.0%

MAXIMUM BID PRICE: $1,790 per acre

CASH FLOWS USING MARKET VALUES

For a level payment loan, the annual mortgage payment based on a land value of $2,000 per acre, 10.00 percent interest, and a 30 year repayment period is $159.12.

This is more than the additional income and tax savings associated with the purchase. Thus, income from other enterprises must be used to supplement this purchase.

Year	After-tax[a] income	Tax[b] Savings	Supplemental[c] income needed	Area land values
1	73.22	52.50	33.40	2,080
2	75.42	52.18	31.52	2,163
3	77.68	61.83	20.61	2,250
4	80.01	51.44	27.66	2,340
5	82.41	51.02	25.69	2,433
6	84.89	50.55	23.68	2,531
7	87.43	50.04	21.65	2,632
8	90.06	49.47	19.59	2,737
9	92.76	48.85	17.51	2,847
10	95.54	48.17	15.41	2,960
11	98.41	47.41	13.30	3,079
12	101.36	46.59	11.18	3,202
13	104.40	45.68	9.05	3,330
14	107.53	44.67	6.91	3,463
15	110.76	43.57	4.79	3,602

[a]After Tax Income = ((1 + Rate of Change in Return to Land) **year) × (1 − Marginal Income Tax Rate) × Return to Land
[b]Tax Savings = Interst Paid × Marginal Tax Rate
[c]Supplemental Income = Annual Principal and Interest Payment − (After Tax + Tax Savings)

Figure 14.4 Maximum bid price for land calculator. *Source:* FX-17, Cooperative Extension Service, Purdue University, West Lafayette, Indiana, 1980. Copyright 1982 Purdue Research Foundation.

price. The results also showed he would have to subsidize the farm at the rate of $33.40 per acre the first year. Because the farm would not begin to generate a positive cash flow until after the fifteenth year, Olie decided not to make the investment.

The main difference between the hand budget and the computer budget is that the latter takes into account changes in returns and changes in land values over time. One could arrive at the figures in the computer budget by making a series of one-year budgets.

The computer budget can be used to determine how changes in the returns to land and in land prices affect the maximum bid price.

Financing land is discussed in Chapter 7.

Summary

Whenever a land purchase is being considered, the following questions should be answered:

1. What is the operating return on investment?
2. What is the total return on investment?
3. How do the returns in points 1 and 2 compare to other alternatives?
4. What impact will land purchases have on net-worth change over time?
5. What impact will land purchase have on cash flow?
6. If a cash-flow deficit is created, will other sources provide adequate surplus to cover the land-purchase deficit?
7. Can payments on this farm be made even under adverse yield and/or farm product-pricing circumstances?
8. How does this land purchase fit my:
   - Farm operation?
   - Debt-risk tolerance?
   - Total goals of land ownership and size?
   - Liquidity and cash availability goals?

A farm operator might seriously consider buying land if the answer to these three questions is yes: Can I pay for it even in adverse conditions? Will this land purchase fit my farm business and personal goals? Does this appear to be a good time to purchase land from a business-investment standpoint?

IMPROVING LAND

Two principal ways to increase production on a crop farm are to increase acreage and to increase production per acre. In this section, some of the ways to increase production per acre will be discussed.

Drainage

Additional drainage is profitable on much of the land in the eastern United States. Production per acre may be increased with proper drainage because plants have better root development and growth and nutrients are used more efficiently when there is no excess moisture. Timeliness can be improved when good drainage allows land to be farmed earlier in the spring and later in the fall. Also, machinery efficiency may be improved with good drainage because machinery can be used more days and there are no wet areas that have to be left for a later time. In addition to increasing yield, drainage reduces variability and uncertainty, allowing an operator to be more aggressive in borrowing and in marketing. For a landlord, good drainage may attract an operator with a high level of management capabilities. Drainage is a subject that every manager should understand.

Evaluating drainage decisions.   Drew Simpson operates a 420-acre crop farm in southern Wisconsin. Field flooding and excessive soil moisture caused substantial losses for Drew during the past several years. Having borrowed heavily to purchase his farm, Drew has been short on cash. He did not consider investing in drainage until his son John told him about some exercises he had worked on in college that showed that drainage can be profitable. John, along with the local agricultural extension agent and the district conservationist of the Soil Conservation Service, convinced Drew to evaluate drainage costs and returns for his farm.

A map of the Simpson farm was developed showing existing tile, waterways, outlets, and areas where drainage problems existed. Cost and returns budgets were developed for drainage projects likely to have high returns.

Surface drainage. Some areas of the Simpson farm could be leveled and shaped to improve surface drainage. The SCS district conservationist judged that surface drainage could eliminate flooding, which occurred once every four years on 30 acres (Figure 14.5). On 50 additional acres, land leveling and shaping would improve drainage and increase corn yields by 10 bushels per acre per year. The surface drainage project would cost about $5,000.

The Simpsons calculated annual returns and costs as shown in Table 14.3.

In addition to calculating annual return, Drew also estimated simple rate of return on average investment (see "Capital Investments," Chapter 3).

$$\text{Simple rate of return on investment} = \frac{\text{Net returns (excluding interest cost)}}{\text{Average investment}}$$

$$= \frac{\$2,537.50 + 400.00}{5,000.00} \times 100 = 58.8\%$$

Drew found that a $5,000 investment in surface drainage would increase his annual gross returns by $3,437.50. It would increase profit by $2,537.50 per year and return about 58.8% on investment.

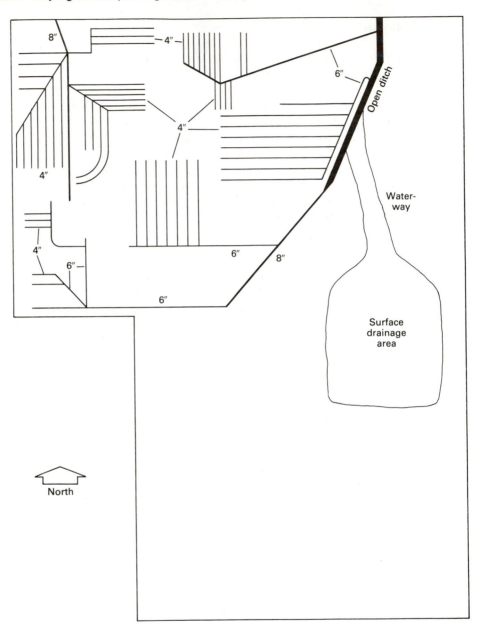

Figure 14.5 Tile plan, Drew Simpson farm.

TABLE 14.3   Surface Drainage Returns and Costs, Drew Simpson Farm

A. Annual Average Returns
1. Increase corn yields from 0 to 100 bu./acre one year out of four.

$$\frac{100}{4} = 25 \text{ bu. annual average yield increase}$$

25 bu. × \$2.75/bu. × 30 acres	\$2,062.50

2. Increase of 10 bu./acre/year on 50 acres due to improved drainage.

50 acres × 10 bu. × \$2.75	1,375.00

3. Total annual increased income (A1 + A2)	\$3,437.50

B. Annual Costs
Establish waterway, shape and level. Total initial investment, \$5,000.

1. 8% interest on average investment of \$5,000[a]	\$ 400.00
2. Waterway upkeep	500.00
	\$ 900.00
C. Annual Net Returns from Surface Drainage (A − B)	\$2,537.50

[a]Interest rate has been adjusted for change in the price level. See Chapter 8, Budgeting Annual Cost of Depreciable Resources.

On the basis of his analysis, Drew decided to make the improvement. He showed the figures to a banker and found it easy to obtain a loan to pay for the surface drainage. Drew even found that he was eligible to receive \$1,000 in payments from the local ASCS office for putting in the waterway. This reduced his cost by 20%, making the project even more profitable.

Since the highest payoff alternative appeared very profitable, Drew elected to budget the second-highest payoff drainage project.

Tiling 200 acres. Drew, John, and the SCS district conservationist developed a tile plan for the 200 acres of wet land (see Figure 14.5). Tile necessary to increase the yield from 90 to 120 bushels per acre included:

2,000 ft 8-in. tile at \$1.30/ft.	\$ 2,600.00
10,000 ft 6-in. tile at \$ .85/ft.	8,500.00
160,000 ft 4-in. tile at \$ .48/ft.	76,800.00
Total	\$87,900.00
Per acre	\$ 439.50

Table 14.4 is a projection of returns, costs, and profitability of the tile investment.

Since an investment in the tiling project would increase net returns \$4,588 per year, Drew decided to borrow money for the tiling project in addition to that already borrowed for surface drainage.

TABLE 14.4 Returns, Costs, and Profitability of Tile Investment, Drew Simpson Farm

I. Increased Returns and Reduced Cost per Acre
   A. Increased Returns
      1. Increase yield 90 to 120 bu. corn at $2.75 due to improved drainage and improved timeliness.

         30 bu. × $2.75/bu. $82.50

   B. Reduced Cost
      2. Reduced cost of machinery because entire unit can be farmed at one time without having to return to plant wet areas later.   10.50

   C. Total $93.00

II. Increased Cost

Investment/acre	$439.50	
Investment tax credit 10% (see Chapter 22)	−43.95	
Net investment/acre	$395.55	

      1. Depreciation (over 20 years, with no salvage value) and interest (13% market interest rate, 5% inflation rate, 8% real interest rate)[a]

         Ain = .1019   40.31

      2. Increased fertilizer, seed and other operating costs $ 29.75

         Total increased cost $ 70.06

III. Net Returns to Drainage per Acre (I minus II) $ 22.94
    On 200 acres $4,588.00

[a]See Chapter 8, Budgeting Annual Cost of Depreciable Resources.

Irrigation

Irrigation is most likely to be profitable on soils that have low moisture-holding capacity, in areas of the country that have low or variable amounts of rainfall, and in the production of high-net-income crops such as vegetables. In some areas of the United States, rainfall distribution is so uniform throughout the year and from year to year that irrigation will not pay. In many instances, however, reduced risk resulting from irrigation is more important than increased profit from irrigation. The reduced risk enables a manager to be more aggressive in farm expansion and marketing strategies, which usually generates increased returns from the total farm.

Gerry Schwartz operates a crop and dairy farm in southern Michigan. Even though the amount and distribution of rainfall are favorable for crop production, Gerry's crop yields are extremely variable because he farms some sandy land. Corn yields have ranged from 25 to 140 bushels per acre during the past five years, while soybean, wheat, and hay yields have been somewhat less variable. By reducing the risk of variable yields, Gerry could enjoy a higher income. He did some budgeting and found that irrigation would increase his net income by $10.00 per acre, or $2,800.00 on the 280 acres he planned to irrigate. A more complete budget showed that by irrigating Gerry could increase his income by $26,854.80. Why? First of all, he could produce more corn, the most profitable crop on his farm. Without irrigation he grew more soybeans, wheat, hay, and pasture to spread the risk. Second, Gerry could do a more effective job of marketing by forward contracting when crop prices are high. Presently Gerry is apprehensive about advance contracting because he can not be sure he will produce the crop, so he forgoes many favorable price opportunities.

Finally, irrigation would allow Gerry to increase the size of his dairy herd because he could produce more feed per acre and could be more certain that the amount of production planned would be available. The reduction of risk from irrigation would enable Gerry to make better use of his management skills in crop selection, marketing, and size.

Clearing Land

Although much of the productive land in the United States has been cleared, there is still a possibility of increasing the acres of productive land on some farms through clearing. The cost of clearing is quite variable, depending on the size and density of tree growth. Usually it is possible to clear good row-crop land for less than the cost of purchasing land. Also, clearing land has tax advantages. One-fourth of taxable income or $5,000, whichever is lower, can be used as an expense in the year the clearing is done. The remainder of the clearing cost can be depreciated. Land clearing enables the owner to borrow a greater amount against the farm, if desired. The cleared trees can sometimes be marketed to help offset part of the cost of clearing.

Land that is cleared may require several years to develop to its full production potential. Additional drainage of cleared land may be necessary, adding to the total cost of developing productive land. It should be kept in mind that some less productive soils or land with severe slopes may be best suited to forest land and should not be cleared.

Fertility

Improving the general fertility of soil at least to the medium level usually increases yield per acre. The principles of diminishing returns discussed in Chapter 3 should be considered when building soil fertility, however.

Drainage, irrigation, clearing, and fertility improvement may increase production from a given land area. Increasing acres of land by renting is discussed in Chapter 15.

DISCUSSION QUESTIONS

1. List and explain some advantages of buying land.
2. List and explain some disadvantages of buying land.
3. What are some ways for a person with a low net worth to purchase land?

4. List the important things to observe when purchasing a farm.

5. List factors that affect land prices and explain the impact of each on land prices.

6. When is the best time and where is the best place to purchase land? Explain.

7. What factors determine whether or not the purchase of land will be profitable? Will have a favorable cash flow?

8. List and explain two methods that can be used for evaluating a land purchase.

9. What are some sources of credit for financing a land purchase?

10. List the factors that should be included in costs and returns when evaluating a drainage investment.

11. What kinds of returns may be gained from irrigation?

12. Is irrigation likely to be profitable for all farms? Explain.

RELATED READINGS

GOODWIN, JOHN W. *Agricultural Economics,* chap. 19. Reston, Va.: Reston Publishing Co., 1977.

JUNDT, DWIGHT W. *Buying and Selling Farmland.* St. Louis, Missouri: Doane Agricultural Service, 1980.

KAY, RONALD D. *Farm Management,* chap. 14. New York: McGraw-Hill, 1981.

LINS, DAVID A., NEIL E. HARL, and THOMAS L. FREY. *Farmland.* Skokie, Ill.: Agri Business Publications, 1982.

LUCKHAM, W. R. "How Much Can You Pay for Agricultural Land?" in *Virginia Agricultural Economics.* Blacksburg, Va.: Virginia Polytechnic Institute and State University, 1975.

MURRAY, WILLIAM G., DUANE G. HARRIS, GERALD A. MILLER, and NEIL S. THOMPSON. *Farm Appraisal and Valuation,* (6th ed.), Ames, Iowa: Iowa State University Press, 1983.

OSBURN, DONALD D., and KENNETH C. SCHNEEBERGER. *Modern Agricultural Management,* chap. 17. Reston, Va.: Reston Publishing Co., 1983.

ROBBINS, P. R., E. E. CARSON, R. Z. WHEATON, and J. V. MANNERING. "Irrigation of Field Crops in Indiana," West Lafayette, Ind.: Purdue University, Cooperative Extension Service ID-119, 1977.

SUTER, R. C. *The Appraisal of Farm Real Estate.* Danville, Ill.: Interstate Printers and Publishers, 1980.

Renting a Farm

15

WHY RENT RATHER THAN BUY?

A farm usually can be rented for less money than the combined annual principal and interest payments on purchased land. For example, most Corn Belt land rented for about 4% to 6% of its market value during the period from 1978 to 1983. Interest and principal payments on land during that same period was about 14% of the purchase price. Typically, renting is a way to gain control of land with a more favorable cash flow than would be experienced if similar land were purchased. Rental land can provide a way to generate income for family living or business expansion.

Martin Rochelle wanted to get started in farming, but his home farm was too small for both Martin and his father. Martin's father Richard owned 136 acres and cash-rented another 185 acres for $125 an acre. Richard agreed to help Martin by allowing him use of his machinery without charge. Having difficulty finding rental land, Martin considered the purchase of 200 acres for $2,000 per acre. With an annual interest rate of 10%, principal of 2%, and taxes of $10 per acre, annual cash-flow requirements for purchased land would be $250. A budget showed that Martin would be $80 per acre, or $16,000, short of meeting his cash flow if he purchased the farm. On the other hand, if he could rent 200 acres for $125 per acre, his cash flow would be improved by $125 per acre, $250 (purchase) minus $125 (rental). This would be a cash-flow improvement of $25,000 compared to purchasing land and, therefore, would change Martin's cash-flow situation from a $16,000 deficit to a $9,000 surplus! Also, Martin would not need to be concerned about getting money for the down payment.

Some operators choose not to purchase land even though they have an adequate cash flow and down payment to do so. Instead, these operators may choose other investments that they believe will pay higher returns.

GAINING CONTROL OF RENTAL LAND

Land is scarce. Because there is a fixed amount available, in most areas numerous operators compete to gain control of the limited land supply. Yet we can observe some established farmers who are able to rent as much land as they want and some beginning farmers who obtain sufficient rental land for an economic size unit. What makes one farmer successful in renting land while another is not? Following are some things an operator can do to help gain control of rental land.

Think in Terms of What the Landlord Wants

In many instances, when an operator rents land, the operator thinks in terms of what "I" want. This attitude might work in a buyer's market, but land rental is usually a seller's market. Therefore, anyone who wishes to rent land should ask this question about each prospective landlord: "What will make this landowner happy about the rental arrangement?" If the renter develops the attitude of thinking in terms of what the landowner wants, this approach can be a key to success in renting land. The following points should be helpful in dealing with landlords. The renter needs to tailor each point to individual landowners, however, because they have different preferences.

Do a good job.   Most established farmers who have been successful in gaining control of rental land have, above all else, done a good job with production. Yields are high as a result of timeliness, good fertilization practices, proper seed varieties, weed control, insect control, disease control, and tillage methods. Most landlords want a good return and a good image for their farm. Both of these goals are accomplished by doing a good job of crop production.

Maintain the land and buildings.   Keeping the farm in good condition is important to many farm owners. Offering to do some of the things listed below can help secure the initial rental of a farm, and performing some of these tasks on a continuous basis can help in retaining the rental land from year to year.

- Test soil
- Clear fence rows
- Maintain sod waterways
- Clip weeds
- Repair gates
- Maintain lanes and driveways
- Replace broken boards on buildings
- Nail down loose roof shingles
- Maintain fences

Provide information to the landlord.   Landowners usually like to have information about such things as costs, progress of field operations, crops, and yields. They also appreciate hearing about any unusual problems or gains. These reports can be made by simply writing the information on a map of the farm. The spring report might show acres of various crops with dates of planting, seed varieties, and fertilization. The fall report might show dates of harvest, yields, and any special information. Liming, tile repair, and installation of new tile can also be shown on the map (see Chapter 6).

Be Willing to Raise Livestock

Some farms have livestock buildings, and most owners would like to see these buildings used. Many renters are not interested in raising livestock, so there is often less competition for livestock farms.

> Jim and Alice Eiker wanted to farm but had no family farm opportunity. Renting was the only way for them to get started in the farming business. They found a small farm with average land for the area and some old high-labor dairy buildings. The landowner agreed to rent the Eikers the land provided that they would be willing to milk cows. Although crop farming was their first choice, this offer provided Jim and Alice an opportunity to begin farming. After getting started with this 240-acre, 35-cow unit, they rented more land in the community and eventually purchased the initial farm unit.

The renter must weigh the value of the rental land against the cost of raising livestock, sometimes in buildings that require large amounts of the operator's labor. It may not always be desirable to rent a livestock farm, but a willingness to raise livestock can make an operator more competitive with some landlords.

Cash-Rent

Cash rental is a way that young farmers can more easily compete with established farmers for land. While the young farmers may not have the experience or large modern machinery desired by the landlord, they may be able to offer a higher cash rent. Before cash-renting, however, farmers must budget carefully to determine the amount that they can pay for rent and still have a satisfactory return (see Table 15.1).

Cash rentals can be high relative to returns because some operators price fixed labor and machinery below costs. Also, some operators may not know their costs and bid too high by mistake.

> Harry Cleveland farmed 640 acres, 320 owned and 320 cash-rented. He did most of the work himself with only a few hours of part-time help at planting and harvest. When the owner of the rented 320 acres died, the land was sold to a neighbor who began farming that unit. This left Harry with only 320 acres to farm. A unit of 200 acres located 1 mile from Harry was to be cash-rented to the highest bidder. Harry was able to outbid the competition because he was willing to accept $50 per acre for the use of his machinery, labor, and management, all of which would not be fully used if he farmed only the 320 acres he owned.

TABLE 15.1   Figuring Break-Even Cash Rent Based on Production Costs[a]

Item	Corn/Acre (125 bu.) Operator	Your Estimate	Soybeans/Acre (40 bu.) Operator	Your Estimate
Fertilizer	$ 51.00	_____	$ 23.00	_____
Seed	14.00	_____	11.00	_____
Chemicals	10.00	_____	12.00	_____
Machine operation[b]	40.00	_____	24.00	_____
Machine ownership cost[c]	40.00	_____	40.00	_____
Storage and drying fixed costs	35.00	_____	11.00	_____
Interest and miscellaneous (including stored grain)	25.00	_____	20.00	_____
Labor and management	36.00	_____	32.00	_____
Total cost excluding cash rent (1)	251.00	_____	173.00	_____

Corn Price	Gross Return (2A)	Break-Even Rent (2A − 1)	Soybean Price	Gross Return (2B)	Break-Even Rent (2B − 1)
$2.50	$312.50	_____	$5.50	$220.00	_____
2.75	343.75	_____	6.00	240.00	_____
3.00	375.00	_____	6.50	260.00	_____
3.25	406.25	_____	7.00	280.00	_____
3.50	437.50	_____	7.50	300.00	_____
3.75	468.75	_____	8.00	320.00	_____

[a]Excluding land.

[b]Fuel, repairs, and oil.

[c]Depreciation, interest, taxes, and insurance.

Anyone who had to purchase machinery and hire labor and management would need approximately $84 per acre to cover these costs (Table 15.1).

> Calculate the maximum amount you could bid on a land tract in your area that is being cash-rented.

Do Custom Work

Doing custom tillage, planting, or harvesting will sometimes open the door to land-rental opportunities because it increases contacts and demonstrates that you have adequate machinery. Also, helping a landowner out of a difficult situation may gain for you the opportunity to rent the farm in subsequent years.

John Borg owned 200 acres and did the tillage and planting himself but hired harvesting of corn and soybeans. In one extremely wet fall John had difficulty finding a custom operator who had time to harvest his crops. A farmer who did custom work in the area agreed to harvest John's crops if he would have first chance if John decided to rent. The next year John Borg did decide to rent his farm, and the operator who did the custom work for him has been operating it since that time.

Keep Good Public Relations with Landowners

Practicing good public relations is almost always helpful, and it may prove especially so with landowners.

Bill Bixley plowed Sara Smith's garden each year and sometimes helped her start her automobile on cold winter mornings. When her renter retired, she offered the farm to Bill on a share-rental arrangement even though several more experienced operators with larger equipment wanted to rent the farm.

Keep Contacts Informed

It can be helpful to keep appropriate people aware that you are looking for land to rent. Bankers, Production Credit, FmHA, and Federal Land Bank representatives, farm implement suppliers, professional farm managers, and others who talk with persons involved in agriculture often hear about the availability of farms for rent.

A 400-acre unit managed by a bank trust department had been farmed for many years by Tom Jordan, who lived 15 miles from the farm. Two farmers who owned land on each side of the 400 acres had hoped to rent the unit when Tom Jordan retired. However, Dennis Whitcant, a farmer living 6 miles away, kept representatives in the local bank (and other places) aware of his desire to rent more land. One of the bankers informed Dennis about Tom's retirement, and Dennis contacted the trust officer and rented the farm before it was generally known that it would be available.

Help an Investor Find Land

Sometimes investors like to purchase farm property and rent it to reliable operators. Seeking out such investors and helping them to find suitable farms can put you in a good position to rent the purchased farm.

Delmar Worth learned from a local realtor about Dr. Hurt's interest in buying a farm as an investment. Delmar wanted to rent more land, so he contacted Dr. Hurt and offered to help him find a farm to purchase in exchange for allowing him to rent the farm. After checking Delmar's references, Dr. Hurt agreed. Delmar is now farming on a share-rental basis the land he found for Dr. Hurt.

Nick Argyropolos, an established farmer, has the policy of purchasing a farm, improving it, and then selling it to any investor who will allow him to farm it. As soon as one sale is made, Nick purchases another farm.

Inquire

Sometimes farmers assume that a farm is not going to be rented and fail to talk with the owner about rental possibilities.

A young woman who was attempting to get started in farming just happened to talk to a landowner and found that the landowner had rented his farm to another young farmer in the community. When the young woman voiced her surprise—"I didn't know you were going to rent the farm"—the landowner responded, "If you are going to get started farming, you'd better learn how to determine when land will be available for rent." The landowner's sharp comment, in addition to the young woman's desire to farm, motivated the young woman to be more aggressive in the future. She is now farming several hundred acres.

Keep Track of Land Sales

Changes in land ownership can mean changes in rental arrangements. Be aware of all land sales, especially to off-farm investors.

Be Flexible

It may be necessary to accept a type of lease that is not your first preference. Being flexible may enable you to rent land and, at a later time, arrange to change the lease.

Mo Wesley offered to rent 260 acres, purchased by an off-farm investor, on a share-crop arrangement. The investor wanted to have the unit custom-farmed. Mo agreed to operate on a custom-hire basis and two years later convinced the owner to rent on the share basis.

Marshall Williams cash-rented a farm from a doctor even though he preferred a share-rental arrangement. A year later, when both prices and yields were high, Marshall prepared a budget showing that share renting that year would have paid a higher return to the doctor than cash renting. The doctor was willing to change to the share arrangement that Marshall preferred because he was convinced there would be lower risk associated with a share arrangement.

CHOOSING A RENTAL ARRANGEMENT[1]

There are four important considerations in choosing a lease:

1. What share of the income do I receive?
2. What portion of the costs do I contribute?
3. What portion of the risk do I carry?
4. What crop and land management practices will be followed?

In any community there are typical leases that answer these questions. If the operator is especially good or if there are a limited number of good operators in the community, the operator might be able to bargain for a better-than-usual lease. On the other hand, if the farm is above average in land quality, if land is scarce in the area, or if the renter has not yet demonstrated superior performance, the renter may have to make concessions to the landlord.

Several types of leases have evolved to allow shifting income, risk, costs, and management between the tenant and the landlord. Following is a discussion of various types of leases.

Cash Leases

With a cash-lease arrangement, the owner agrees to provide a specific tract of land (and sometimes buildings) for a specified time period for a certain amount of money. Cash rentals have a number of advantages and disadvantages for the operator and landlord (see Table 15–2).

Flexible cash rent. A flexible cash-rent arrangement can be used to tie rental rates to prices, yields, and gross income, and stipulations in the lease can provide some management control. Flexible cash rents involve adjustments in the amount of rent paid as product price or yield varies. Table 15.3 illustrates two flexible cash-rent plans. Some important steps in establishing flexible cash rents are:

1. Establish a base rent at an agreed-upon base product price and/or yield. For example, land rent might be $105.00 per acre when soybeans are $6.50 per bushel and yield is 40 bushels per acre.
2. Agree upon a time and place for establishing price. Agree, for example, that prices will be determined at a local elevator between the dates of January 1 and harvest and that the dates for establishing prices will be selected by the owner. Yield is usually determined at harvest.

---

[1] Some of the material in this section is from "Leasing Arrangements for the 1980s," booklet developed by the Agricultural Economics Department, Purdue University, West Lafayette, IN, 1980. Authors of papers in the publication include: G. A. Harrison, E. C. Carson, Paul R. Robbins, David C. Petritz, and David H. Bache. Also included is material from unpublished papers written by J. H. Atkinson.

TABLE 15.2   Advantages and Disadvantages of a Cash Lease

Advantages	Disadvantages
Operator	
Operator reaps full benefits from superior management, which results in higher yields, lower cost, higher prices.	Operator takes all the risks associated with fluctuating prices, adverse weather, and increasing costs.
Simplifies record keeping, eliminates need to divide and keep track of jointly owned crops and livestock. Eliminates most joint decisions and pressures from the landlord to plant and harvest early.	Operator must make essentially all management decisions.
Good way to gain control of additional land. Operator can bid what the land is worth and is not so tied to custom or tradition as in crop-share leasing.	Operator often pays a rent equal to or higher than under a crop-share lease and, in addition, assumes much more of the risk and management responsibility.
Operator may acquire added drying and storage facilities and gain benefits resulting from them for the entire crop instead of for only a part of the crop.	Operator has larger capital requirements for inputs, storage, etc. In addition, operator must have cash to pay the rent.
Greatly reduces the opportunity for disagreements and the need to consult with the landlord as would be true where joint decisions must be made under the crop-share lease.	Usually, at least part of the rent will have to be paid early in the year, before the crop is planted.
Landlord	
More stable, secure income.	Operator may go broke and fail to pay the rent.
Landlord no longer needs to worry about keeping up on the latest technologies, market information, etc. These worries are transferred to the operator.	Landlord may want to share the management and risk responsibilities.
Should the landlord die, spouse would more likely feel comfortable with the arrangement under a cash agreement than under a share agreement.	Since the landlord has given up most of the decision making to the tenant, there may be more chance that the farm will be exploited—depletion of soils, poor care of buildings, failure to cut weeds, etc.
Landlord may get at least a part of the rental income several months earlier than under a crop-share lease.	Landlord forgoes the opportunity to gain from yield-improving technologies, improving markets, etc., except as these may be reflected in following years' rents.
Cash expenditures are greatly reduced.	Landlord forgoes the opportunity to gain from storage, skillful marketing, etc.
Greatly reduces opportunities for disagreements and need for consultation with the operator.	

TABLE 15.3 Example of Flexible Cash Rent

Plan A[a]		Plan B[b]	
Soybean Price	Cash Rent	Gross Income	Cash Rent
$5.50	$ 80.00	$220.00	$ 85.00
6.50	105.00	260.00	105.00
7.50	130.00	300.00	125.00

[a]Cash rent is $105.00 per acre with soybean price of $6.50. Rent is adjusted ±25 cents for each 1-cent change in the price of soybeans at a specified time and place.

[b]Gross income with $6.50 soybeans at 40 bu./acre is $260.00. For each $1.00 change in gross income, cash rent is adjusted $0.50.

3. Agree on how much the rent will fluctuate from the base with unit changes in price, yield, and/or gross income. For example, it might be agreed that with each 1-cent change in the price of soybeans, rent will change 25 cents and/or with each 1-bushel change in yield, rent will change $3.00 per acre, or with each $1.00 change in expected gross income, rent will change 50 cents per acre.

Specifying an adjustment in rental rate based only on price could create financial difficulty for the operator in low-yield, high-price years, so it is advisable to have a maximum cash rent or to use gross income as the adjustment factor. A provision could be included that would reduce or eliminate increases in rents should yields for the farm fall below a predetermined level. On 40-bushel soybean land, for example, this figure might be 25 bushels or less. It should be low enough so as not to occur very often but high enough to give the operator reasonable protection against low yields caused by forces beyond human control. The flexible lease may appeal to operators and landlords who want the lease to continue over a period of years. The amount of rent paid will automatically be adjusted as prices of products change. All leases should be in writing, and this is especially true for flexible cash-rent leases because of their complexity.

Management control.   The landlord can maintain some management control over cash-rented land by specifying desired conditions. These conditions could include acres of various crops, level of fertilization, weed and insect control practices, tillage practices, waterway maintenance practices, and drainage maintenance. Requirements specified in a lease by a landowner for a 450-acre rental unit included the following:

1. The annual acreage of soybeans shall not exceed 275 acres.
2. Fertilization will include a minimum annual application of 50 pounds of phosphate per acre and 50 pounds of potash per acre.
3. Weeds shall be controlled.

4. Sod waterways shall be maintained.
5. Tile drains shall be maintained and repaired as breaks occur.
6. Open ditches shall be maintained and sprayed for weed and brush control.
7. The landowner and the operator will meet quarterly to discuss the implementation of these and other crop-management practices.

To encourage improvements and maintenance of the farm, landowners might specify a certain amount of money to be used each year for tile, waterways, lime, and so on.

Cash-rental rates.   Each geographic area has market cash-rental rates. These vary over time depending on the crop yields, prices, and costs. Table 15.4 illustrates the types of information available in some states.

TABLE 15.4   Average Estimated Cash Rents, Bare Tillable Land, 1982 and 1983, Purdue Land Values Survey, Indiana, July 1983

Area	Land class	Rent/A		Rent as a percentage of June land value	
		1982	1983	1982	1983
		Dollars		Percent	
North[a]	Top	127	129	5.5	6.2
	Average	97	97	5.5	6.0
	Poor	68	69	5.6	6.0
Northeast[a]	Top	115	114	5.9	6.4
	Average	89	90	6.1	6.5
	Poor	64	67	6.3	6.9
West Central[a]	Top	142	138	6.0	6.1
	Average	115	116	6.0	6.4
	Poor	87	89	6.5	6.6
Central[a]	Top	135	135	5.4	5.9
	Average	111	112	5.5	5.9
	Poor	86	87	5.8	6.0
Southwest[a]	Top	115	108	5.0	5.4
	Average	86	83	5.0	5.6
	Poor	59	63	5.5	5.8
Southeast[a]	Top	96	91	6.3	7.0
	Average	72	70	6.4	7.0
	Poor	48	50	6.2	6.6
Indiana[b]	Top	124	122	5.6	6.1
	Average	98	97	5.7	6.2
	Poor	71	73	5.9	6.4

[a]Based on the surveys returned from this region.

[b]Based on all the surveys returned.

Source: J. H. Atkinson, "Turnaround in Land Values," *Purdue Agricultural Economics Report,* August 1983.

Share Leases

Share leases involve allocation of the crops on a percentage basis as payment for the resources that the landlord and the operator contribute. With many share leases, some of the costs also are divided. Share leases reverse many of the advantages and disadvantages presented earlier for the cash lease (see Table 15.5).

Each geographic area of the country has typical or most usual share arrangements that have evolved as a result of experience over many years. The share of income and costs varies from area to area because of differences in land, weather, risk, and management skill. In the Corn Belt, the 50–50 sharing of both income and costs is often followed; in the Mississippi Delta, the 75% operator–25% landlord lease is frequently used; and in Kansas, the arrangement is often 60% operator–40% landlord.

Table 15.6 shows typical crop-lease arrangements determined by a survey of Corn Belt farmers. Variations from these typical arrangements are often made

TABLE 15.5   Advantages and Disadvantages of the Share Lease

Advantages	Disadvantages
Operator	
Spreads the risk by paying landlord a share of the crop rather than a fixed amount of income.	Complex; operator must consult with landlord about decisions.
Operator may receive some management help.	Hard to rent, especially for beginning farmer.
Net rent payment is often less than for a cash lease.	Increases chances of disagreements.
Less capital required than for cash renting.	Operator must share gains from outstanding management.
	Landlords may not be satisfied with the timing of planting and harvesting and the way jobs are done.
	More bookkeeping is required to keep expense and receipts separated for each landlord.
Landlord	
Return from higher prices and yields are shared by landlord.	Increases worries about getting the job done.
Landlord more certain to obtain returns than with a cash lease.	Creates variable, uncertain income.
Farm more likely to be maintained and improved because landlord has more control.	Possibly less income than with a cash lease.
Landlord can gain from management in crop selection, crop-management practices, and marketing.	More complex than a cash lease, thus more possibility for disagreement.

TABLE 15.6   Common Crop-Lease Arrangements in the Corn Belt

| Item | Type of Lease | | | |
| | 50–50 | | $\frac{2}{3} = \frac{1}{3}$ | |
	Operator	Landlord	Operator	Landlord
Crops	50%	50%	67%	33%
Costs				
Fertilizer	50	50	100	0
Lime	0	100	100	0
Seed	50	50	100	0
Herbicide	50	50	100	0
Insecticide	50	50	100	0
Machinery	80	20[a]	100	0
Labor	100	0	100	0
Storage	50	50	67	33
Land and land improvements	0	100	0	100

[a]Landlord pays operator for half of harvesting and operating costs of drying grain.

through bargaining between the operator and the landlord. Areas in which bargaining most frequently occurs are:

1. Harvest costs: Operator may provide all harvesting, or costs may be shared with the landlord.
2. Storage: Landlord or operator may provide all storage.
3. Dryer: Operator or landlord may provide the dryer.
4. Custom application of fertilizer and chemicals may be paid for by the operator or shared with the landlord.
5. Crops may be hauled to market by the operator, or the landlord may pay for his or her share of marketing the crops.

> What are the usual leasing arrangements in your area? What are the most usual bargaining points?

LEASE EFFICIENCY

The term of the lease and the sharing of costs and returns can cause a rental farm to yield a lower income than would be attained on an owner-operated farm.

Lease Term

Short term leases may discourage investments in land and buildings that pay high returns over a period of several years but do not pay for the first one or two years. Farm owners may be reluctant to rent on a long-term basis because they want the opportunity to change renters if a good job is not being done, or they might want to sell the property in the near future and do not wish to be committed to a long-term lease arrangement. A long-term lease guarantees the renter the farm for the term of the lease; however, if the renter chooses to quit, it is usually not feasible to force the renter to continue to operate. The main benefit a landlord can obtain from a long-term lease is improvement of the farm, eventually resulting in higher rental returns.

Many leases are written so that they are automatically renewable if not terminated by either party in writing before a given date. Landlords and renters should work toward long-range leasing either on a formal or informal basis because long-term leasing tends to generate higher income from the farm. Should the lease be terminated before improvements made by the operator are used, the operator may be repaid for the unused portion as specified in the lease.

Sharing Costs and Returns

When income is not shared in the same proportion as costs, inequities may result. For example, suppose that a building investment by the landlord would reduce labor costs sufficiently to pay for the investment and make a substantial profit as well. However, the renter, who provides all of the labor, would receive the entire cost saving, while the landlord, who provides the buildings, would incur the entire cost. Under these circumstances the landlord may be reluctant to invest in the building. The landlord and the renter must discuss the benefits to be gained and make an adjustment in the lease or in the farm organization so that the building investment would be profitable for the landlord as well as the renter.

Sharing returns and costs in the same proportion tends to encourage efficiency. For instance, an arrangement under which the renter provides all of the fertilizer but receives only half the crop would encourage lower-than-optimum fertilizer use.

The landlord and the renter should continually consider how total net returns from the farm can be maximized. The lease should be designed so that it is profitable for both the landlord and the renter to contribute resources to the optimum farm plan.

LEASE EQUITY

All types of leases can be adjusted to shift net returns from one party to the other. For example, cash rents can be raised or lowered, costs such as harvesting can be shared or the entire cost borne by one party, and the shares of returns can be changed. The share of returns to each party should be proportional to the value of resources that each contributes. This principle is a good reference point, but the problem in applying the principle is that there are subtle differences in the quality of resources contributed, and these subtle differences greatly affect the value of the resources. Assume that, on the average, the operator's management ability is worth 7% of the gross income. Superior management may be worth 14%, while poor management may have a negative value. On the average, land may have an annual rental value of $100 per acre. But well-drained, fertile land with good moisture-holding capacity that lies in large tracts with few physical barriers is worth much more than the average. Further, land has an accompanying landowner whose association with the land may increase or decrease its value.

In addition to resource quality differences, prices of resources change over time because of international as well as local supply and demand conditions. In a given time period there may be a shortage of good operators in a particular geographic area, and the price of good operating management may be high compared to other areas. As good operators observe the opportunities and move into the area, the price for good operating management will decline.

Thus, when deciding on the returns to each party from a rental arrangement:

1. Determine the typical cash- and share-rental characteristics for the area.
2. List the resources and their annual value that each party will contribute (Table 15.7).
3. Budget the returns to each party and compare this return to the contributions (discussed later in this chapter).
4. Make adjustments in the shares of costs and returns to bring resource contributions more in line with returns.

Of overriding importance is the individual situation. For example, if a landlord has an outstanding operator that he or she calculates is receiving a higher proportion of returns than is justified by the operator's resource contribution, the landlord must consider what other alternatives there may be. The landlord might be able to secure a higher share of the returns with a less capable operator, but this may result in lower total returns than would be the case with a lower proportion of returns with an excellent operator: 40% of $20,000 is more than 50% of $12,000. Likewise, an operator who has machinery and labor to farm 600 acres may be better off paying more than what is typical in the area to rent a 280-acre farm if the only other alternative is not renting the farm and operating only 320 acres.

Thus, the return to each party should be determined not only by the value of contributions made by each but also by considering current and past arrangements on other farms in the area, the unique characteristics of the resources offered by each party, and the alternatives open to the landlord and the operator.

TABLE 15.7   Determining the Value of Resource Contribution by the Landlord and the Tenant Under a Share-Rental Arrangement (Hypothetical)

Item of Expense	(A) Estimated Total Value	(B) Estimated Capital Charge	Estimated Annual Cost		
			(C) Whole Farm	(D) Landlord's Share	(E) Tenant's Share
Capital expenses					
1. Land	$1,200,000	4%	$ 48,000	$ 48,000	$ 0
2. Building	150,000	10	15,000	15,000	0
3. Machinery and equipment	200,000	10	20,000	2,000	18,000
4. Livestock	60,000	10	6,000	3,000	3,000
5. Feed and supplies	10,000	10	1,000	500	500
6. Other					
7. Other					
Farm operation expenses					
8. Labor					
Tenant labor and management			$ 25,000	$ 0	$ 25,000
Landlord labor and management			2,000	2,000	
Hired			12,000	0	12,000
9. Repairs					
Buildings, fences, etc.			2,500	2,500	0
Machinery			6,000	0	6,000
10. Depreciation					
Buildings, fences, etc.			15,000	15,000	0
Machinery			25,000	2,500	22,500
11. Tractor fuel			15,000	3,000	12,000
12. Custom fertilizer spreading			1,000	500	500
13. Seed			5,000	2,500	2,500
14. Fertilizer and lime			26,000	13,000	13,000
15. Other crop expenses			2,000	1,000	1,000
16. Feed purchased			30,000	15,000	15,000
17. Other livestock expenses			2,000	1,000	1,000
18. Insurance					
Buildings			1,000	1,000	0
Personal property			1,000	200	800
19. Taxes					
Land and buildings			5,000	5,000	0
Personal property			1,600	200	1,400
20. Miscellaneous			3,000	1,000	2,000
21. Total expenses			270,100	133,900	136,200
22. Percent contributed			100%	49.6%	50.4%

PASTURE RENTAL

Throughout the country, pastures vary widely in quality and in supply and demand conditions. Because of these variations, considerable differences are found in leasing rates and methods from state to state. The following general relationships between pasture rental rates and the prices of other commodities are typical for the Midwest:

- Rental rate per cow per month has generally been equal to 2.2 times the price of a bushel of corn.
- Rental rate per cow per month has generally been equal to the price of hay per ton divided by a factor of 8.5.
- Rental rate per cow per month has generally been equal to the price of fed cattle divided by a factor of 11.

Rental rates per acre for the grazing season are determined from these per-cow-per-month estimates by multiplying by the number of months in the grazing season. This value is then divided by the number of acres of pastureland needed to carry a cow during the grazing season. For example, the rent for an eight-month grazing period would be $24 per acre if a monthly rate of $6 per cow is common in the locale and if the pasture is of such quality that 2 acres are required to carry each cow during the season.

One difficulty in establishing rental rates per head is varying the rental rate for different sizes and classes of animals. A series of coefficients has been developed as an aid for making these calculations. A 1,000-pound animal is referred to as an "animal unit." A yearling steer has an animal-unit equivalent of 0.75, indicating that the yearling has three-fourths the pasture requirements of a 1,000-pound cow. A calf six to twelve months of age has an animal-unit equivalent of 0.5; a three- to six-month-old calf, 0.3; and a 1,000- to 1,400-pound bull, 1.25.

Using these coefficients, rental rates can be varied to reflect the different sizes of animals being grazed. For example, if a rental rate of $5.00 per head has been established for a 1,000-pound cow, the rental rate for grazing a nine-month-old calf would be $2.50 per month.

Local supply and demand conditions play an important role in determining pasture rent. If there is a large quantity of pasture for rent in an area and very few producers need pasture, the rental rate will likely decline. Pastures must be used where grown and must be used during the grazing season rather than stored for later use. Generally speaking, few alternative uses exist for pastureland, so the agreed-upon rent must be established by bargaining between the owner and the renter. In many cases, a buyer's market exists, and the buyer can negotiate a bargain.

In estimating what they can afford to pay for pasture rent, operators need to consider profit potential from using the pasture. For instance, if a rented pasture will be used to graze steers, the operator should consider the price for feeder cattle in the spring and the expected selling price in the fall. Other costs associated with the pasturing program that must also be considered include supplementary feed, water supply, minerals and salt, medication, implants, and interest on investment in cattle. The operator should also estimate labor costs and possible travel costs if some distance exists between home and the cattle. Using these costs, the maximum amount the operator can afford to pay for pasture rent can be estimated. This will be tempered by quality of pasture, location to the home farm, and water supply.

The costs of fertilizer, fence repair, and maintenance of water supply may be borne by either the landlord or the tenant, and the amount of rent should reflect these costs.

A written lease should specify rental rates, stocking rates, and the responsibilities of each party in terms of fence inspection and repair, maintenance of water systems, supervision of water supply, salt and mineral supply, fly control, return of stray animals to pasture, and calling of a veterinarian in case of emergency.

BUDGETING RETURNS TO ALTERNATIVE LEASING ARRANGEMENTS

In determining the profitability of renting additional land, a manager should use the budgeting procedures illustrated in Chapters 8 and 10, but the returns and costs should be specified for both the renter and the landlord. The budgeting procedure for evaluating different types of rental arrangements is illustrated with the Sally Field case.

Sally Field Case

Sally and Tom Field farmed a 320-acre unit for many years. When Tom died last winter, Sally elected not to continue operating the farm but instead to rent to Roger Hunt, one of the best farmers in the community. Sally and Roger considered cash and share arrangements and also examined the possibility of Roger farming for Sally on a custom-hire basis. They considered the following seven rental alternatives:

1. Cash lease: $110.00 per acre, tenant pays all expenses except lime, land tax, and maintenance (see Table 15.8 for costs).
2. Flexible cash rent based on price: Rent is $110.00 per acre with corn at $3.00. For each 1-cent change in corn price from $3.00, cash rent changes 35 cents per acre. Landlord determines date of sale between rental date and November 1 of the crop year.
3. Flexible cash rent based on gross income: Rent is $110.00 per acre with corn yield of 120 bushels and corn price of $3.00. For each one dollar change in gross income per acre from $360 per acre, rent changes 50 cents per acre.
4. In-kind lease: 40 bushels per acre of #2 corn to owner, tenant pays all expenses except lime, land tax, maintenance, and storage cost of 35 cents per acre for the 40 bushels.
5. 50–50 lease: Typical crop share (costs as shown in Table 15.8).

TABLE 15.8 Estimated Costs per Acre of Producing Corn and Typical Division between Landlord and Tenant under 50–50 Crop-Share Lease and Custom-Hire Arrangement[a] (Sally Field and Roger Hunt)

Item	50–50 Lease (120 bu./acre)			Custom Hire		
	Total Cost	Landlord	Tenant	Total Cost	Landlord	Tenant
Fertilizer	$ 50.00	$25.00	$ 25.00	$ 50.00	$ 50.00	$ 0
Lime	2.00	2.00	0	2.00	2.00	0
Seed	15.00	7.50	7.50	15.00	15.00	0
Chemicals	10.00	5.00	5.00	10.00	10.00	0
Machine operation	45.00	10.00	35.00	45.00	12.00	33.00
Machine fixed cost	43.00	0	43.00	43.00	0	43.00
Land tax and maintenance	13.00	13.00	0	13.00	13.00	0
Storage	42.00	21.00	21.00	42.00	42.00	0
Interest and miscellaneous	12.00	6.00	6.00	12.00	10.00	2.00
Total	$232.00	$89.50	$142.50	$232.00	$154.00	$78.00

[a]Does not include labor and management or interest cost on land.

6. Custom-incentive lease: $70.00 per acre payment to operator plus one-third of the corn yield over 90 bushels per acre. Operator provides machinery and labor. Each party is responsible for corn drying at $0.10 per bushel and storage at $0.35 per bushel.

7. Custom-hire agreement: Flat payment of $100.00 per acre to operator. Operator provides labor and machinery. Owner pays all other expenses including all drying and storage (see Table 15.8).

Sally and Roger calculated the return each would receive for each type of lease on the basis of the cost and yield information in Table 15.8. They judged that a normal yield was 120 bushels per acre and the most likely price was $3.00 per bushel. They also computed returns for a price of $2.50 per bushel and a yield of 80 bushels per acre. The returns to Roger and Sally are presented in Table 15.9.

Sally observed that she would make the most money with a custom lease, but Roger was unwilling to provide his good management and machinery on a custom basis. Sally liked the idea of the high returns and low risk of the cash lease. Observing that his returns were highest and risk relatively low with a 50–50 cash lease, Roger asked Sally to rent on a 50–50 basis. Because Roger was an excellent crop farmer and because Sally had confidence that Roger would be reliable and do a good job, she agreed.

> If Sally had been discussing lease arrangements with a starting farmer, which arrangement do you think they would have selected?
>
> Do you think Sally was wise in renting to Roger on a 50-50 lease, or should she have found an operator who would rent for cash or custom-farm?

TABLE 15.9 Returns to Owner and Operator under Various Lease Arrangements, Yields, and Prices, Sally Field and Roger Hunt

Type of Lease	Returns When Corn Yields 120 Bushels per Acre Price $3.00		Returns When Corn Yields 80 Bushels per Acre[a] Price $3.00		Returns When Corn Yields 120 Bushels— Price $2.50	
	Operator[b]	Owner[c]	Operator	Owner	Operator	Owner
1. Cash	$33.00	$ 95.00	− $69.00	$95.00	− $27.00	$95.00
2. Flexible cash—Price	33.00	95.00	− 69.00	95.00	− 9.50	77.50
3. Flexible cash—Gross income	33.00	95.00	− 9.00	35.00	3.00	65.00
4. In-kind	37.00	91.00	− 65.00	91.00	− 3.00	71.00
5. 50–50	37.50	90.50	− 13.50	39.50	7.50	60.50
6. Custom incentive	17.50	110.50	− 8.00	34.00	12.50	55.50
7. Custom hire	22.00	106.00	22.00	4.00	22.00	46.00

[a] Lower yield due to bad weather; uses same costs as for 120 bushels of corn except for storage at $0.35 per bushel and drying at $0.10 per bushel.

[b] This represents return to labor plus a management/risk return.

[c] This represents return to land valued at $1,600 per acre plus a management/risk return.

LEASE PROVISIONS

A farm lease should be written so that there will be no misunderstanding regarding the specific terms of the rental agreement. If a lease is not in writing, the parties may have different views of what was thought to be an agreement on a particular point. Provisions that seemed entirely clear at the signing of the lease may not be clear several months later. Finally, should one party fail to fulfill his or her lease obligations, the other party will be on more solid ground, from a legal standpoint, in protecting his or her rights if the lease is in writing. Perhaps most important of all, a written lease may help avoid a legal battle. Generally, everyone loses when disagreements must be settled in court.

The North Central Regional livestock share lease in Figure 15.1 illustrates the important things to be included in a lease. Similar lease forms are available from many state extension services and commercial organizations.

> Read the lease in Figure 15.1 carefully, including the instructions. Make a list of important elements of the lease and indicate why each of these is important. Secure a similar kind of lease for your area from the extension service, a commercial agency, or a renter. How does it differ from the North Central lease?

Livestock Share Farm Lease North Central Regional

Publication No. 108

This form can provide the landlord and tenant with a guide for developing an agreement to fit their individual situation. This form is not intended to take the place of legal advice pertaining to contractual relationships between the two parties. Because of the possibility that a farm operating agreement may be legally considered a partnership under certain conditions, seeking proper legal advice is recommended when developing such an agreement.

This lease is entered into this _____ day of _____, 19_____, between

_____, landlord, of _____

_____

(address)

_____, spouse, of _____

_____

(address)

hereafter known as "the landlord," and

_____, tenant, of _____

_____

(address)

_____, spouse, of _____

_____

(address)

hereafter known as "the tenant."

I. PROPERTY DESCRIPTION

The landlord hereby leases to the tenant, to occupy and use for agricultural and related purposes, the following described property:

_____
_____

consisting of approximately _____ acres situated in _____ County (Counties), _____ (State) with all improvements thereon except as follows:

_____
_____
_____

II. GENERAL TERMS OF LEASE

A. Time period covered. The provisions of this agreement shall be in effect for _____ year(s), commencing on the _____ day of _____, 19_____. This lease shall continue in effect from year to year thereafter unless written notice of termination is given by either party to the other at least _____ days prior to expiration of this lease or the end of any year of continuation.

B. Review of lease. A written request is required for a general review of the lease or for consideration of proposed changes by either party, at least _____ days prior to the final date for giving notice to terminate the lease as specified in IIA.

C. Amendments and alterations. Amendments and alterations to this lease shall be in writing and shall be signed by both the landlord and tenant.

D. No partnership intended. It is particularly understood and agreed that this lease shall not be deemed to be nor intended to give rise to a partnership relation.

E. Transfer of property. If the landlord should sell or otherwise transfer title to the farm, he will do so subject to the provisions of this lease.

F. Right of entry. The landlord reserves the right for himself, his agents, his employees, or his assigns to enter the farm at any reasonable time to: a) consult with the tenant; b) make repairs, improvements, and inspections; and c) (after notice of termination of the lease is given) do plowing, seeding, fertilizing, and any other customary seasonal work, none of which is to interfere with the tenant in carrying out regular farm operations.

G. No right to sublease. The landlord does not convey to the tenant the right to lease or sublet any part of the farm or to assign the lease to any person or persons whomsoever.

H. Binding on heirs. The provisions of this lease shall be binding upon the heirs, executors, administrators, and successors of both landlord and tenant in like manner as upon the original parties, except as provided by mutual written agreement.

I. Landlord's lien for rent and performance. The landlord's lien provided by law on crops grown or growing shall be the security for the rent herein specified and for the faithful performance of the terms of the lease. If the tenant fails to pay the rent due or fails to keep the agreements of this lease, all costs and attorney fees of the landlord in enforcing collection or performance shall be added to and become a part of the obligations payable by the tenant hereunder.

J. Additional provisions.

_____
_____

III. LAND USE

A. General provisions. The land described in Section I will be used in approximately the following manner. If it is impractical in any year to follow such a land-use plan, appropriate adjustments will be made by mutual written agreements between the parties.

For further information see: "Livestock-Share Rental Arrangements for Your Farm" NCR publication number 107.

Figure 15.1   Livestock share farm lease, north central regional. *Source:* Cooperative Extension Service, Pub. No. 108.

1. Cropland
   a) Row crops   _____ acres
   b) Small grains   _____ acres
   c) Legumes   _____ acres
   d) Rotation pasture   _____ acres

2. Pasture: _____ _____ acres

3. Other: _____ _____ acres
   _____ _____ acres

4. Total   _____ acres

B. Restrictions. The maximum acres harvested as silage shall be _____ acres unless it is mutually decided otherwise.

    The pasture stocking rate shall not exceed:

PASTURE IDENTIFICATION:

_____ _____ acres/animal unit
_____ _____ acres/animal unit
_____ _____ acres/animal unit

(1,000 pound mature cow is equivalent to one animal unit.)

Other restrictions are:

_____
_____
_____

C. Government programs. The extent of participation in government programs will be discussed and decided on an annual basis. The course of action agreed upon shall be placed in writing and be signed by both parties. A copy of the course of action so agreed upon shall be made available to each party.

IV. LIVESTOCK PRODUCTION AND SHARING ARRANGEMENTS

A. It is agreed the tenant and landlord will engage in the production of livestock. Real property including land and the type and number of livestock to be contributed to production by each party are reported in Table 1.

Table 1—Contributions of Property to be Furnished by Each Party

	Approximate number to be kept	Share furnished by Landlord %	Tenant %
1. Land and fixed improvements at beginning of this lease described in Section I		_____	_____
2. Fixed improvements constructed during period of this lease:			
Materials and skilled labor		_____	_____
Hauling materials to farm		_____	_____
Farm labor		_____	_____
_____		_____	_____
_____		_____	_____
3. Livestock:			
Breeding: _____	_____	_____	_____
_____	_____	_____	_____
_____	_____	_____	_____
Replacements: _____	_____	_____	_____
_____	_____	_____	_____
_____	_____	_____	_____
Feeders: _____	_____	_____	_____
_____	_____	_____	_____
_____	_____	_____	_____
4. Machinery and equipment: (crop, livestock, etc.)			
_____		_____	_____
_____		_____	_____
_____		_____	_____
_____		_____	_____
5. Portable farm buildings:			
_____		_____	_____
_____		_____	_____

2

Figure 15.1 (*continued*)

B. Annual operating expenses shall be supplied by the landlord and tenant as reported in Table 2 except as discussed in Section VI.

Table 2—Percentage Share of Operating Expenses to be Furnished by Each Party

	(L)	(T)
1. Crop Expenses:		
• Fertilizer		
• Lime		
• Seed		
• Herbicide		
• Crop insurance		
• Other supplies		
• Other: _____		
2. Livestock Expenses:		
• Feed purchased		
• Veterinary		
• Breeding fees		
• Medicines and drugs		
• Feed grinding and mixing		
• _____		
• _____		
3. Fuel:		
• Tractor		
• Truck		
• Harvesting		
• Crop drying		
• Feed processing		
• Heating buildings		
4. Electricity		
5. Telephone		
6. General hired labor		
7. Custom:		
• Hauling crops and livestock		
• Harvesting:		
Corn		
Small grain		
Soybeans		
_____		
_____		
8. Insurance:		
• Buildings		
• _____		
9. Taxes		
10. Interest:		
• Operating capital		
• Intermediate term loans		
11. Other		

C. Additional agreements in regard to livestock production.

1. Breeding replacements shall be furnished as follows:

_____
_____
_____

2. Sale of breeding stock shall be shared as follows:

_____
_____

3. Other breeding stock provisions are:

_____
_____

D. Neither landlord or tenant shall have the authority to bind the other in any contract with third parties. Expenses other than those reported in Tables 1 and 2 shall be shared as follows:

_____
_____

E. Buying and selling. The tenant shall consult with the landlord regarding time, price, sales agency, and similar matters regarding the purchase and sale of livestock, feed, and crops whenever the transaction exceeds $_____ in value. Additional agreements are as follows:

_____
_____

F. Livestock restrictions. Neither the tenant nor the landlord shall bring to the farm livestock not included in the agreement without express written permission of the other party.
   Additional agreements relative to livestock are:

_____
_____

G. Equipment and machinery replacements. The cost of additional and replacement livestock equipment and machinery will be shared as follows:

_____
_____
_____
_____

V. DIVISION OF INCOME AND CASH RENT ON NON-SHARED ITEMS

A. Division of income. The tenant shall pay rent to the landlord for the use of the landlord's property described in this lease (Table 1) an amount equal to _____ percent of the gross income. Gross income shall consist of the proceeds from the sale or exchange of all grain, forages, livestock, and other products produced under the provisions of this lease, except for:

_____
_____
_____

3

Figure 15.1 (*continued*)

B. Cash rent on non-shared items. The tenant agrees to pay cash rent annually for the use of the following non-shared items:

Table 3—Amount of Annual Cash Rent
(complete at beginning of lease)

Farmstead: Dwelling	$_____
Service buildings	$_____
Timber and waste	$_____
Other: _____	$_____
_____	$_____
Total cash rent	$_____

Payment of cash rent: The tenant agrees to pay cash rent as follows:

$_____ on or before _____ day of _____ month

$_____ on or before _____ day of _____ month

$_____ on or before _____ day of _____ month

$_____ on or before _____ day of _____ month

If rent is not paid when due, the tenant agrees to pay interest on the amount of unpaid rent at the rate of _____ percent per annum from due date until paid.

VI. OPERATION AND MAINTENANCE OF FARM

In order to operate this farm efficiently and to maintain it in a high state of productivity, the parties agree as follows:

A. The tenant agrees:

1. General maintenance. To provide the unskilled labor necessary to maintain the farm and its improvements during his tenancy in as good condition as it was at the beginning. Normal wear and depreciation and damage from causes beyond the tenant's control are excepted.

2. Land use. Not to: a) plow pasture or meadowland, b) cut live trees for sale or personal use, c) pasture new seedlings of legumes and grasses in the year they are seeded without consent of the landlord.

3. Insurance. Not to house automobiles, motor trucks, or tractors in barns, or otherwise violate restrictions in the landlord's insurance policies without written consent from the landlord. Restrictions to be observed are as follows:

_____

_____

_____

4. Noxious weeds. To use diligence to prevent noxious weeds from going to seed on the farm. Treatment of the noxious weed infestation and cost thereof shall be handled as follows:

_____

_____

_____

_____

5. Addition of improvements. Not to: a) erect or permit to be erected on the farm any nonremovable structure or building, b) incur any expense to the landlord for such purposes, or c) add electrical wiring, plumbing, or heating to any building without written consent of the landlord.

6. Conservation. Control soil erosion as completely as practicable; keep in good repair all terraces, open ditches, inlets and outlets of tile drains; preserve all established watercourses or ditches including grassed waterways; and refrain from any operation or practice that will injure such structures.

7. Damages. When he leaves the farm, to pay the landlord reasonable compensation for any damages to the farm for which he, the tenant, is responsible. Any decrease in value due to ordinary wear and depreciation or damages outside the control of the tenant are excepted.

8. Costs of operation. To pay all costs of operation except those specifically referred to in Sections IV, VI-A-4, and VI-B.

9. Repairs. Not to buy materials for maintenance and repairs in an amount in excess of $_____ within a single year without written consent of the landlord.

B. The landlord agrees:

1. Loss replacement. To replace or repair as promptly as possible the dwelling or any other building regularly used by the tenant that may be destroyed or damaged by fire, flood, or other cause beyond the control of the tenant or to make rental adjustments in lieu of replacements.

2. Materials for repairs. To furnish all material needed for normal maintenance and repair.

3. Skilled labor. To furnish any skilled labor for tasks which the tenant himself is unable to perform satisfactorily. Additional agreements regarding materials and labor are:

_____

_____

4. Reimbursement. To pay for materials purchased by the tenant for purposes of repair and maintenance in an amount not to exceed $_____ in any one year, except as otherwise agreed upon. Reimbursement shall be made within _____ days after the tenant submits the bill.

5. Removable improvements. To let the tenant make minor improvements of a temporary or removable nature, which do not mar the condition or appearance of the farm, at the tenant's expense. He further agrees to let the tenant remove such improvements even though they are legally fixtures at any time this lease is in effect or within _____ days thereafter, provided the tenant leaves in good condition that part of the farm from which such improvements are removed. The tenant shall have no right to compensation for improvements that are not removed except as mutually agreed.

6. Compensation for crop expenses. To reimburse the tenant at the termination of this lease for field work done and for other crop costs incurred for crops to be harvested during the following year. unless otherwise agreed, current custom rates for the operations involved will be used as a basis of settlement.

4

Figure 15.1 (*continued*)

C. Both agree:

1. **Capital improvements.** Costs of establishing hay or pasture seedings, new conservation structures, improvements (except as provided in Section V-B-5), or of applying lime and other long-lived fertilizers shall be divided between landlord and tenant as set forth in the following table. The tenant will be re-imbursed by the landlord either when the improvement is completed, or the tenant will be compensated for his share of the depreciated cost of his contribution when he leaves the farm based on the value of the tenant's contribution and depreciation rate shown in the following table. (Cross out the portion of the preceding sentence which does not apply.)

Rates for labor, power, and machinery contributed by the tenant shall be agreed upon before construction is started.

Compensation for Improvements Table

Type of improvement	Date to be completed	Estimated total cost (dollars)	Proportion to be contributed by tenant			Total value of tenant's contrib. (dollars) *	Rate of annual depreciation
			Material	Unskilled labor	Mach.		
			%	%	%		%

* To be recorded when improvement is completed.

2. **Mineral rights.** Nothing in this lease shall confer upon the tenant any right to minerals underlying said land, but same are hereby reserved by the landlord together with the full right to enter upon the premises and to bore, search, and excavate for same, to work and remove same, and to deposit excavated rubbish, and with full liberty to pass over said premises with vehicles and lay down and work any railroad track or tracks, tanks, pipelines, power lines, and structures as may be necessary or convenient for the above purpose. The landlord agrees to reimburse the tenant for any actual damage he may suffer for crops destroyed by these activities and to release the tenant from obligation to continue farming this property when development of mineral resources interferes materially with the tenant's opportunity to make a satisfactory return.

VII. FARM RECORDS AND FINANCIAL SETTLEMENTS

A. Records of joint interest shall be kept by _____ and shall be made available to the landlord/tenant (cross out one) upon request. Financial and production records shall include a complete inventory of all property used in the farm business. Inventories shall be recorded and financial records summarized by _____ day of _____ (month) or at intervals mutually agreed upon. Specify:

B. The record system to be used shall be:

C. All joint receipts and disbursements shall be handled through _____ bank as follows:

- Receipts: _____

- Disbursements: _____

D. Cash financial settlement shall be made by the _____ day of each month or at intervals mutually-agreed upon. Specify:

VIII. ARBITRATION OF DIFFERENCES AND DIVISION OF PROPERTY

A. **Arbitration of differences.** Any differences between the parties as to their several rights or obligations under this lease that are not settled by mutual agreement after thorough discussion, shall be submitted for arbitration to a committee of three disinterested persons, one selected by each party hereto and the third by the two thus selected. The committee's decision shall be accepted by both parties.

5

Figure 15.1 (*continued*)

B. Division of property. Upon termination of this lease, unused production shall be divided as follows:

1. Feed grain and supplies. All grain, silage, other feeds, and all co-owned supplies including straw and other bedding materials shall be divided by measure or value, whichever is more equitable, with the landlord and tenant each receiving title to his respective share as reported in Section V-A.

2. Livestock. If the livestock are owned equally (50-50), the tenant shall divide each class of livestock, as cows, steers, calves, hogs, etc., into two groups and the landlord shall take his choice of the two groups of each. In case the groupings cannot be made equal, a difference in monetary value shall be assigned before the choice is made and added to the choice.

3. Undivided interest of co-owned property. If both parties mutually agree not to accept the above described plan for dividing co-owned classes of property including livestock, it is agreed the tenant shall set a value on the entire amount of the respective co-owned classes of property on the basis of which he will either sell his undivided interest or buy that of the landlord, at the option of the landlord; or the co-owned property may be disposed of by private or public sale arranged for that purpose at a reasonable time and place.

4. Home use. The tenant and landlord may take annually for home use the following kinds and quantities of jointly owned crops, livestock, and/or livestock products:

_____

_____

_____

_____

Executed in duplicate on the date first above written:

_____
(tenant)

_____
(tenant spouse)

_____
(landlord

_____
(landlord spouse)

STATE OF _____

COUNTY OF _____ } SS:

On this _____ day of _____ A.D., 19____, before

me, the undersigned, a Notary Public in said State, personally appeared _____

_____, _____, _____,

and _____, to me known to be the identical persons named in and who executed

the foregoing instrument, and acknowledged that they executed the same as their voluntary act and deed.

_____
(Notary Public)

Issued in furtherance of Cooperative Extension work, Acts of Congress of May 8 and June 30, 1914, in cooperation with the U.S. Department of Agriculture and Cooperative Extension Services of Illinois, Indiana, Kansas, Michigan, Minnesota, Missouri, Nebraska, North Dakota, Ohio, South Dakota and Wisconsin. John O. Dunbar, Director, Cooperative Extension Service, Kansas State University, Manhattan.

Figure 15.1 (*continued*)

DISCUSSION QUESTIONS

1. What are the advantages of renting land compared to purchasing land? Disadvantages?
2. What strategies can be employed in gaining control of rental land?
3. What are the advantages and disadvantages for the operator of a cash lease? Of a share lease?
4. How can the risks of a cash lease be reduced for an operator?
5. What factors determine how costs and returns from crop production should be shared between the operator and the landowner?
6. Give some examples of how a share lease can lead to inefficiency.
7. What procedure should be used by an operator or a landowner to determine the returns that could be expected with various types of leases?
8. List the important factors an operator should consider when deciding whether to rent a particular farm.
9. How should the value of rental pasture be determined?
10. Why is a written lease important? What provisions should be included in a lease?

RELATED READINGS

ATKINSON, J. H. "Adapting the 50-50 Crop Share Lease to Different Levels of Land Productivity," *Journal of the American Society of Farm Managers and Rural Appraisors,* April, 1983, 47, 43–48.

DUNAWAY, ROBERT M., and ALVIN J. MORROW. *Farm Lease Guide.* Des Moines, Iowa: Wallace-Homestead Book Company, 1980.

FORSTER, LYNN D., and BERNARD L. ERVEN. *Foundations for Managing the Farm Business,* chap. 10. Columbus, Ohio: Grid Publishing Co., 1981.

HERBST, J. H. *Farm Management Principles, Budgets, Plans,* chap. 14. Champaign, Ill.: Stipes Publishing Co., 1983.

KAY, RONALD D. *Farm Management, Planning, Control, and Implementation,* chap. 14. New York: McGraw-Hall, 1981.

"Leasing Arrangements for the 1980's, Answers to Common Leasing Questions," unpublished booklet, Department of Agricultural Economics, Purdue University, West Lafayette, Ind., 1980.

REISS, FRANKLIN J. "Farm Leases for Illinois," Champaign, Ill.: University of Illinois, Cooperative Extension Service, Circular 1199, 1982.

Farm Production Systems: Machinery Investment, Selection, and Management

16

PLANNING PRODUCTION SYSTEMS

Planning the production system involves the choice of the types and amounts of buildings, machinery, equipment, labor, and land and the organization of these resources to produce farm products. Decisions concerning crop production systems include size of tractors and various types of equipment, number of tractors and units of equipment, tillage practices, time of tillage practices, hours worked per day, new versus used equipment, amount of custom hire, amount of labor, and methods of drying, processing, storage and hauling.

Livestock production-system decisions include amounts of housing, lots, and/or pasture for various phases of the life cycle, equipment and labor for moving feed to livestock, equipment and labor for moving manure away from livestock, equipment and labor for handling livestock (milking cows, weaning calves, castrating pigs, etc.), and the scheduling of various functions.

Following are some principles for planning farm production systems. Crop and livestock production systems are discussed subsequently.

PRINCIPLES FOR PLANNING AND SELECTING FARM PRODUCTION SYSTEMS

- The production system affects the efficiency of crop and livestock production. It is important to have a production system that will result in relatively high crop yields and good livestock performance.
- There are wide ranges in the amounts of capital, machinery, buildings, equipment, labor, and management that can be used to produce a certain amount of crops or livestock. The most profitable system for a particular farm will depend largely on the availability and cost of capital and labor and the kind of management on the farm. A young beginning farmer might choose a system that requires more labor and less capital. As time goes by, more capital may become available, which would encourage a system requiring less labor per unit of production.
- The production system is likely to vary over time. Because of changes in amounts of capital available, the desire for leisure time, the size of the farm business, and technology, the "optimum" production system will change. Managers should anticipate change and try to plan the system they expect to

have ten or twenty years in the future before they begin investing in a system. This can reduce the amount of investment that must be "abandoned" as the production system is changed.

- Sometimes there are cost-of-production differences among systems. Be sure to secure information about costs of production before choosing a production system.

- Different types of production systems require different kinds of labor and management skills. Choose a system that fits your management ability and skills. For example, a livestock producer who raises livestock in confinement needs to have more mechanical skills than one who raises livestock on pasture.

- Existing machinery, equipment, and buildings should be taken into consideration.

- Different parts of the production system should be synchronized so that bottlenecks are minimized and capacity use is maximized.

- Price-level changes, interest rates, and income taxes affect both the system selected and the time when investments should be made.

Keeping these principles in mind, we will now proceed to plan a crop machinery system in this chapter and a building system in Chapter 17.

SIZE, KIND, AND AMOUNT OF MACHINERY

Hal and Ruth Jacoby have an opportunity to rent his grandmother's 320-acre crop farm in southern Minnesota. The farm is located only 3 miles from Hal's 400-acre home farm unit which his father operates. Hal and Ruth have decided to farm independently rather than join in a partnership with his parents, but they are considering joint ownership of a single set of equipment with Hal's parents. Hal decided to evaluate the type of machinery system needed and to compute costs and returns for alternative machinery systems. To make the evaluation, Hal has assembled the following information.

Information Needed

Crops.   Although they expect to adjust the acreage of various crops each year depending on the market outlook, the Jacobys plan to have approximately half corn and half soybeans.

Acres of crop.   The Jacoby home farm has 380 tillable acres, and Hal's farm has 300 tillable acres. Hal would like to rent another 200 acres but is not sure when that will be possible. If he farms alone, he will need to plan for 300 acres. Hal and his parents would have a total of 680 acres. The possible rental of 200 acres would need to be considered for each of these two situations.

Field operations.   The Jacobys anticipate having the following field operations for corn and soybeans.

Corn	Soybeans
Spread fertilizer	Spread fertilizer
Plow	Plow
Disk twice	Disk twice
Plant	Plant
Rotary-hoe	Rotary-hoe
Cultivate	Cultivate
Combine	Combine
Chop stalks	

Timing of operations.   Through research publications the Jacobys have learned that yields of corn in their area decline 1 bushel per acre per day when planted after May 10 and 2 bushels per acre per day when planted after May 23. Soybean yields decline $\frac{1}{3}$ bushel for each day they are planted after May 15. In the fall, corn yields decline $\frac{1}{4}$ bushel per day for each day corn is harvested after October 1 and soybean yields decline about $\frac{1}{10}$ bushel per day after October 1. These are most likely results and will vary from year to year and from farm to farm. To sway the odds of high yields in their favor, the Jacobys decided on a goal of completing corn planting by May 15, soybean planting by May 20, and harvesting by November 15.

Time required.   The Jacobys used Figure 16.1 to estimate the amount of field work that could be accomplished with different sizes of machinery. Rates of accomplishments of selected machinery systems will be discussed later in this chapter.

Time available.   Data from the crop-reporting service and extension publications enabled the Jacobys to estimate the number of days they could work in the field at various times of the year. They summarized these data along with specific activities that could be done at different times (Table 16.1). The number of days available for field work will vary from farm to farm depending on soil type, drainage, and the weather.

Choosing a Machinery System

Considerations.   From the information assembled, the Jacobys arrived at the following conclusions:

- Timeliness is very important in corn and soybean production, with highest yields attained if all of the corn can be planted in 4.2 working days (before May 10) and all corn and soybeans can be planted in 6.0 working days (before May 15).

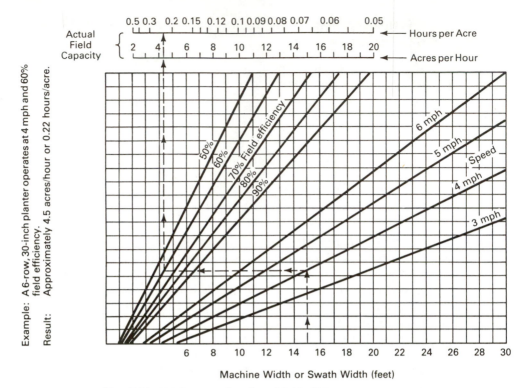

¹See Table 16.2 for an explanation of field efficiency.

Figure 16.1 Field capacity chart (any machine). (See Table 16.2 for an explanation of field efficiency.) *Source:* Purdue University Agricultural Extension Circular EC-541, August 1981.

- As the size and amount of machinery increase for a specified acreage, fixed machinery costs increase. Therefore, there is a trade-off between getting the crops planted and harvested in the optimum time and the cost of machinery.

- Because of the very limited time available for planting without yield penalty, it would be desirable to have as much field work as possible completed in the fall or in early spring. Of course, some soil cannot be plowed in the fall because of erosion. If soil type and slope rule out fall plowing, one might chisel or ridge till instead. Other alternatives might be to switch to spring tillage and run longer hours or to use larger equipment to get the job done on time.

- Running equipment long hours will allow more timely planting and harvesting without requiring increased equipment size.

Selection of the "best" machinery system is complex, because (1) yields are affected by timeliness, (2) several activities can be done in each of several time periods, (3) the size and amount of equipment affect machinery and labor costs, and (4) crop

TABLE 16.1   Number of Days to Work in Field and Jobs That Can Be Done during Those Days for Corn and Soybeans, Jacoby Farm

Time Period	Length in Weeks	Number of Working Days[a]	Activities That Could Be Done	
			Corn	Soybeans
1. November 29–April 25	21	16.0	Spread fertilizer, chop stalks, plow	Spread fertilizer, plow
2. April 25–May 9	2	4.2	Spread fertilizer, chop stalks, plow, disk, plant	Spread fertilizer, plow, disk, plant
3. May 10–June 5	4	12.0	Period 2 activities, rotary-hoe, cultivate	Period 2 activities, rotary-hoe, cultivate
4. June 6–July 11	5	17.0	Rotary-hoe, cultivate	Rotary-hoe, cultivate
5. September 27–November 29	9	31.0	Harvest, chop stalks, spread fertilizer, plow	Harvest, spread fertilizer, plow

[a] The ground is suitable for working at least this number of days in eight of ten years.

production costs vary by time of planting and harvesting. Because of the complexity of machinery-selection decisions, a computer program has been developed to aid in planning machinery selection. The Jacobys elected to use this computer program.[1] It also would be feasible to develop a linear programming model (see Chapter 8) to plan machinery selection for production of various crops in any area of the country. For those who do not have access to a computer, the following procedure may be useful in choosing a machinery system.

The size of equipment needed to accomplish the most limiting and important activities should be determined. On the Jacoby farm, these activities are planting and harvesting because if these activities are not accomplished on time, a substantial yield penalty must be paid. The Jacobys made the following calculations in deciding on the size of corn planter needed:

1. The number of acres that can be planted per hour with different-size planters (see Table 16.2).
2. The number of planting days before May 20: nine (Table 16.1).
3. Acres that need to be planted per good working day:

$$680 \text{ acres} \div 9 \text{ working days} = 75 \text{ acres}$$

[1] For more information, see the Purdue Crop Budget Model, B-96, Department of Agricultural Economics, Purdue University, West Lafayette, Ind. The model plans machinery for corn, soybeans, and wheat.

TABLE 16.2 Rate of Planting for Various-Size Corn Planters

Planter Size	Width	Oper. Speed	Field Efficiency%[a]	Acres per Field Hour[b]	Acres per 12-Hour Day
4 rows, 40 in.	13.3 ft.	4 mph	71	4.58	55
6 rows, 30 in.	15.0 ft.	5 mph	69	6.27	75
8 rows, 30 in.	20.0 ft.	5 mph	67	8.12	97
12 rows, 30 in.	30.0 ft.	5 mph	65	11.82	142
16 rows, 30 in.	40.0 ft.	5 mph	63	15.27	183

[a]Field efficiency is the percent of total field time spent operating at the desired speed and width. (It cannot be 100% because time is wasted during turns, adjustments, planter refills, refueling, and maintenance).

[b]$\text{Acres per field hour} = \dfrac{\text{Width (ft)} \times \text{Speed (mph} \times \text{Field efficiency)}}{8.25}$

The Jacobys could complete corn and soybean planting for the total 680 acres by their May 20 target date with a six-row planter operated 12 hours per day. A twelve-row planter would allow them to complete planting before May 15 and provide insurance for very bad years. How much would a twelve-row planter cost, and would it pay? To answer these questions, the Jacobys prepared the following budget from the cost figure in Table 16.3.

Annual fixed cost	
6-row	$2,054
12-row	$4,252
Increased annual fixed cost of a 12-row planter	
over a 6-row planter	$2,198

The Jacobys assumed that variable costs of repairs and pulling the planter would be the same on a per-acre basis for the two different-size planters. In fact, labor cost would be lower for the large planter because more could be accomplished per hour.

TABLE 16.3 Prices and Annual Costs of Different-Size Corn Planters, Jacoby Farm

Planter Size	Price	Annual Fixed Cost[a]
4 rows, 40 in.	$ 9,190	$1,507
6 rows, 30 in.	$12,524	$2,054
8 rows, 30 in.	$20,656	$3,388
12 rows, 30 in.	$25,926	$4,252
16 rows, 30 in.	$45,384	$7,443

[a]Interest 8% and machinery life 10 years, Ain = .1490. Taxes 1% and insurance .5% of new value. For procedure see "Budgeting Annual Cost of Depreciable Resources" in Chapter 8.

The return difference was also budgeted. By May 10, in 4.2 days (Table 16.1), 315 acres of corn could be planted with a six-row planter (4.2 × 75). This would leave only 25 acres to be planted after May 10, and there would be so little yield penalty that it will be ignored.

By May 15, with approximately 1.8 more good working days, corn planting would be completed and 110 acres of soybeans planted, leaving 230 acres of soybeans and requiring three more working days (230 ÷ 75). The remaining 230 acres of soybeans would be planted an average of approximately 3.5 days late with a loss of $1,868 (1.16 bu./acre at $7.00 = $8.12 × 230 acres).[2]

In summary:

Added return of the 12-row planter	$1,868
Added cost	$2,198
Net return	−$ 330

Three advantages of the twelve-row planter were not considered in the budget: (1) It will enable the Jacobys to complete planting in a more timely fashion in very bad weather years. (2) It will save labor at planting time. (3) It will provide some excess capacity in the event that it would be possible to rent more ground. The Jacobys decided these advantages were of sufficient value to warrant the purchase of the twelve-row planter even though the budget shows a negative $330.

The Jacobys made a similar analysis of harvesting requirements. They considered a 15-foot, six (30-in.)-row combine that cost $90,000 and would harvest 2.5 acres of corn or 4.5 acres of soybeans per hour. They assumed they could operate an average of ten hours per day for corn and eight hours per day for soybeans, with the soybeans usually harvested first and the corn second.

Good days required for harvest were: $\dfrac{340 \text{ acres soybeans}}{36 \text{ acres/day}}$ = 9.4 days

$\dfrac{340 \text{ acres corn}}{25 \text{ acres/day}}$ = 13.6 days

A total of 23 days (9.4 + 13.6) would be required. Harvest could be completed by early November, thus meeting the harvest goals set by the Jacobys. The Jacobys reasoned that if they could finish planting earlier, crops would be ready for harvest earlier, resulting in more good field days available for harvest. They made their decision in favor of a twelve-row planter and a six-row combine.

Next, the Jacobys thought it would be desirable to evaluate plowing, another possible bottleneck because it is a relatively slow operation. Planning to have two 110-hp. tractors, they wanted to determine whether or not one five, 16-in. plow would be adequate.

---

[2] Working days estimated on the basis of Table 16.1.

$$\text{Acres per hour} = \frac{6.7 \text{ width} \times 5 \text{ mph} \times 0.80 \text{ field efficiency}}{8.25} = 3.25 \text{ acres/hour}$$

The Jacobys would be able to plow 52 acres in a 16-hour day. Thirteen good field days would be required to plow 680 acres. These good field-operating days would be available either in the fall after crop harvest or in the spring (Table 16.1). The Jacobys decided that one plow would be sufficient. Based on their analysis and judgment, the Jacobys chose the set of machinery in Table 16.4 for their operation.

To aid in the evaluation of their machinery systems, the Jacobys used a computer program. They specified their resources (land, machinery, labor), yields, crop prices, resource costs, and expected number of working days, and the computer model provided the following information.

With 340 acres in soybeans and 340 acres in corn, the expected return to management for the 680 acres is $27,274. (Table 16.5). This return is in addition to a $15,000 labor payment to both Jacoby families and a land-rental payment of $133.48 per acre. (Table 16.6). Part B of Table 16.5 shows the shadow prices for items that limit crop production. The shadow price is part of the linear programming solution (Chapter 8) and shows the amount that one more unit of a limiting factor would increase gross income. The shadow prices are all relatively low, except for land. This confirms that the Jacobys would have sufficient machinery for the 680 acres with the machinery selected. It would be desirable for the Jacobys to make another computer run to determine if the machinery is adequate to farm yet another 200 acres.

The computer model also provides information (not shown here) about the schedule of field operations, income above variable cost for each crop, and amount of resources used. The model is useful to crop farmers in helping them plan the size and amount of machinery, scheduling of production, crop selection, and labor.

Large versus Small Machinery

This question is often asked "Am I better off with one set of large crop machinery or two sets of smaller crop machinery?" There is only one way to be sure of the

TABLE 16.4   Machinery Selected for Jacoby Farm

Machinery Item	Rating or Size	Number of Units
Tractors	110 hp	2
Fertilizer spreader	6 ton	1
Plow	5, 16 in.	1
Chisel	10 ft.	1
Disk	14 ft.	1
Planter	12 row, 30 in.	1
Rotary hoe	6 row, 30 in.	1
Cultivator	6 row, 30 in.	1
Combine and small grain head	15 ft.	1
Corn head	6 row, 30 in.	1

TABLE 16.5   Return to Management, Farm Plan,
and Shadow Prices, Computer Output for Jacoby Farm

A. Jacoby Farm Cropping Budget

Net returns to management	$27,274
Acres corn grain	340
Acres corn silage	0
Acres soybeans	340
Acres wheat	0
Acres double-crop beans	0
Acres not used	0
Acres rented out	0
Acres rented in	0
Hours custom combine hired out	0

Limiting Resource	Shadow Prices[a] Value in Dollars per Additional Unit
B. Value of an extra hour of permanent labor	
1. Apr. 26–May 2	$ 1.75
2. May 10–May 16	3.23
3. Oct. 18–Nov. 7	5.00
Value of an extra acre used for	
4. Corn	252.95
5. Soybeans	217.28
6. Wheat	254.88
Value of an extra hour at harvesting time:	
7. Soybeans–corn-soybean combine,	
Sep. 27–Oct. 17	10.95
8. Corn–corn-soybean combine,	
Sep. 27–Oct. 17	29.59

[a]One more unit of limiting resource would increase gross returns
by the amount shown. To determine profit, cost of the added
unit would need to be subtracted.

answer—by budgeting both systems. It should be kept in mind that large machinery reduces the number of operators needed, thus reducing labor cost per acre. If the Jacobys had chosen to farm independently with smaller machinery, machinery costs would probably not have been much different, but each independent set of equipment would have required an operator. With large equipment requiring only one operator, the second person has time to provide crop support help (hauling, repairs, etc.), raise livestock, look for more ground to farm, or work at another job. Therefore, large machinery often is more profitable if it can be used the same number of hours as smaller equipment. More acres are needed to run large equipment to equal the number of hours smaller machines are used. Operators who are planning to expand in the near future but who lack sufficient land to warrant large machinery might consider doing some custom work. But the custom work must not interfere with their doing a good job with their own farm.

TABLE 16.6 Profit and Loss Comparison, Computer Output for Jacoby Farm

Item	
Income	
1. Dry corn sales	$ 0
2. Wet corn sales	0
3. Stored corn sales	135,973
4. Dry soybeans sales	0
5. Wet soybean sales	0
6. Stored soybean sales	104,621
7. Wheat sales	0
8. Silage	0
9. Land rented out	0
10. Combining hired out	0
Total income	$240,594
Allocated variable costs	
1. Fertilizer	$ 29,240
2. Seed	8,680
2. Insecticide and/or herbicide	9,350
4. Fuel, lubricant, and repairs	16,595
5. Drying at farm	4,291
6. Drying at elevator	0
7. Interest on operating funds and miscellaneous	7,140
8. Custom combining hired in	0
Total allocated variable costs	$ 75,296
Unallocated variable costs	
1. Added land rental	$ 0
2. Part-time hired labor	138
Total unallocated variable costs	$ 138
Fixed costs	
1. Fixed machinery costs	$ 32,120
2. Fixed labor costs	15,000
3. Fixed land costs	90,766
Total fixed costs	$137,886
Total costs	$213,320
Returns to management before income taxes	$ 27,274

Hours per Day

When more acres are farmed with a given set of machinery or the same acres farmed with less equipment by operating longer hours, machinery investment per acre is reduced. This results in reductions of several costs associated with the level of investment: interest, taxes, insurance, and a portion of depreciation.

As smaller machinery is operated a greater number of hours, labor costs increase. Also, a larger labor force makes management and supervision more complex. The operator must figure labor and machinery costs for alternative sizes of machinery before making a decision.

One farm operator figured that machinery investment could be reduced from $200,000 to $160,000 by increasing the hours operated from 12 to 15. With fixed costs of 16.4% the fixed machinery costs of the two systems would be:

16.4% [3] × $200,000	$32,800
16.4% × $160,000	$26,240
Reduction in machinery costs	$ 6,560

Assuming the machinery would be operated about sixty days per year, the increased hired labor would be sixty days times three hours, or 180 hours. If good seasonal labor could be hired for $6 per hour, the total labor cost with the smaller machinery would be 180 hours times $6.00, or $1,080. Costs would be $5,480 less ($6,560 minus $1,080) with the smaller machinery than with larger machinery.

New versus Used Machinery

The choice of new or used machinery depends on the amount of capital available, the machinery selected, and the maintenance and repair ability of the operator.

Sam Sutton started farming with low equity. He obtained a limited amount of financing from FmHA for machinery and operating capital for a 320-acre unit he was able to rent on a share lease. Because Sam did not have sufficient capital to purchase new machinery, he was forced to buy used machinery. He lacked good mechanical skills but had a strong determination to farm. Although he worked hard to keep the used equipment operating, Sam experienced some breakdowns during critical planting and harvesting times and had many expensive repair-service calls. After three years he had accumulated sufficient equity to enable him to switch to new machinery. Sam judged his time would be best used on crop and livestock production rather than machinery repair.

Ralph Whitter, on the other hand, finds that used machinery fits his 280-acre operation very well. He can locate good used machinery because he has excellent machinery management and selection skills. Having a relatively small farm, he is able to purchase equipment other farmers have traded in. Using his own labor, Ralph has the ability to put the used equipment in top shape.

[3] See [a], Table 16.3.

Because of his small acreage, he is not hurt as much by a machinery breakdown during planting and harvesting as a farmer with a larger unit would be. Also, with a small farm unit, Ralph has adequate time to devote to machinery repairs and improvements, work that he enjoys. Purchasing used machinery enables Ralph to keep his machinery fixed costs per acre at about half what they would be if he purchased new machinery.

When to Trade

When to trade depends on skill in keeping used machinery operating, the need for a change in equipment because of a change in the farm operation, the higher fixed cost of new machinery compared to the higher repair cost of used machinery, availability of money, the tax situation, the amount of risk of breakdown the operator is willing to accept, the improved features of new machinery, and the personal satisfaction gained from operating new machinery. A good way for a farmer to analyze whether it would be profitable to trade machinery would be to prepare a simple budget (Table 16.7). This budget can be used for a single piece of machinery or for trading all machinery. Some factors are difficult to forecast, such as risk of breakdown. But if a manager calculates the difference in cost and direct benefits, this information will help determine how high the difficult-to-measure factors must be in order for a trade to be profitable.

Extras

The extras on many tractors and combines—cabs, air conditioning, stereos—are quite expensive, and a farmer who is short on capital can operate without them. However, if the working environment is so improved with these options that the operator can work longer hours, they may actually pay a return. Some operators may be willing to work in unpleasant weather when protected by a cab, whereas they would not be willing to operate a tractor without protection from the weather.

Leasing

Leasing is a way to obtain the use of a machine with less capital outlay and financial commitment than would be required if the machine were purchased. Some leases are for short periods of time (day, week, month), while others are on a yearly or multiyear basis.

In most cases, it is cheaper to buy a machine than to rent it because the transfer costs and profits of the lessor can be saved by purchasing.

There are some situations, however, in which leasing may be profitable. When capital is extremely limited, the control of a machine may be obtained through leasing with a smaller capital outlay than through purchasing, thus allowing available capital to be stretched for more uses. One can sometimes avoid a long-term capital

TABLE 16.7   Hypothetical Machinery Budget

A. Reduced cost and increased income	
1. Reduced repair cost	$ 3,500
2. Lower risk of breakdowns in critical time periods	5,000
3. Reduced income taxes	5,000
4. Benefits of technical improvements on new machinery	2,000
5. Allowable rental of more acres if additional land becomes available	2,000
6. Personal enjoyment from owning new machinery	1,000
Total reduced cost and added returns	$18,500
B. Added costs of trading machinery	
Interest, depreciaiton, taxes, and insurance	
16.4% of $100,000 increase in machinery investment	$16,400
C. Net income (loss) from trading (A − B)	$2,100

commitment by leasing. Suppose that additional land has been rented but availability beyond the present year is uncertain. Machinery to farm this land might be obtained through leasing for a one-year period. On the other hand, if the machinery is purchased, a longer-term financial commitment must be made. While the purchased machinery can be sold if no longer needed, there is always some uncertainty about the price that can be obtained at the time of sale. Leasing may eliminate this uncertainty. In some instances, leasing can be cheaper than owning. A dealer who is oversupplied with machinery may be willing to lease it for a relatively low rate of return rather than have it stand idle on his lot. Also, some dealers lease at low rates as a competitive device to get their machinery in the fields where farmers will see it in operation.

Tax implications of leasing versus purchasing should be considered. In some instances, leasing may be advantageous, and in other instances, purchasing may have greater tax advantages.

John Hart is considering the purchase of a new tractor that would cost $40,000. He expects to keep this tractor five years. Checking with his local dealer, John found that he could get a five-year lease for $8,211 per year.

John calculated the annual cost of owning a tractor for 5 years, using the procedure for budgeting annual cost of depreciable resources presented in Chapter 8.

$$\text{Annual cost} = (\text{Total depreciation} \times \text{Ain}) + \text{iSV} + \times\% \text{ of new cost}$$
$$\text{for taxes and insurance}$$

John estimated market interest at 13%; inflation, 5%; taxes, 1% of new cost; insurance, .5% of new cost; and ending salvage value in current dollars of $20,000. Hence,

$$\text{Annual Cost} = (\$20,000 \times .2505^4) + 8\% \text{ of } \$20,000 + 1\tfrac{1}{2}\%$$
$$\text{of } \$40,000 = \$5,010 + \$1,600 + \$600 = \$7,210$$

In this case, John has figured his cost (excluding income tax considerations and assuming operating costs would be the same) in favor of purchase. Should the rate of depreciation or interest increase, it might become more profitable to lease than buy, provided the rental rate remained the same. John should consider the amount of initial down payment on the purchased tractor compared to the single-year lease and should also consider income tax.

Leasing should be kept in mind as one possible alternative for securing the use of machinery. Depending on economic conditions and the particular farm situation, leasing could be more profitable than purchasing.

Custom Hiring

Another way to obtain the use of machinery without purchasing it is through custom hiring, which provides labor and management as well as machinery. It may be a good alternative for operators who have an acreage so small that the fixed costs per acre of owning machinery are high relative to the cost of hiring. Farmers who are short on capital might prefer to let someone else own the machinery, saving their scarce capital for other farm needs. Custom hiring can be a good way to secure labor and management in cases where part-time help is needed.

A potential disadvantage of custom hiring is loss of timeliness. Sometimes custom operators will do your work only after their own or other customers' work has been completed. In years of poor weather, this can cause late planting or harvest and result in severe yield penalties. Select an operator who is not overcommitted and establish an agreement about time of operation before the season starts. Pay a sufficiently high rate (well above usual, if necessary) so that the custom operator will agree that your farm is important. Typical custom rates are often available from surveys conducted by the state agricultural extension services or commercial agencies.[5]

Joint Use of Machinery[6]

Sharing equipment enables operators to gain the labor-saving advantage of large machinery while avoiding the high machinery fixed costs resulting from the use of large machinery on small acreage.

[4] From Appendix A.

[5] For example, Doane Agricultural Report, St. Louis, Mo.

[6] This section based on an unpublished paper by D. H. Doster, Dept. of Agricultural Economics, Purdue University.

Both Roger Bursten and Phil Hesh farm 320 acres, feed 1,000 cattle, and hire one worker. The machinery that each farmer uses fits the 320 acres he owns. Roger and Phil attended a farm management extension seminar recently and heard that "machinery costs per acre are the same for large and small equipment if they are both operated the same number of hours." Together they did some budgeting and found that by increasing machinery size, one set of machinery would handle both farms in a timely manner. The set of large machinery would cost the same as both sets of small machinery, but only one operator would be needed. With one large-machinery set, it would be possible to eliminate one of the hired workers. Also, since Roger and Phil work closely together, they have agreed that if either is incapacitated, the other will provide backup management. Roger and Phil get along very well personally and have respect for each other's management ability.

Although joint use of machinery may reduce machinery and labor costs, such an arrangement is not always practical. Personality conflicts, lack of mutual respect for management practices, and lack of a system for joint machinery use are three reasons why joint ownership of machinery may not provide satisfaction.

The following ideas may be helpful in evaluating whether or not joint machinery use will work for you:

Personalities. Can you get along with the other party or parties when each of you has an equal voice? When sharing equipment, there is usually no boss, no person who will have the final word or make the final decision. This can lead to situations where both parties arrive at different decisions. If neither is willing to yield and if the parties cannot reason together about the issue and come to a common conclusion, there will be a problem. Decisions will be made that are not always in your own best interest.

Management. Do you have respect for the machinery management skill of the other party? Does the other party take as good care of machinery as you do? Do you take as good care of machinery as the other party? Keep in mind that this is an area that can lead to friction.

Organization. Can all parties plan, organize, and develop a system or policy that answers most questions that may arise as to priority use of the machinery? Some people are willing to follow a policy, while others do not feel comfortable with a structured plan. In most machinery-sharing arrangements, a sharing policy is necessary. Here are some possible policies:

1. Alternate good field days.
2. Alternate amounts of accomplishment (you plant 100 acres, I plant 100 acres).
3. Alternate shifts (you use machinery midnight to noon, I use it noon to midnight).
4. Alternate years (I am first this year, you are first next year).

　　Economic gains can result from the joint use of equipment, but due to varied personalities, machinery management skills, and organizational preferences of different operators, only a few joint-ownership ventures are successful.

General Comments about Machinery

Keep machinery maintained and ready to go. Time may be worth $100, $300, even $1,000 per hour during the critical planting and harvesting periods. If you spend an hour, a day, a week, getting machinery ready when it is already time to go, you may be substituting a $6-per-hour job for a $100- to $500-per-hour job. A machinery workshop may make the difference between having machinery ready to operate and not having it ready.

　　Follow good safety practices. Machinery is dangerous if not operated properly. Never be in such a hurry or so lackadaisical that you do not give proper attention to safety. One mistake can result in disaster.

　　Machinery provides personal satisfaction to some people. A big new tractor provides as much enjoyment as a new automobile to some operators. There is nothing wrong with buying machinery simply because you want it as long as you know the cost and you can afford it.

DISCUSSION QUESTIONS

1. How might the production system affect crop or livestock efficiency? Give some examples.
2. How might management ability affect the type of production system that should be selected?
3. If two different production systems result in the same cost per unit of production but have widely different capital and labor requirements, which one should a manager choose? Explain.
4. Why do some farmers change production systems over time? What implications does this change have for farm planning?
5. What information is needed for making machinery-selection decisions?
6. What steps should be followed in choosing machinery type and size? Why?
7. What factors determine the number of hours per day that machines should be operated?
8. List the important factors a manager should consider in deciding whether to purchase new or used machinery.
9. What are the advantages and disadvantages of leasing versus owning machinery?
10. Under what circumstance might custom hiring be a good source of machinery? What is the major disadvantage of custom hire?
11. What are the advantages and disadvantages of joint machinery use?
12. Plan machinery type and size for a farm with which you are familiar.

RELATED READINGS

BOWERS, W. *Modern Machinery Management.* Champaign, Ill.: Stipes Publishing Co., Inc., 1970.

DOSTER, D. H. "Purdue Crop Budget," West Lafayette, Ind.: Purdue University Department of Agricultural Economics, EC- 541 and 542, 1981.

FULTON, CRAIG V., EARL O. HEADY, and GEORGE E. AYERS. "Farm Machinery Costs in Relation to Machinery and Farm Size," *CARD Report 80.* Ames, Ia.: Iowa State University, 1978.

HARSH, STEPHEN B., LARRY J. CONNOR, and GERALD D. SCHWAB. *Managing the Farm Business,* chap. 12. Englewood Cliffs, N.J.: Prentice-Hall, Inc., 1981.

HERBST, J. H. *Farm Management Principles, Budgets, Plans,* chap. 9. Champaign, Ill.: Stipes Publishing Co., 1983.

KAY, RONALD D. *Farm Management, Planning, Control, and Implementation,* chap. 16. New York: McGraw-Hill, 1981.

PARSONS, S. D., and D. H. DOSTER. "Days Suitable for Fieldwork in Indiana with Emphasis on Machinery Sizing," West Lafayette, Ind.: Purdue University Agricultural Experiment Station Bulletin 239, 1980.

PARSONS, S. D., and D. H. DOSTER. "Determining Required Field Capacities for Machinery Sizing Decisions," West Lafayette, Ind.: Purdue University, Cooperative Extension Service, ID-155, 1983.

SCHLENDER, JOHN R., and D. LEO FIGURSKI. *Examining Your Machinery Costs,* rev. ed. Manhattan, Kansas: Kansas State University, Cooperative Extension Service, C-375, 1971.

Farm Production
Systems: Buildings

17

IMPORTANT CONSIDERATIONS ABOUT FARM BUILDINGS

The same production system principles that apply to machinery apply also to buildings (review the first section of Chapter 16), but buildings have a unique characteristic that often make building investments one of the most important decisions a manager makes. Buildings, once constructed, are very difficult to sell. They are usually integrated with a farmstead and cannot be separated for sale. Managers who need buildings usually prefer to have them in a specific location and of a specific type. Purchasers may discount considerably the price of existing buildings because of location and type. Even when the total farm is sold, buildings usually do not add half their replacement cost to the price of the farm.

In most cases, the only way that farm-building investments are profitable is when the buildings are used for storage of crops or machinery or for housing livestock for the total period for which they were planned.

Ron Lopez wanted to return to the home farm after graduating from college with a major in animal sciences. The Lopez farm, consisting of 320 owned and 200 rented acres, was a one-person unit and needed to be expanded to support two families. Although Paul, Ron's father, liked to raise crops better than milking dairy cows, Ron suggested they expand the dairy operation because land was difficult to rent and expensive to buy. Following Ron's suggestion, Paul invested $150,000 in a modern dairy unit and another $75,000 in inventories. The production system worked fine, but after two years, Ron decided he did not like to work with dairy cows. He left the farm and took a job in feed sales. Paul has $200,000 in remaining debt and a dairy production facility that cannot be sold and will return only $10,000 per year if rented. The fixed cost of the building (interest, depreciation, taxes, repairs, insurance) is $22,500. Paul now has the following options:

1. Rent the buildings and lose $12,500 per year.
2. Let the buildings remain idle and lose $22,500 per year.
3. Hire an operator and continue the dairy operation.

Unfortunately, Paul does not like any of these alternatives, but he has no other choices. If he had purchased or rented land and purchased machinery, the land and machinery could be much more easily sold or rented.

Buildings are expensive to move after they have been constructed. Once a building has been located in the wrong place from the standpoint of expansion or efficiency, the manager faces the undesirable alternatives of moving the building or living with the inefficiency.

Plans for expansion should be developed before any buildings are constructed. There is usually little additional cost to planning a building system so that it can be expanded, but there could be a great cost to building an initial unit in such a way that expansion is not economically practical. Plan as if you will eventually expand the building system to several times its initial capacity.

Buildings have an important impact on the efficiency of livestock performance and on crop quality. Be sure to study and observe other buildings before planning and constructing one of your own. Some builders have knowledge about the important requirements of livestock buildings; others do not. Select a builder who knows about ventilation, insulation, floor layout, and proper strength of materials. Building-plan booklets from such sources as the Midwest Plan Service can be helpful.[1] Contact managers who have constructed similar buildings and check out the features of their buildings that they like and dislike. Sketch your proposed building and show it to other farmers, extension specialists, agricultural researchers, building contractors, and others. Incorporate their ideas for improvement into your plan. Study the plan yourself and think about ways to improve the building. This exhaustive research and preplanning is likely to lead to a better building. Keep in mind that you must live with your decision because it is very costly to change buildings once construction is completed.

BUILDING DECISIONS

Impact on Farm Organization

A new building almost always has an impact on the total farm organization and is accompanied by a change in farm organization. The evaluation of a building investment, therefore, usually requires a total farm budget in which costs and returns of the present organization are compared with the new farm organization being considered. Even a decision about replacing an existing building may affect the total organization.

> The 32-year-old farrowing barn at the Alex Gerry farm is almost beyond repair and is also obsolete. If the barn is not replaced, Alex will have to change from farrow-to-finish production to feeding out hogs. If Alex constructs a new farrowing house, he will probably select a slatted-floor, low-labor unit so he could either expand volume with the same labor or reduce his labor supply. In either case, the costs and returns from the building change will extend beyond the building itself to other parts of the business. Also, since a building is a long-

[1]Midwest Plan Service, 122 Davidson Hall, Iowa State University, Ames, Iowa 50011.

term investment, costs and returns resulting from the change must be considered for the length of the planning period (see "Farm Capital Investment Decisions" in Chapter 3).

Will a New Building Pay?

Harold Price and his family have been operating 380 acres with thirty-five dairy cows on a Grade A system in a stanchion barn. Over the years Harold has depended on help from his four sons and has operated a relatively high-labor system with only family labor. Now that his youngest son is graduating from high school, Harold must hire a full-time employee if he is to continue in the dairy business. In Harold's judgment, he and the employee could handle eighty cows if he constructs a new milking parlor, converts the stanchion barn to free stalls, and automates his feed- and manure-handling systems. He estimates the expansion would require an added building and equipment investment of $115,000, an added livestock investment of $79,000, plus an expanded feed inventory of $6,500. Harold considers the planning period for this investment to be ten years. He knows that to project net income accurately, he must estimate returns, costs, and profits for his entire planning period and then observe his net worth at the end of that period (see Chapter 3). Using the computer, he plans to make a total farm analysis with the help of his extension agent.

In the meantime, Harold has done some partial budgeting and has determined the differences in the new system from his present plan (Figure 17.1). He is receiving a gross income per cow of $1,987 for milk plus $314 for cull cows and bull calves. His direct costs (feed, fuel, utilities, veterinarian, etc.) are $1,201 per cow. The return to the added buildings, equipment, cows, and feed inventory would be $2,301 minus $1,201, or $1,100 per cow. The added costs for the buildings and equipment include depreciation, interest, repairs, taxes, and insurance.

Harold's plan is for a ten-year period, and he judges that the buildings will last ten years and the equipment five years; interest will be 8%. The depreciation and interest will be amortized with equal annual charges. The building rate is 14.9% and the equipment rate is 25.1% (Table 17.1). Harold summarized added returns to be $49,500 (Figure 17.1) and added costs to be $33,830, of which $26,990 was transferred from Table 17.1. The total cost of interest, taxes, and insurance on the added cows and feed inventory is $6,840. The cows are not depreciated because the herd will be maintained at the same level through replacements. Total increased returns minus increased costs is $15,670. Harold decided that this return is adequate to warrant taking the risk of adding the $200,500 investment associated with the increase in herd size from thirty-five to eighty. If a more comprehensive analysis confirms the results of the partial budget, he plans to make the investment.

Remodel or Build?

Remodeling old buildings can save investment money and allow a manager to produce livestock or store crops with lower overhead costs and fewer financial commit-

TABLE 17.1 Calculation of Annual Ownership Cost of Dairy Buildings and Equipment, Harold Price Farm

Item	Percent of New Cost	Initial Investment
A. Buildings		$65,000
Depreciation and interest[a]	14.9	
Repairs and maintenance	2.0	
Taxes	1.0	
Insurance	0.5	
Total	18.4	
Annual ownership cost	$11,960	
B. Equipment		$50,000
Depreciation and interest[b]	25.1	
Repairs and maintenance	4.0	
Taxes	1.0	
Insurance	0.5	
Total	30.6	
Annual ownership cost	$15,300	

[a]Depreciation 10 years, interest 8%, amortized over the planning period (see Appendix A). Procedure is presented in Chapter 8 under "Budgeting Annual Cost of Depreciable Resources".
[b]Depreciation 5 years, interest 8%, amortized (see Appendix A).

ments. These advantages are especially significant for the operator who has very limited capital or who may not want to make a long-term commitment. However, if the cost of remodeling exceeds one-third of the cost of a new building, the benefits of a new building should be carefully considered. These benefits are:

1. Labor efficiency may be improved and management simplified, thus making expansion easier.
2. Location can be selected.
3. Performance might be improved.
4. Labor, energy, and repair costs might be reduced.
5. Complexity and difficulties of remodeling can be eliminated.
6. The general appearance of the farmstead might be improved.

It is advisable to make a partial budget, such as the one in Figure 17.1, to evaluate remodeling versus a new building. An important question in remodeling is, "If I later abandon the remodeled building, can much of the added equipment be used in the new building?" If the answer is yes, remodeling becomes more attractive.

PARTIAL BUDGET
Harold Price Farm
(Estimation of Changes from Present Situations)

A. TEST OF MY PLAN TO: _Construct a new milk parlor and expand from 35 to 80 cows_

A.   Additional Annual Receipts

Income over direct cost for _____

45 cows at $1,100 each $49,500

    Total additional receipts · $49,500

B.   Reduced Annual Costs

None   _____

_____   _____

    Total reduced costs · ___

    Total of additional receipts and reduced costs · $49,500

C.   Additional Annual Costs

Ownership costs   _____

1. Buildings (Table 17.1) $11,960

2. Equipment (Table 17.1)   15,030

3. Interest, taxes, insurance   _____

on cows and feed   _____

inventory, 8% of $85,500   6,840

    Total additional costs · $33,830

D.   Reduced Annual Receipts

None   _____

    Total reduced receipts · _____

    Total of additional costs and reduced   receipts · $33,830

E.   Net Change in Farm Income

    Total of additional costs and reduced receipts subtracted from
    total of additional receipts and reduced costs · $15,670

Figure 17.1   Partial budget, Harold Price farm.

Tom and Leona Wilson started farming on a small share-rental unit that required raising livestock to provide sufficient volume to earn an adequate income. Tom discussed livestock possibilities with his landlady. She was interested in livestock but did not want to invest much money in buildings. Tom made plans for remodeling an existing henhouse, barn, and shed to make them suitable for swine production.

The remodeled buildings required a great deal of Tom's time for feeding and observing livestock, handling waste, and moving livestock. The forty-sow, two-litter farrow-to-finish enterprise not only increased Tom's income but the landlady's as well. As income increased, the landlady was willing to invest more to reduce labor requirements and increase volume. Eventually the landlady replaced the old converted buildings with new buildings that reduced labor requirements and enabled Tom to expand to 100 sows.

High Investment, Low Labor versus Low Investment, High Labor

There is great variance in the relative amount of capital, labor, and management required by different livestock production systems. Often (but not always) these systems have similar total costs per unit of production, though the components of cost are different (Table 17.2).

Low-investment systems tend to be encouraged if:

1. Capital is short
2. Capital is expensive
3. Surplus and low-cost labor is available
4. The planning horizon is short
5. Good alternative investment opportunities are available
6. Volume of production is low
7. The farm produces straw or pasture
8. The farm is landlord-owned and the future is uncertain
9. Production is not intensive
10. Management is oriented more toward husbandry than mechanics.

High-investment systems tend to be encouraged if:

1. Labor is short
2. Volume increase is desired
3. Land is suited to row crops

TABLE 17.2 Labor and Capital Requirements and Labor, Facility, and Total Cost of Swine Production

Item (per hog produced)	Low Investment	High Investment
Labor	3.0 hours	1.5 hours
Capital invested in buildings and equipment	$ 69.00	$102.00
Labor cost	15.00	7.50
Building and equipment cost	12.42	19.38
Total cost[a]	$107.00	$108.00

[a]Include all costs: feed, veterinary, overhead, labor, etc.

4. Capital is available
5. Production is sufficiently intensive to utilize buildings fully
6. The farm is owner-operated
7. The planning horizon is long
8. Management is oriented toward mechanics as well as husbandry.

Once a high-investment system is constructed, it should be used intensively to reduce overhead costs of production as much as possible.

> Which system do you think would be better in each situation in Figure 17.2?

Construct or Hire Construction?

Farmers who plan and supervise the construction of their own crop storage and live-stock buildings sometimes report savings of 20% to 50% compared to the costs of hiring the entire unit constructed by a contractor. Investment funds can be saved and overhead costs reduced substantially *if* you have the skill to do the job and *if* the construction project does not adversely affect the total farm operation.

> Bob Lord heard about potential savings operators could gain by constructing their own buildings. Even though he had little construction experience and did not understand how to obtain needed information about ventilation, insulation, and strength of material, Bob decided to build a cattle-finishing unit. He did all of the construction himself, including pouring the concrete slats. The construction was not well done. Inadequate ventilation resulted in a disease problem, which adversely affected feed conversion and caused above-average death loss. Also, the cattle had problems from standing and walking on the poorly constructed slats. Performance was not good, and some cattle died. Bob would have been better off to get expert advice and construction help rather than build the facility himself.

> Charlie Jordan, on the other hand, saved 35% of a $100,000 investment in a cold-confinement cattle-feeding unit. Charlie is skillful at construction and had time in the summer after the corn was laid by to work on the cattle building. The construction project used his full-time hired labor better, and it was easy to find part-time student help in the summer to work on the project. Constructing his own building was profitable for Charlie Jordan.

Finish at Once or over Several Years?

Spreading construction over several years allows a manager to test out advanced technology before making a total commitment, to do some or all of the construction personally, and to reduce risk by adjusting the rate of investment to income. But if

Type of Production System

	High Investment, Low Labor	Low Investment, High Labor
Land		
1. Flat and productive	_____	_____
2. Rolling pasture, bedding available	_____	_____
3. Fenced, water available	_____	_____
4. Location near residential area	_____	_____
Management, Labor		
5. Short on experience	_____	_____
6. Top-notch livestock ability	_____	_____
7. Good mechanical ability	_____	_____
8. Can supervise or manage labor	_____	_____
9. Seasonal labor supply	_____	_____
10. Constant but limited	_____	_____
11. Spouse likes to work with livestock	_____	_____
12. Large amount of low-cost labor	_____	_____
Capital Situation		
13. Willing to make long-term commitment	_____	_____
14. Short of capital	_____	_____
15. Need steady income	_____	_____
16. Old buildings available	_____	_____
Changing Cost Situation		
17. System has cost advantage	_____	_____
18. Energy costs rising	_____	_____
19. Building costs rising	_____	_____
Business Organization		
20. Landlord, share rented	_____	_____
21. Owner-operator	_____	_____
22. Specialized livestock-producing unit	_____	_____

Figure 17.2   Which building production system is better?

construction is to be spread over several years, the plan for the total building complex, including projections of income and costs, should be made at the beginning. The projections should be compared to budgets of completing the entire project at one time. Spreading construction can often limit volume and income substantially. Also, from a management standpoint, it is easier to make the total change at one time than make adjustments each year for several years.

Building Rental

Building rental possibilities depend largely on whether you can find the type of building needed in the location needed at the time needed. If buildings that meet these conditions are available, a comparison of the rental cost and the owned cost can be made (see the earlier section, "Will a New Building Pay?").

If livestock buildings are available, it is usually because the owner has quit rather than because the buildings were constructed for rental. This being the case, the would-be renter is in a good bargaining position for obtaining a low rental fee. The renter should want to know why the farmer quit using the building. Was there a problem in attaining good livestock performance? Was this caused by design features of the building?

DISCUSSION QUESTIONS

1. Why might the construction of a farm building be a more important decision than the purchase of land or machinery of equal value? Explain.
2. Why is planning before construction very important for farm buildings?
3. What methods should one use for determining whether a new building will pay?
4. Budget the payoff of an added building for a farm with which you are familiar.
5. What advice would you give to a manager who asks, "Should I remodel my old building or save the remodeling money and construct a new building?"
6. What factors determine whether a manager should construct a high-investment, low-labor building or a low-investment, high-labor building?
7. What advice would you give an operator who asks if it is better to construct one's own buildings or hire them constructed?
8. List the advantages and disadvantages of completing the construction of a building complex over several years compared to completing construction in a relatively short time.
9. What possibilities exist for building rentals? What are the important considerations when renting buildings?

RELATED READINGS

AMERICAN SOCIETY OF FARM MANAGERS AND RURAL APPRAISERS. *Rural Appraisal Manual,* 5th ed., Denver, Colorado, 1979.

BOYD, JAMES S. *Practical Farm Buildings.* Danville, Ill.: The Interstate Printers Publishers, Inc., 1973.

HERBST, J. H. *Farm Management Principles, Budgets, Plans,* chap. 10. Champaign, Ill.: Stipes Publishing Co., 1983.

MIDWEST PLAN SERVICE. *Midwest Plan Service Structures and Environment Handbook,* 11th ed., Ames, Iowa: Iowa State University, 1983.

MURRAY, WILLIAM G., DUANE G. HARRIS, GERALD A. MILLER, and NEILL S. THOMPSON. *Farm Appraisal and Valuation,* chaps. 10–11. Ames, Iowa: The Iowa State University Press, 1983.

NEUBAUER, LOREN W., and HARRY B. WALKER. *Farm Building Design.* Englewood Cliffs, N.J.: Prentice-Hall, 1961.

SUTER, ROBERT C. *The Appraisal of Farm Real Estate,* 2nd ed. Danville, Ill.: Interstate Printers and Publishers, 1980.

WHITAKER, JAMES H. *Agricultural Buildings and Structures.* Reston, Va.: Reston Publishing Co., 1979.

Farm Marketing
and Purchasing

18

IMPORTANCE OF MARKETING AND PURCHASING

Farmers have very little control over prices received for products or prices paid for resources. But a slight percentage change in prices received for products and paid for resources has a tremendous impact on farmers' profits.

Jim Kelly, a Kansas farmer, figured his cost of producing wheat to be $3.90 per bushel. The same year the average price received for wheat by farmers in the area was $4.10, resulting in a profit for Jim of $0.20 per bushel. Now Jim reasons that he can reduce costs 5%, or $0.19 per bushel, simply by purchasing more wisely (checking prices of inputs in several places, taking maximum advantage of various discounts, and keeping in tune with price trends). In other words, the practice of careful purchasing could nearly double profit. Jim also believes that he can increase price received by $0.10 per bushel by checking alternative grain markets and studying price movements. The modest percentage gains from careful buying and selling could more than double Jim Kelly's farm profit.

TYPES OF FARM MARKETING DECISIONS

Farm marketing decisions and practices are of two types. One type, which we will call *marketing techniques,* involves such decisions and practices as choosing the best market, keeping many marketing options open, controlling quality to obtain a higher price, and checking stored products to be sure they are in good condition. Having considerable control in these decisions, a manager has the opportunity to increase profits by doing the correct thing at the proper time.

The second type of marketing decision is the *when-to-price-the-product decision*. Farm products are sometimes—but not always—priced at the time of delivery. There are arrangements whereby some commodities can be priced prior to delivery (indeed, even prior to production), and it is also possible to price some products long after they have been delivered. Prices of many farm products are continually changing, so the date of pricing has a great impact on profit. But the when-to-price decision is closely related to the amount of risk a manager is willing to accept. Would the manager prefer a more certain income or a possible higher income with a significant chance of a lower income (see Chapter 4)?

Billy Hedrick is contemplating selling soybeans on January 2, before planting, for fall delivery for $6.50, estimating that his cost of production will be $6.25. But should he sell in January or wait in anticipation of a higher price? To answer this question, Billy collected the following information from outlook experts: "Supplies of soybeans are short, and if there is a poor crop in South America or a drought this summer, the soybean price could go as high as $10.00. On the other hand, if there is sufficient rain and a large crop, the price could be as low as $5.50 at harvest."

Billy knows that as the year progresses, the soybean price will be affected by information regarding planting acreage, world production, exports, weather, stocks of soybeans, consumption, inflation, and other factors. He realizes he is facing a range of possible prices each of which has a probability:

Soybean Price	Probability
$9.00 or higher	.05
8.00 - 8.99	.10
7.00 - 7.99	.10
6.00 - 6.99	.60
5.99 or lower	.15

What should Billy do? First of all, he has done the correct thing in analyzing the likelihood of various prices in the future. A manager should revise his estimates of price probabilities whenever there is a major change in such factors as weather and exports. Second, Billy must evaluate his risk preference. As previously stated, this decision involves the choice of a certain good income or a possible higher income with a significant chance of lower income. Finally, Billy must determine his cash needs.

Managers seeking to avoid risk must be careful not to contract too much in advance since production is uncertain, or else a major loss might be incurred. When contracting for delivery of a farm product not yet produced, one risks the possibility that difficulties may be encountered in producing the product.

Bruce Carr, a highly levered young farmer, read a magazine article that said, "If you are in a tight cash-flow situation, don't be greedy; if price is above cost of production, forward-contract production." In April, Bruce contracted 80% of a normal corn crop of 100 bushels per acre for $3.30 per bushel for December delivery because costs were only $3.00. It was a dry year; Bruce's corn yielded only 50 bushels per acre, and the corn price increased to $4.00 by November. When Bruce hauled his corn to the elevator, he received the following payment per acre: 50 × $3.30, or $165.00. Then, to fulfill his contract of 80 bushels, Bruce had to purchase 30 bushels of corn at $4.00 and sell it for $3.30. On this transaction, Bruce lost ($4.00 − $3.30) × 30 bushels, or $21.00. His gross return per acre was $165.00 − $21.00, or $144. With costs of $300 per acre, Bruce lost $156 per acre; only a government disaster loan kept him from going bankrupt.

Farm inputs such as fertilizer, seed, and soybean meal can also be priced at different times, and these pricing decisions are similar to product pricing decisions.

SOME TECHNIQUES TO IMPROVE PRICES RECEIVED AND PAID

Check Several Markets

Checking prices of several buyers is a simple procedure that might result in price increases of $0.01 to $0.10 per bushel for grain and $0.25 to $1.50 per hundredweight for livestock. Managers sometimes neglect obtaining prices from different farm-product buyers or farm-input sellers because, not realizing the impact of a few cents per unit on profit, they trade at the most convenient market or with the market operator they like best.

> Check today's prices of products you might sell at all markets in your area. How much variation did you find? What differences would this have on profit of a typical-size farm in your area?

Look for Special Markets

Sometimes higher product prices can be obtained by finding special markets. Louise Hitchcock sells her corn for $0.06 per bushel over the local market price to a specialized cattle feeder in her area. If the cattle feeder purchased corn from the local elevator, he would have to pay $0.12 above the amount paid to farmers. Thus, both Louise and the cattle feeder gain $0.06 through this arrangement.

Seed production, breeding livestock, and direct selling of farm products to consumers are other examples of special markets. Each year Evan Green feeds out 300 cattle, which he processes through a local plant, selling the beef directly to consumers. Joseph Borelli sells vegetables directly to consumers with a roadside stand and a u-pick system.

Keep Buyers Informed

Buyers and distributors of agricultural products occasionally receive orders for products they do not have in stock. To fill these orders, they must secure additional products and are sometimes willing to pay premium prices. If buyers are aware that you have commodities available and that you will consider selling if the price is favorable, they might call you to fill the order. In such cases, you might receive an above-market price for a portion of your product.

Avoid Being Forced to Sell Storable, Seasonal Crops at Harvest

Depressed prices at market time are typical for crops that mature during a single season, especially in good crop years. Crop production is sometimes more than either the transportation system or the local storage facilities can handle during harvest. The result is discounted prices.

How can farmers avoid being forced to sell at harvest? One way is to construct on-farm storage. Of course, costs of storing crops should be compared to returns.

Rollie Springer, an Iowa farmer, analyzed market prices and found that he could expect to receive 50 cents per bushel more for corn stored until April than for corn sold at harvest in October. Using the figures in Table 18.1, Rollie estimated the cost of storing corn for six months to be 31.8 cents per bushel. This allows 18.2 cents per bushel return (above all costs) for risk and management. Producing 60,000 bushels of corn per year, Rollie would increase profit $10,920 by storing.

TABLE 18.1   Farmer Costs of Storing and Holding Shelled Corn from Harvest to Varying Delivery Times

Cost Item	Months Grain Stored			
	1	3	6	9
	On-farm storage (cents per bushel sold)			
Storing				
Annual bin costs	8.0	8.0	8.0	8.0
Extra handling labor and shrink	2.0	2.0	2.0	2.0
Total storing	10.0	10.0	10.0	10.0
Holding				
Insurance and conditioning	0.1	0.3	0.4	0.5
Interest at 10% ($2.50 per bu.)	2.1	6.2	12.5	18.7
Extra shrink (15.5%–13.0%)	?	?	7.2	7.2
Extra drying	?	?	1.7	1.7
Total holding	2.2	6.5	21.8	28.1
Total storing and holding	12.2	16.5	31.8	38.1
Rented elevator storage				
Storage services ($0.10 minimum + $0.015)	10.0	10.0	13.7	18.2
Shrink (15.5%–14%)	4.4	4.4	4.4	4.4
Interest at 10%	2.1	6.2	12.5	18.7
Total storing and holding	16.5	20.6	30.6	41.3

Source: Price Forecasting and Sales Management. Urbana, Ill.: Cooperative Extension Service, University of Illinois, 1980.

A second way to avoid the disadvantage of forced selling would be to rent storage space in grain elevators. In Rollie's case, renting would be 1.2 cents cheaper than constructing on-farm storage (Table 18.1). However, harvest delays can be caused by elevator storage if the elevator is a long distance from the farm or if long lines of trucks and wagons must wait to deliver grain at harvest. Another drawback of elevators is that they occasionally go bankrupt and farmers lose their stored crops. To help insure against this, farmers should store in a bonded elevator and insist on a warehouse receipt.

Evaluate the Cost of Discounts

Crop prices are discounted if crops fail to meet standards for moisture, quality, and absence of foreign materials. Farmers should evaluate the economics of quality discounts, which may be greater than the cost of drying or cleaning crops to meet the minimum requirements. Crops might first be dried or cleaned at the farm before delivery to the elevator. Drying grain on the farm usually pays good returns, but drying crops below the minimum standard is usually less profitable than delivering crops that just barely meet the standard. This is because no more is paid per bushel, but the crop weighs less.

Stored crops should be checked frequently. Thousands of dollars are lost each year because crops are allowed to deteriorate and spoil. Excess moisture, lack of ventilation, or changes in outside temperature can cause problems. A wise man once commented, "If a farmer stored $50,000 in a building, he would check it each day to be sure the money was still there. Why, then, do farmers put crops worth $50,000 in storage and not check them for months?"

Sometimes there is a cost associated with avoiding discounts. This cost must be compared to potential gains. For example, the price of grain crops harvested early might be discounted due to moisture above acceptable levels. On the other hand, early harvest may result in less field crop loss, and grain saved from early harvest may be more valuable than the amount of the discount.

> List the types of discounts that often occur with crops produced in your area. Check on the effect discounting could have on price and then estimate the possible impact on profit for a selected farm.

DECIDING WHEN TO PRICE

Know Your Income-Risk Preference

As indicated earlier in this chapter, a major consideration regarding when to price is the amount of risk you are willing to accept (see also Chapter 4). Give careful thought to the amount of risk you are willing to accept for the chance of a higher income; then plan a marketing strategy to coincide with your income-risk preference.

Know Your Cash Needs

If you are in a tight cash-flow situation, be cautious about holding crops too long. In any event, you should have a projected cash-needs plan that shows when income is needed to cover expenses and service debts (see Chapter 6).

Know the Cost of Production

In a competitive industry such as agriculture, price over the long term tends to move around the average cost of production for average producers. When price is above cost of production, more product is produced by existing and new farms, and price declines. When price is below cost of production, cutbacks are made in production because producers eventually become discouraged. Reduced supplies move prices up. The price can be substantially above or below cost of production while producers are adjusting their businesses to current and expected prices. But eventually, prices move toward cost of production. It is helpful for managers to know average costs of production for their products.

> Determine the cost of production for products produced in your area. Are current prices above or below cost of production?

Know Price Characteristics
and Factors That Influence Price

The forces that determine the annual average price of corn, wheat, soybeans, barley, and oats are weather conditions both in the United States and the world, numbers of acres planted, livestock numbers, and other demand factors. Month-to-month crop prices are related to time of year, with lowest prices typically at harvest. Then, because of the cost of holding the crop, prices tend to increase until the next harvest period approaches and another market glut occurs (Figure 18.1). Typically, production cycles as well as seasonal price differences influence cattle, hog, poultry, and egg prices (Figure 18.2). These cycles are caused by farmers' making production decisions on the basis of present price rather than future price and by the delay between the time farmers make production decisions and the time products are ready for market. The time delay is the result of the biological nature of farm production. Prices generally fluctuate around the cost of production.

    Knowledge of the types of price movements associated with products produced can be helpful to the farmer in making marketing decisions.

> Obtain information about monthly prices for products produced in your area for a period of several years. What factors caused price changes over this period of time? What are the prices of these products likely to be in the next year? Why?

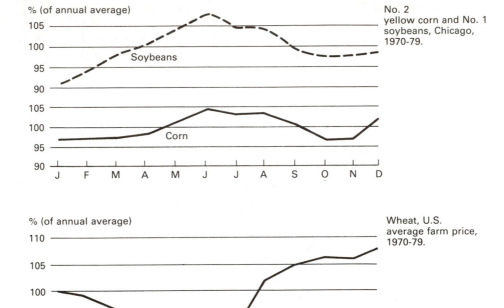

Figure 18.1 Seasonal price patterns for selected farm crops, 1970–79 average. *Source:* USDA.

Have a System for Securing Price Information

The Department of Agriculture periodically releases reports that have implications for price changes. The Agricultural Extension Service and various private forecasting agencies continually issue updated reports on price expectations. It is advisable to follow a system of keeping yourself up-to-date with these reports, which may give you insight regarding changes in the price probability range. Keep in mind that while the price probability range may shift, the producer faces a range of prices, each of which has a probability and not a certain price.

Fundamental versus Technical Price Explanations

There are two schools of thought with regard to explaining and forecasting price movements. The fundamentalist school contends that price is the result of supply and demand and that if one can correctly forecast supply and demand, one can correctly forecast price. The technical school believes that the market tells its own story and

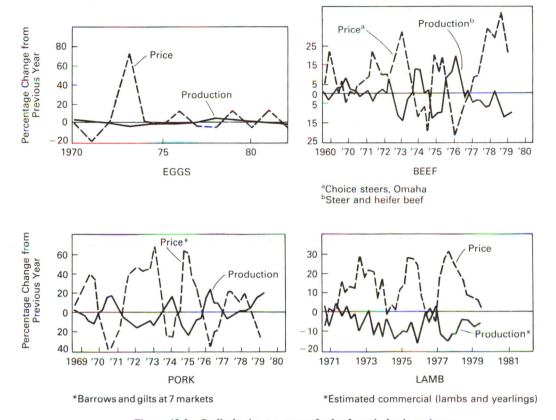

Figure 18.2 Cyclical price movement for beef, pork, lamb, and eggs.

that it moves in patterns that can be predicted by a set of rules or guidelines related to current and past prices. Some market analysts contend that in the short run (day to day or week to week), the market is greatly affected by technical forces. In the long run, prices are determined by the fundamentals. The farm manager should be aware of both technical and fundamental forces.

Use the Futures Market or a Cash Forward Contract

Farmers have the opportunity to sell many farm products on the futures market or sell to a buyer with a cash forward contract for delivery in the future. If a manager observes a price he or she considers acceptable, the price can be established before the product is produced. An advantage of selling on the futures market, when appropriate, instead of cash forward contracting is the ease in "repurchasing" the futures contract if price expectations change. In the case of a cash forward contract, the producer is required to deliver the crop contracted; a change in plans after the contract has been made can be costly. A disadvantage of the futures market is that substantial payments of margin money may be required by the broker should prices move opposite to the direction anticipated by the seller.

The futures market and cash forward contracts are useful marketing tools for the manager to use at appropriate times. Options are available for some commodities and allow the seller to be assured of a price without foregoing the opportunity for a higher price.

Understand the Basis When Marketing

The basis is the difference between cash price of a commodity at a particular place and time and the price of that commodity on the futures market on a given exchange. The basis is affected by the cost and availability of storage at each location and of transportation between the cash and futures markets. Among other factors, it is also affected by local supply and demand conditions compared with supply and demand conditions at the futures market.

In some years the basis may be wider than usual for a particular time of the year whereas in other years it may be much narrower. An advantageous basis can sometimes be assured with a basis contract. Some producers sell their crop for cash when the basis is narrow. If they anticipate a price increase, they may repurchase, for a later sale, the amount of cash commodity sold on the futures market.

> Leo Croy produces corn in central Ohio. In March Leo's local elevator received a corn order to fill a ten-car train. The elevator did not have sufficient corn in storage, and therefore increased price in order to attract more corn. Normally the basis for March corn in the area is 20 cents under the Chicago future price for March, but because of the train order and resulting higher cash price the basis narrowed to only 2 cents. It is unlikely that the basis will ever get narrower for Leo. By selling now he will receive 18 cents more than usual. However, expecting corn prices to go up during the next three months, Leo was reluctant to sell. When he talked with a market analyst, he was advised to sell the corn for cash to take advantage of the narrow basis and to buy corn back on the futures to take advantage of the price increase he expected. Following the analyst's advice, Leo purchased a futures contract of 10,000 bushels for $2.63 a bushel, later selling it for $3.13 and making $5,000 on the price rise. If prices had declined, he would have lost money. In any event, Leo's action was similar to holding his corn for later sale with the added advantage of a low basis at sale time.

Government Programs and Marketing Orders

Government price-support programs should not be overlooked when developing a marketing strategy. Some programs provide a "floor," or minimum price, for certain commodities for farmers who qualify. The guaranteed government minimum price allows a manager to hold for a higher price without risk of extremely low prices. Managers should be aware of government programs and use strategies to obtain high base acreages of profitable crops and high established yields. The attractiveness of government programs is usually enhanced as the base acreage and yield increase.

Marketing orders.   Marketing orders are arrangements, sanctioned by law, that allow producers to choose to have certain products marketed through a central decision maker. Essentially, marketing orders provide monopoly selling powers to a commodity group in a particular area. Once the majority of this commodity group approves a marketing order, all producers must market through the order. Because marketing orders do not control production, their impact on average price and net income is debatable. Marketing orders do result in more orderly marketing, and they reduce variability in prices.

Marketing orders are authorized for a limited number of commodities, such as milk, fresh fruits and vegetables, tobacco, peanuts, turkeys, and processing apples, to name a few. Marketing orders are not allowed by law for food and feed grains, soybeans, livestock, poultry (excluding turkey), and eggs.

Once under a marketing order, most selling and product pricing decisions are delegated to the order administrator.

DEVELOPING A PRODUCTION AND MARKETING STRATEGY

Some steps for developing a marketing strategy are listed and are subsequently illustrated with the Leo Croy example.

1. Forecast for the next production and marketing season the range of prices and probability of each price for products you produce.
2. Decide what you will produce and plan how much you will have to sell. Production plans should be based on prices and profit, risk preference, cash needs, and a variety of management factors, which are discussed in Chapters 10 and 11.
3. Determine profit and cash-flow needs and other goals.
4. Determine the range in dates over which sales can be made.
5. Estimate production costs and the relationships between price received, profit, and cash flow.
6. Make a general plan of when to sell or the conditions under which you will sell, taking into consideration price probabilities, cash needs, and risk preference.
7. Update your price probability listing periodically, usually after events that have a major impact or after important market reports are released.
8. Adjust your selling plans to the changing price conditions.

Marketing Strategies

The following are some possible marketing strategies. Elements in these strategies can be recombined to create additional possibilities.

1. *Aim for the average price by making five to ten sales throughout the marketing period.* This strategy might be used by minimaxers or managers who perceive themselves to have limited market-forecasting skills (see Chapter 4).

2. *Hold for prices to be in the upper 30% of the price probability range.* This strategy might be followed by a maximaxer. The danger in using this strategy is that the marketing period might end with no sales having been made. Should this happen, a forced liquidation of commodities at a low price could occur.

3. *Sell if price is above cost of production.* Although it sounds as if this strategy would result in sure profits, this is not necessarily true. First of all, it is possible for prices to remain below cost of production for the entire marketing period, thus forcing a sale at the end of the marketing time.

Prices of some commodities (especially livestock) cycle, with long periods of time when prices are above costs of production and long periods of time when prices are below costs of production (Figure 18.2). If a farmer fails to sell when prices are below cost of production and declining, losses will be greater. If, on the other hand, the farmer sells when prices are above cost of production but increasing, profit will be limited. There is an old market axiom, "Cut your losses, but let your profit run." By selling only at times when and as soon as prices are above costs of production, managers may be cutting their profits but letting their losses run.

Perhaps a more appropriate way of stating strategy 3 is: Sell if price is above cost of production unless you believe it is going higher. If you do not believe prices will be higher, sell even if it is below cost of production.

Leo Croy Production and Marketing Plan

An example of how a production and marketing strategy might be developed is presented here using the plan Leo Croy initiated in November.

Price forecast and production plan.   Leo farms 420 acres in central Ohio. On the basis of long-range crop budgets (Chapter 10), he would plant a corn-soybean rotation, 210 acres of each. However, for next year Leo expects prices to be more favorable for corn than for beans. Because of a large crop of soybeans in South America, there is likely to be a substantial stock of soybeans remaining next October 1. On the other hand, the corn crop was short this year because of a severe drought in the Corn Belt. Should further dry weather occur next year, Leo expects corn prices to increase rapidly. Consequently, Leo has tentatively decided to plant 280 acres of corn and 140 acres of soybeans next year. He expects production to be 120 bushels of corn per acre, or 33,600 bushels, and 45 bushels of soybeans per acre, or 6,300 bushels. Of course, if market conditions change, this production plan would be reevaluated.

Risk-income preference.   Leo is about halfway between being a minimaxer and maximaxer; in other words, he is neither extremely conservative nor extremely liberal from a risk-income standpoint (see Chapter 4). He is concerned about making payments on a $425,000 debt that he owes for land, machinery, and operating capital.

Storage, markets, and marketing period.   In a normal production year, Leo has sufficient storage on the farm for both corn and soybeans. However, because of the shift to corn, he will be short of on-farm storage by about 8,500 bushels. There are three elevators in the area, and all are willing to contract for future delivery. Leo has decided that he would rather forward-contract than hedge on the futures market because he does not want to face the possibility of having to secure margin money.

Corn and soybeans can be contracted beginning November 1 of this year and can be stored (except for 8,500 bushels of corn) until September 1 of the year after next. So there is a twenty-two month marketing period for all crops except the 8,500 bushels of corn for which Leo has no storage. Wishing to avoid off-farm storage, Leo decided to forward-contract the 8,500 bushels between November 1 of this year and September 30 next year.

Production cost and cash flow.   Leo has estimated his production costs to be $2.86 per bushel of corn and $6.58 per bushel of soybeans. If he can sell at least two-thirds of his crop at these prices, he will likely have sufficient money to meet his mortgage payments and living expenses.

Marketing strategy.   Leo decided that if corn and bean prices were above $2.86 and $6.58, respectively, he would contract up to one-third of the crop when he judged that prices were near their peak. He observed in early November that he could sell next year's corn for $3.03 and soybeans for $7.08. He studied price charts and talked with a marketing analyst about whether corn and bean prices were in an upward, downward, or stable trend. It appeared from the technical charts that both corn and soybean prices were increasing. Leo decided to wait until prices signaled a downturn before selling. Prices continued to increase for several days but then started to decline. On December 12 the market broke through a lower support and signaled a downward trend; corn price fell below $3.10 and beans below $7.25. Leo contracted about one-third of his crop (11,000 bushels of corn and 2,100 bushels of soybeans) for fall delivery. He opted to sell no more than half of his crop before next August 1, at which time he could assess yields. He did not want to risk contracting more than he could produce.

With two chances in ten of drought conditions and of corn reaching $4.00 and soybeans reaching $9.00, Leo opted to wait until spring and summer to market the remaining 5,500 bushels of corn and 1,050 bushels of soybeans that he would consider selling before harvest. He would sell this sixth of his crop only if corn prices reached $4.00 and soybeans $9.00.

In marketing the half to two-thirds of the crop that remained to be sold after harvest, Leo spread corn and soybean sales into three periods, November–January, February–April, and May–August. He used technical charts and long-term price expectations to determine when to sell in each period. If price did not equal production plus storage costs, Leo would sell half of the planned sales and carry the other half into the next period. Any crop not sold by August 15 of the year after next would be sold regardless of price.

As conditions changed, Leo continued to review and evaluate his marketing plan. The astute manager makes marketing a continuous part of the farm business plan.

> Develop a marketing strategy for the next production period for a product produced on a particular farm in your area. Explain the reason for the plan you developed.

DISCUSSION QUESTIONS

1. How much impact does buying and selling have on farm profit? Budget the impact for some hypothetical enterprises.
2. What are some techniques for increasing price received for products sold and lowering price paid for resources purchased?
3. What is the difference between selling a product and pricing a product? Why might they be done at different times? How might they be done at different times?
4. What are the important factors to consider for deciding when to price a product?
5. What is the difference between the technical and fundamental methods of forecasting prices?
6. What are the advantages and disadvantages of selling a product on the futures market versus contracting with a buyer?
7. What are the steps for developing a production-marketing strategy?
8. List alternative marketing strategies. Which would you recommend to a manager?

RELATED READINGS

BRANSON, ROBERT E. and DOUGLASS G. NORVELL. *Introduction to Agricultural Marketing.* New York: McGraw-Hill, 1983.

CHICAGO BOARD OF TRADE. *Commodity Marketing.* Chicago: Board of Trade of the City of Chicago, 1982.

DOWNEY, W. DAVID and JOHN K. TROCKE. *Agribusiness Management,* Part 3. New York: McGraw-Hill, 1981.

GOOD, DARREL L., THOMAS A. HIERONYMUS, and ROYCE A. HINTON. *Price Forecasting and Sales Management.* Urbana, Ill.: Cooperative Extension Service, University of Illinois 1980.

KOHLS, RICHARD L., and JOSEPH N. UHL. *Marketing of Agricultural Products*. New York: Macmillan, 1984.

KOTLER, PHILIP. *Marketing Management Analysis, Planning, and Control*. Englewood Cliffs, N.J.: Prentice-Hall, 1984.

Marketing for Farmers. St. Louis, Mo.: Doane-Western, Inc., 1982.

SHEPARD, GEOFFREY S. and GENE A. FUTRELL. *Marketing Farm Products*. Ames, Iowa: Iowa State University Press, 1982.

Getting Started
in Farming

19

Two ways to begin farming are with your family or independent of your family. This chapter presents some of the considerations, problems, and solutions of joining the family operation. Also discussed are ways to get started in farming without family help.

JOINING THE FAMILY FARM

Farming with other members of the family can be a very rewarding experience if the arrangement is a successful one. A family farming arrangement provides not only a career but the satisfaction of keeping the family closer together. On the other hand, if the arrangement is unsuccessful, it not only may result in job dissatisfaction but also may create personal stress in the family.

A successful arrangement for a family farm-operating arrangement depends on both personal and economic factors. Economic considerations are whether or not the farm will generate sufficient income for all parties and whether or not the income is fairly divided. Important personal factors are whether goals are similar or dissimilar and whether or not family members can get along with one another. Each of the economic and personal considerations is discussed and is illustrated with a case example.

Will the Farm Provide Sufficient Income?

When a new person or family joins the farm business on a permanent basis, one of two things must happen: The party or parties presently operating the farm must share, thereby reducing their income, or the farm organization must be changed so that the farm will generate more income. The first step in developing a suitable farming arrangement is to estimate the amount of income the farm will earn without making any organizational changes (see Chapter 12). Does budgeted income correlate to the amount of money the farm has been making in the past? If not, appropriate adjustments should be made in the basic planning data so that budgeted income is similar to income earned in the past. Second, all parties should decide how much income they would like. Will there be sufficient income to meet these goals? If not, how will the deficiency be met? If income is to be increased through farm organization changes or off-farm employment, the income resulting from these changes should be projected. The question ''Is there sufficient capital to make the changes needed to provide income desired by all parties?'' should be answered. If an organization cannot be found that will generate sufficient income, a satisfactory operating arrangement may not be feasible.

> Kenny Fore, a student at a state college, wanted to return to the home farm and become a partner with his father and brother Jim after graduation. The Fores, a close-knit family, enjoyed doing things together. Jim joined the farm during Kenny's sophomore year, and the entire family looked forward to having Kenny become a partner in the family farm business.
>
> During his senior year Kenny observed that his brother was having difficulty making payments on an 80-acre farm he had purchased. Kenny found that, while his father wanted to help his sons get started in farming, he was unable to help Jim with the mortgage payments because he had reduced his own income to bring Jim into the business. In a farm management class, Kenny budgeted current income; after asking Jim and his father about their income goals, he realized that there was barely enough money for his father and brother. In order for the farm to earn sufficient income to include Kenny in the business, the farm would need to be improved or expanded. This would require more machinery, buildings, land, livestock, and operating capital. Jim had borrowed up to his limit to get started, and Kenny's father did not want to go further in debt. It became obvious after the analysis that Kenny, who had no savings, should take the job offered him in a community bank, save some money, and grow into a partnership with his family. Had he not done a good job of analysis, Kenny might have joined the farm only to find that his need for income was causing stress and disagreements among the family members.

Estimate income for a farm with which you are familiar that might have a son or daughter interested in joining the business in the near future. What are the income goals of each party? Is there sufficient income to meet all the needs? What are some possibilities for farm organization changes that might increase income? Are there sufficient capital and management to make organizational changes?

Sharing Income

Farm income is the return to labor, management, land, machinery, buildings, breeding livestock, and operating capital. From an economic standpoint, a fair arrangement is one in which each party is rewarded for his or her contributions. From a personal standpoint, one of the parties may decide to accept less income than is ''deserved'' to allow the other party to have more. There are limits as to the amount of transfer allowable without tax implications. If such a transfer is to be made, a tax adviser should be consulted.

Let's look at some alternatives for sharing income.

1. Wage.   The advantages of the ordinary salary for the person joining the farm are that it is simple, has no risk for the person joining the farm, and allows easy exit from the business if the arrangement does not work satisfactorily. The disadvantages are that a salary does not involve the young person in ownership of the farm resources, nor does it provide a profit incentive for doing a better job. Also, the starting person is less likely to be involved in management decisions when there is no sharing of ownership, profit, or risk.

Salary is a good way to begin for a trial period while the father, mother, son, or daughter observes how the beginner gets along in a business environment. The wage should be at a rate that is being paid for similar jobs. The son or daughter might inquire at farms and industries in the area to determine the amount being paid to workers and managers with similar responsibilities.

> If you were returning to a farm business, what salary level would be fair?

2. Wage plus a share of the profit.   This plan adds profit sharing and incentive to the regular salary and otherwise has similar advantages and disadvantages.

3. Cotenancy.   The parents and the son or daughter could become partners, with the child renting the farm from the parents. The type of rental arrangement would depend on the preferences of the parties involved and on typical arrangements for the area. The rental could be either cash or share. If the farm is rented for cash and if there is a 50-50 cotenancy arrangement, receipts and costs would probably be allocated as in Table 19.1.

If the farm is rented on the share basis, the division between the operators and the owner would be on the basis of tradition in the geographic area. If the farm is

TABLE 19.1   50-50 Cotenancy Cash Rental Arrangement

	As Operators		As Farm Owners
	Parents	Son or Daughter	Parents
A. Receipts			
1. Crops	50%	50%	
2. Livestock	50%	50%	
3. Cash rental of farm			100%
B. Expenses			
1. Operating costs	50%	50%	
2. Machinery	50%	50%	
3. Labor	50%	50%	
4. Cash rent	50%	50%	
5. Land and buildings, taxes, insurance, repairs			100%

TABLE 19.2 50-50 Cotenancy Share Rental Arrangement

	As Operators		As Farm Owners
	Parents	Son or Daughter	Parents
A. Receipts			
1. Crops	25%	25%	50%
2. Livestock	25%	25%	50%
B. Expenses			
1. Operating costs, seed, fertilizer, chemicals	25%	25%	50%
2. Machinery operations, fuel, repairs	50%	50%	
3. Machinery ownership	50%	50%	
4. Labor	50%	50%	
5. Land and buildings, taxes, insurance, repairs			100%

located in an area where the 50-50 lease is typical, the receipt and expense distribution would be similar to that shown in Table 19.2.

The advantage of the cotenancy arrangement is that it involves both parties totally in investment, risk, management, and profit sharing. One disadvantage is that it may not provide sufficient income to the new partner if the farm is small. Also, it is not easy to make gradual changes in expense and income sharing if the parents choose to reduce their contribution and shift machinery and inventory ownership as well as management and labor input to the son or daughter.

4. Operating arrangements. An operating arrangement is a flexible system that can be easily changed over time and still reward individuals for their specific resource contribution. It can be either a partnership or a corporation. Various farm assets can be held by individuals or the corporation or partnership. One way it could work is illustrated in Figure 19.1. The parties involved in the operating arrangement provide the management. After all other resources are paid, the return to management is divided among the parties in relation to their management contribution. For example, initially a son might be compensated for 10% of the management and receive 10% of the return. Over time this might grow to 50%. Later, when the parents retire, the percentage of the son's share could increase to 60%, 70%, or 80%.

Salaries are paid to all parties according to the amount they work. Initially both father and son might receive a $14,000 salary. Once the son becomes established, the father might work fewer hours and take longer vacations. His salary might be reduced to whatever amount is appropriate for the amount of time he devotes to the farm.

In the beginning, *land* may be rented from the parents and others in the community. But as the children accumulate capital, they may wish to purchase land and rent it to the arrangement.

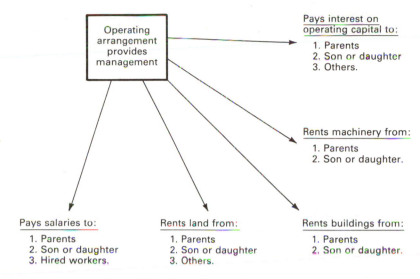

Figure 19.1   Example operating arrangement.

Buildings and machinery can be owned by various parties and rented to the operation in a similar manner.

The operating arrangement facilitates making any necessary changes in management and ownership over time. It allows the parents to give land and other farm assets to nonfarm children while excluding the operating income earned by farm children. It also enables any number of parties to join the arrangement, provide varied amounts of management, capital, labor, land, buildings, and machinery, and be rewarded for their individual contributions. If a farm business has an unusually good employee, this arrangement can even be used to enable the employee to own part of the operating arrangement without owning part of the farm. This might help retain the employee and keep motivation high.

Some important questions must be answered in setting up an operating arrangement:

1. If there is not sufficient income to pay all resources, who gets first claim?
   - One alternative would be to sum all payments, calculate the percentage of all payments relative to income, and then pay each resource that percentage of the initial plan. As an example, let us assume that the initial plan for an operating arrangement was to pay a father and son for their contributions as shown in the table on page 346.

   Any income above $140,000 would be divided 50-50. However, suppose that the year's income is only $100,000:

   $$\frac{\$100,000}{\$140,000} \times 100 = 71.43\%$$

	Father	Son	Total
Labor	$ 15,000	$15,000	$ 30,000
Land	50,000	0	50,000
Buildings	20,000	0	20,000
Machinery	15,000	5,000	20,000
Interest	10,000	10,000	20,000
Total	$110,000	$30,000	$140,000

The father would be paid $110,000 times 71.43%, or $78,571; the son would be paid $30,000 times 71.43%, or $21,429.

- A second alternative is to pay labor the full amount and distribute the remainder on the basis of the percentage that total payments, excluding labor, are of income minus labor payments.

2. How much should various resources be paid? Some guidelines are:
   - *Labor:* Pay a salary that is comparable to the amount paid for similar work in the area.
   - *Land:* Rent on a typical share basis for the area.
   - *Machinery and crop equipment:* Annual use cost (see Chapter 16).
   - *Buildings:* Annual use cost (see Chapter 17) or typical share bases for the area.
   - *Livestock equipment:* Annual use cost (see Chapter 17) or typical share bases for the area.
   - *Interest on operating capital:* Pay the rate that lenders charge.

The operating arrangement should have a written provision that protects all parties in the arrangement but also protects the arrangement. This protection can be accomplished by specifying the procedure to be followed when a party wishes to withdraw from the arrangement. The written provision should indicate when payment to the withdrawing party is to be made and the procedure for establishing the value of assets in the arrangement. This recommendation applies to all types of arrangements, not to the operating arrangement exclusively.

5. Cooperative arrangements.   There may be circumstances when it is not advisable to have two parties tied together in an entire operation. For instance, the farm may be too small, the goals of the parties may be quite different, or the personalities of the parties may not be compatible in a farm business arrangement. However, it still may be possible to cooperate in some areas for mutual benefit.

Jon Ladinski wanted to farm with his father, but the home farm was too small to provide an income for two families. Jon's father agreed that if Jon could find some land to rent, he would allow his son the use of his machinery in exchange for Jon's labor. Jon rented 60 acres and began farming on his own with the use of his father's machinery. This arrangement not only enabled Jon to get started but also reduced his father's labor load.

Two brothers, Peter and Herbert Klein, farm about 500 acres each in the same community. Each brother has complete management control over his own unit, paying all expenses and retaining all receipts individually with one exception—they have a common set of machinery. This not only allows the Kleins to operate large, labor-efficient machinery and to have backup labor and management in the case of illness, but it also allows them to make most farm decisions independently.

> Recommend an operating arrangement for a farm with which you are familiar. How might this arrangement change over time?

Put It in Writing and Make Sure It Is Legally Sound

Operating arrangements should be in writing to help avoid any misunderstandings between the parties involved. Sometimes details may be viewed differently or may even be forgotten if they are not carefully recorded in writing. Also, in the event of the death of one or all of the parties, the heirs may find themselves involved in the arrangement without any knowledge of the initial agreement. The written agreement should be reviewed by an attorney and an accountant to be sure it is legally sound and does not lead to tax challenges by the Internal Revenue Service or state tax authorities.

Tax Considerations

The transfer of assets into corporations and partnerships and the rental, sale or giving away of assets can have important income and estate tax implications. It is important to have the counsel of a knowledgeable tax adviser before making sales and transfers.

Personal Considerations

Goals. Before entering into a farm-operating agreement, each party should list personal goals and recommendations for the organization of the farm business (see Chapter 2). Are preferences for debt, hours of work, and type of farm operation compatible? If not, can compromises be made that would be satisfactory to all parties? If goals are not similar and conflicts cannot be resolved, it may not be advisable to bring a new person into the business.

Management abilities and job description.   The management abilities of persons who are to be involved with the business should be evaluated (see Chapter 2). These abilities, along with personal likes and dislikes as well as farm needs, should be considered in developing a job description for each person (see Chapter 21). The job description defines the responsibility and authority of each person. A good job description should enable the business to be more efficient because it leads to the assignment of job responsibilities to persons who can do them best. Also, because there is an understanding about who has authority and responsibility for various jobs and decisions, personal conflicts should be reduced.

> Develop a description of jobs and areas of responsibility for persons on a family farm with which you are familiar.

Changing responsibility.   Most likely the parents have had responsibility for all farm decisions before the children became partners in the business. Parents should begin shifting a small portion of that responsibility to their children so that experience can be gained by the new partners. More and more responsibility may be shifted until responsibilities of all parties are equal. The day may come when the parents would like to shift even more of their responsibility to the children. The parents will likely be involved in the farm business to some extent throughout their lives. Usually the business can be much more productive and profitable if parents continue to contribute their wisdom and understanding even after retirement. This shift in responsibility is one of the most important and delicate factors in determining whether or not a family operating arrangement can be successful. Some common mistakes in transferring responsibility are:

1. Mom and dad won't let go. The son or daughter joins the farm with assurance that he or she will be a partner, but one year goes by, then five, ten, fifteen, and the son or daughter has lots of work but no responsibility. One of two things usually happens under these circumstances: The son or daughter leaves, or the child stays but fails to develop the management skills necessary for handling the farm when the parents pass out of the picture.

2. The son or daughter wants to be boss immediately. Some children develop an attitude that once they return to the farm, they are in charge. Usually they do not have the management skills, nor have they earned this promotion. For this reason, it may be desirable to have an apprenticeship before having a partnership. Sons or daughters who wish to avoid friction should practice patience in assuming a role of authority.

3. Mom and dad expect the son or daughter to do everything right, exactly the way they would have done it. Each person has a personal style of doing things, and

everyone makes mistakes while learning. Partners must be tolerant of each other. Sons and daughters must realize that parents, like any other business managers, will make mistakes from time to time, too.

Personal relations. Because they work with people in a number of ways, farmers should make an effort to understand and apply the principles of good personal relations. The subject matter of numerous books, the principles of personal relations cannot be covered adequately in this section, but some important considerations will be discussed briefly.

1. Have mutual respect. If you do not have respect and appreciation for your business partner, it will be difficult to accept that partner's decisions and to have a harmonious relationship. If parents and children think of each other as nice people who do not know much about farming and do not have much management ability, it is not very likely that a family arrangement can be successful.

2. The new party to the arrangement should initially recommend changes that are almost sure to work and will have visible quick results. An improved livestock medication for sick animals, proper weed-control chemicals, and proper fertilization are examples of practices that can quickly show improvement, thus gaining the respect of the parents.

3. Approach decisions in a logical, analytical manner. Instead of saying "We *must* buy the 80 that is for sale next door," make an analysis of costs and benefits associated with the decision. Estimate the returns, costs, return on investment, cash flow, risk, impact on morale of workers, impact on the total operation, and so on. Once all of the facts are assembled and the analysis is complete, an argument often dissolves into agreement. "We would like to own that 80, but we cannot make the mortgage payments, so we won't buy it."

4. Save your good will for the important issues. With more than one person involved, there will always be differences of opinion about what to do and how to do it. Some of these issues do not have much consequence, such as "Which side of the barn should I start feeding?" while issues such as "Should we build a new dairy barn?" are very important. Persons who argue strongly over the small decisions often create tensions that make it difficult to approach major decisions objectively. It is a good policy to avoid controversy over things that do not have much impact on the farm business.

5. Consult a trusted outsider. There can occasionally be some emotion and bias associated with farm decisions when a strong difference of opinion arises. It is sometimes helpful to have a person from outside the farm business assist with the analysis. The outsider, or "member of your farm board of directors," should be a person who has the confidence and respect of all parties and who understands personal as well as economic considerations. It could be a profes-

sional farm manager, banker, farmer, business executive, or extension agent. This person should have a good understanding of the farm and the people who own and operate it.

6. Be a student of personal relations. Farm managers spend a great deal of time deciding on the best seed varieties, fertilizer, accounting system, crops to produce, livestock to raise, and so forth. Since these decisions are put into action by people, it is logical for managers to spend time studying and contemplating how to work more smoothly and effectively with people to ensure their happiness and success in performing specified jobs. Time spent reading, attending seminars, and thinking about how to get along with people is time well spent.

The following is a case study of the Johnson farm that will give you an opportunity to evaluate important economic and personal factors for a specific situation.

The Johnson Case

Joe and Betty Johnson, both age fifty, and their son and daughter-in-law, Pete and Sue, both age twenty-two, are considering farming together beginning next spring when Pete finishes school. The farm consists of 200 acres owned and 200 acres rented 50-50. Fifty sows farrow-to-finish are on the owned farm, and fifty sows farrow-to-finish are on the rented farm; all hogs are produced with the low-investment system.

Henry Wilson, 64, who has been working for the Johnsons for many years, in-

TABLE 19.3 Personal Goals and Objectives, Johnson Farm

	Joe (Father)	Pete (Son)	Betty (Mother)	Sue (Daughter-in-Law)
Maximum amount of debt	$250,000	$1,000,000	$50,000	$100,000
Maximum percentage of debt	50%	100%	20%	50%
Minimum income desired	$20,000	$12,000	$20,000	$12,000
Minimum hours with family per day	1 hour	3 hours	3 hours	5 hours
Hours in service activities per week	2 hours	2 hours	8 hours	2 hours
Hours work on farm per week	40 hours	60 hours	5 hours	5 hours
Rated goals[a]				
Stay active in management	10	10	8	1
Be in charge	10	10	5	1
Work with livestock	10	5	1	1
Work with crops	5	10	1	1
Retire in 15 years	10	1	10	1
Have a lot of responsibility	7	7	1	1
Make a lot of tough decisions	7	7	1	1
Keep farm in family	10	10	10	10
Help children get started	10	10	10	10

[a]1 = not important, 10 = extremely important.

formed Joe that he would probably retire on social security and move closer to town if Pete decides to return home. The young couple, therefore, would be able to live in the recently remodeled house Henry would vacate.

To aid in evaluating their situation, the four Johnsons prepared information about family goals (Table 19.3) and management abilities (Table 19.4). The Johnsons considered the following arrangements, calculating returns for each.

1. *Wage:* Pete would be paid $1,100 per month (see Tables 19.5 and 19.9).

2. *Wage plus incentive:* Pete would receive $900 per month plus 10% of the profit. Profit would be calculated by determining returns and costs from information in Table 19.5. Labor expense and interest on Joe's $80,000 mortgage at 8.5% interest should be included as costs. Pete's salary would be considered a cash labor expense (see Table 19.9).

TABLE 19.4 Organizational Preferences and Management Assessment, Johnson Farm

	Parents (Joe and Betty)	Son and Daughter-in-Law (Pete and Sue)
A. Farm Strategy[a]		
Rent more land	8	10
Buy more land	1	10
Hire labor if needed	10	10
Do custom work	5	10
Begin a new enterprise	5	5
Expand hogs, build more hog buildings	8	5
Expand rapidly	3	10
B. Management and labor strengths and weaknesses[b]		
Crop	8	10
Livestock	10	5
Personnel supervision	10	8
Buying	10	8
Selling	5	8
Record keeping	5	8
Securing capital	10	5
Mechanical ability	8	8
Buildings skills	8	8
Emotional endurance	10	6
Physical endurance	6	10

[a]Ratings: 1 = not important, 10 = extremely important.
[b]Ratings: 1 = very low ability, 10 = very high ability

3. *Traditional 50-50 share arrangement:* Income and expenses would be shared equally (see Table 19.5). The landlord provides land, buildings, and swine equipment. The operators provide all labor and farm machinery. Pete must purchase one-half of Joe's machinery and inventory (see Joe's financial statement, Table 19.6). In calculating interest, assume that Pete would borrow the money for the machinery and inventory purchase at 8.5% interest (see Pete's financial statement, Table 19.7). The money received from Pete would allow Joe to reduce his land mortgage (see Tables 19.10 and 19.11).

4. *Operating partnership or corporation:* Joe would contribute his machinery ($50,000) and part of his inventory ($33,375) to the arrangement, while Pete would purchase $30,000 of Joe's inventory, allowing Joe to reduce his mortgage by that amount. Thus, Joe and Pete would own 73.5% and 26.5% of the arrangement, respectively. The arrangement would share-rent Joe's farm and pay a $15,000 salary to Joe and $15,000 to Pete. The remaining income would be divided according to ownership (see Tables 19.12 through 19.14).

The Johnsons prepared budgets of returns to each party for each of the above arrangements (see Tables 19.8 through 19.14). Check their figures in the tables. Will there be sufficient income for two families? Will they be able to get along? Would you recommend that they farm together? Explain. Which plan would you recommend for the next year or two? After one or two years? Why? What additional decisions must the Johnsons make to complete their arrangements?

TABLE 19.5 Receipts and Expenses per Unit of Production, Johnson Farm

	Total	Operator	Landlord
Receipts per unit			
Corn, 120 bu. per acre at $2.75	$ 330	$165	$165
Swine (per sow and 2 litters)			
32 cwt. at $50.00 and 2 cwt at $45.00	1,690	845	845
Expenses per unit[a]			
Corn, per acre			
Total direct costs	$ 130	$ 78	$ 52
Indirect costs			
Land taxes and maintenance	15	0	15
Machinery ownership cost	40	40	0
Grain storage ownership cost	14	0	14
Total indirect costs	$ 69	$ 40	$ 29
Swine (per sow and 2 litters)			
Direct costs (includes corn fed)	$1,150	$575	$575
Indirect costs	300	75	225

[a] excluding labor, management and interest on owned land

TABLE 19.6   Financial Statement, Joe and Betty Johnson, January 1, 1984

Assets		
Land, 200 acres	$450,000	
Machinery	50,000	
Buildings and equipment	38,500	
Livestock		
Sows and growing pigs	36,375	
Crops, feed, and supplies	27,000	
Total assets		$601,875
Liabilities		
Land mortgage	$ 80,000	
Total liabilities		80,000
Net worth		$521,875

TABLE 19.7   Financial Statement, Pete and Sue Johnson, January 1, 1984

Assets		
Automobile	5,500	
Total assets		$ 5,500
Liabilities		
School loan	$ 2,500	
Automobile	1,000	
Total liabilities		3,500
Net worth		$ 2,000

TABLE 19.8   Budgeted Returns for Each Party for the Different Arrangements for a Normal Year, Johnson Farm (from Tables 19.9–19.14)

	Parents (Joe and Betty)	Son and Daughter-in-Law (Pete and Sue)
Wage	$37,350	$13,200
Wage plus incentive	35,775	14,775
50–50 share	36,218	14,332
Operating arrangement	35,900	14,650

TABLE 19.9   Johnson Farm Budget: Arrangements 1 and 2

Item	Number of Units	Dollars per Unit	Total per Item	Total
Arrangement 1				
A. Receipts				
1. Corn, owned	200	$ 330	$66,000	
2. Corn, 50–50	200	165	33,000	
3. Sows, owned	50	1,690	84,500	
4. Sows, 50–50	50	845	42,250	
5. Total				$225,750
B. Expenses				
1. Corn, owned	200	$ 199	$39,800	
2. Corn, 50–50	200	118	23,600	
3. Sows, owned	50	1,450	72,500	
4. Sows, 50–50	50	650	32,500	
5. Labor, Pete	—	—	13,200	
6. Interest, 8.5% of $80,000	—	—	6,800	
7. Total				188,400
C. Net farm profit (Joe)				$ 37,350
Arrangement 2				
D. 1. Add labor for arrangement 1 to net farm profit				$ 13,200
2. Total				$ 50,550
3. Subtract labor for arrangement 2				− 10,800
4. Net farm profit for arrangement 2				$ 39,750
E. 1. Joe's share for arrangement 2—90% of farm profit				$ 35,775
F. 1. Pete's salary				$ 10,800
2. Pete's 10% of profit				3,975
3. Pete's share for arrangement 2				$ 14,775

> Prepare budgets for situations in which farm receipts are 10% higher than a normal year and 10% lower than a normal year. Will there be sufficient income in a low-income year?

TABLE 19.10   Johnson Farm Budget: Arrangement 3, 50–50, Joe's Share

Item	Number of Units	Dollars per Unit	Total per Item	Total
A. Receipts				
1. Corn, ½ operator	400	$ 82.50	$33,000.00	
2. Landlord	200	165.00	33,000.00	
3. Hogs, ½ operator	100	422.50	42,250.00	
4. Landlord	50	845.00	42,250.00	
5. Total				$150,500.00
B. Expenses				
1. Corn, ½ operator	400	$ 59.00	$23,600.00	
2. Landlord	200	81.00	16,200.00	
3. Hogs, ½ operator	100	325.00	32,500.00	
4. Landlord	50	800.00	40,000.00	
5. Interest, 8.5% of $23,312.50			1,981.56	
6. Total				114,281.56
C. Joe's farm profit				$ 36,218.44

TABLE 19.11   Johnson Farm Budget: Arrangement 3, 50–50, Pete's Share

Item	Number of Units	Dollars per Unit	Total per Item	Total
A. Receipts				
1. Corn, ½ operator	400	$ 82.50	$33,000.00	
2. Hogs, ½ operator	100	422.50	42,250.00	
				$75,250.00
B. Expenses				
1. Corn, ½ operator	400	$59.00	$23,600.00	
2. Hogs, ½ operator	100	325.00	32,500.00	
3. Interest, 8.5% on $56,687.50			4,818.44	
				60,918.44
C. Pete's farm profit				$14,331.56

TABLE 19.12   Johnson Farm Budget: Arrangement 4, Total Operating Arrangement

Item	Number of Units	Dollars per Unit	Total per Item	Total
A. Receipts				
1. Corn, operator's share, 50–50	400	$ 165	$66,000	
2. Hogs, operator's share, 50–50	100	845	84,500	
				$150,500
B. Expenses				
1. Corn, operator's share, 50–50	400	$ 118	$47,200	
2. Hogs, operator's share, 50–50	100	650	65,000	
3. Salaries	2	15,000	30,000	
				142,200
C. Operating arrangement profit				$ 8,300

TABLE 19.13   Johnson Farm Budget: Arrangement 4, Joe's Share

Item	Number of Units	Dollars per Unit	Total per Item	Total
A. Receipts				
1. Salary			$15,000	
2. 73.5% of operating arrangement profit			6,100	
3. Corn, landlord's share, 50–50	200	$165	33,000	
4. Hogs, landlord's share, 50–50	50	845	42,250	
				$96,350
B. Expenses				
1. Corn, landlord's share, 50–50	200	$ 81	16,200	
2. Hogs, landlord's share, 50–50	50	800	40,000	
3. Interest, 8.5% on $50,000			4,250	
				60,450
C. Joe's total farm income				$35,900

TABLE 19.14   Johnson Farm Budget: Arrangement 4, Pete's Share

Item	Number of Units	Dollars per Unit	Total per Item	Total
A. Receipts				
1. Salary			$15,000	
2. 26.5% of operating arrangement profit			2,200	
3. Total				$17,200
Expenses				
1. Interest on borrowed capital, 8.5% of $30,000			$ 2,550	
				2,550
C. Pete's total farm income				$14,650

GETTING STARTED WITHOUT FAMILY HELP

Joining an Established Farmer

Joining an established farm can provide experience and in some cases can allow one to gain an ownership interest in a farm business.

What to look for.   Since experience is one of the main benefits of joining an established farmer, look first for an outstanding operator of the type of farm and in the geographic area in which you are interested. It is important that the operator is easy to work with and is willing to take time to teach you the things that should be known about the business. The job should be well defined so that there is a clear understanding of responsibilities as well as of opportunities for pay increases, profit sharing, and ownership.

Last but not least, the farm should be large enough to provide sufficient income for you as well as the operator and should be in sound financial condition.

How to find an established farmer to join.   Sources that might be helpful in locating a farmer that you might join include farm management consultants, university school of agriculture placement offices, extension agents, farm managers, and bankers and other members of financial agencies. Advertising in local papers and farm magazines might also be helpful. Before advertising, prepare a résumé indicating your accomplishments, background, abilities, and job interests.

Renting a Farm

If capital can be obtained for machinery and operating capital, it may be possible to get started by cash- or share-renting a farm. Although gaining control of capital and finding a farm without family help may be difficult, a few young people do accomplish this each year (see the Kirk and Sue Henly case in Chapter 5). Strategies for finding and keeping rental land are discussed in Chapter 15.

To start farming by renting a farm with very little equity capital usually requires a willingness to accept a low standard of living until the farm business is off the ground. This may mean several years with an old automobile, used furniture, and a modest house. It takes a great deal of initiative and some good fortune to locate the farm and the operating capital.

Buying a Farm

The need for a down payment and the negative cash flow make it difficult but not impossible to start farming with a purchased farm. Anyone considering buying a farm with limited equity should project cash flow carefully before making a final decision (see Chapters 6 and 14).

> Carl Weaver located a 240-acre farm with many old dairy buildings that was for sale in his home community. He obtained a first mortgage from the owner and secured the second mortgage and operating capital from FmHA. Carl milked many cows in the old buildings to generate cash for the mortgage payments. He and his wife, Gloria, lived very modestly for several years until their equity had increased.

Summary

It is still possible today for a young person to get started in farming with limited capital. To be successful requires determination, management skill, eagerness to work very hard, and willingness to live modestly in the early years. If you are working for an established farmer but would like to own a farm, start to invest early. Invest in the farm where you are working or buy a small farm and rent it out. The importance of saving and investing early can not be overemphasized if you hope to own and operate a farm some day (see Chapter 7).

DISCUSSION QUESTIONS

1. How can one determine if a farm will generate sufficient income to support an additional person who wishes to join the farm business?
2. What are some alternative ways of sharing income among operators? Give the advantages and disadvantages of each arrangement.

3. What are some guidelines for deciding how much each resource in an operating arrangement should be paid? What should be done if the farm does not generate sufficient income to pay all resources?

4. Is it possible for the goals of each individual in a family farming arrangement to affect whether or not the arrangement will be successful? How can one determine if the goals of all who would like to be involved with the business are compatible? If serious goal conflicts exist among those who would like to be involved, how might these conflicts be resolved?

5. Is it desirable for sons or daughters joining a farm business to have management strengths that are similar to those of their parents, or should they be different? Does the same apply to management weaknesses? Discuss.

6. "Transfer of responsibility and authority from parents to children can be one of the most important factors in determining the success of a family operating arrangement." Do you agree with this statement? Why? How can transfer problems be avoided?

7. Can personal relations be learned? Explain.

8. List five important personal-relations principles.

9. Is it possible to get started in farming without family help? Explain.

10. What should one look for when determining whether or not joining an established farmer would be a good opportunity?

11. If you hope to own a farm and do not have family help, what is the most important practice that you should follow?

RELATED READINGS

ATKINSON, J. H., ROBERT W. TAYLOR, GEORGE F. PATRICK, and JOHN F. MARTEN. *Farming Together: A Farm Management Perspective,* West Lafayette, Ind.: Cooperative Extension Service EC-473, Purdue University, 1978.

BOEHLJE, MICHAEL D. and VERNON EIDMAN. *Farm Management,* chap. 9. New York: John Wiley and Sons, 1984.

DONNERMEYER, JOSEPH F., and EDWARD E. CARSON. *Getting Started in Farming,* North Central Regional Extension Publication No. 81. West Lafayette, Ind.: Cooperative Extension Service, Purdue University, 1979.

MOORE, C. L., SR., and F. E. JUSTUS, JR. *Getting Started in Farming: Via the Home Farm,* North Central Regional Extension Publication No. 84. Lexington, Ky.: Cooperative Extension Service, University of Kentucky, 1979.

THOMAS, KENNETH H., and MICHAEL D. BOEHLJE. *Farm Business Arrangements: Which One for You?* North Central Regional Extension Publication No. 50. Minneapolis: Cooperative Extension Service, University of Minnesota, 1982.

THOMAS, KENNETH H., M. D. BOEHLJE, and R. A. LUENING, *Getting Started in Farming: Mostly on Your Own,* North Central Regional Extension Publication No. 82. Minneapolis: Cooperative Extension Service, University of Minnesota, 1979.

WARREN, G. F. *Farm Management,* pp. 268–269. New York: Macmillan, Rural Text-Book Series, 1918.

THE CHRISTIAN FARM

Farm Corporations and Partnerships[1]

20

[1] Tax regulations and laws pertaining to partnerships, corporations, and other forms of legal organization are likely to change from year to year. Consequently, certain specifics in this chapter may not be up-to-date, but the general principles apply. Updates of many of the listings in "Related Readings" at the end of the chapter can be used to obtain appropriate up-to-date information.

PURPOSE OF CORPORATIONS AND PARTNERSHIPS

A corporation or partnership may be used as an official legal organization that defines how labor, land, management, machinery, and capital are to be contributed to the business and how much each of these resources will be paid. The legal organization should include procedures for persons entering the farm business, leaving the farm business, and transferring ownership. The type of legal organization has important tax consequences for those involved with the business.

Neither the corporate structure nor the partnership structure answers questions about the issues raised in the preceding paragraph; they merely provide a mechanism for giving legal validity to plans that have already been formulated. A young man who was planning to return to his home farm said, "We didn't know how much to pay Dad or me for our labor and management and how much to pay Dad for the farm he owns, so we incorporated." Corporations and partnerships do not solve these kinds of problems. The persons involved must decide what they want. An attorney and an accountant are often needed to initiate the legal structure, but they should not be the ones who make decisions about entry, exit, resource contributions, and income sharing. Accountants and attorneys may provide ideas and alternatives, but if the legal organization is to accomplish the goals of the owners, managers, and operators, the business and management relationships and transfer alternatives must be thought through and specified by the people involved.

Joe Johnson has been operating his business as a sole proprietorship (see Chapter 19). He owns all of the operating resources of the business (machinery, crop inventory, livestock inventory) and part of the land. Joe has full management responsibility, although he delegates some of this responsibility to his employee, Henry. A sole proprietor makes the decisions, bears the responsibility, pays the taxes, and receives or distributes the profits as he or she sees fit.

But now Joe has invited his son and daughter-in-law, Pete and Sue, to join the business and share in the labor, management, and ownership. Life can no longer be as simple for Joe as it was with the sole proprietorship. He and Pete have been advised that they need to form an operating partnership or corporation as a legal structure to formalize their operating arrangement.

Pete and Joe began reading publications about corporations and partnerships. They talked with their attorney and accountant about various aspects of a legal structure. They also visited neighbors who had incorporated or formed partnerships and obtained information about the neighbors' experiences. The following are some of the important considerations the Johnsons discovered about corporations and part-nerships.

IMPORTANT CONSIDERATIONS ABOUT CORPORATIONS

What Is a Corporation?

If the Johnsons incorporate their operating arrangement, they will create a separate legal entity. Since the operating arrangement would include machinery and other in-ventory valued at $113,375 (see Chapter 19), the Johnsons might issue 114 shares of stock (one share for each $1,000 contributed to the corporation). Pete and Sue would each own 15 shares, having contributed $30,000; Joe and Betty would each own 42 shares having contributed $84,000.

The usual operating procedure is for the stockholders or owners to select a board of directors, which chooses officers to execute the board's policy with regard to major corporate decisions. The officers of the corporation, along with hired managers, carry out the day-to-day decisions. Managers generally make operational decisions.

In a small business corporation, the same people are often involved at all levels or in all functions. The Johnsons would be stockholders, directors, officers, and also employees. If the Johnsons were to incorporate, Joe would be president; Pete, vice-president; Betty, treasurer; and Sue, secretary.

However, even though Joe, Pete, Betty, and Sue would make decisions for Johnson Farms, Inc., the corporation is a separate legal (and tax-paying) entity with its own rights and responsibilities. For instance, it buys machinery, fertilizer, and livestock and sells crops and hogs. It also pays rents, salaries, taxes, and bonuses or profit sharing.

What a corporation—especially a farm corporation—can do, must do, and cannot do are defined by state law. Iowa, Kansas, Minnesota, North Dakota, South Dakota, Wisconsin, Missouri, Nebraska, and Oklahoma have special restrictions on farm corporations.[2] The purposes of the corporation are described in the articles of incorporation, and these must be approved by the state. The bylaws, which define the operating procedures of the corporation, are established by the board of directors or the stockholders. State approval is not required for bylaws.

Ease of Transfer

It is relatively easy to transfer ownership of a corporation from one individual to another. When Pete and Sue can afford to increase their ownership of the farm-operating arrangement, if incorporated, they could do so by purchasing stock from

---

[2] See Neil E. Harl and John C. O'Byrne, *The Farm Corporation,* North Central Regional Extension Publication No. 11, rev. ed. (Ames, Iowa: Cooperative Extension Service, Iowa State University, 1983).

Joe and Betty. If more capital is needed in the business or if Joe and Betty do not wish to sell, additional shares could be purchased from the corporation.

It is easier to keep track of proportionate ownership when individuals hold stock than when they hold specific assets such as machinery, livestock, or grain.

Continuity

The ease of transfer associated with corporations may encourage transfer of property from the older stockholders to the younger stockholders through gifts or purchases. This transfer enhances continuity. Also, when one of the stockholders dies, the assets of the corporation are not affected. However, the shares of stock must be transferred, and the transfer can put financial or personal stress on the people involved.

Limited Liability

A stockholder is liable for the actions of the corporation, but only to the extent of ownership of shares in the corporation. Property held outside the corporation is protected against any financial deficiencies of the corporation. However, the employees, officers, and directors may be held individually responsible for negligent actions and, therefore, may or may not have limited liability. Some credit institutions require stockholders of small corporations to sign notes and mortgages as individuals as well as corporate officers. So, while all corporations have limited liability, this advantage is often reduced for closely held farm corporations because of lender requirements and director responsibility.

Taxes

Incorporating the farm business has *many* tax consequences. Careful study and consultation with persons knowledgeable about corporate tax can reduce surprises. Publications on the subject of corporations are not always comprehensive, and not all tax advisers have an adequate understanding of corporate tax laws and their implications for farms. Because of these limitations and the frequency of changes in tax laws, some surprises may occur. The following are some of the important tax considerations.

Federal income tax.   As individual income tax at the margin exceeds 15%, there is likely to be some savings in federal income taxes through incorporation *if corporate profits remain in the corporation*. The savings are the result of lower corporate tax rates and the strategy of dividing income between the salaries of workers and managers and corporate profits. Because tax rates are progressive, dividing income puts each entity into a lower tax bracket. The first $25,000 of corporate profit is taxed at 15%, the second $25,000 at 18%, the third $25,000 at 30%, and the fourth $25,000 at 40%. Income over $100,000 is taxed at 46%.

The higher the individual's taxable income, the greater the tax benefit to incorporate *if the profits remain in the corporation.* If money is withdrawn from a corporation above salaries and bonuses, as a dividend, the money is taxed twice, once as corporate profit and then as income to the stockholder. Dividends are not a tax deductible expense to the corporation.

For example, if a nonincorporated operator had taxable income of $100,000, individual federal income tax would be $37,935.[3] If the business were incorporated and the operator takes a $50,000 salary, the farm business federal tax would be:

	$50,000	Salary[3]	$13,889 (individual)
1st	$25,000	Corporate profit at 15%	3,750 (corporation)
2nd	$25,000	Corporate profit at 18%	4,500 (corporation)
			$22,139

Current federal tax would be reduced by $15,796 if $50,000 corporate profit remained in the corporation. If some day the $50,000 is distributed, the tax must be paid at that time. In the meantime, the business has the use of the $15,796 in delayed tax money for operating and expanding the business.

State tax. Some states have taxes applicable to corporations, which in some instances are higher than the tax paid to the state by sole proprietorships or partnerships.

Social security tax. In 1984 a corporation as an employer was required to pay social security taxes of 7% on wages up to $37,800 per year, and each employee was required to pay 6.7% of his or her wages, for a total of 13.7%. A self-employed person was required to pay a total of 11.3%. However, the level of income on which tax is based could be lower with a corporation. Assume, for example, that in 1984 a farm business had a return to the operator of $37,800. If the business were not incorporated, self-employment social security tax would be paid on the entire amount. But if the business were incorporated and a salary of $20,000 were paid to the operator (the remaining $17,800 left in the corporation), social security tax would be paid only on the $20,000. An important consideration, of course, is that the amount of social security tax paid affects the amount of benefits for which one is eligible.

Capital gains. A corporation has a 28% capital gains tax rate, or the regular corporate rate if taxable income is below $50,000. This is often higher than the sum that would be paid by a nonincorporated farm.

Employee benefits. Under most circumstances, benefits that are tax-deductible expenses for the corporation can be provided to corporation owners and

[3] See tax table 22.1 Chapter 22.

operators who are corporation employees. Medical insurance, life insurance, pension plans, and even housing and meals are among these benefits if they can be justified from the employer's standpoint.

Since sole proprietors or partners cannot work for themselves or their partnership, corporations have an advantage in providing employee benefits to owners. However, before an employee benefit plan is initiated, various restrictions on corporation employee benefits should be thoroughly examined.

Transfer of assets into the corporation.   Sometimes farm property held by owners has a higher market value than the price paid minus depreciation. When this occurs, the gain may be taxable on transfer. To transfer farm assets into the corporation without being required to pay income tax on the gain, two conditions must be met: (1) Those transferring property into the corporation must own 80% or more of the corporate stock after incorporation, and (2) the property must be exchanged for corporate stock and securities only. Most transfers would meet these requirements.

Taking property out of the corporation.   If property of the corporation is traded for stock and there is a gain, income tax must be paid. In some instances the corporate transfer is taxed as ordinary income and in other situations as capital gains. If the entire corporation is liquidated, the income tax consequences differ with the choice of liquidation procedure. In some cases, corporate reorganization may be a preferred alternative to liquidation. It is very important to have competent counsel before liquidating a corporation or transferring assets out of a corporation. Tax implications should be studied well in advance of the anticipated asset withdrawal or liquidation.

Selling land.   If land held by the corporation is sold, capital gains tax is applicable at the corporate level. The money from the land sale is trapped in the corporation, and tax may have to be paid again on the gains when they are taken from the corporation. If land with substantial capital gain is to be sold, it is often disadvantageous to incorporate, except under a subchapter S form.[4]

Losses.   Operating losses on farms organized as sole proprietorships, partnerships, or S corporations can be used to offset other income and thereby reduce income taxes. Losses in a regular corporation remain in the corporation and can be used only to offset taxable income of the corporation three years back and fifteen years forward.

Tax laws and tax rates change from time to time for both corporations and individuals. It is advisable to evaluate whether or not a farm business or some portion of the business would pay more or less tax if it were incorporated. In general, regular corporations tend to gain tax advantage as taxable incomes increase and while profit

---

[4]S corporations are discussed later in this chapter.

remains in the business for expansion, capital improvements, or debt repayment. Accumulations of over $250,000 in earnings and profits are subject to an additional tax unless the funds are needed for business purposes.

S corporations.   If incorporation is desirable for reasons other than income taxes and if being taxed as a corporation is disadvantageous compared to a partnership or sole proprietorship, the corporation can elect to become an S, or tax-option, corporation. No income taxes are paid by an S corporation; corporate income, capital gains, credits, and operating losses go directly to the owners in proportion to their ownership. For S corporations, employees owning more than 2% of the stock are treated as partners in a partnership and are not eligible to participate in employee benefits. Most other corporate provisions (other than taxes and benefits) are the same as for a regular corporation.

To qualify as an S corporation, certain conditions must be met: Only one class of stock can be issued (but voting rights can differ within the class), there may be no more than thirty-five stockholders, all stockholders must be individuals, estates, grantor trusts, or voting trusts, and all stockholders must consent to the election. If the corporation has accumulated profits and if more than 25% of the corporation's gross receipts come from rents, royalties, interest, dividends, annuities, or dealings in securities, a special income tax is imposed at the 46% rate. After three years of passive income above 25%, the S corporation status is lost.

The S corporation tends to be advantageous if corporate income is low, if there is substantial capital gains income, if there are corporate operating losses and shareholders have income from other sources, if there is substantial investment tax credit, and if owners wish to take profits out of the business.

A tax analysis is necessary to determine which form of organization minimizes taxes at a particular time. Some operators find it advantageous to change organizational structure over time. During the early growth years, when taxable income is low and investment credit is substantial, an S corporation may be advantageous. Later, as the established operation stops growing and debts are retired, taxable income may be substantial. It might be advantageous to convert to a regular corporation when this occurs.

A corporation and its stockholders may elect S corporation status by filing IRS Form 2553. Once an S corporation election has been voluntarily or involuntarily terminated, the election generally cannot be made again for a period of five years.

Buy-Sell Arrangements

Minority stockholders of small, closely held corporations could encounter severe disadvantages if the corporate bylaws do not include a good buy-sell provision. When a stockholder desires to sell stock, it may be difficult to find an interested buyer. It may not be possible to sell the stock or to obtain property in trade for the stock. In addition, the stock may not pay a dividend.

One way to avoid this trap is with a buy-sell agreement designed to provide protection to both the minority stockholder and the corporation. The agreement should have a provision with regard to how a stockholder can sell stock. For instance, the stock might first be offered to the corporation and then to other stockholders. If they are not interested, it could be offered to outside buyers acceptable to all stockholders. If it is still not sold, the corporation might be required to purchase the stock at some stated percentage of fair market price (established by independent appraisers) or trade property of equal value for the stock. The corporation or current stockholders might be permitted to make payments for the stock over a three- to ten-year period with interest paid on the outstanding balance of the stock.

A good procedure for selling that is acceptable to stockholders should be included in the bylaws of every farm corporation.

Overhead

Incorporation involves the development of articles of incorporation and bylaws. Costs for initial incorporation will likely range from $500 to $2,500, depending on the complexity of the arrangement and the state and professionals involved. Corporate tax reports, records, and minutes of annual meetings must be kept. In general, a corporation requires more paperwork and time expenditure than a partnership or a sole proprietorship.

Philosophy of Returns to Labor, Capital, and Management

In a family farm business, the returns to labor, management, and capital are intertwined and may not be recognized as separate sources of income. By paying salaries, bonuses, and dividends, a corporation tends to recognize different sources of income. This recognition can be beneficial to managerial planning.

Checklist for Initiating a Corporation

A list of factors that need to be considered before incorporating, developed by Neil Harl, appears in Appendix B.

GENERAL PARTNERSHIP

One alternative to a corporation is a partnership. A partnership consists of two or more people joining together to operate a business for a profit. In fact, if the Johnsons do not incorporate but agree on the operating arrangement discussed in Chapter 19, they may automatically be a partnership. The formation of a partnership can be done orally or in writing; no formal filing of documents is necessary. Compared to a corporation, partnerships are easier to form, have fewer tax implications, and are easier to dissolve. However, transfer of ownership is not as easy in a partnership as in a corporation. There is also less tax protection for money held in the business, individual liability is greater, and continuity may be more difficult with a partnership than with a corporation.

Taxes

A partnership pays no income taxes and files only an annual information return, IRS Form 1065. Operating gains or losses and investment tax credit are distributed to the partners in proportion to their share of the partnership. Neither income nor losses are trapped in the partnership.

From an income tax standpoint, a partnership is much like an S corporation. Partners are self-employed and receive income in the proportion indicated in the partnership agreement. In a corporation (including an S corporation), owners may work for the corporation and receive a salary (which is an expense to the corporation), with the remaining income (or losses) going to the owners in proportion to the stock held. Since partners are self-employed, there is less opportunity for provision of employee benefits than is true with a corporation. Deferred-income retirement plans can be established for a partnership (or an individual) under the Keogh rules or as IRAs (Individual Retirement Accounts).

Transfer of property into a partnership does not usually trigger capital gains or investment tax credit recapture unless a portion of the property is transferred to another party. Then the selling party must pay gains and recapture of investment credit on the portion sold. Investment tax credit may be recaptured if the change in organizational structure is not a mere change in the form of doing business. The partnership generally takes over the individual's tax basis and depreciation schedule for the transferred property.

Liability

Each partner is personally liable for the obligations of the partnership. Should a partnership have financial difficulties, creditors first exhaust the holdings of the partnership. If debt remains after the equity of the partnership has been exhausted, the creditors have legal access to the individual holdings of the partners. It is critically important to have partners who are dependable and trustworthy. Avoid "implied partnerships" that may not be planned but are considered to be partnerships because management and net income are shared. Courts may also examine how the parties presented themselves to the public in determining whether a partnership existed.

Limited partnerships.   A limited partnership provides the opportunity for certain "investor partners" to contribute capital but to be liable for partnership obligations only to the extent of their share of partnership holdings. A limited partnership must have at least one general partner who is personally liable for all partnership activities. If any of the limited partners participate in management, they become general partners from a legal standpoint. In contrast to the general partnership, the limited partnership is required to submit certain information required by the state.

To discourage the use of limited partnerships for tax-loss purposes by high income investors, the Tax Reform Act of 1976 placed restrictions on when deductions can be taken for the purchase of inputs. Also, if a limited partnership has numerous "corporate characteristics," it can be treated as a corporation for income tax purposes.

Termination

A partnership is usually terminated at the death of a partner or when one or more partners decide to withdraw, unless otherwise specified in a partnership agreement. When the partnership is terminated, (1) the assets can be liquidated and the money distributed, (2) the assets and liabilities can be distributed in proportion to ownership, or (3) the remaining partners can form a new partnership, corporation, or one or more sole proprietorships. Dissolving any business organization takes time and money and often slows the thrust of the business. Therefore, provisions that would enhance continuity should be included in the agreement. If one partner dies or withdraws, the partnership agreement might grant the remaining partner or partners the option of purchasing that share of the partnership within a specified period of time.

Written Agreement and Records

Because a partnership is so fragile, it is very important to have a written agreement that indicates:

1. Goals and future plans of the business
2. Labor provided by each person and amount paid to each
3. Management responsibilities for each person and amount of pay (if separate from labor)
4. Resource contributions of each person and the market value, tax basis, and depreciation schedule for each resource
5. Ownership of the assets
6. How income and losses are to be shared
7. Termination date or circumstances of the partnership
8. Kinds of records to be kept and who will have responsibility for keeping records, paying bills, etc.
9. Procedure for distribution of assets at termination of the partnership
10. Procedure for purchase of assets of a departing partner (buy-sell arrangement)
11. Limit on each partner's authority to act for the business

It would be advisable to follow the procedure in Chapter 19 for establishing a farm-operating arrangement and for evaluating whether or not persons are compatible for a partnership arrangement.

CHOOSING A LEGAL ORGANIZATION FOR THE FARM

The objective in selecting a legal organization is to choose one (or more) that meets as many of the following criteria as deemed desirable by those involved with the business:

1. The legal organization will allow more than one person to contribute labor, management, land, buildings, machinery, and operating capital to a farm business and to share income in proportion to each person's contribution.
2. The organization will permit ease of transfer of ownership, labor functions, and management responsibility.
3. It will minimize taxes or shift them to a time that is most advantageous for the individuals and the business.
4. The legal structure should minimize the liability assumed by each person from the actions of other persons in the business and the actions of the business itself.
5. The legal structure should be simple, easy to form, easy to operate, and easy to dissolve.
6. The structure should allow for continuity if that is one of the goals of those involved with the farm.

No one legal structure meets all of the foregoing criteria. The question of which legal structure is best cannot be answered permanently. Changes occur in the business and in the goals and objectives of those associated with the business. Changes also occur in government laws and tax policies; tax consequences vary considerably according to level of income and the nature of business. Therefore, managers must keep up to date on the characteristics and options of legal organization. They must review their legal organization whenever there has been a major change in goals, income, the business organization, laws, or taxes. It is advisable to obtain competent advice from a knowledgeable professional.

The two following procedures will be helpful in choosing a legal organization.

1. Evaluate the importance of the six objectives just listed. Rate each of them 1 to 10, from least to most importance.

The Johnsons discussed the six objectives with each other and determined which ones were most important to them (Table 20.1). They are most interested in a structure that would encourage Pete and Sue to come home, facilitate the transfer to Pete, and allow the business to continue. Because they plan to expand the farm business, they reasoned that taxes would not be a major consideration at this time (see Chapter 22). Having confidence in one another and expecting to have nearly all of their assets in the farm business, they see no great benefit from limited liability. Although they dislike the prospect of more paperwork, the Johnsons are willing to accept the additional paperwork as a small price to pay for being able to work together.

TABLE 20.1 Evaluation of Objectives for a Legal
Structure, Johnson Farm

Objective	Importance[a]
1. Encourage contributions of:	
Labor	10
Management	10
Land	10
Buildings	10
Machinery and equipment	10
Operating capital	10
2. Ease of transfer	10
3. Minimize taxes	5
4. Minimize personal liability	5
5. Simplicity: easy to form, operate, dissolve	5
6. Encourage continuity	10

[a]1 = least important, 10 = most important.

2. Compare personal objectives to the characteristics of each legal organization (Table 20.2).

    The Johnsons believe that their long-term objectives can best be met by the corporation. However, they agreed to remain a sole proprietorship for the next two

TABLE 20.2 Characteristics of Different Legal Structures

Legal Structure	Characteristics[a]					
	(1) Encourage contributions of resources and fair sharing of income	(2) Ease of transfer	(3) Minimize taxes	(4) Minimize liability	(5) Simplicity	(6) Encourage continuity
Sole proprietorship	1	1	X[b]	1	10	1
General partnership	5	5	X	1	5	5
Limited partnership	10	5	X	5	1	5
Corporation	10	10	X	10	1	10
S corporation	10	10	X	10	1	10

[a]1 = low, 10 = high.
[b]Must be evaluated for each farm situation and income level. See the discussion on taxes for partnerships, corporations, and S corporations in this chapter.

years, allowing Pete to work for a salary and bonuses while making sure he really wants to join the farm on a permanent basis. If Pete and Sue decide after two years that they want to be a permanent part of the business, the Johnsons will form a corporation. Whether or not it will be an S corporation will be determined after careful study by the Johnsons and their tax and legal advisers.

MULTIPLE LEGAL ORGANIZATIONS

Two or more legal organizations may help to reach the objectives of all persons involved with the farm business. For example, Joe and Betty Johnson would like to shift the operation and management of the farm to Pete and Sue and provide full compensation for the younger Johnsons' management, labor, and capital. Joe and Betty may also want to give equal parts of their farm to all of their children, including two who live away from the farm and do not wish to be involved in the management of the farm business.

Joe and Betty considered including the farm with the operating corporation and annually giving shares to each child to minimize estate taxes (see Chapter 22). But Joe reasoned that the nonfarm children would then own part of the operating arrangement and might share in the returns to management even though they did not participate in the management decisions. All the Johnsons agreed that it would not be fair to share operating profit with the off-farm children and that it would be easier to identify operating profit by having a separate operating corporation.

Joe solved this conflict with an operating corporation, like the operating arrangement discussed in Chapter 19. The plan is for the operating corporation to rent the farm on a share basis. Joe and Betty will give all three of their children shares of the farm, and each will share the returns to the farm in proportion to his or her ownership.

Two legal organizations will allow Joe, Betty, Pete, and Sue to get the full return to their management skill and will allow the parents to give a portion of their farm to their nonfarm children without eroding the return to management.[5] Multiple legal organizations can have important income and estate tax implications and should be evaluated carefully before being initiated.

This chapter covers only an introduction to legal organization. Before making legal-organization decisions, read specialized publications, visit with people who have had experience with various organizations, and obtain competent legal and accounting advice. Be aware that not all professionals have had adequate experience with farm legal organization. Gaining necessary knowledge and the ability to ask the right questions is your best protection.

---

[5] A trust is another alternative that can be useful for estate planning purposes.

DISCUSSION QUESTIONS

1. Will a partnership or corporate legal structure answer such questions as who will contribute labor, management, and capital and how will each partner be rewarded for his or her contribution? Explain.

2. What is a corporation? What are the advantages of a corporation?

3. What factors should be considered before incorporating?

4. Will a corporation reduce federal income tax? State income tax? Capital gains tax? Social security tax?

5. How might employee benefits provided by a corporation result in less income tax than the same benefits paid by an individual?

6. What is the difference between a corporation and an S corporation? Under what circumstances might the S corporation be preferable?

7. What is a buy-sell arrangement? Why is it desirable to have a buy-sell arrangement in corporate bylaws?

8. Why might a corporate legal structure be helpful to a manager in recognizing that farm profit is the return to labor, management, and capital?

9. What are the main differences between a corporation and a general partnership?

10. Why is it especially important that a partnership agreement be in writing? List some of the things that should be included in the partnership agreement.

11. What important criteria should one consider when choosing a farm legal structure?

12. Under what circumstances are multiple legal organizations advantageous?

13. Explain how you would approach planning a legal structure for a farm with which you are familiar.

RELATED READINGS

BOCK, C. ALLEN. "Farm Partnership Formation and Operation," *Agricultural Law Journal*, 3, no. 3 (Fall 1982): 504–534.

BOEHLJE, MICHAEL D., and KENNETH KRAUSE. *Economic and Federal Tax Factors Affecting the Choice of a Legal Farm Business Organization*, United States Department of Agriculture, Agricultural Economics Report No. 468. Washington, D.C.: 1981.

BROCK, RICHARD A., EDDY L. LaDUE, and ROBERT S. SMITH. *Pre-incorporation Considerations for the Farm Firm*. Department of Agricultural Economics, Ithaca, N.Y.: Cornell University, 1976.

HARL, NEIL E. *Agricultural Law*, vols. 7–8. New York: Matthew Bender, 1983.

———— *Farm Estate and Business Planning*. Skokie, Ill.: AgriBusiness Publications, 1982.

———— and JOHN C. O'BYRNE. *The Farm Corporation: What It Is, How It Works, How It Is Taxed*, North Central Regional Extension Publication No. 11. Ames: Cooperative Extension Service, Iowa State University, 1981.

HARSH, STEPHEN B., LARRY J. CONNOR, and GERALD D. SCHWAB. *Managing the Farm Business*, pp. 61–69. Englewood Cliffs, N.J.: Prentice-Hall, 1981.

HEPP, RALPH E. and MYRON P. KELSEY. *General Partnerships for Agricultural Producers,* Bulletin E-731. East Lansing: Cooperative Extension Service, Michigan State University, 1972.

PRETZER, DON D. *Business Organization of the Family Farm,* MF-279. Manhattan: Kansas State University, 1980.

THOMAS, KENNETH H., and MICHAEL D. BOEHLJE. *Farm Business Arrangements: Which One for You?* North Central Regional Extension Publication No. 50. Minneapolis: Cooperative Extension Service, University of Minnesota, 1982.

Farm Labor-Management Considerations

21

In this chapter, total labor planning and management are considered, including operator, family, part-time hired, and full-time hired labor. The labor-management resource is different in agriculture than in most other types of businesses. Workers tend to operate separately, and the jobs performed by each worker change often because of weather and the biological progression of crops and livestock. Hence it is necessary that most farm workers be keen observers who are able to make decisions should the need arise. Crops, livestock, machinery, and equipment are valuable, and if they are not cared for properly by each worker, substantial losses may be incurred.

Three types of farm labor-management situations are presented to illustrate the most significant farm labor considerations and decisions. Factors that determine the optimum amount of labor are also presented.

SITUATION 1: OPERATOR, FAMILY, AND PART-TIME HIRED LABOR

Many farms are run by one operator using family and part-time labor. The manager may simply prefer a one-person farm, may not have capital resources for a larger farm, or may not want to deal with full-time labor. The principal labor and management concerns of the one-person farm are discussed here.

Labor Efficiency

Wide differences exist in the amount of farm work that can be accomplished in a given amount of time. On a one-person farm, labor efficiency not only affects the cost of labor per unit of production, but, more significantly, it also determines volume of production. If a manager elects to operate with a given size labor force—self, family, and limited part-time help—the volume of business is controlled by the accomplishments of the limited labor force. To increase volume of business, the operator must either use labor more efficiently or use labor-saving capital investments.

Productive man work units per person (PMWU/P) compared to similar farms is a means of measuring labor efficiency, but the capital invested per person is not reflected and must be taken into account by the evaluator. It should also be taken into account that increasing labor efficiency is seldom profitable if it is achieved at the expense of crop and livestock efficiency. Therefore, one must view PMWU/P in light

TABLE 21.1   Total Labor Required, Using Standard Requirements per Unit of Production, Paul Kirsch Farm

Enterprise	Number of Units	PMWU[a]	Total PMWU
Corn	160	0.5	80
Soybeans	160	0.4	64
Sows (farrow to finish)	40	4.4	176
Total			320

[a]Productive man work units, number of 10-hour days typically required for these enterprises.

of crop and livestock efficiency and the amount invested in machinery and equipment (see Chapter 6).

Measuring labor efficiency.   To illustrate how to measure labor efficiency, let us examine a hypothetical situation. Paul Kirsch operates a 320-acre farm and farrows 40 two-litter sows in groups of 20 four times each year. He feeds out the hogs, about 640 per year. Paul has been analyzing his labor situation to determine whether or not his labor efficiency is adequate and, if not, how it can be improved. First he compared the total labor usually required for enterprises similar to his (Table 21.1) with the total estimated labor being used on the Kirsch farm in these enterprises (Table 21.2).

Paul found that the required amount of labor for his operation was 320 ten-hour days per year, based on productive man work units obtained from an extension publication (Table 21.1). Approximately 384.5 ten-hour days were actually being worked (Table 21.2). Also, Paul determined that while the PMWU/P from records of similar farms was 300 (see Chapter 6), his PMWU/P was:

$$\frac{\text{Total PMWU}}{\text{Man equivalent}} = \frac{320}{1.28} = 250$$

TABLE 21.2   Hours Worked, Paul Kirsch Farm

Person	Hours per Week	Total Hours
Paul (operator)	50 hours average for 49 weeks	2,450
Millie (wife)	5 hours for 49 weeks (keeps books, picks up supplies)	245
Mike (son)	10 hours for 35 weeks during school, 50 hours for 13 weeks in summer	1,000
Part-time	25 hours for 6 weeks (planting and harvest)	150
Total		3,845 or 384.5 10-hour days

The Kirsch farm has been using about 20% more labor to get the job done than is being used by similar farms.

Compare labor available and labor required.   Paul discussed the analysis with his agricultural extension agent, Don Worthington, who asked if more sows could be handled with the same labor. Paul explained that at certain times of the year he has more labor than needed, whereas at other times they can barely complete the work even by working long days. Don suggested that labor distribution be checked to determine whether or not labor requirements or labor availability could be adjusted to eliminate bottlenecks and possibly to allow expansion of the swine herd (Table 21.3, Figure 21.1). Paul discovered that he had about 789 hours of surplus labor during the winter and summer months but a labor deficiency at planting time (132 hours) and during harvest (12 hours).

Realizing that a May labor shortage could result in neglect of crops and livestock and reduced efficiency, Paul and Don discussed two changes in farm organization that could better balance peak with nonpeak requirements. First, the farrowing months for sows were shifted one month ahead, reducing May requirements substantially (60 hours) and increasing labor requirements in June when Mike is out of school and is available to look after the sows. Second, Paul scheduled more of the indirect jobs, such as planning, repairs, and bookkeeping, into the December–February and June–August slack periods. Initiating these two changes along with acquiring some

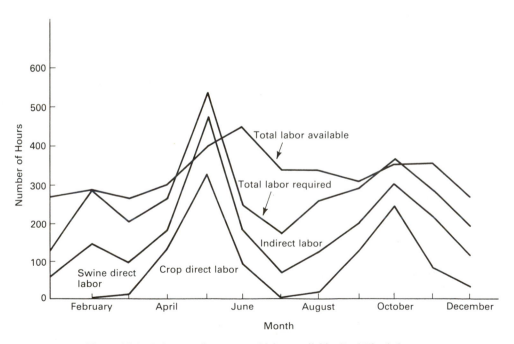

Figure 21.1   Labor requirements and labor available, Paul Kirsch farm.

TABLE 21.3 Monthly Labor Requirements, Paul Kirsch Farm (in hours)

Month	Corn (160 acres)				Soybeans (160 acres)				Swine (40 sows)				Total Labor Required			Total Labor Available					Labor Surplus or Deficit	
	Direct	Indirect	Total per Acre	Total Corn	Direct	Indirect	Total per Acre	Total Soybeans	Direct	Indirect	Total per Sow	Total Hogs	Total Direct	Total End	Total	Paul	Millie	Mike	Part-Time	Total	Surplus	Deficit
January	—	—	—	—	—	—	—	—	1.5	2.0	3.5	140	60	80	140	200	30	40	—	270	130	
February	—	0.2	0.2	32	—	0.2	0.2	32	3.5	2.0	5.5	220	140	144	284	210	35	40	—	285	1	
March	0.1	0.2	0.3	48	—	0.2	0.2	32	2.0	1.0	3.0	120	96	104	200	200	20	40	—	260	60	
April	0.5	0.1	0.6	96	0.3	0.1	0.4	64	1.5	1.0	2.5	100	188	72	260	240	20	40	—	300	40	
May	1.0	0.1	1.1	176	1.0	0.1	1.1	176	3.5	1.0	4.5	180	460	72	532	240	20	40	100	400		132
June	0.3	0.1	0.4	64	0.3	0.1	0.4	64	2.0	1.0	3.0	120	176	72	248	220	20	210	—	450	202	
July	—	0.1	0.1	16	—	0.1	0.1	16	1.5	2.0	3.5	140	60	112	172	110	10	210	—	330	158	
August	—	0.1	0.1	16	—	0.1	0.1	16	3.5	2.0	5.5	220	140	112	252	110	10	210	—	330	78	
September	—	0.2	0.2	32	0.7	0.1	0.8	128	2.0	1.0	3.0	120	192	88	280	240	20	40	—	300	20	
October	1.0	0.1	1.1	176	0.5	0.1	0.6	96	1.5	1.0	2.5	100	300	72	372	240	20	50	50	360		12
November	0.5	0.1	0.6	96	—	—	—	—	3.5	1.0	4.5	180	220	56	276	240	20	40	—	300	24	
December	0.2	0.1	0.3	48	—	0.1	0.1	16	2.0	1.0	3.0	120	112	72	184	200	20	40	—	260	76	
Total	3.6	1.4	5.0	800	2.8	1.2	4.0	640	28.0	16.0	44.0	1,760	2,144	1,056	3,200	2,450	245	1,000	150	3,845	789	144

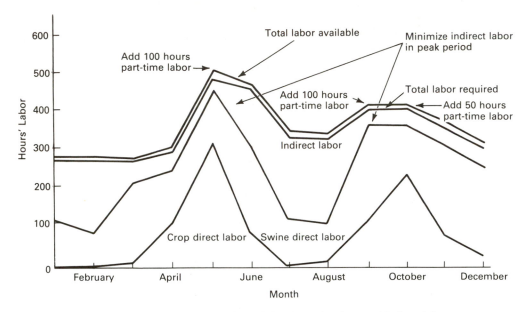

Figure 21.2 Labor requirements after shifting farrowing dates and indirect labor and adding twenty sows, Paul Kirsch farm.

additional part-time help (250 hours) in May, September, and October enabled Paul to increase his swine herd to sixty sows. Not only is his labor more fully utilized, but there is also less stress in May (Figure 21.2).

Plan the work schedule. One way to reduce stress in peak labor periods and to improve farm timeliness is to do as many jobs as possible during slack labor periods. A written job schedule may be helpful at least until the time of doing a job becomes a habit (Table 21.4).

Analyze each job. The time required to do different farm jobs varies greatly. Studies show that it is not uncommon for the labor forces in the top 25% in labor efficiency to accomplish twice as much as those in the bottom 25%. Some practices to ensure good labor efficiency are:

1. Keep equipment well maintained so that breakdowns will not slow the job.
2. Organize tools so that they can be easily located.
3. Study jobs to be done and simplify them if possible. Hardin and Vaughan[1] give some general procedures for work simplification:

[1]Lawrence W. Vaughan and Lowell S. Hardin, *Farm Work Simplification,* p. 5 (New York: Wiley, 1949).

TABLE 21.4   Sample Job Schedule

Job Description	Earliest Date Job Can Be Done	Latest Date Job Can Be Done	Date When Job Becomes High Priority
1. Overhaul tractor	December 1	February 1	January 10
2. Plowing corn ground	October 1	April 1	March 1
3. Get corn planter ready to go	January 1	April 15	February 1
4. Spread manure on crop ground	December 1	April 15	March 1
5. Plowing soybean ground	October 1	May 1	April 1
6. Maintenance of farm livestock, buildings	May 1	September 1	August 1

Procedure

1. List all jobs to be completed during the year in approximate chronological order using the latest date by which the job should be done (middle column).
2. Circle jobs in middle column as date is reached and do these jobs immediately. They are top priority.
3. Circle jobs in right-hand column as date is reached and do these jobs soon—they are high priority.
4. Circle jobs in left-hand column when date arrives and do as many jobs as time will permit.
5. Cross out jobs when they are completed.

- Eliminate all unnecessary work.
- Simplify the hand and body motions used in doing the work.
- Provide a more convenient arrangement of work areas and location of materials for doing the work.
- Improve on the adequacy, suitability, and use of equipment needed for the work.
- Organize the work routine for full and effective use of men and machines.

Labor used in the production of livestock and livestock products is primarily concerned with the movement of materials, such as grain, forage, milk, and manure. Herbst[2] provides the following principles for simplifying farm jobs:

1. Do not move the material if you can satisfactorily avoid doing so.
2. If the material must be moved, minimize the distance.
3. Move a large amount at one time.
4. Consider using gravity to move materials.

[2]J. H. Herbst, *Farm Management Principles, Budgets, Plans,* p. 148. (Champaign, Ill.: Stipes Publishing Co., 1983).

5. Consider ground-level storage for bulky materials, such as hay.
6. Store concentrates overhead, or use mechanical equipment to remove from ground-level storage.
7. Make materials flow if possible, continuously when so desired, and preferably unattended.
8. Use hauling, loading, and storage equipment to handle materials in bulk form.

The arrangement of buildings, the interior of buildings, and equipment can have an important influence on labor efficiency. Points to keep in mind are:

1. Provide for a circular path to eliminate backtracking.
2. Keep buildings and work areas relatively close together to reduce travel distances.
3. Use unobstructed, all-weather travel routes.
4. Make gates and doors sufficiently wide, and keep them functioning properly.
5. Build equipment into a matching system and be sure it fits the job.
6. Coordinate crew size and equipment.
7. Locate tools and supplies where the work is to be done; duplicate small tools and keep at each work site.
8. Combine jobs whenever possible; do another job while a machine is running if safety is not jeopardized.
9. Plan to complete one operation when another begins.
10. Work at reasonable speed; do not waste motions.
11. Consider using electric controls to time equipment.

In summary, time required per job often can be reduced by studying each job carefully. Work simplification is especially important with livestock enterprises where numerous functions are performed and large amounts of feed and waste are moved daily.

One good way to get ideas for improving labor efficiency is to observe other farmers who are doing similar jobs. Also, farm magazines often feature good ideas for work simplification.

Select a farm and evaluate labor efficiency. Calculate manwork units per person. How do work units on this farm compare to those on similar farms? Compare labor availability with labor requirements at different times of the year. Prepare a job schedule. Study jobs that are major labor users on your farm and determine how to reorganize those jobs to improve labor efficiency.

Part-Time Labor

Good part-time labor can increase profits by improving crop or livestock efficiency or by substituting for expensive machinery and equipment or for a full-time employee. One of the major challenges with part-time labor is being able to find dependable people who have the skills that are needed and who are willing to work when they are needed. Most communities have good potential part-time employees who need only to be located, hired, and then trained. For example, retired persons, factory workers, students, and teachers may enjoy farm work as well as the extra money that can be earned. The manager's challenge is to identify good workers and make plans with them so that they will be available when needed. Often one can afford to pay good, dependable part-time workers a higher-than-usual wage because they are needed for relatively few hours and yet their contribution to crop and livestock efficiency and cost reduction is substantial.

> Jim Brown obtains good part-time help during crop planting and harvesting by renting out an "extra" house on his farm to Pete, who works at a local store 40 hours per week. Wanting to make extra money, Pete is happy to work longer days in the spring and fall. On the other hand, the house which Pete rents at a bargain rate obligates him to work for Jim who hired Pete because of his skill in using and repairing machinery.

> Sarah Wilson meets labor needs at harvest by having her crops custom-harvested by a neighbor. Custom harvesting not only provides labor for the two-person requirements of harvest but also eliminates the need for Sarah to own a combine for her small farm. One of the big problems with custom work, however, is timeliness. Sarah has obtained a commitment from her neighbor to be first on his custom list by paying $2.00 extra per acre, planning in advance, and hiring him on a continuous basis as long as her work is completed first.

Management and Labor Expertise

On a farm with two or more managers or operators, each person can specialize in certain parts of the farm business. One person might be responsible for the dairy while another is in charge of crops. One person's expertise might be in marketing farm products while another's is in maintaining machinery. Specialization allows one to devote more time to a given area, enabling that person to do a better job. The one-operator farm, on the other hand, must devise ways to stay on top of the many jobs that need to be done and the management decisions that must be made. One way of achieving this is by keeping the business simple. Select production systems that are simple and easy to manage. Keep the number of crops and livestock enterprises low. Another way for the one-operator unit to stay on top is to specialize by family member. The wife might do the marketing, a son could handle machinery maintenance, a daughter could be in charge of the milking, and so on. There are certain times, however, when the one-operator farm necessarily must hire some specialized help. Machinery repairs and maintenance, marketing, accounting, and veterinary services are but a few of the areas in which assistance can be provided by specialists who service farmers.

Backup Labor and Management

One danger of a one-operator farm is the possibility that the operator may become incapacitated due to illness or injury at a critical time. Who would perform the duties of the operator if he or she were unable to do so? Perhaps it would be possible to have a cooperative arrangement with a neighbor. An arrangement with another one-operator farm might be devised in which both units share a worker who would move full-time to the unit where the operator has become incapacitated. This kind of planning allows the farm business to run more smoothly in case of an emergency or if the operator simply wishes to take a vacation.

SITUATION 2: OPERATOR, FULL-TIME HIRED, FAMILY, AND PART-TIME HIRED LABOR

The manager of a farm with a full-time hired laborer must be as concerned about labor efficiency and labor distribution as the manager who employs only part-time labor. The manager of a two-person farm has the possible advantage of backup labor and management as well as the possibility of specializing some of the labor and management functions. The following are some considerations, in addition to those discussed in the preceding sections, that should be kept in mind by those who run a two-person farm.

Job Descriptions

It is difficult to hire a good farm worker without first knowing what you expect the worker to do, and it is unlikely that the worker will be happy with the job unless the assignment is clearly understood. A good job description is essential so that each person knows what is expected of him or her with regard to work and decision making.

The same Paul Kirsch who was farming 320 acres, raising sixty sows farrow-to-finish, and running a one-person farm operation decided to expand to 640 acres and 150 sows and to add a full-time hired worker. Before beginning his search for a worker, Paul determined what jobs and management he would prefer doing himself and what he would expect the employee to do. Rating himself high in livestock skills and low in mechanical aptitude, Paul looked for someone who could be responsible for equipment maintenance, accept major responsibility for the crop work, and be willing to work with the hogs if needed. He prepared a detailed list of jobs and responsibilities for himself and the worker. When the worker was hired, the two of them went over the list together, making some minor adjustments.

> Develop job descriptions for persons who work on a farm with which you are familiar. Show your description to the manager and workers. What modifications did they suggest?

Recruiting Qualified Workers

The type of recruitment will depend on the kind of person being sought. If the job involves menial labor with very little management, a newspaper ad may be sufficient. But if the job is for a person who will have responsibility for some phase of the business, a more formal procedure is likely to attract qualified persons. The procedure might include the following six steps:

1. Develop a brief (less than one page) job announcement. Describe the type of person you want to hire and the characteristics of the job. Be sure to include the procedure for interested parties to contact you.

2. Circulate the job announcement to people who have contacts with the kinds of persons you are seeking and in places where candidates are likely to see it. This might include banks, PCA, farm supply stores, county extension agent, university college of agriculture placement services, and commercial employment agencies. Magazine and newspaper advertisements may also help locate job candidates.

3. Interview prospective employees who appear likely to fit the job and collect information from them about their:
   - Background
   - Experience
   - Tenure (how long they will likely stay on the job)
   - Long-range goals and objectives
   - Special abilities and limitations
   - References—one financial, one work, and one character reference.

   Make judgments to the extent possible about their:
   - Character: Are they honest and trustworthy? Do they pay their bills?
   - Personal characteristics: Do they have initiative and enthusiasm? Are they willing and able to learn? Can they get along well with others? Are they neat?

   Develop a checklist and grade each applicant.

4. Describe the farm to the interviewee, reflecting your own enthusiasm about the

total operation and the job opportunity. Some typical advantages of farm work over nonfarm work are:

- Varied work
- Work with nature, plants, and animals
- Work both outdoors and indoors
- Opportunity to observe growth of crops and livestock, gaining a sense of accomplishment
- Opportunity to learn about many things, including decision making.

5. Indicate how soon you will let the interviewee know if you will make a job offer.
6. Offer the best person from those interviewed a competitive wage (considering salary, health insurance, life insurance, housing, food, etc.).

Keep in mind that while fringe benefits are often necessary from the standpoint of both employee and employer, one dollar in fringe benefits is almost always considered to be of less value by the employee than one dollar of salary.

Attaining Performance

After a good employee has been hired, there are a number of ways to attain optimum performance.

Training.   A good place to start is with the job description. First, review it in total. Then systematically go through the jobs to be done, step by step, allowing sufficient time between jobs (even days or weeks) to enable the employee to become proficient at each successive job.

If jobs are complex, such as grinding different feed mixes for different kinds and sizes of farm animals, it is advisable to have detailed written instructions about the procedures. Written policy statements that provide guidelines for when certain jobs should be done may be helpful to both the employee and the manager.

Policies such as "Milking will begin at 6 A.M. and 6 P.M." and "Feed tanks will be checked each day at 1:30 P.M. and will be refilled if they are less than half full" can be very helpful when a new employee is being initiated into the business. After a time, policies become routine and there is no longer any need for a policy book. But whenever employees change, written policies and job descriptions can save a great deal of time.

A good labor manager must be a good teacher. Training is an ongoing job. Changing methods as well as new equipment, buildings, production systems, and enterprises require continual learning. Workers should be encouraged to attend short courses, extension meetings, and other applied training programs when these are relevant to the job. Employees should understand how their job fits in with the total operation, and it is the manager's responsibility to see that they do. Last but not least,

TABLE 21.5   Ranking of Job Characteristics
by Farm Employees

Factor	Ranking	Average Rank
Good wages	1	1.6
Good labor relations	2	2.9
Good facilities, equipment to work with	3	3.9
Adequate house, plus privileges	4	4.1
Vacation and time off	5	4.6
Bonuses	6	5.2
Incentive plan	7	5.6
Other	8	7.1

Source: Hired Farm Labor (West Lafayette, Ind.: Purdue University, Cooperative Extension Service, April 1977).

everyone gets satisfaction from a job well done. Therefore, good training enhances employee motivation—and that is good for any business!

Compensation.   In a farm labor research survey, employees were asked to rank, in order of importance, various job characteristics (Table 21.5). Good wages was chosen by the employees as the most important factor of those listed in the survey. Sometimes employees do not realize the value of their total compensation package. Thus, it is recommended that the monetary value of all benefits be listed for the employees at least once each year. For example, a manager listed the following for his employee, pointing out that few nonfarm jobs would provide the use of a house and a truck to the employee.

Wages ($1,000/month)	$12,000
House (rental value, $200/month)	2,400
Truck	1,000
Social security (employer)	800
Medical insurance	635
Food (garden, meat)	250
10% of net income of $25,000	2,500
	$19,585

Opportunity for ownership.   After a trial work period of one or two years, a key employee might be given the opportunity of owning part of the operating portion of the business. Ownership can increase morale, retain an employee on a permanent basis, bring more capital into the business, and increase farm profits.

An operating corporation or partnership of the type discussed in Chapter 19 is ideal for providing ownership possibilities to the employee. The ownership arrangement could provide the opportunity to:

1. Purchase a percentage of the operating part of the business each year, perhaps up to 5%
2. Share profit according to ownership
3. Sell the stock back to the arrangement in a systematic way should the employee leave. If the value of stock is small, it may all be purchased within thirty days. As the value of stock becomes greater, the majority owner may want to specify that equal amounts of stock will be purchased each month for a year or over several years. The agreement should allow the employee to recover the stock investment but should not put the business in financial difficulty if the employee decides to leave. The plan for repurchase of stock should be formulated in advance to accomplish these two objectives.

Income incentive programs.   Numerous incentive programs have been considered, proposed, and used (Figure 21.3). While incentive systems can be helpful in motivating employees, there are two dangers of incentive programs that should not be overlooked. First, an incentive system on a narrow aspect of the business, such as milk per cow or bushels per acre, can encourage an employee to concentrate so much effort in a specific area that business profit is hampered. For example, suppose that an employee is responsible for the dairy herd and a bonus is paid on milk per cow. In this situation, there may be a tendency to feed liberal amounts of grain and spend a great deal of time milking and caring for the cows. As a result, feed costs might be high, and the nonmilking herd and equipment may be neglected. To avoid such occurrences, some farmers use only percentage of the net income as an incentive, even though it is somewhat complex and requires a number of assumptions to be calculated.

A second danger of an incentive system, especially one offering a bonus given at the discretion of the manager and not related to specific performance of the farm business, is that the employee may come to expect it and may become dissatisfied in a year when a bonus or incentive is not given. Also, the employee may become dissatisfied if the bonus *is* related to business performance and through no fault of his or her own—bad weather, low prices—production and profit are low.

Whether or not an incentive should be used depends on the management style of the manager and the preference of the employee. In the case of a permanent key employee who is highly qualified and substantially involved with management, an incentive such as a percentage of the net income should be strongly considered.

Employee relations.   The development of good personal relations was discussed briefly in Chapter 19. Presented here is a list, compiled by Paul Robbins [3], of some important aspects of a good farm employer-employee relationship.

---

[3]See *Hired Farm Labor* (West Lafayette, Ind.: Purdue University, Cooperative Extension Service April 1977).

Incentive Guide

The following examples of incentive payment programs are meant to serve only as a guide. Any plan should be adjusted to fit your particular situation. For example, payment rates on a large, productive, highly mechanized farm, employing several workers, should be different than those on a small, unproductive, poorly mechanized farm. Incentive payments should be tied to work responsibilities carried out by the employees and over which they have some control.

Whole Farm

Percent of Gross Income
- ¼-1% of all gross receipts (adjust to size and type of farm)

Percent of Net Income
- 1-4% of returns left after all cash operating expenses are deducted from gross income

Percent of Taxable Income
- 2-10% of taxable income as computed on form Schedule F

Percent of Profits
- 10-40% of profits derived by subtracting from the taxable income a labor and management charge for the operator, and a return on the operator's equity in the business. Adjust this amount by the inventory change that took palce in the farm's personal property during the last taxable year.

Wage Adjustments and Bonuses
- End of year bonus of 1-10% of cash wages
- Paid vacation of 2-4 weeks per year during the low labor load periods.
- An annual increase in cash wages of 3-10% per year if the employee stays

Livestock

Hogs

Feeder pigs purchased and fed out
- 25-50¢/feeder pig bought and fed out.
- ¼-1% of hog sales less cost of feeder pigs.
- If death losses are less than 4%, the employee receives 25-40% of the market value of these market hogs saved. (Example: 98% of feeder pigs purchased live to be sold on the market. The employee receives 25-40% of the market value of 2% of all market hogs sold.)

Feeder pigs produced (for sale or fed out on the farm)
- 25-50¢/pig weaned
- $1-3/pig weaned above 7/litter
- $3-5/sow that weans more than 8 pigs/litter
- ¼-1% of gross income from hogs, including inventory changes

Complete hog program
- 25-50¢/hog marketed during the year if employee stays until end of year
- $2-5/market hog sold above 7/litter
- ¼-1% of gross income from hogs—including inventory changes

Pure Bred Livestock
- ¼-⅓ of premiums when purebred livestock are exhibited

Dairy
- ½-2% of milk sales, paid monthly
- Start at ½% of milk check and increase pay by gradually moving up to 2% of milk check
- 5¢/cwt. milk sold, and rate is increased by 2¢/yr. employee stays, up to a maximum of 25¢
- 1-3% of returns above feed cost based on DHLA records
- 25-50¢/cwt. milk sold above 10,000 lbs./cow & 50-75¢/cwt. milk sold over 15,000 lbs./cow
- $5-10 for each calf saved over an 85% calf crop at the end of the year
- 15-25¢ for each one thousand pounds of milk sold per worker over 300,000 pounds

Beef

Cow herds (calves sold at weaning)
- $1-3 for each beef calf weaned
- 10% of gross income above $160/cow
- $10-20 for each calf weaned over 90% calf crop

Feeder cattle purchased
- 25¢-$1/head of fed cattle marketed
- ⅛-1% of beef sales less cost of purchased feeders
- 10-20% of return over all cash costs including home-grown grain fed

Crops

- ¼-1% of small grain produced, including grain equivalent in silage
- 5¢/bu. corn produced over 100 bu. per acre
- 10¢/bu. of soybeans produced above 30 bu./acre
- $1-3/ton of alfalfa that yields over 3.5 ton/acre
- ⅛-1% of gross crop sales
- $100 bonus if corn and soybeans are planted without a single row missed. Hired workers get bonuses if they catch and replant missed rows on their own.

Figure 21.3 Incentive program guideline. *Source:* Kenneth H. Thomas and Michael D. Boehlje, *Farm Business Arrangements: Which One Are You?* North Central Regional Extension Publication 50 (Minneapolis: Cooperative Extension Service, University of Minnesota, 1982).

- Friendly attitude and the ability to get along with others
- Loyalty, trust, and mutual respect
- Knowing how to delegate responsibility and knowledge about the job to be done
- The ability to correct and supervise without making the employee appear stupid
- The ability to plan ahead so as to reduce hasty decisions
- Putting the employee in surroundings where he or she can be productive (people like to feel that they are productive)
- The ability to give orders so that the employee knows what is expected
- The ability to be patient while an employee is adjusting to a new situation
- Giving the employee an opportunity to advance
- Frequent praise and expression of gratitude for a job well done
- Giving the employee and family a feeling of belonging. This may mean taking the employee to farm meetings occasionally, encouraging the entire family to become active in church, school, and community affairs, and encouraging the children to participate in 4-H, scouts, athletics, etc.
- Giving added responsibility when the employee is willing and able to assume it
- Making sure that the employee gets necessary training
- Asking for advice and counsel where and when you feel the employee is competent to give it
- Sharing unpleasant tasks that must be done
- Providing a home the employee's family is proud to live in
- Preparing and reviewing the written agreement from time to time
- If appropriate, giving the employee a title (herdsman, assistant manager, crop assistant) that adds dignity to the job (Do not refer to employee as the ''hired hand.'')
- Making it clear that the employee has just one boss
- Giving the employee time off to do what he or she wants and needs to do
- Considering the fact that the employee has family responsibilities and obligations.

Modern buildings and equipment.   Two important benefits are derived from a modern operation. Most employees get satisfaction from being associated with a progressive business. Also, modern buildings and equipment often eliminate the work that is least desirable—carrying bales, shoveling grain, scraping manure, lifting feed bags, and so on. Hence, in addition to improving labor productivity, modern buildings and equipment can be a very important morale factor for hired employees.

Evaluation.   Periodically, a minimum of once each year, employees should be evaluated. The purpose of the evaluation is to formally recognize an employee for work well done and to point out areas of needed improvement. The evaluation should be specific and on points directly related to the job. Each manager will want to develop evaluation criteria and may wish to take into consideration the abilities and characteristics listed below. In addition, the manager may also list and evaluate specific jobs from the job description prepared earlier.

	Excellent	Good	Adequate but needs improvement	Unsatisfactory
Timeliness	_____	_____	_____	_____
Job quality	_____	_____	_____	_____
Initiative	_____	_____	_____	_____
Cost consciousness	_____	_____	_____	_____
Maintenance	_____	_____	_____	_____
Safety	_____	_____	_____	_____
Communications ability	_____	_____	_____	_____
Personal relations	_____	_____	_____	_____

Government Regulations and Requirements

The farm employer should become familiar with government labor laws and regulations. Regulations have been increasing in number in recent years, a trend that is likely to continue. Farms with one full-time worker and limited part-time workers will be most concerned with the first four regulations listed. All regulations listed, and possibly others, may be applicable to farms with more than one hired worker.

1. *Social Security.* Employers are required to withhold social security taxes from their employees' wages and match the employees' tax with an equal amount. Social security or Federal Insurance Contribution Act (FICA) taxes must be withheld if over $150 in cash wages is paid to an employee or if the employee works over 20 hours in a week. Persons under 21 employed by their parents and farm spouses are excluded.

2. *Workmen's compensation* insurance is required in most states. It is an insurance system that provides financial protection for workers injured on the job and frees the employer from liability for this type of injury.

3. *Occupational Safety and Health Administration (OSHA)* regulations must be followed by all employers, and they should check to be sure they are following regulations.

4. *Federal income tax withholding* is not required by law but may be done if requested in writing by the employee.

5. *Unemployment insurance* must be paid by farm employers who have ten or more workers in each of twenty or more weeks or who pay over $20,000 for hired labor in any calendar quarter.

6. *The federal minimum wage* law applies to farms that hire more than 500 worker-days of labor in any calendar quarter.

7. *Housing regulations* apply to farms hiring migrant workers.

8. *Federal civil rights laws* apply to farms with fifteen or more workers.

9. Federal laws specify limitations for the employment of persons under 16 years of age.

SITUATION 3: SEVERAL FULL-TIME HIRED EMPLOYEES

Multiemployee farms have an opportunity to capitalize on the specific strengths of each employee. Specialization enables employees to become more proficient in their particular duties and to keep up-to-date on new developments in their area of specialty, such as crop or livestock management, machinery maintenance, or record keeping.

Personnel Policies

As the number of employees increases, the need for a personnel policy statement becomes necessary to ensure that all employees are treated fairly, know what to expect, and know what is expected of them. The following items were included in an employee policy statement of a large farm.

1. Employees are expected to work 50 hours per week—9 hours per day plus Saturday morning. Every month each employee has one Monday afternoon off for personal business.

2. One day of vacation is earned each month. The employee must plan the vacation time with the manager.

3. One day of sick leave is earned each month.

4. Personal automobiles are never to be used for business because of insurance considerations.

5. Farm automobiles can be used for personal use, up to 100 miles per week, but the employee is to furnish fuel.

6. If an employee travels on farm business, actual expenses are paid and receipts are required.

7. The employee must have the written approval of the manager before disclosing any information about the business.

8. It is the duty of each employee to keep his or her area of responsibility neat.

Visit a farm that employs several workers. What personnel policy statements are followed on the farm? What others would you recommend?

Organizational Chart

Job descriptions and an understanding of responsibilities become even more important as the number of employees increases. What are the functions of each job? Who has responsibility for various decisions? To whom does each employee report for instructions and decisions beyond his or her authority? The very large farm may even use an organizational chart such as the one in Figure 21.4.

Some principles that are generally followed in large organizations are:

1. Each person should have only one supervisor.
2. There is a limit to the number of people that any one person can supervise.

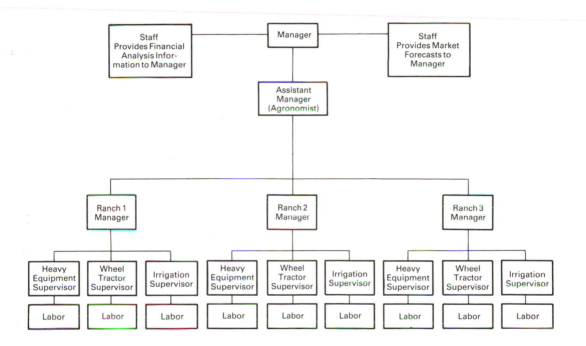

Manager makes decisions about acres of various crops and the sale of crops and reviews decisions about personnel, fertilization, other crop inputs, and machinery with assistant manager and ranch managers.

Assistant manager plans location of crops and all crop management practices and develops a general production schedule after consulting with ranch managers.

Each ranch manager is responsible for carrying out the cropping plan.

Machinery and irrigation supervisors are responsible for jobs assigned by ranch managers.

Figure 21.4

3. Frequently made decisions should be routinized with the use of policies. For example:

   • Milking begins at 6 A.M. and 6 P.M..
   • Cows are fed $\frac{1}{2}$ pound of grain for each pound of milk produced.
   • Crop planting begins in the spring after April 15 when the soil temperature reaches 63° F and the ground is not too wet for machinery operations.

4. Responsibility must be accompanied by authority.

The objective of organization is to coordinate people, land, machinery, and other resources to achieve the goals of the farm. Gains can be made through specialization that accompanies organization. The challenge is to avoid excessively high overhead, which is typical of large organizations.

People, their ideas, and their work determine whether or not the farm will be profitable. Thus the selection, training, motivation, and management of labor is crucial to the success of a farm or any business.

HOW MUCH HIRED LABOR?

The amount of labor needed is closely related to farm size (see Chapter 13). But for a particular farm, a manager can usually choose from several production systems, each of which has different labor-capital requirements (see Chapters 16 and 17). For a given production system, the amount of labor can affect crop and livestock efficiency. Too little labor will result in low efficiency while too much labor will have an adverse effect on profit.

How do managers choose the optimum amount of labor? First, they must budget the costs and returns of changing the amount of current labor (see Chapters 8 and 12). They should take into account that a minimum of two persons not only provides some insurance in case of accident or illness but also allows for specialization of responsibilities. Finally, managers must recognize that a key factor in the productivity and return to labor is their own labor-management ability.

In summary, whether or not it would be profitable and desirable to add more labor depends on:

1. Added income from increased size
2. Added income from improved crop and livestock efficiency
3. Reduced building and machinery costs resulting from better maintenance
4. Lower cost as a result of reduced capital investment
5. Benefits of backup labor and management in case of illness or accident
6. Cost of labor, including wages, social security, insurance, and other benefits
7. Labor-management ability of the operator
8. Operator's preference regarding the number of people to be supervised.

DISCUSSION QUESTIONS

1. What is labor efficiency?
2. How can labor efficiency be measured?
3. Should farmers aim to maximize labor efficiency? Why?
4. What are some ways that labor efficiency can be improved?
5. Prepare a list for yourself of the jobs you should complete during the next three months.
6. Why is labor efficiency especially important on a one-person farm?
7. What are the advantages and disadvantages of a one-person farm?
8. What compensation should the following types of hired persons be paid:
   (a). Part-time
   (b). Full-time for routine jobs
   (c). Full-time with management responsibility for an enterprise or part of an enterprise
   (d). Major management responsibility
9. Should substantial fringe benefits such as housing and insurance be provided for employees, or should employees be paid higher wages in lieu of fringe benefits? Why?
10. How would you recruit needed farm workers?
11. What factors affect worker performance? Recommend an employee management program that will keep workers motivated and performance high.
12. What are personnel policies? What purposes do they serve?
13. Under what circumstance might an organizational chart be useful? What function would it serve?
14. How should a manager determine whether or not additional labor will pay?

RELATED READINGS

BEACH, DALE S. *Instructors Manual, Personnel: The Management of People at Work*. New York: Macmillan, 1980.

FORSTER, D. LYNN, and BERNARD L. ERVEN. *Foundations for Managing the Farm Business,* pp. 227–248. Columbus, Oh.: Grid Publishing, 1981.

GILES, TONY, and MALCOLM STANSFIELD. *The Farmer as Manager,* pp. 143–156. London: George Allen and Unlin, Ltd., 1980.

HARSH, STEPHEN B., LARRY J. CONNOR, and GERALD D. SCHWAB. *Managing the Farm Business,* pp. 279–289. Englewood Cliffs, N.J.: Prentice-Hall, 1981.

HERBST, J. H. *Farm Management Principles, Budgets, Plans,* chap. 8. Champaign, Ill.: Stipes Publishing Co., 1976.

HYER, EDGAR A., and JOHN A. ROGALLA. *Farm Management,* pp. 163–173. San Luis Obispo, Calif.: Farm Management Publishing Co., 1978.

PETERS, THOMAS, J. and ROBERT N. WATERMAN, JR. *In Search of Excellence*. New York: Harper and Row, 1982.

ROBBINS, PAUL. *Hired Farm Labor,* EC-459. West Lafayette, Ind.: Cooperative Extension Service, Purdue University, April 1977.

Tax Management[1]

22

[1] Tax rates and regulations are likely to change from year to year. Certain specifics in this chapter may not be up-to-date, but the general principles apply. Updates of many of the listings in "Related Readings" at the end of the chapter can be used to obtain appropriate up-to-date information.

The purpose of this chapter is to review the major tax considerations that should be taken into account by managers of farm businesses. There are two types of mistakes that a manager can make with regard to taxes. The first is to ignore tax consequences entirely, losing after-tax income by failing to take advantage of tax-reducing opportunities. The second mistake is to concentrate so hard on reducing taxes that the farm organization is controlled by the tax laws rather than by the manager. Quite often this latter type of management error reduces before-tax income so much that even though taxes are minimized, after-tax income is less than if tax consequences were ignored altogether. The manager's job is to be aware of taxes and tax laws but not to let taxes overly influence the organization of the farm.

INCOME TAXES

Tax Rates

Tables 22.1 and 22.2 list tax rates for single and married persons. Two observations can be made from these tables. First, with the tax rates shown plus an additional

TABLE 22.1 Federal Income Tax Rates for Single Persons Beginning 1984

Taxable income	Tax on lower amt.	Rate on excess
$ 2,300	No tax	11%
3,400	121	12
4,400	241	14
6,500	535	15
8,500	835	16
10,800	1,203	18
12,900	1,581	20
15,000	2,001	23
18,200	2,737	26
23,500	4,115	30
28,800	5,705	34
34,100	7,507	38
41,500	10,319	42
55,300	16,115	48
81,800	28,835	50

Source: Internal Revenue Code, Section I.

TABLE 22.2 Federal Income Tax Rates for Married
Persons Filing Joint Returns Beginning in 1984

Taxable income	Tax on lower amt.	Rate on excess
$ 3,400	No tax	11%
5,500	231	12
7,600	483	14
11,900	1,085	16
16,000	1,741	18
20,200	2,497	22
24,600	3,465	25
29,900	4,790	28
35,200	6,274	33
45,800	9,772	38
60,000	15,168	42
85,600	25,920	45
109,400	36,630	49
162,400	62,600	50

Source: Internal Revenue Code, Section I.

11.3% to 13.7% for social security plus state taxes, individuals with taxable incomes above $20,200 must pay over one-third of their taxable income above $20,200 in federal and state income taxes and social security tax. Second, federal tax rates are progressive, increasing from 11% to 50%. Tax management therefore becomes more important as farm family income increases.

Farm Growth and Cash Reporting to Delay Taxes

Two methods of reporting income taxes are the cash method and the accrual method. The main difference between the two is that the cash system requires reporting income when received and expenses when paid, but no inventories, whereas the accrual method requires the reporting of income when it is earned and expenses when they are incurred. Under the accrual method, an increase in the value of inventory of farm products is treated as a receipt and a decrease is treated as an expense in the year in which it occurs.

One advantage of the cash system over the accrual system of tax reporting is that a growing farm can accumulate income in the form of inventory and delay the income tax until the asset is sold, sometimes a great many years later. Until the tax is paid, the farmer has the use of the money. Another advantage is that when using the cash reporting system, it is somewhat easier to shift income between taxable years, keeping annual income more uniform.

Bill and Sally Grundy found that the expansion of their farm business helped them defer income tax. Before expanding, they farmed 300 acres of owned land and 200 acres of cash-rented land. Filing a joint tax return on their taxable income, which averaged $32,000 per year, the Grundys paid $5,378 in income taxes (Table 22.2).

In 1984 Bill and Sally cash-rented an additional 200 acres, which yielded 45 bushels of wheat per acre. The wheat was sold in 1985.

The Grundy's 1984 tax situation was as follows:

Present operation (taxable income)		$32,000
Rent, 200 acres at $70/acre	$14,000	
Crop expense, 200 acres at $70/acre	14,000	
Total expense	$28,000	
Taxable income		$ 4,000
1984 tax (Table 22.2)	$ 66	
Added wheat in inventory, 8,000 bu. at $4/bu.	$32,000	
1984 accrual income		$36,000

The Grundys reduced their income tax from $5,378 to $66 in 1984 because they paid the expenses for the 100 acres in 1984 but did not sell the wheat until 1985. So their taxable income in 1984 was only $4,000, but with the additional $32,000 in wheat inventory their real income was $36,000. If they had reported tax on the accrual basis, taxable income would have been $36,000.

Having delayed payment of $5,312 in income taxes, the Grundys have that money to use in their business, for living expenses, or to put into savings until they reduce size and stop renting the additional 200 acres. For 1985 the Grundys must pay taxes on the $36,000 income unless there is further expansion that could provide another opportunity to delay taxes. A continuously growing farm can finance part of its expansion with delayed tax provided the cash tax-reporting method is used.

Capital Gains

Farm property that is part of the "production plant" and has been held for more than one year before being sold (two years for cattle and horses) can qualify for income tax treatment as a long-term capital gain. Only 40% of the increased value of capital items is taxed, so taxes may be reduced by 60% on a capital gain compared to ordinary income. (The untaxed 60% is subject to alternative minimum tax in some instances.) Land, breeding livestock, and timber are typical items that can qualify for capital gains treatment.

There are several ways that farmers can take advantage of the capital gains provision. Some of these ways are discussed in the following sections.

Invest in assets for which there is a high return in increased asset value.   Bill and Mary Quigg operate a 320-acre unit. They wish to expand their farm operation and are planning to invest $100,000 to rent or purchase more land. If they buy more land, the $100,000 will purchase 60 acres, which can be farmed with their present machinery. If they rent more land, the $100,000 will enable them to trade machinery as well as cover the added operating costs for 300 acres.

Bill and Mary budgeted a 15% return from both alternatives. If they rent land, they expect to net $50 per acre, or $15,000. If they buy 60 acres, they expect to net $150 per acre, or $9,000, and, in addition, they expect the land to increase in value $100 per acre each year. The Quiggs' taxable income would be $6,000 less if they buy rather than rent because tax is not paid on the land value increase until the land is sold. When the 60 acres are sold, only 40% of the gain will be taxed, provided the land is held more than one year. Assuming that they are in the 33% tax bracket, the Quiggs' current taxes would be $1,980 less if they buy rather than rent land.

Of course, there are other more significant management factors than tax considerations when deciding whether to buy or rent land (see Chapters 14 and 15).

Sell breeding stock.   Lin Choi, who has 125 beef cows, has a policy of culling 25 cows raised in his herd per year, for which he receives $550 per cow, or $13,750. Because cows held twenty-four months or more are taxed as long-term capital gains, he pays tax on only 40% of the $13,750, or $5,500. Assuming that Lin is in the 30% tax bracket, he will pay $2,475 less tax on the culled cows than if the $13,750 income had been from market cattle sales (30% times the $8,250 reduction).

Lin could save back more heifers and sell 50 cows per year rather than 25 and reduce his taxes another $2,475. He should evaluate whether or not the tax saving would be greater than the management impact of turning over the breeding herd at a faster rate. Cull dairy cows also qualify for long-term capital gains treatment if held twenty-four months or more, and sows or ewes qualify if held over twelve months.

Clear land.   Land-clearing costs of up to $5,000 or one-fourth of taxable farm income (whichever is less) can be reported as an ordinary farm expense. Thus taxable income is reduced by the amount of the clearing cost. The return, that is, the increased value of the farm, is not taxed until the farm is sold, at which time it is taxed as a capital gain. If the land is held for less than ten years, part or all of the land-clearing expense may be recaptured as ordinary income.

Investment Tax Credit

A tax credit of 6% or 10% of the purchase price is allowed for investment in certain agricultural property including machinery, equipment, storage facilities for crops or livestock products, single-purpose livestock-production facilities, tile, fences, breeding livestock, and some other depreciable items.

Property falling into the five- or ten-year category of accelerated cost recovery qualifies for a 10% credit. This applies to single-purpose livestock facilities, machinery, equipment, breeding cattle, fences, and tile. Three-year property, such as automobiles, pickup trucks, and breeding swine, qualify for a 6% credit. Land and general-purpose farm buildings, such as a machine shed, do not qualify for tax investment credit. For farmers who have tax to pay, investment credit is similar to cash as it reduces taxes, dollar for dollar, by the amount of the credit. If the property is disposed of in less than five or three years, respectively, a portion of the credit is taken back, or "recaptured." If investment credit is taken, the cost basis must be reduced by one-half of the amount of the credit or the credit must be reduced by two percentage points.

Ross Whitsel constructed a new dairy facility for $236,000 including equipment. Both facility and equipment fall into the five-year cost-recovery category. Ross received a $23,600 investment credit to be used to reduce the present year's tax. If the current year's taxes are less than $23,600, the credit can be carried back three years and then forward for fifteen years.

Maximizing Legal Depreciation

The cost of a resource that lasts more than one year usually must be spread over the years of life of that resource. The Economic Recovery Tax Act of 1981 specifies four depreciation categories for farm property as well as the particular items that must be included in each category (Table 5.1).

As an alternative, the farmer can choose the straight-line method, which allows some tax management in regard to the length of the depreciation period. Optional cost-recovery periods for the straight-line method are:

3-year personal property	3, 5, or 12 years
5-year personal property	5, 12, or 25 years
10-year personal property	10, 25, or 35 years
15-year real property	15, 35, or 45 years

If a farmer buys a number of assets in a particular recovery class during a tax year, all of these assets must be treated the same, except for fifteen-year property. If the farmer buys a tractor and a combine in one year, the same cost-recovery method must be used for both assets.

Should current income put a farmer in a relatively high tax bracket, rapid depreciation may be desirable. On the other hand, when current income is low, the best tax management may be to choose a longer life for the depreciable item with the straight-line method (see Chapter 5).

The laws allows for expensing capital item purchases up to $7,500 per year in 1984 and 1985 and $10,000 thereafter. If this expense option is chosen, investment credit may not be taken on these items.

Distributing Income among More Individuals

Because of progressive tax rates, taxes can be reduced if a given amount of income can be distributed among several persons rather than concentrated in one person. Of course, the persons to whom the money is paid must have earned it from the business.

Bill and Mary Quigg have a taxable farm income of $36,000. Each of their fifteen-year-old twin sons does $3,000 work a year. Rather than pay the boys an income, Bill planned to pay for their college education, provide spending money, and let them use his car. Bill's tax adviser has recommended instead that he pay his sons a $3,000 salary for their work and have the boys pay for part of their education. The tax adviser developed the following budget for the Quiggs:

Income tax if boys not paid:		
Taxable income, Bill and Mary Quigg	$36,000	
Tax (Table 22.2, Schedule Y, Joint)		$6,538
Tax if boys are paid $3,000:		
Taxable income, Bill and Mary Quigg	$30,000	
Tax (Table 22.2), Bill and Mary		$4,818
Taxable Income[a], Mick	$ 2,000	
Tax		0
Taxable Income[a], Mack	2,000	
Tax		0
		$4,818

[a]Paid income ($3,000) minus personal exemption ($1,000).

By paying Mick and Mack for their work rather than paying directly for their education, Bill and Mary reduced total taxes from $6,538 to $4,818, a savings of $1,720. Also, since the boys are working for their parents, it is not necessary for them to pay social security tax so long as they are under twenty-one. Being able to show that they provided over half the support for Mick and Mack, the Quiggs did not lose the twins as tax exemptions.

Income Averaging

Because of progressive tax rates, it is generally good tax management to keep income uniform from year to year. It is especially important for income to be at least as high as is necessary to use all deductions and personal exemptions. Once these are lost, there is no way to recover them. Losses can be carried forward and back, but if income is negative, thousands of dollars of personal exemptions are lost (unless the farm is incorporated).

A manager can shift receipts and expenses from one tax year to another to keep income uniform. Nevertheless, because of differences in production and prices from year to year, large variations in income are apt to occur. The Murphys' income is a good example of this. During the five years from 1978 to 1982, their taxable incomes have been:

1978	1979	1980	1981	1982
$40,000	$10,000	$20,000	$10,000	$50,000

If incomes were not averaged, the Murphys' 1982 federal income tax payment would be $13,305. However, by averaging income (using tax schedule 1040G), 1982 tax would be $11,307, a savings of $1,998.

Records

Shopping for a tractor part in town, Jerry Haskins stopped in a new farm store. Not having a charge account, he paid $30.00 cash and put the receipt in his shirt pocket. The receipt was destroyed when the shirt was washed, and Jerry failed to obtain a duplicate. Since the Haskins are in the 33% tax bracket, the loss of the receipt was the same as losing 33% of $30.00, or $9.90. Losses of this kind throughout the year can amount to several hundred dollars. One good way to have a double record is to keep a separate farm checking account and to pay *all* bills by check, writing on the check the item for which the payment was made.

Good tax records serve not only to minimize taxes but also to verify expenses in case of a tax audit.

Incorporating

Incorporating the farm business can have tax advantages or disadvantages. This has already been discussed in Chapter 20.

ESTATE TAXES

Farming requires tremendous amounts of capital, commonly in excess of $1 million. Transfer of this amount of farm property to children at the death of both parents could result in substantial estate taxes. Payment of estate tax in addition to other existing financial obligations could force liquidation of part or all of the farm business or result in a tight financial situation for the heirs for many years. Through careful estate planning, the estate tax can be reduced and the goals of all parties still achieved. It is important for *all* farmers, regardless of age, to have an understanding of estate management and to have an estate plan. The further ahead plans are made, the more likely the desired goals can be reached. Estate planning is a topic too large and complex to be covered in this book, but a few statements of philosophy regarding estate planning will be presented.

• Persons who either own or might inherit a farm estate should understand estate taxes. One way to become more knowledgeable about estate taxes is to read one or more of the publications listed in "Related Readings" at the end of this chapter. You should become aware of the amount of estate taxes that would be paid under different estate-transfer methods.

• The same advice applies to estate tax planning as to income taxes: persons involved must focus mainly on the management of the business and not be overly influenced to minimize taxes with methods that might hurt or detract from the efficient management of the business.

• The property owner is the person who must decide how and when to transfer the property to the next generation.

• Several tools can be utilized to reduce estate taxes including gifting, trusts, and "special use" estate evaluation. These tools should be thoroughly understood.

• Estate planning may be crucial for the continuity of the farm and the harmonious relationship of those involved with the business. It can include procedures that enable farm-operating heirs to purchase property from nonfarm heirs in such a way that the business need not be liquidated.

• Developing a good estate plan can be achieved through careful study combined with a great deal of discussion among all parties. It should be recognized that estate plans have costs as well as benefits.

• Obtaining competent counsel is critical in setting up an estate plan.

In summary, consider taxes but manage the business to maximize after-tax earnings. Do not allow taxes to manage you.

DISCUSSION QUESTIONS

1. Why do growing farms that report tax on the cash basis usually pay less income tax?
2. What is capital gains tax? How can a farmer convert ordinary income to capital gains income? What is the tax consequence of this shift?
3. What is investment tax credit? What type of resources are eligible for investment credit? If a manager purchases a $50,000 tractor, how much will income taxes be reduced through investment credit?
4. Should a manager depreciate farm assets as rapidly as possible? Why?
5. Why does distributing income among more individuals reduce taxes?
6. What is income averaging?
7. How might good records reduce income taxes?
8. Why is an estate-transfer plan important?
9. Who should make the decisions about estate transfer?
10. What are the most important considerations for reducing estate taxes?
11. List some ways to reduce family conflicts that sometimes occur over estate transfers.

RELATED READINGS

ACKER, D. L., P. L. WRIGHT, and G. A. HARRISON. *Tax-Sheltered Retirement Plans or Farm Investments,* North Central Regional Extention Publication No. 55. Columbus, Ohio: Ohio State University, 1978.

Farmers Tax Guide. Internal Revenue Service Publication No. 225. Washington D.C.: U.S. Department of the Treasury, 1983.

HARL, NEIL E. *Agricultural Law,* vols. 7–8. New York: Matthew Bender, 1983.

———. "The Economic Recovery Tax Act of 1981," *Agri-Finance,* October 1981.

——— *Farm Estate and Business Planning.* Skokie, Ill.: AgriBusiness Publications, 1983.

HARRIS, PHILLIP E., R. EDWARDS BROWN, JR., and W. A. TINSLEY. "Income Tax Management for Farmers," North Central Regional Publication No. 2. Madison, Wis.: University of Wisconsin, 1982.

HARSH, STEPHEN B., LARRY J. CONNER, and GERALD D. SCHWAB. *Managing the Farm Business,* chap. 13. Englewood Cliffs, N.J.: Prentice-Hall, 1981.

O'BYRNE, JOHN C., and CHARLES DAVENPORT. *Doane's Tax Guide for Farmers.* Indianapolis: The Allen Smith Co., 1981.

——— *Farm Income Tax Manual.* Indianapolis: The Allen Smith Company, 1981.

SMITH, ROBERT S. and R. N. WEIGLE. "Taxmanship in Buying or Selling a Farm," North Central Regional Publication No. 43. Madison, Wis.: University of Wisconsin, 1977.

SUTER, ROBERT C. *Estate Planning: The Book for Farmers.* Danville, Ill.: The Interstate Printers and Publishers, 1983.

——— *When Your Case Matures: Estate Planning for Entreprenuers.* Danville, Ill.: The Interstate Printers and Publishers, 1983.

U.S. Master Tax Guide. Chicago: Commercial Clearing House, Inc., 1984.

Professional Farm Management

23

WHAT IS PROFESSIONAL MANAGEMENT?

The principal job of the professional farm manager is to manage, for a fee, a farm business owned by someone living away from the farm or by someone who lacks the time, farming knowledge, or personal relations ability required to manage the farm. Typically, professionally managed farms are owned by an heir of the previous owner-operator, such as a surviving spouse, son, or daughter, or by investors.

In addition to direct management of farms, some professional managers also provide services such as real estate brokerage, farm appraisal, estate and income tax counseling, record keeping, and even management advice to farmers. Professional farm management is an interesting, challenging occupation that enables a person to be involved in farm management with limited amounts of personal capital.

MANAGING A FARM

Managing a farm usually entails carrying out the following eight steps:

1. Determine the Goals of the Owner

It should be kept in mind that the professional manager is working for the owner and that the farm should be managed in such a way that the goals of the owner are accomplished. Hence the first step in managing a farm is to determine the goals and desires of the owner. Sometimes the owner is unable to express these goals directly, and the professional manager must identify them by observation. For instance, a widow may say she wants to make farm improvements, but the farm manager may discover that the farm is her only source of income and that the first priority is making sure there is sufficient income for the widow's living expenses. An investor who has purchased a farm may say that his or her main objective is to make money. The manager may soon learn, however, that the investor likes to take friends to visit the farm and that keeping the buildings painted and weeds clipped is almost as important as making money. In still another case, the operator has been on the farm for many years and is a friend of the owner. A major goal may be to keep the operator on the farm even if this means less income.

2. Select an Operator

Having determined the goals and objectives of the owner, the farm manager must find a capable operator who fits the farm. Typically, the farm manager visits the farm eight to thirty times per year, so if any plan is to be successful, a farm operator who can carry out a plan in the manager's absence is essential. Moreover, if an operator is to remain enthusiastic and provide continuity by farming the unit for several years, the farm must meet the needs of the operator. The manager's responsibility, therefore, is to choose a capable operator who wants and needs the farm. The importance of choosing the right operator cannot be overemphasized. If a good operator is selected and a sound plan developed, the farm operation is almost certain to be successful. If, on the other hand, an incompetent operator is chosen, it will be impossible for the farm operation to be successful even with an excellent plan.

How does one find an outstanding operator? Usually, potential operators inform the professional managers of their desire to rent a farm should one become available. As word spreads through the community that a farm is for rent, several operators may express interest. Also, the professional manager may already know some good operators in the area and may ask them if they would like to rent the farm. If these informal methods do not turn up good candidates, an ad may be placed in a local newspaper or even a farm magazine. Information should be collected from each potential operator regarding experience, machinery owned, and financial situation. It is helpful to know why the operator is changing farms and why the operator wants to rent your particular farm. Operators' applications should provide several references including persons who have had financial dealings with them and persons who can evaluate their farming ability.

The top candidates should be selected and their past performance evaluated. Past performance is the best single indicator of future performance. Questions that each candidate's references might be asked are: Does the candidate do a good job of farming? What are typical crop yields and rate of gain and production of livestock? Does this person pay bills on time? Get along well with people? Keep the farm neat?

When an operator is found who measures up favorably in all of the considerations mentioned, proceed to rent the farm. It is usually most profitable in the long run to make rental concessions, if necessary, to get the best possible operator.

3. Develop a Plan

A tentative farm-operating and capital-improvement plan should be developed, keeping in mind the goals of both the owner and the operator and the abilities of the operator. After review of the plan, first by the owner and then by the operator, make any necessary modifications. Sometimes it is necessary to modify a plan more than once before it is acceptable to all parties.

The plan should show the number of acres and the location of all crops. It should have specific information regarding production practices, including fertilization, seed, chemicals, and time of operations. Numbers of livestock, production methods, and schedule of livestock production should be specified. A list of resources needed and the times that they are needed should be indicated, as well as marketing and storage plans. Finally, a projected receipt and expense budget should be included in the plan for each quarter of the year.

Conditions will undoubtedly force some changes in the plan as the year progresses, but having an initial agreement on the jobs to be done is crucial.

4. Check on Plan Execution

The professional manager must visit the farm periodically to check if the operation is moving according to plans and to make adjustments in the plan if necessary. Perhaps excess rainfall might require changing some acreage from corn to beans, or price changes of feed ingredients might make a new feed mix less costly.

The number of farm visits needed depends on the complexity of the operation, the amount of capital improvement under way, the length of time the plan has been in operation, and the ability of the operator. An intensive livestock farm might be visited each week. A crop farm may require only eight visits at key times during the year. Many times the telephone can be used to discuss and solve minor problems, avoiding the time and expense of driving to the farm.

5. Keep Records, Sell Products, Pay Bills

It is the farm manager's job to sell products at the appropriate time, keep records, pay bills, and send the balance of cash not needed in the operation to the owner. Also, at various times, papers must be filed in order for the farm to take advantage of property tax exemptions, government program payments, and so forth. It is usually the responsibility of the professional manager to do all of these things, acting like a judicious farm owner.

6. Evaluate Profitability

Expenses, receipts, and production should be compared to the plan at the end of each quarter. Any substantial deviation of actual performance from planned performance should be explored with the operator and explained to the owner. Finally, a careful financial analysis of the farm should be made at the end of the year. This would include a comparison of receipts, expenses, and profits to the budget and to similar farms as well as an evaluation of volume and efficiency.

7. Report to the Owner

Each quarter the owner should be sent a listing of expenses, receipts, and production information. A brief report of farming operation progress should be provided. At the end of the year a comprehensive analysis of profitability and production should be prepared for the owner. Most owners like to have information from the manager's report in order to observe farm earnings and to be able to discuss the farm's progress with family and friends. Of course, any unexpected changes, both favorable and unfavorable, should be reported to the owner immediately.

8. Plan Farm Improvements

Most farms require periodic capital investments if they are to reach their potential. Possible areas needing attention include tiling, sod waterways, land leveling, building construction, removal of rocks from fields, repair of tile, clearing fence rows, and irrigation. The farm manager should prepare a list of proposed improvements, in order of priority, and the cost of each and discuss these with the owner. The owner, of course, must make the final decision regarding what should be done and how much should be spent on farm improvements.

ABILITIES REQUIRED

From the foregoing description of the various responsibilities of the farm manager, it is obvious that a key to the farm manager's success is an ability to work with, evaluate, and motivate people. The manager must be able to get along with both the owner and the operator and to resolve conflicting preferences between the two. A professional manager is sometimes hired to manage a farm because personal conflicts exist between owners and operators. The manager must be able to communicate effectively not only with the owner and operator but also with farm-supply and marketing agencies. In addition to using good judgment in selecting a suitable operator, as previously stated, the manager must also be able to motivate the operator to follow the plan that has been developed jointly.

A final key to the professional manager's success is the ability to obtain desired results from the farm. This involves an understanding of soils and crop production, livestock production, agricultural engineering, marketing, and management. The professional manager may counsel with specialized experts, such as a nutritionist or soil-fertility agronomist, but the manager must personally have a good background in all of these areas.

HOW MANY FARMS?

The number of farms managed by a professional manager varies considerably, depending on such factors as farm size, farm type (crop or livestock), concentration of farms in a geographic area, the operating arrangement on the farm, and the productivity and amount of service provided by the manager. Farms on which operators are hired for a salary require more supervision than farms rented on shares. The number managed may be as low as one or two very large farms or as high as fifty farms, the most usual number being twenty to thirty.

RATE OF CHARGE AND INCOME

Farm managers usually charge in one of three ways:

Flat Fee

Managers charge a fixed fee per acre, established by considering farm size and intensity. In the Midwest, for example, the charge would most likely be between $6 and $10 per acre. Owners and managers like the certainty of this type of charge. The owner knows the precise cost, and the manager has a precise income. However, this method lacks incentive for the manager and does not have an automatic increase or decrease with price level changes. In an inflationary period the fee may need to be adjusted quite often, and this may cause concern among owners.

Percentage of the Landlord's Share of Gross Income

Many management agencies in the Midwest charge 5% to 12% of the landlord's share of gross income. Purchased feed and livestock are deducted from gross receipts, and sale of capital items are excluded. If a farm produces $300 worth of crops per acre and the landlord's share is $150 and the fee rate is 6%, a $9 charge per acre would be made. If the crop is fed to livestock, the percentage is figured on the basis of the value of livestock or livestock products produced.

This system automatically increases or decreases fees with price level changes as farm-product prices increase or decrease. It has an incentive for the manager to increase output but not to control costs.

Percentage of Net Income

Some management agencies charge 10% to 20% of the landlord's share of the net income. All costs except interest on investment are typically included. This system adjusts automatically to price level changes and, from the owner's point of view, has the best incentive for the manager. It results in more risk and income variability for the manager. Sometimes a manager takes over a poor farm with a low net income. It takes time to improve the farm and increase the income. The manager has no assurance of being retained to manage the farm after having improved it. To avoid this disadvantage, some farm managers charge a certain amount per acre or a percentage of the net income, whichever is higher. Some charge a flat fee plus a percentage of the net income. A gross income charge is sometimes combined with a flat fee charge.

The income of the professional manager depends on the number of farms managed, farm size, and direct and overhead costs.

OTHER SERVICES FARM MANAGERS RENDER

In addition to the traditional farm management jobs described, managers are involved in many other professional activities.

Real Estate

Many professional managers are real estate brokers. They aid sellers in offering their farms to best advantage to receive the highest price, and they find buyers for these farms. Professional managers also assist buyers (farmer and investor) to locate farms to purchase. The charge for these services may be a percentage of the sale or an hourly charge for the time involved.

Consulting Services to Owners and Farmers

Some owners may not desire complete management service but may need advice about production, marketing, financial, or personnel problems. Such owners may hire a professional manager to give advice or to provide a plan for solving a problem. Similarly, some farmers hire a professional farm manager for help with financial management, personnel management, record keeping, farm organization, or estate planning. For these services the professional manager usually charges a fee per hour or per day.

Consulting Service to Businesses and Institutions

Industries that are involved with agriculture may hire a professional manager to help in the solution of certain problems. One professional manager was hired to help a potato chip manufacturer plan the sale of salvage to cattle feeders. A city hired a professional manager to help plan the disposal of sewage sludge as a fertilizer for crops. An attorney hired a professional manager to do an analysis that would be useful in a court trial.

Record Keeping and Income Tax Reporting

Professional farm managers sometimes provide record-keeping and tax-reporting services to farmers. It is likely that in the future, professional farm managers will offer an increasing number of services to owner-operators, agribusiness, and investors in addition to the traditional work that they now do for owners.

FINDING A PROFESSIONAL FARM MANAGEMENT JOB

Professional farm-management jobs are not easy to find, as only a limited number of entry-level positions are available each year. Interested persons should obtain a list of professional farm-management agencies in the geographic areas in which they would like to be employed. Write to the American Society of Farm Managers and Rural Appraisers for the names of the secretaries of the state management associations. The state secretaries can provide a list of farm managers. Ask the secretaries to indicate the names of management agencies. Contact these agencies about job opportunities and spend time riding with farm managers and talking with them about their management methods. Some banks in agricultural communities also hire farm managers.

After establishing contact with professional farm-management agencies and banks, indicate your interest in them and continue to check with them periodically to remind them of your interest.

DISCUSSION QUESTIONS

1. What is the principal job of a professional farm manager?
2. When managing a farm, what should be the goals of the professional farm manager?
3. List some of the services performed by a professional farm manager for an owner.
4. What kinds of abilities are needed to be a successful professional farm manager?
5. Which is more important, developing a sound farm plan or selecting a good operator? Explain.
6. What other services do professional farm managers perform in addition to direct management of farms?
7. How are professional farm managers paid for their services?
8. How might one go about finding a professional farm-management job?

RELATED READINGS

ANDREWS, J. B. "Experience and Training Necessary for a Professional Farm Manager," *Journal of the American Society of Farm Managers and Rural Appraisers,* 19, no. 2 (October 1955).

——— "Some Observations of the Procedures and Practices of Professional Farm Managers," *Journal of the American Society of Farm Managers and Rural Appraisers,* 20, no. 2 (October 1956).

DOANE, D. H. "The Future of Our Profession," *Journal of the American Society of Farm Managers and Rural Appraisers,* 16, no. 1 (April 1952).

GUITHER, H. D. "Opportunities for Expanding Professional Farm Management Service," *Journal of the American Society of Farm Managers and Rural Appraisers,* 28, no. 1 (April 1964).

HERTZ, C. F. "Development and Diversification of a Professional Management, Rural Appraisal, and Farm Real Estate Business," *Journal of the American Society of Farm Managers and Rural Appraisers,* 32, no. 2 (October 1968).

HOLCOMB, J. M. "Managerial Services," *Journal of the American Society of Farm Managers and Rural Appraisers,* 29, no. 2 (October 1965).

—— and C. D. POWELL. "Why Corn Belt Farm Owners Terminate Professional Farm Management Agreements," *Journal of the American Society of Farm Managers and Rural Appraisers,* 31, no. 1 (April 1967).

HOLZGRAEFE, DAVID. "Legal Relationships between Landowner and Professional Farm Manager," *Journal of the American Society of Farm Managers and Rural Appraisers,* 38, no. 2 (October 1974).

KADLEC, JOHN E. "Business Strategies for Growth, Profit and Client Satisfaction in the Farm Management Business," *Journal of the American Society of Farm Managers and Rural Appraisers,* 37, no. 1 (April 1973).

KAY, RONALD D. *Farm Management,* chap. 19. McGraw-Hill, 1981.

Professional Farm and Ranch Management Manual. Denver, Colo.: American Society of Farm Managers and Rural Appraisers, 1977.

SUTER, ROBERT C. *Professional Farm Management,* Station Bulletin No. 177. West Lafayette, Ind.: Purdue University Agricultural Experiment Station, 1977.

Size of Periodic Payment to Pay Off a Loan of $1.00

Appendix

TABLE A-1 Annuity Whose Present Value is $1[a] $i/[1 - (1 + i)^{-n}]$

Period (n)	Rate/Period (i)								
	4%	5%	6%	7%	8%	9%	10%	11%	12%
1	1.0400	1.0500	1.0600	1.0700	1.0800	1.0900	1.1000	1.1100	1.1200
2	0.5302	0.5378	0.5454	0.5531	0.5608	0.5685	0.5762	0.5839	0.5917
3	0.3603	0.3672	0.3741	0.3811	0.3880	0.3951	0.4021	0.4092	0.4163
4	0.2755	0.2820	0.2886	0.2952	0.3019	0.3087	0.3155	0.3223	0.3292
5	0.2246	0.2310	0.2374	0.2439	0.2505	0.2571	0.2638	0.2706	0.2774
6	0.1908	0.1970	0.2034	0.2098	0.2163	0.2229	0.2296	0.2364	0.2432
7	0.1666	0.1728	0.1791	0.1856	0.1921	0.1987	0.2054	0.2122	0.2191
8	0.1485	0.1547	0.1610	0.1675	0.1740	0.1807	0.1874	0.1943	0.2013
9	0.1345	0.1407	0.1470	0.1535	0.1601	0.1668	0.1736	0.1806	0.1877
10	0.1233	0.1295	0.1359	0.1424	0.1490	0.1558	0.1627	0.1698	0.1770
11	0.1141	0.1204	0.1268	0.1334	0.1401	0.1469	0.1540	0.1611	0.1684
12	0.1066	0.1128	0.1193	0.1259	0.1327	0.1397	0.1468	0.1540	0.1614
13	0.1001	0.1065	0.1130	0.1197	0.1265	0.1336	0.1408	0.1482	0.1557
14	0.0947	0.1010	0.1076	0.1143	0.1213	0.1284	0.1357	0.1432	0.1509
15	0.0899	0.0963	0.1030	0.1098	0.1168	0.1241	0.1315	0.1391	0.1468
16	0.0858	0.0923	0.0990	0.1059	0.1130	0.1203	0.1278	0.1355	0.1434
17	0.0822	0.0887	0.0954	0.1024	0.1096	0.1170	0.1247	0.1325	0.1405
18	0.0790	0.0855	0.0924	0.0994	0.1067	0.1142	0.1219	0.1298	0.1379
19	0.0761	0.0827	0.0896	0.0968	0.1041	0.1117	0.1195	0.1276	0.1358
20	0.0736	0.0802	0.0872	0.0944	0.1019	0.1095	0.1175	0.1256	0.1339
21	0.0713	0.0780	0.0850	0.0923	0.0998	0.1076	0.1156	0.1238	0.1322
22	0.0692	0.0760	0.0830	0.0904	0.0980	0.1059	0.1140	0.1223	0.1308
23	0.0673	0.0741	0.0813	0.0887	0.0964	0.1044	0.1126	0.1210	0.1296
24	0.0656	0.0725	0.0797	0.0872	0.0950	0.1030	0.1113	0.1198	0.1285
25	0.0640	0.0710	0.0782	0.0858	0.0937	0.1018	0.1102	0.1187	0.1275
26	0.0626	0.0696	0.0769	0.0846	0.0925	0.1007	0.1092	0.1178	0.1267
27	0.0612	0.0683	0.0757	0.0834	0.0914	0.0997	0.1083	0.1170	0.1259
28	0.0600	0.0671	0.0746	0.0824	0.0905	0.0989	0.1075	0.1163	0.1252
29	0.0589	0.0660	0.0736	0.0814	0.0896	0.0981	0.1067	0.1156	0.1247
30	0.0578	0.0651	0.0726	0.0806	0.0888	0.0973	0.1061	0.1150	0.1241
31	0.0569	0.0641	0.0718	0.0798	0.0881	0.0967	0.1055	0.1145	0.1237
32	0.0559	0.0633	0.0710	0.0791	0.0875	0.0961	0.1050	0.1140	0.1233
33	0.0551	0.0625	0.0703	0.0784	0.0869	0.0956	0.1045	0.1136	0.1229
34	0.0543	0.0618	0.0696	0.0778	0.0863	0.0951	0.1041	0.1133	0.1226
35	0.0536	0.0611	0.0690	0.0772	0.0858	0.0946	0.1037	0.1129	0.1223
36	0.0529	0.0604	0.0684	0.0767	0.0853	0.0942	0.1033	0.1126	0.1221
37	0.0522	0.0598	0.0679	0.0762	0.0849	0.0939	0.1030	0.1124	0.1218
38	0.0516	0.0593	0.0674	0.0758	0.0845	0.0935	0.1027	0.1121	0.1216
39	0.0511	0.0588	0.0669	0.0754	0.0842	0.0932	0.1025	0.1119	0.1215
40	0.0505	0.0583	0.0665	0.0750	0.0839	0.0930	0.1023	0.1117	0.1213
41	0.0500	0.0578	0.0661	0.0747	0.0836	0.0927	0.1020	0.1115	0.1212
42	0.0495	0.0574	0.0657	0.0743	0.0833	0.0925	0.1019	0.1114	0.1210
43	0.0491	0.0570	0.0653	0.0740	0.0830	0.0923	0.1017	0.1113	0.1209
44	0.0487	0.0566	0.0650	0.0738	0.0828	0.0921	0.1015	0.1111	0.1208
45	0.0483	0.0563	0.0647	0.0735	0.0826	0.0919	0.1014	0.1110	0.1207

[a]Size of periodic payment to pay off a loan of $1 or an annuity worth $1 today.

Source: Stephen B. Harsh, Larry J. O'Conner, and Gerald D. Schwab, *Managing the Farm Business* (Prentice-Hall: Englewood Cliffs, N.J., 1981), pp. 372–373.

TABLE A-1   Annuity Whose Present Value is $1[a] $i/[1 - (1 + i)^{-n}]$ (cont.)

Period (n)	Rate/Period (i)								
	13%	14%	15%	16%	17%	18%	19%	20%	25%
1	1.1300	1.1400	1.1500	1.1600	1.1700	1.1800	1.1900	1.2000	1.2500
2	0.5995	0.6073	0.6151	0.6230	0.6308	0.6387	0.6466	0.6545	0.6944
3	0.4235	0.4307	0.4380	0.4453	0.4526	0.4599	0.4673	0.4747	0.5123
4	0.3362	0.3432	0.3503	0.3574	0.3645	0.3717	0.3790	0.3863	0.4234
5	0.2843	0.2913	0.2983	0.3054	0.3126	0.3198	0.3271	0.3344	0.3718
6	0.2502	0.2572	0.2642	0.2714	0.2786	0.2859	0.2933	0.3007	0.3388
7	0.2261	0.2332	0.2404	0.2476	0.2549	0.2624	0.2699	0.2774	0.3163
8	0.2084	0.2156	0.2229	0.2302	0.2377	0.2452	0.2529	0.2606	0.3004
9	0.1949	0.2022	0.2096	0.2171	0.2247	0.2324	0.2402	0.2481	0.2888
10	0.1843	0.1917	0.1993	0.2069	0.2147	0.2225	0.2305	0.2385	0.2801
11	0.1758	0.1834	0.1911	0.1989	0.2068	0.2148	0.2229	0.2311	0.2735
12	0.1690	0.1767	0.1845	0.1924	0.2005	0.2086	0.2169	0.2253	0.2684
13	0.1634	0.1712	0.1791	0.1872	0.1954	0.2037	0.2121	0.2206	0.2645
14	0.1587	0.1666	0.1747	0.1829	0.1912	0.1997	0.2082	0.2169	0.2615
15	0.1547	0.1628	0.1710	0.1794	0.1878	0.1964	0.2051	0.2139	0.2591
16	0.1514	0.1596	0.1679	0.1764	0.1850	0.1937	0.2025	0.2114	0.2572
17	0.1486	0.1569	0.1654	0.1740	0.1827	0.1915	0.2004	0.2094	0.2558
18	0.1462	0.1546	0.1632	0.1719	0.1807	0.1896	0.1987	0.2078	0.2546
19	0.1441	0.1527	0.1613	0.1701	0.1791	0.1881	0.1972	0.2065	0.2537
20	0.1424	0.1510	0.1598	0.1687	0.1777	0.1868	0.1960	0.2054	0.2529
21	0.1408	0.1495	0.1584	0.1674	0.1765	0.1857	0.1951	0.2044	0.2523
22	0.1395	0.1483	0.1573	0.1664	0.1756	0.1848	0.1942	0.2037	0.2519
23	0.1383	0.1472	0.1563	0.1654	0.1747	0.1841	0.1935	0.2031	0.2515
24	0.1373	0.1463	0.1554	0.1647	0.1740	0.1835	0.1930	0.2025	0.2512
25	0.1364	0.1455	0.1547	0.1640	0.1734	0.1829	0.1925	0.2021	0.2509
26	0.1357	0.1448	0.1541	0.1634	0.1729	0.1825	0.1921	0.2018	0.2508
27	0.1350	0.1442	0.1535	0.1630	0.1725	0.1821	0.1917	0.2015	0.2506
28	0.1344	0.1437	0.1531	0.1625	0.1721	0.1818	0.1915	0.2012	0.2505
29	0.1339	0.1432	0.1527	0.1622	0.1718	0.1815	0.1912	0.2010	0.2504
30	0.1334	0.1428	0.1523	0.1619	0.1715	0.1813	0.1910	0.2008	0.2503
31	0.1330	0.1425	0.1520	0.1616	0.1713	0.1811	0.1909	0.2007	0.2502
32	0.1327	0.1421	0.1517	0.1614	0.1711	0.1809	0.1907	0.2006	0.2502
33	0.1323	0.1419	0.1515	0.1612	0.1710	0.1808	0.1906	0.2005	0.2502
34	0.1321	0.1416	0.1513	0.1610	0.1708	0.1806	0.1905	0.2004	0.2501
35	0.1318	0.1414	0.1511	0.1609	0.1707	0.1806	0.1904	0.2003	0.2501
36	0.1316	0.1413	0.1510	0.1608	0.1706	0.1805	0.1904	0.2003	0.2501
37	0.1314	0.1411	0.1509	0.1607	0.1705	0.1804	0.1903	0.2002	0.2501
38	0.1313	0.1410	0.1507	0.1606	0.1704	0.1803	0.1903	0.2002	0.2501
39	0.1311	0.1409	0.1506	0.1605	0.1704	0.1803	0.1902	0.2002	0.2500
40	0.1310	0.1407	0.1506	0.1604	0.1703	0.1802	0.1902	0.2001	0.2500
41	0.1309	0.1407	0.1505	0.1604	0.1703	0.1802	0.1902	0.2001	0.2500
42	0.1308	0.1406	0.1504	0.1603	0.1702	0.1802	0.1901	0.2001	0.2500
43	0.1307	0.1405	0.1504	0.1603	0.1702	0.1801	0.1901	0.2001	0.2500
44	0.1306	0.1404	0.1503	0.1602	0.1702	0.1801	0.1901	0.2001	0.2500
45	0.1305	0.1404	0.1503	0.1602	0.1701	0.1801	0.1901	0.2001	0.2500

[a]Size of periodic payment to pay off a loan of $1 or an annuity worth $1 today.

Checklist[1]
for Farm Incorporation

Appendix B

[1]*Source:* Neil E. Harl, *Farm Estate and Business Planning* (Skokie, Ill.: AgriBusiness Publications, 1982.

1. **Name.** What is to be the corporate name? Consider application to reserve corporate name.

2. **Duration.** Is the corporation to be organized to exist perpetually? Or for a term of years?

3. **Purpose.** What are to be the purposes of the corporation? Narrowly defined or broadly stated?

4. **Stock and Debt Capital Structure.**

   a. How many classes of stock are to be authorized? How many shares of stock are to be issued? What are characteristics of each as to:

      (1) Voting rights—voting stock, nonvoting stock, proxy voting, cumulative rights
      (2) Dividend rights
      (3) Preference on liquidation
      (4) Conversion rights, if any
      (5) Par value—consider low par value to minimize annual fee on stated capital (possible in some states)
      (6) Fair market value on issuance
      (7) Preemptive rights.

   b. Is debt capital to be used? (Watch tax-free incorporation limitations and debt-equity ratio).

      (1) Type of debt security (note, bond, debenture) and amount
      (2) Time of maturity
      (3) Conversion to stock
      (4) Interest rate
      (5) Priority on liquidation.

5. **Stock Transfer Restriction.** What type of restriction is to be used (consent, first option, buy-sell agreement)? Method of stock valuation (book value, appraised value, periodically renegotiated fixed value)? Arrangements for payment by purchasers?

6. **Shareholders.** Names and addresses? Date of annual meeting? Place of annual meeting? Voting requirements? Quorum requirements? Pooling agreements? Voting trusts? Shareholders' agreements? For minor shareholders, consider us-

ing Uniform Gifts to Minors Act custodianship. Custodian should be someone other than donor.

7. **Board of Directors.** Number of directors on board? Names of first directors? Voting requirements? Quorum requirements? Arrangements for meetings? Director fees? Is preincorporation agreement desirable?

8. **Officers.** What offices are to be authorized? Who is expected to be elected to each office? What salary is to be authorized for each officer? Is corporation to pay entire social security tax or only one-half? Is a bonus policy to be authorized? What authority are officers to have in terms of signing other documents? Explain proper format for signatures on corporate documents.

9. **Other Employees.** What individuals are to be employed by the corporation in addition to the officers? What are terms of employment? Is an employment contract to be drafted? Arrangements for compensation? Is corporation to pay entire social security tax or only one-half?

10. **Assets to Be Owned by Corporation.** What property is to be transferred to the corporation?
    a. Prepare inventory for each transferor and list each item by name of owner, description of asset, income tax basis, fair market value, indebtedness, and holding period. Preserve copies to be submitted with income tax returns and for the permanent file.

    Watch gifts between and among transferors of property, especially upon conveyance of property held in co-ownership. Land held by a husband and wife in joint tenancy and acquired since December 31, 1954, merits special attention in this regard, especially for transfers before 1982. After 1981, any gift (to the other spouse) on conveyance to a corporation of property co-owned by a husband and wife is covered by the 100% federal gift tax marital deduction. Note insurance carried on assets and assets under special registration.
    b. Is transfer to be tax-free or taxable? Check eligibility requirements for one desired.
    c. Who is to value assets?
    d. Have property taxes been paid by transferor to date of incorporation?
    e. Are documentary stamp taxes required on land transferred?
    f. Abstracts of title?
    g. Prepare deeds and bills of sale.

11. **Assets to Be Leased by Corporation.** What property is to be leased to the corporation? List each item by name of lessor, description of property, and rental to be charged. Prepare leases.

12. **Bank.** What bank is to be the depository bank? Resolve officer authority to borrow money and sign negotiable instruments to be prepared and sent to bank.

13. **Income Taxation.** What method of income taxation to be followed?
    a. Regular—File Form 1120 annually.

b. Subchapter S—review eligibility requirements for election; prepare Form 2553 with consents by each shareholder; if corporation has operated previously as regular corporation, check operating loss carry-over, investment tax credit carry-over, and recapture of investment tax credit; file Form 1120-S annually.

14. **Identification Number.** Prepare and submit Form SS4, "Employer's Application for ID Number."

15. **Registered Office.** What is the address of the registered office of the corporation?

16. **Registered Agent.** Who is to be the registered agent of the corporation?

17. **Notice of Incorporation.** If required by state law, as in Iowa, prepare notice of incorporation, forward to publisher of eligible newspaper, and, where required, send affidavit of publication to secretary of state.

18. **Incorporation Kit.** Order corporate kit, specifying type of seal, if any; number and type of stock certificates (have stock transfer restriction printed thereon or type restriction on certificate when received); minute book.

19. **Loans, Mortgages.** What loans or mortgages are to be assumed or taken subject to by corporation? Give special attention to Federal Land Bank, Production Credit, Farmers Home Administration loans.

20. **Basis.** Determine corporation's income tax basis of assets for purposes of depreciation and sale. Calculate and make a record of shareholder's basis for stock and securities received. Because of "galloping basis," repeat every year for subchapter S corporations.

21. **Fiscal Year.** What is to be the corporation's fiscal year? Consider fiscal year other than calendar year for subchapter S corporations.

22. **Method of Accounting.** Is the corporation to be on the cash or accrual basis? Is the corporation required to be on accrual accounting by virtue of gross receipts, method of taxation, and stock ownership? How are inventories to be valued?

23. **Special Elections.** Check on elections for treatment of commodity credit loans, soil and water conservation expenses, and land-clearing expenses.

24. **Residences.** Are houses to be transferred to corporations? Reasonable rental to be paid by occupants? Or occupants to report value of occupancy as additional income? Or rely on I.R.C. section 119?

25. **Motor Vehicles.** What vehicles are to be transferred to corporation? Insurance arrangements? Title transfer? What vehicles are to be individually owned? Rate of compensation for business use? Insurance coverage for accidents involving employee-owned vehicles within scope of employment?

26. **Recapture.** If corporation is not a mere change in form of doing business, will investment tax credit be recaptured? If subchapter S taxation is elected after operation as a regular corporation, file shareholder consent to be responsible for recaptured investment tax credit with last Form 1120. If the transfer of

assets for the corporation is a taxable exchange, other amounts may be recaptured.

27. **Fringe Benefits.** What fringe benefits are to be provided? Check health and accident plan, group term life insurance (minimum number of employees required by state law—ten or more in most states—or "baby group" plan), and deferred compensation for retirement.

28. **Doing Business in Other States.** Will the corporation be doing business in another state? How much? Necessary to qualify to do business as foreign corporation?

29. **Minority Shareholders.** Is stock to be permitted to pass to off-farm shareholders? Consider assuring management rights, current income, and market for stock in planning for protection of minority shareholders.

30. **Wills.** Do wills and estate plans of shareholders need to be updated by codicil or completely rewritten? Consider provisions to direct executor not to object to subchapter S election and to comply with restrictions on stock transfer. For holders, or potential holders of subchapter S corporation stock, consider substitute provisions in lieu of trusts—for example, legal life estate rather than marital deduction trust.

31. **Memberships.** What about memberships in cooperatives? Farm organizations? Breed associations?

32. **Insurance.** Check on casualty insurance, liability insurance, workers' compensation, and motor vehicle liability.

Index